The UNIX
Operating System

SECOND EDITION

The UNIX†
Operating System

SECOND EDITION

Kaare Christian
The Rockefeller University
New York, New York

†UNIX is a trademark of Bell Laboratories.

WILEY

JOHN WILEY & SONS
New York • Chichester • Brisbane • Toronto • Singapore

CP/M is a trademark of Digital Research.
IBM is a registered trademark of International Business Machines Corporation.
Intel is a registered trademark of Intel Corporation.
MS, MS-DOS, OS/2, and XENIX are registered trademarks of Microsoft Corporation.
PDP and VAX are trademarks of Digital Equipment Corporation.
UNIX is a trademark of AT&T Bell Laboratories.

Library of Congress Cataloging in Publication Data:
Christian, Kaare, 1954-
    The UNIX operating system / Kaare Christian. 2nd ed.
        p.   cm.
    Includes index.
    ISBN 0-471-84782-8.   ISBN 0-471-84781-X (pbk.)
    1. UNIX (Computer operating system)   I. Title.
QA76.8.U65C45 1988
005.4'465 — dc19

Printed in the United States of America

10 9 8 7 6 5 4 3 2 1

For Edward Josiah Bunker

Contents

Preface to the Second Edition

The most important feature of the first edition of this book was its staying power. It was the kind of book that novices could read easily but also the kind of book that more advanced UNIX users could learn from and use profitably. I have tried to keep that goal in sight during many months of work on this edition.

Although this book is officially a second edition, it contains as much new material as the first edition. A few chapters have been carried through more or less intact, but most have experienced extensive revision. More importantly, many new chapters have been added, especially in the second part of the book.

The basic design of this book is to provide introductory information in the first half and to provide information on advanced topics in the second half. The first part of the book contains a brief history of the UNIX system, a discussion of the UNIX filesystem, information on many important UNIX utilities, and instructions for using the vi text editor. The latter half of the book contains information on shell programming, tutorials for sed (a powerful scripted editor) and awk (a programming language for modifying text files), several chapters for UNIX programmers, a chapter that shows you how to benchmark UNIX systems, two chapters on UNIX system administration, and a chapter each on shell internals and the UNIX kernel. The appendices cover the traditional ed editor and provide reference material for the vi editor.

Space limitations have forced some of the material in the first edition of this book to migrate to more spacious quarters. The first edition contained an appendix summarizing 40 of the most important UNIX commands; that material has been greatly expanded into a separate book titled *The UNIX*

Command Reference Guide (John Wiley, 1987). The first edition also contained a chapter on the `nroff/troff` text processing system. That chapter expanded so much that it too became a separate book, *The UNIX Text Processing System* (John Wiley, 1987).

The first edition of this book was written in 1981, when Version 7 was probably the most widely used UNIX flavor. Work on this edition of the book started in late 1985 and continued until August 1987. Years from now we may look back on the mid 1980s as the height of the clash between System V and Berkeley. System V, though proclaimed a standard by AT&T (in 1984), is just beginning to emerge as a technically accomplished system. Efforts are currently under way to merge System V with Berkeley and with Xenix, and UNIX standardization efforts are under way in Europe and the Far East. Future books on UNIX may not need to be so concerned with what feature is available in what version. In those occasional areas where features differ between System V and Berkeley, I've tried to include both. Most of the material presented here applies to both System V and Berkeley and also to Xenix, Ultrix, and most other modern versions of the UNIX system.

Maria Taylor was my editor at John Wiley during the start of this revision. Work started inauspiciously, but after about six months of writing I realized that I had far too much material for a single book. Maria supported my decision to split the material into three books, and she helped get the two new books officially under way at Wiley. When Maria's duties at John Wiley were changed, Diane Cerra became my editor. Diane skillfully shepherded these three books through their final editorial and production stages. Thanks go to both Diane and Maria for their help and understanding. Phyllis Brooks at John Wiley was instrumental during the production of these three books. And finally, thanks must also go to Jim Gaughan, my original editor at John Wiley.

The major part of this revision was carried out while I worked at the Neurobiology Laboratory headed by Torsten Wiesel, at The Rockefeller University in New York city. The majority of the new examples were run on a VAX 11/780 running version 4.2 of the Berkeley UNIX system. In many cases the output of the commands was captured by the `script` program and then transferred into the manuscript. Many people at Rockefeller lent assistance to this project, including Dan Ts'o, Charles Gilbert, and Owen Smith.

The original secretarial work on this project was done by Jan Heissinger. Later in the project, Julie Dollinger helped with many different aspects of the work. My wife, Robin, also lent occasional word-processing assistance.

Brigitte Fuller and Bruce Steinberg at the Santa Cruz Operation supplied a copy of Xenix System V/286 to run on my personal computer. That system was used to test and create many of the examples, and it was used as my UNIX system away from home when I completed work on this book at the Max Planck Institute, in Tübingen, West Germany. In Tübingen, Jürgen Bolz helped bring the project to completion.

Please write if you have comments or suggestions. Direct them to me at my permanent address, The Neurobiology Laboratory, The Rockefeller University, RU Box 138, 1230 York Ave., New York, New York 10021. Comments can also be addressed to me electronically via the UUCP network at cmcl2!rna!kc.

KAARE CHRISTIAN

Tübingen, West Germany
December 1987

Preface to the First Edition

UNIX is the name of a family of computer operating systems. Many experts feel that the UNIX system is the most important development in computer operating systems in the past decade. The impact of the UNIX system is being compared with that of FORTRAN, the first major portable high-level programming language, or that of IBM's System/360, the first compatible series of computers spanning a wide performance range. The UNIX system is becoming increasingly important because it runs on a wide range of computers and because it has many applications.

Originally used on Digital Equipment Corporation minicomputers for computer science research, program development, and document preparation, current versions of the UNIX system are now available for computers as small and inexpensive as the Zilog Z-80 and computers as large as the Amdahl 470/V7. The UNIX system is now used for a large range of business, scientific, and industrial applications.

Operating systems are also called executives, because they (like business executives) administer and control the operation of a complicated device. In the narrowest sense, the UNIX system parcels computer time into a number of portions and allocates the portions among the various users. It also controls the flow of information between the central computer and the disks, tapes, terminals, and printers and manages the long-term storage of information.

In a broader sense, the UNIX system is a large collection of programs that rely on the basic services just mentioned. The programs allow a user to create and examine files, to write and test new programs, to perform sophisticated document preparation—in short, to manage information. The UNIX system is simple, useful, and intelligible.

One of the most important advantages of the UNIX system is that it runs on many types of computers. Ordinary programs that run on one type of computer (under the UNIX system) can usually be run on other types of computers with little or no modification. This allows companies that sell computer programs to produce a single product for a large market, and it allows computer users to learn a single operating system that is available on many different machines. Even though this sounds simple and obvious, it has taken three decades of work with computers to achieve.

The work of Ken Thompson and Dennis M. Ritchie at Bell Laboratories in the early 1970s started a revolution. In the mid-1970s, the excitement spread to the academic community, which was seeking a solution to many difficulties of modern computer science. In the 1980s, this phenomenon reached the business community, which sees the UNIX system as an important part of the struggle to provide better and longer-lasting software products and services.

The original goal of Thompson and Ritchie was to create a productive environment for pursuing computer science research. The original goal, and much more, has been achieved. Thompson and Ritchie have demonstrated that individuals can make important contributions in a difficult field, and the UNIX system has demonstrated that new and better ideas are eventually accepted in the marketplace.

I would like to thank Robert Schoenfeld, Owen Smith, and Paul Rosen of The Rockefeller University for their encouragement, comments, and criticism; Tom Krausz and Eric Rosenthal of IMI Systems for their extremely helpful comments; and Edward Gershey of The Rockefeller University for his support. Ed Catmull and Alvy Ray Smith of Lucasfilm Ltd. generously supplied the cover artwork. Finally I would like to thank Jim Gaughan and Jenet McIver at John Wiley for their encouragement and assistance throughout this project.

KAARE CHRISTIAN

New York, New York
May 1982

The Cover Illustration

The illustration on the cover is a single frame of a one-minute sequence known as the "Genesis Effect," which was created in 1982 for the motion picture *Star Trek II: The Wrath of Khan* from Paramount Pictures. Members of the Computer Group at Lucasfilm Ltd. used computer graphics techniques to create the one-minute sequence. No physical artwork or physical models were used—instead, computers running the UNIX system created the 1620 images in the sequence.

Computer graphics has progressed from simple black-and-white line drawings systems to sophisticated color animation systems. Most advanced computer animation systems are capable of creating impressive images— images that are obviously computer-generated. At Lucasfilm, the state of the art has advanced to the point where computer-generated images are so "real" and "lifelike" that they can be smoothly intercut with images of reality.

The Genesis Sequence opens with a view of a dead planet as seen from a nearby spacecraft. The spacecraft fires a projectile at the planet; the result of the impact is a wall of fire that spreads across the planet, transforming the lifeless rock into a Garden of Eden. During the planet's evolution, the spacecraft flies close by the surface to observe the dramatic biogenesis occurring on the planet. Finally the spacecraft pulls back to reveal the verdant planet, complete with rivers, plains, mountains, oceans, and atmosphere.

Alvy Ray Smith, the head of the Genesis Project at Lucasfilm, supervised the talented group that created the Genesis Sequence. He likes to think of the group as an "off-line rock group." He said, "We work together on our individual instruments for months, and only later do we face the music.

The point is that all members of the team are creative contributors, and a project requires all of them.''

Each frame of the Genesis Sequence was assembled from many pieces using computers running the UNIX system. First the background images were created, and then the foreground images were sandwiched on top. It took the UNIX system up to five hours to perform all of the calculations for some of the most complicated frames, and up to 50 programs were used for some of the frames. Besides the complexity of the individual frames, the magicians at Lucasfilm had to worry about continuity from frame to frame and the constantly changing perspective as the spacecraft flies past the planet.

I am indebted to Ed Catmull, director of the Computer Division at Lucasfilm, and Alvy Ray Smith, Graphics Project Leader at Lucasfilm, for supplying the cover image. The following members of the staff at Lucasfilm Ltd. were the principal creators of the Genesis Sequence:

Loren Carpenter	Fractal mountains, atmosphere, shockwave
Pat Cole	Projectile
Tom Duff	Cratered sphere, texture-mapped sphere
Chris Evans	Painted the pull-away planet surface
Tom Porter	Stars, compositing, paint
Bill Reeves	Fires
Alvy Ray Smith	Concept, direction

The UNIX Operating System

SECOND EDITION

CHAPTER 1

The History of the UNIX System

1.1 BACKGROUND

The UNIX system is one of the major advances in the progression of computers from the esoteric realm of high technology into the mainstream of people's daily activities. It has demonstrated that a powerful operating system can be largely machine-independent, and it has shown that powerful software tools can be used effectively by people in the course of using a computer to solve problems.

The UNIX system provides essentially the same services as those provided by all operating systems: it allows you to run programs, it provides a convenient and consistent interface to the wide variety of peripheral devices (printers, tapes, disks, terminals, etc.) that are connected to most computers, and it provides a filesystem for long-term information storage. The UNIX system's uniqueness is largely due to the way it evolved. We can best understand the system's growing popularity by adopting a historical perspective.

In the late 1960s Bell Laboratories was involved with an operating system called Multics. Multics is a multiuser interactive system using a GE mainframe computer. Bell Labs withdrew from the Multics project in 1969, but Multics had a major influence on the UNIX system. In fact, the name UNIX is a play on the word Multics. One of the most striking differences between the UNIX system and Multics is complexity—the UNIX operating system is relatively simple, while Multics is extremely complex.

At about the same time as Bell's withdrawal from Multics, the "granddaddy of the UNIX system," Ken Thompson, began tinkering on a reject Digital Equipment Corporation PDP-7 minicomputer. Ostensibly,

1

Thompson sought to create an operating system that could support the coordinated efforts of a team of programmers in a programming research environment. In retrospect, this objective has been successfully accomplished. Also, in order to appease management, Thompson proposed that further UNIX systems development be supported by Bell Labs in order to provide a document preparation tool for the Bell Laboratories patent organization. An early version of the UNIX system using a PDP-11/20 was actually delivered to the Bell Laboratories patent organization in 1971.

From the very beginning, two seemingly incompatible disciplines, programming and document preparation, have been the cornerstones of the UNIX system. In practice, the UNIX system has demonstrated that text management tools are central to many disciplines, including programming. People have criticized the UNIX system for being just a fancy word processor. While there are some types of applications that require operating systems other than the UNIX system, the focus on text manipulation has served to make it an extremely general-purpose operating system. Text is an accepted medium for communication, a key feature for a general-purpose interactive operating system.

Ken Thompson's original efforts culminated in the creation of an operating system, a PDP-7 assembler, and several assembly language utility programs. In 1973, Dennis Ritchie rewrote the UNIX system in his new creation, the C programming language. C is a general-purpose, medium-level programming language that Ritchie developed specifically to further work on the UNIX system. C has proved to be adaptable to many different types of computer architecture, and it is now a common programming language on all types of computers, especially minicomputers and microcomputers. If the UNIX system had not been rewritten in a portable language, it would have been chained to the machine (the outdated PDP-7) that it was developed on. Once the original assembly language version of the UNIX system was rewritten in C, it was suddenly possible to move the entire system from one environment to another with a minimum of difficulty.

The first move (port) to a different type of computer was accomplished by Ritchie and Stephen Johnson in 1976, when they transported the UNIX system to the Interdata 8/32. Since then, the UNIX system has been moved to virtually every popular computer architecture, ranging from single-chip microprocessors such as the Zilog Z-80 and Z-8000; the Motorola MC68000, 68010, and 68020; and the Intel 8086/8088 80286 and 80386, to large, mainframe computers such as IBM 370, the Amdahl 470, and the Cray II.

As Thompson gained acceptance from his colleagues and management during the early 1970s, the UNIX system began to be used internally throughout the Bell System. As word of the operating system spread, it generated interest at several prestigious academic institutions. In 1975, Western Electric started licensing the UNIX system. The fee was nominal for academic institutions, encouraging them to use and further develop the UNIX system.

Perhaps because the UNIX system was looked upon so favorably by the academic community, it was initially met with skepticism by the business community. Recently, the business community has realized the ease with which the UNIX system can be adopted for a wide variety of applications, and commercial use of the UNIX system is growing rapidly. Starting in the late 1970s a multibillion dollar industry emerged to supply UNIX hardware, software, and related services.

As you may have gleaned from the story related above, the origin of the UNIX system is unlike that of any other operating system. Most other operating systems have been developed by computer manufacturers to sell computers. AT&T was not in the business of selling computers during the first decade of the UNIX system's development, and the UNIX system was not originally envisioned as a commercial product. The UNIX system has only become a commercial venture in response to the enormous demand that has developed.

Some of the difficulties today stem from early reluctance by AT&T to devote significant resources to husbanding the UNIX system. Into that void stepped many would-be UNIX guardians, but the most successful (and the most heavily funded) was the University of California at Berkeley. Unlike an ordinary commercial operating system, which is completely controlled by its maker, the UNIX system today is buffeted by four major forces and a hundred or more lesser players.

The four major forces in the UNIX arena are AT&T, the University of California at Berkeley, Sun Microsystems, and Microsoft Corporation. AT&T's interest in UNIX is obvious, and now that it is allowed to compete in the data-processing field, its major strength is the UNIX system. U.C. Berkeley is the home of Berkeley UNIX, which is the most technically advanced UNIX version in several areas. Sun Microsystems manufactures a line of workstations that run the UNIX system, and they are responsible for several major technical advancements including the first diskless UNIX workstations and the NFS network filesystem. Microsoft is the vendor of Xenix, the most popular commercial version of the UNIX system.

Today the major problem with the UNIX system is its lack of standardization. Only a meeting of the minds of the four major powers, plus at least tacit consent and cooperation by dozens of second-tier vendors (many of which are powerful corporations, such as IBM), can resolve the problem. There are two major variants (Berkeley and System V) plus dozens of minor variations. Most people would like to see a convergence of these systems, but there are significant technical and corporate barriers.

The UNIX system has pioneered several important ideas other than its most important innovation—portability. One of the most important innovations is the *pipe,* which has in turn led to the idea that complicated functions can be programmed as a set of programs working together. Typesetting provides the best example. The UNIX system contains several different typesetting programs—one for conventional chores, one for mathematics, one for tabular data, and one for diagrams. *Pipe* connections let you use as many of these programs as are necessary. Each typesetting program does not duplicate the features in the other programs; instead, there is a complementary relationship. Solving a complicated problem using a body of cooperating processes has proved to be convenient for both program developers and program users.

Another idea that pervades the UNIX system is the notion of a *software tool*. This idea is not unique to the UNIX system, but it certainly has been developed further here than in other systems.

Most software tools are small, cohesive programs that do one thing well and that can cooperate with other tools to perform more sophisticated chores. For example, wc counts words, and ls lists files. Together they can count files in a directory. Two of the most programmable software tools are sed and awk. Both are programming languages for text file manipulation: sed is a programmable editor, while awk takes the more familiar programming language approach, but with many special features for handling text.

To simplify programming chores involving the recognition of a command language, the UNIX system has yacc and lex. These two programs allow a programmer to implement a command language interpreter by describing the command language in a tabular form rather than by writing a unique interpreter for the language. lex and yacc require study before they can be mastered, but once mastered they make it possible to conveniently program new applications which use command languages.

Two other examples of sophisticated tools are make and the Source Code Control System (SCCS). make is used to specify the interdependencies in a software system so that the system can be maintained automatically. SCCS is used to track a software system throughout its mature lifetime so that old versions can be retrieved and new versions can be documented.

At this point, the UNIX system appears to be emerging as a standard operating system for use on a wide spectrum of computers. The UNIX system is not likely to be used widely in situations where a computer is used for a special purpose that lends itself to a specialized operating system (e.g., transaction processing, reservation systems, real-time systems). From a pragmatic point of view, the UNIX system is likely to be important in the years to come because it is widely used. The UNIX industry is still in its infancy, and in monetary terms it cannot be compared with the industry that services some of the established mainframe operating systems. However, the prospects are very good for the companies in the UNIX system service industry, and some analysts are predicting that the UNIX system industry may come to rival the support industries that exist today for the more established operating systems.

Another aspect of the UNIX system's future relates to its nearly universal acceptance and use in the academic computing community. In the same way that the programming language ALGOL (and more recently PASCAL) is widely used in the academic literature to describe algorithms, the UNIX operating system is frequently used to illustrate operating system topics. The UNIX system has become a standard against which new developments in operating systems are measured.

1.2 VERSIONS OF UNIX

In July of 1974, Ken Thompson and Dennis Ritchie published their classic paper "The UNIX Time-Sharing System" in the Communications of the ACM (Association for Computing Machinery). That paper led to widespread interest in the UNIX system, especially when people learned that a copy of the Version 5 system, as described in the paper, could be acquired for just $150, unsupported but with complete source code.

By 1976, Version 6 of the UNIX system was distributed, both within the Bell System and to universities throughout the world. Version 6 featured a primitive shell, the ed text editor, and a set of about 100 utilities strikingly similar to those supplied with the latest UNIX systems. The programming features of the Version 6 shell were rudimentary—it contained a goto statement for flow of control, variables named A to Z, and simple expression testing. However, its interactive features were similar in form and function to those found on today's shells; there were I/O redirection, pipelines, and background processing.

Version 6 served as a basis for development of several variants of the UNIX system, including the MERT real-time UNIX derivative, the PWB (programmers' workbench) systems, and the early work on the UNIX system at Berkeley. Version 6 also gained the distinction of being the first UNIX system to be copied by a commercial firm, when Whitesmiths Inc. produced its Version 6 work-alike called Idris. Version 6 is also remembered as the system that was featured in John Lions' revealing book, *A Commentary on the UNIX Operating System*. Lions' sometimes suppressed book was the first independent discussion of the UNIX system; further books were not forthcoming until 1983, when the first edition of this book and several other books were published.

In 1978, Version 7 of the UNIX system was released by Bell Laboratories. Version 7 of the UNIX system is clearly recognizable as "UNIX" to anyone who is accustomed to the more modern systems. Version 7 is important for many reasons. It featured the first release of the Bourne shell, the first shell to combine a powerful interpretive programming language with powerful features for interactive command entry. Version 7 had an important influence on the PWB systems, and it was the basis for the UNIX 32V system for Digital Equipment VAX computers. Many of the important subsystems attained their nearly final form in Version 7. Some UNIX system veterans have a nostalgic feeling for Version 7. It was the last of the small, clean UNIX systems, yet it was certainly a "modern" UNIX system.

Inside of the Bell System, the PWB UNIX system became Release 3.0, then 4.0, and finally in 1982 it evolved to 5.0. In the early 1980s, as AT&T regained its interest in the UNIX system, they prepared commercial UNIX distributions. The name was changed from Release 5.0 to System V, a few additional documents were prepared, and then System V was proclaimed to be a standard. The original version of System V still contained only the ed line editor, although later releases of System V contain the vi editor adopted from Berkeley.

During the late 1970s and early 1980s, when the UNIX system was nurtured but little by AT&T, it was being aggressively supported and improved by gifted graduate students at the University of California at Berkeley. Starting with the 32V system, Berkeley created 3 BSD and 4 BSD (Berkeley Software Distribution) for the VAX series of computers. Berkeley UNIX system enhancements include the C-Shell, the vi visual editor, the Franz Lisp programming language, the Pascal programming language, networking support, improved interprocess communication via sockets and pseudo-ttys, virtual memory support, and many significant performance enhancements. This stunning string of technical achievements has made Berkeley UNIX systems very popular, especially with the most technically demanding users.

Today the two major variants of the UNIX system are AT&T's System V and Berkeley's 4 BSD. Most other versions are derived from one of these sources. For example, Ultrix is a Berkeley variant that also contains several major System V features. The coexistence of two major variants is a big problem, because the systems have various incompatibilities, both large and small. AT&T is trying to garner industrywide acceptance for its self-proclaimed standard Version V system. However, AT&T must enhance System V substantially to create a system that will be acceptable to the whole spectrum of UNIX system users. Many of the independent vendors of UNIX hardware and software are supporting both System V and 4 BSD by providing hybrid systems containing the functionality of both systems.

CHAPTER 2

Fundamentals

The difference between computers and other machines is that computers are general-purpose. Their generality is the central difficulty in learning to use computers. As a first step in understanding the UNIX system, or any other operating system, you should have a general understanding of the building blocks that underlie a computer. This chapter presents some of these fundamentals.

One of the major functions of an operating system is to disguise the building blocks of computers. You don't have to understand motors and circuit theory to operate an electric appliance, and you shouldn't have to understand computer architecture to use a computer. However, a basic understanding of the fundamentals will make it easier to understand some of the ebb and flow of ideas in the following chapters. If you have some experience with computers, then you should probably skip to Chapter 3.

2.1 LOW-LEVEL FUNCTIONS

A typewriter is easy to use, because there is a specific button to press to get a specific letter printed on the page. Common operations such as rolling the carriage up and returning to the start of the line are built into the mechanism even though they are quite complicated. The typewriter contains a mechanism that translates a keystroke into a series of mechanical events that produce the desired result. The purpose of the translator is to disguise the basic mechanical events in order to make the typewriter easy to use.

Let's get more specific to make this idea clear. When you strike the letter "a" on a typical typewriter keyboard, the following events occur: (1)

7

the ribbon raises; (2) the "a" striker bangs against the platen; (3) the ribbon lowers; (4) the assembly moves to the next print position (unless you are at the margin); and (5) the bell rings if you are a certain number of spaces from the right margin. The typewriter mechanism translates a key depression into a series of internal actions resulting in a letter being printed.

We can imagine a typewriter that lacks the mechanism that translates the keystrokes into the sequence of mechanical events. One of the meanings of the prefix "proto" is "the earliest form." Let's use the term prototypewriter to describe a machine that can perform all of the low-level functions of a typewriter. A prototypewriter can raise and lower the ribbon, move the mechanism back and forth, bang the symbols against the platen, and so on. However, our imaginary prototypewriter lacks the high-level capability of a typewriter to print a letter in response to a single keystroke. In order to use the prototypewriter you would have to memorize the sequence of primitive operations that are required to perform each advanced function (e.g., printing an "a"). One could argue that a prototypewriter is more powerful than a regular typewriter because it is more general-purpose. You could make a prototypewriter type right to left, diagonally, or vertically. However, a prototypewriter would be tremendously awkward, and I suspect that we will never see one on the market.

A computer is somewhat like a prototypewriter. It has potential for being very useful, but it isn't endowed with a convenient, high-level control mechanism. It is conceptually easy to build a translator into a prototypewriter in order to create a convenient and useful device, because a typewriter is a single-purpose device. It is much harder to endow a computer with a convenient set of operations, because computers are general-purpose machines. The role of an operating system is to make it easy to use a general-purpose computer. An operating system endows a computer with a set of useful functions just as the keyboard translator endows a prototypewriter with a set of useful operations.

2.2 TYPICAL COMPUTERS

Many different types of computer are manufactured. Even though there is great variety among computers, the pressures of the marketplace and the path of technology have led to a certain standardization of the major functional units. (See Figs. 2.1 and 2.2.)

Basically, a computer is a machine that follows a sequence of instructions. The instructions perform operations such as adding two numbers, moving some information from one location to another, or branching to a different place in the sequence of instructions. The part of the computer that executes the instructions is called the *processor* (the central processing unit, abbreviated CPU), and the place where the instructions are stored is called the *memory*. The CPU is the part of a computer where information

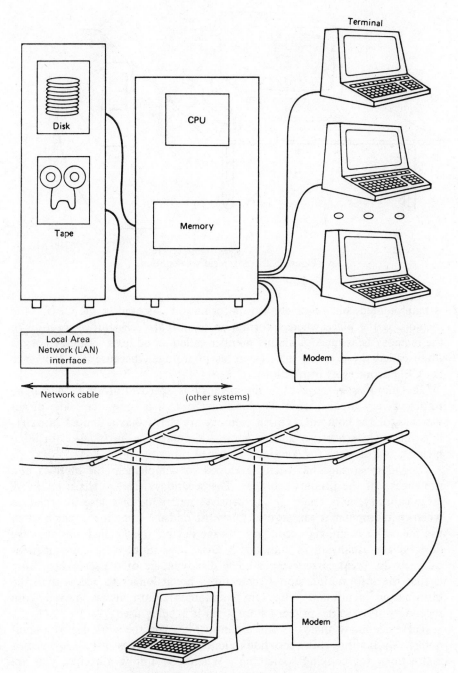

Figure 2.1.   A typical multiuser computer.

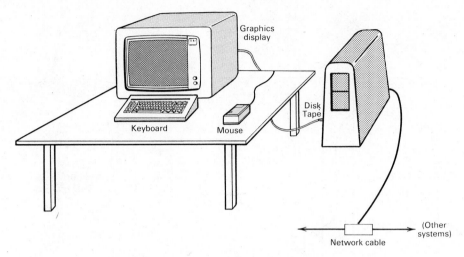

Figure 2.2.   A typical workstation.

is manipulated, but relatively little information is stored in the CPU. The memory is the place where information is stored; each storage location in the memory is assigned a unique number called an address. The memory is often called the primary store (store as in storage), because it is the place the CPU acquires its instructions.

The major advantage of main memory is speed. Information can be retrieved very rapidly from the main memory of a computer. The disadvantages of the computer's main memory are that it has a limited capacity, it is relatively expensive, and on most computers the information in main memory is lost when the computer is turned off.

Secondary storage has been developed to complement the abilities and drawbacks of the primary storage. The secondary storage has a relatively large capacity, it is relatively inexpensive, and it doesn't lose information when the computer is turned off. On most midsize computers, which often use the UNIX system, the secondary storage devices (also called mass storage devices) are usually disks and tapes. Disks and tapes store data magnetically, as do audio cassette tapes. The disadvantage of the secondary store is that the information stored there takes much longer to access than the information in primary store. Information is almost always moved from secondary store to the primary store when it is being used.

There are many analogies that attempt to explain the workings of a computer. My favorite is the cookbook analogy. A recipe is just a sequence of instructions for cooking something. When you follow a recipe, you are doing the same thing that the CPU is doing when it is running a program. Just as there are many different recipes in a cookbook, there can be many different programs in a computer.

I suspect that computers seem so mysterious because they work electrically and they store information in patterns of ones and zeroes. If computers were able to read a cookbook and prepare meals (a much harder task), then people might not be so impressed.

A collection of information on a disk or a tape is called a *file,* and files are usually identified by names. The way files are organized is one of the central features of a computer system. Disks and tapes usually contain many files (often thousands), so it is important for a computer to be able to locate a given file quickly. Therefore, computers maintain lists of files and their locations. You have to understand the basic organization of these lists in order to direct the computer to access files. This very important topic is discussed in Chapter 5.

You communicate with most minicomputers by using a *computer terminal.* A computer terminal has a typewriterlike keyboard and an output device. A display terminal uses a television-style output device, and a printing terminal uses a printer output device. A few terminals have displays and printers in one package. Some other names for display terminals are video terminals and CRT (cathode ray tube) terminals. General-purpose voice entry is still years away, so if you want to use computers, you should become familiar with the layout of the keyboard.

Personal computers usually have an integral (or closely attached) display and keyboard. The difference between a terminal and a personal computer is features and flexibility. A personal computer typically has its own peripherals, such as disks and tapes; it has a more powerful CPU, more memory, and its own operating software. If you have a personal computer such as an IBM PC, you can run UNIX directly on it, or you can run the simpler DOS operating system on your PC, and then run a communications program (a software package that mimics a terminal) to access the UNIX system running on some other computer system.

Computer terminals can be connected to a computer over telephone lines or by direct connections. Direct connections are preferable, because they are faster and simpler, but they work only when the computer terminal and the computer are physically close (within a half mile or so).

A *modem* is a device that allows computers and terminals to communicate over great distances, usually using the public telephone system. Modems translate electrical signals into audible chirps and squeals that can be sent through the telephone network.

2.3   OPERATING SYSTEMS

An *operating system* is a program that manages the resources of a computer. Operating systems send information to the communication devices, manage the storage space on disks, load information and programs into memory, and so on. In computer systems that allow several people to use the system simultaneously, the operating system arbitrates the various requests in order to distribute the computer's resources fairly and effectively.

There is nothing mysterious about using a well-designed operating system. You just have to know how the system is organized. Unfortunately, some people have a bad impression of operating systems, because some of the early operating systems were almost more of a hindrance than a help.

The complexity of operating systems usually varies with the complexity of the host computer system. Very simple computer systems usually have very simple operating systems. For example, the IBM personal computer uses a simple operating system called MS-DOS. (Actually, MS-DOS is a good example of a simple system only in its early versions. MS-DOS is evolving in the direction of the UNIX system, and later MS-DOS systems exhibit a complexity nearing that of the UNIX system.) It performs many of the same tasks as the UNIX system, but only for a single user.

Computers in the middle range of complexity, price, and performance are called *minicomputers*. The UNIX system was originally designed to run on minis, although now there are versions of the UNIX system for very small computers *(microcomputers)* and very large computers *(mainframes)*. On some minicomputer operating systems, only one program can be run at a time, whereas others allow several programs to run simultaneously. Running several programs at once is called *multiprogramming* or *(multitasking)*, and it is difficult to achieve. Therefore, operating systems that don't include multiprogramming (e.g., MS-DOS) are usually much simpler than those that do.

The UNIX system is a moderately complex operating system. It is far simpler than the operating systems that run on most maxicomputers, but it has much more capability than most operating systems that run on microcomputers. For example, the UNIX system allows you to run several programs simultaneously, and it has an advanced system for storing files.

2.4   TIME SHARING

Time sharing is a technique that has been developed for making a computer perform several jobs at once. The goal of time sharing is to give each user the illusion of exclusive use of the machine. Time sharing works because modern computers can perform millions of operations in a second. At that rate, a computer is able to devote thousands of operations to your tasks, and thousands to your neighbor's, and thousands to the job of coordinating everything—all in a single second.

In an interactive computer system, the computer is always waiting for you to tell it what it should do. When you ask the computer to run a program, it starts running immediately, and the computer works diligently on it until it is finished. The computer may be doing some other operations at the same time, but basically your program starts as soon as you enter the command and the computer makes continuous progress.

Time sharing works by dividing each unit of time into a number of slices. Each executing program receives a slice of time. When more programs are executing, each program receives a smaller slice than when only a few programs are executing. Since computers are very fast devices, they can switch rapidly from one job to another, creating the appearance that the computer is performing many tasks simultaneously. In fact, the computer is making progress on one task and then switching to the next, and the next, and so on.

Some time-sharing systems become very inefficient when they are overloaded. Inefficiency strikes when the demand is so large that the computer spends most of its time switching between programs and very little time actually running programs.

2.5 NETWORKING

When computers were rare, each could be utilized fully in isolation. However, today, with the ever increasing numbers of computers, it is increasingly important to be able to move information easily between computers. A *network* is a group of computers that have hardware and software that enable them to communicate.

A *wide-area network* (WAN) is a network consisting of computers that are far apart. Machines in a WAN typically communicate using the public telephone system, higher-speed leased telephone lines, microwaves or other high-speed terrestrial data links, or satellites. One of the earliest, and probably the most famous, WAN is the Advanced Research Projects Agency (ARPA) network developed to support defense industry projects. In the UNIX community, there is a UUCP (UNIX-to-UNIX copy) network connecting, mostly via ordinary dial-up telephone lines, thousands of UNIX systems.

When computer systems are physically close, high-performance, cost-effective *local area networks* (LANs) are feasible. A LAN requires special cabling and interfaces, and typical LANs are limited to a distance of about a mile. Usually the term LAN is reserved for high-speed communications (at least 1 million bits per second). For example, two computers in a building might be connected by a serial data line operated at 10,000 bits per second. Such a connection wouldn't usually be called a LAN, even though it might perform many LAN functions. One of the most common LANs in the UNIX environment is the Ethernet. UNIX networking is discussed more in Chapter 20.

2.6   THE KERNEL

Certain operating system functions are used almost continuously. For example, the part of the UNIX system that is involved in switching from one program to another (time sharing) is needed many times each second. In the UNIX system, all of the functions that are needed immediately are constantly kept in memory. The memory resident part of an operating system is called the *kernel*.

Other operating system functions are needed only occasionally, such as the capability to move a file from one place to another. These types of functions are provided by *utilities,* standard programs that are invoked upon demand by the computer users. In the UNIX system, it is easy for people to add to the stock of utilities by simply writing a new and useful program.

In many operating systems, the kernel contains a great many features. The UNIX system attempts to endow the kernel with relatively few features, so that most operating system functions can be provided by utility programs. If you are curious about the kernel, you should read Chapter 25. The UNIX system kernel is simple enough to be understood in principle by most users.

2.7   PROGRAMS

A *program* is a sequence of instructions that the computer follows to achieve a certain result. Programs are important because they are the only interface between people and the power of computers. When a program is not being executed, the sequence of instructions is stored in a mass storage device (usually a disk). To run the program, a copy of the instructions must be loaded into memory.

When a UNIX program is running, it is called a *process*. If several people are running the same program at about the same time, then there are several processes but only one program.

Well-designed programs work flexibly. It would be foolish to write a program that changed the name of a file from 'alex' to 'alicia.' The program would be used once and then discarded. Instead, there is a program that renames a file, and it is your responsibility when you run the program to supply the two names, which are called parameters.

Although well-designed programs work flexibly, all programs have limits. Sometimes the limits seem arbitrary. For example, you can't use the program that changes the names of files to change other types of names in the system, such as the name that you use in your dialogues with the UNIX system (your login name). When you use a program, it is important to know what information the program requires from you, what the program can do, and what it cannot do.

Most UNIX programs perform just one function. A complicated operation such as using the computer to write and distribute a memo requires a sequence of programs. It is up to you to decompose complicated operations (e.g., writing a memo) into a series of steps that correspond to the available set of programs. As you become proficient with the UNIX system, you will realize that there are usually several different approaches to most complicated operations.

Programs can be divided into two general classes: utility programs and application programs. Utility programs usually perform general functions, whereas application programs are designed for specific purposes. For example, a program that an accounting firm runs to automate its bookkeeping would be classified as an application program, whereas a program that displays the time would usually be considered a utility. Some utilities are usually supplied with an operating system, whereas application programs are often acquired separately.

One purpose of this book is to acquaint you with the most useful UNIX system utility programs. Chapters 6, 7, and 8 present many of the most common and useful of the UNIX system utility programs. The majority of these programs are simple, effective tools for performing simple functions. The presentation of the programs in these three chapters shows typical applications. The idea is to acquaint you with these programs, not to present an exhaustive treatment of each program. After reading the general descriptions in this book, you should be able to learn the details of the important utilities from the documents supplied with your system, or from *The UNIX Command Reference Guide*.

2.8   THE SHELL AND THE EDITOR

Typical UNIX users spend much of their time using two programs: the shell and the editor. To use the UNIX system flexibly, you need to have a working knowledge of many other programs, but these two programs are especially important.

An editor is a program that allows you to create and modify text files. You control the editor by entering commands. All editors contain commands to display lines of a file, commands to add text to a file, and commands to change text that has already been entered.

There are two common types of editors, *line* editors and *visual* (also called *screen*, or *display*) editors. In a line editor the focus of your work is always on one (or several) lines of the file. Most line editor commands operate on whole lines, such as adding lines, deleting lines, moving lines, or altering the text on a line. In a line editor, each time you display lines of the file they appear on the bottom of the screen, causing past work to scroll off the top. While using a line editor, the screen is a record of your activities; it is not an up-to-date display of the contents of the file.

A visual editor makes the screen a window into the file. Whenever changes are made to the file, the screen is immediately updated. Commands in a visual editor often work with units of text other than lines, e.g., characters, words, and paragraphs. Visual editors are good for interactive use, but line editors are usually better at executing prepared editing scripts.

UNIX systems contain several different text editor programs. The original editor was ed, a simple but effective line editor. ed is important because it is universally available and because the style of operation pioneered by ed has been adopted by many other programs. ed is discussed in Appendix III.

However, for interactive use, better editors are now available for UNIX systems. In this book the focus is on vi, a descendant of ed that was developed at Berkeley. vi is powerful, flexible, and almost universally available. Hence it is the program best able to claim to be the "standard" UNIX editor.

You can acquire a basic working knowledge of the vi editor in Chapter 9. A basic understanding will allow you to use vi, but if you plan to use it extensively, you should also become familiar with the advanced functions discussed in Chapter 10. Appendix I summarizes the vi command set, and Appendix II describes vi's options.

The shell is one of the most important programs in the UNIX system. Like the editor, the shell is an interactive program. You control the shell by entering commands which the shell interprets (decodes) and executes. Therefore, the technical name for the shell is *command interpreter*.

The function of a command interpreter is to execute the commands that you enter. For instance, if you want to run the program that prints the date and time on your screen, you enter the command date, and the shell then arranges for that program to be executed.

On many systems, the command interpreter is a part of the internal structure of the operating system. However, in the UNIX system, the shell is just an ordinary program, similar to the date program or any other program. The only thing that is special about the shell is that it is central to most of your interactions with the UNIX system. If you are a typical user, you will spend much of your time entering shell commands. The shell has many features that can increase your effectiveness.

The UNIX system is really a tool for information management. The power of the UNIX system stems from its ability to let programs work together to produce the information you need. On some computer systems, each program is a world unto itself. In the UNIX system, most utilities are simple tools that can be combined with other programs to produce more powerful tools.

The shell is the key to coordinating and combining UNIX system programs. Several chapters present the features of the shell. About half of Chapter 3 is a very simple introduction to the shell. Chapter 4 focuses entirely on the shell as an interactive command interpreter. The information in Chapter 4 may seem dry on first reading; try to work through it a second time after you have some experience with the UNIX system.

Besides being an interactive command interpreter, the shell is a very sophisticated programming language. Most users ignore the programming language features of the shell, simply because most users are not computer programmers. However, if you want to use the shell as a programming language, read Chapter 11 and work through the examples given in Chapter 12.

CHAPTER 3

UNIX System Basics

Learning about a new computer system is like visiting a foreign country—the experience is intimidating at first. Even though the UNIX system is well designed, as a novice you may occasionally be frustrated. The purpose of this chapter is to help you during your first few encounters with the UNIX system. You should skip this chapter if you are already familiar with it.

Some people want to read a short paragraph that will tell them everything they need to know in order to use the UNIX system. Perhaps a typewriter or a toaster can be described that briefly, but a computer operating system can't. To use the UNIX system effectively, you have to master a fairly large body of knowledge. However, most of the ideas are straightforward, and if you are patient, you will soon be an effective UNIX system user.

The UNIX system is harder to use than a toaster, but then it does more than a toaster. Learning the UNIX system is somewhat like learning a complex skill such as swimming or bicycle riding. At first none of your reflexes seem appropriate, but eventually the skill is mastered.

3.1 LOGGING IN

The first thing you have to do to use the UNIX system is to *log in*. The purpose of logging in is twofold: to let the UNIX system verify your right to use the system, and to let it set up your environment. In computer systems that allow access over the telephone, it is very important to restrict use to authorized people, and in computer systems where people are charged, it is important to know who is using the computer so that the billing can accurately reflect use. One of the functions of the UNIX system is to manage the

18

computer resource so that several people can share the computer. In order to do this, the UNIX system maintains a separate environment for each user. The UNIX system remembers who each user is, when each logged in, how much computer time each has used, what files each owns, what files are immediately accessible, what type of a terminal is being used, and so on.

In most single-user computer systems (e.g., home computers), there is no login procedure, because physical access to the hardware confirms your right to use the system. In some mainframe operating systems, there is no formal login process; instead, each submitted job is identified for billing and scheduling purposes. In the UNIX system, once you have completed the login process, you don't have to identify yourself each time you run a program.

Before you can log in for the first time the system administrator must create your account. It is usually simple to set up an account at a UNIX system installation that doesn't charge the user for computer time. Setting up an account at installations that charge for computer time is more difficult, because information about billing and money is required. See Chapter 23 for more information.

From your point of view, the major issue in setting up an account is deciding on your login name and password. The login name is the name that you want to use during your interactions with the UNIX system. Short, lowercase names are usually easiest. Many people use their initials, nickname, or first name. The names "betsy," "kc," and "m" are all acceptable. (Note that some installations impose additional restrictions on your login name, such as making you use your last name, your employee ID number, or your student ID number.)

Once you have an account, you can try logging in. If you are using a dial-up terminal, set the full-duplex/half-duplex switch to full and set the speed of the terminal to the correct speed. Dial the number of the computer, and wait for it to answer. Things are easier from a hardwired terminal—simply strike return or Control-d once or twice in order to get a fresh "login:" message.

Once you have established a connection, the computer will type something on your terminal. If the message is

```
login:
```

or something similar, then the communication speeds (of the terminal and the computer) are synchronized, and you can go ahead and enter your login name. If the message on your screen is garbled, then hit the *break* key on your terminal. The break causes the UNIX system to change its communication speed in an attempt to synchronize with your terminal. The UNIX system will type a fresh login message. If the message is garbled, try hitting the break key again. The UNIX system may cycle through a list of four or five speeds to match speed with your terminal. If after four or five attempts you can't get the UNIX system to print a clear login message on your terminal, you should seek the help of a resident expert.

Eventually you will see the "login:" message. Enter your login name and hit return. After a brief pause, the UNIX system will ask for your password. A password is a secret word that you enter to confirm your identity. (Your initial password is usually assigned when your account is created; you can change it at any time.) Enter your password and hit return.

During most of your interactions with the UNIX system, you will see each character that you type. However, while you are entering your password, the UNIX system will try to maintain the privacy of your password by not echoing the characters that you are typing. The UNIX system is listening, but not echoing. You must type your password very carefully, because you will not see it as it is entered. If you make a typing mistake, you will probably have to restart the login process from the beginning.

Once you have entered your password, the system checks it. If it passes inspection, then the login process will continue. If the password or login name is incorrect, you will be asked to enter your login name and password again. Many UNIX systems allow one or two incorrect login attempts before they hang up the phone. On some systems, the password system is not used. Other systems have an additional layer of security; they require you to enter a dial-up password before you are asked to enter your login name and personal password.

The UNIX system may print several messages at the end of the login process. The messages may divulge news about system scheduling, new programs, users' meetings, and so forth. After the messages the UNIX system will print a prompt to indicate that the system is ready to accept your commands. The default prompt is usually a currency symbol ($) on System V or a percent symbol (%) on Berkeley systems.

The following dialogue shows the login process. In this dialogue, as in most dialogues in this book, user input is in a slightly bolder typeface than the computer's output. (Here the user input is the word *kc*.)

```
login: kc
Password:
NOTICE  - The system will be down
from 17:00 to 19:00 tomorrow
for routine maintenance.
Remember, monthly users meeting
this Weds at 5 pm.
$ _
```

In this dialogue, you should notice that the user name, *kc*, is echoed on the screen, but the password is not visible (because it is not echoed, to maintain security).

A command is a request for the UNIX system to do something. Following a prompt, you type in a command followed by a carriage return, then the

UNIX system attempts to perform the command. When the UNIX system has finished running the command, it displays a fresh prompt. Three of the most common UNIX commands—date, who, and echo—are discussed in the next section.

3.2 SOME SIMPLE COMMANDS

The best way to learn about the UNIX system is to use it. Try the date command.

```
$ date
Weds July  5  11:08:17 EDT 1987
$ _
```

Remember that the currency symbol is the standard UNIX prompt. (The prompt may be different on your system.) To enter the date command, type the letters *d, a, t,* and *e* followed by a carriage return (often marked *Enter* on the keyboard). The carriage return says to the computer, "I've finished typing the command, now it's your turn." Don't forget to type the carriage return at the end of every entry. In the diagrams of UNIX dialogues in this book, I don't show the carriage return explicitly. That's because using the carriage return key quickly becomes a reflex, and I don't want to clutter the dialogue text with information that everyone understands.

Next try the who command.

```
$ who
td      tty10    Jul 5     7:03
kc      tty18    Jul 5     8:18
alvy    tty11    Jul 5    11:03
karl    tty03    Jul 5    11:03
$ _
```

The system lists people who are currently using the system along with the time they first logged in and the identification name of the terminal they are using. Notice that your login name (*kc* in the above dialogue) is in the list.

Now let's explore the echo command.

```
$ echo hello
hello
$ _
```

In this dialogue the word *echo* is the name of the command, and the word *hello* is an argument to the command. Arguments are used to supply additional information to a command. The echo command simply repeats its arguments. Several uses for the echo command will be seen later in this book.

In the dialogue shown above, the user entry, *echo hello*, is often referred to as a *command line*. A command line is a single line of text that you type to tell the UNIX system to do something. The first word on the line is typically the command name; additional words are the arguments.

In the UNIX system, commands and their arguments (there can be several arguments) are separated by spaces or tabs. The white space (spaces or tabs) is extremely important. If you omit the white space, the system will not understand your command. The following command fails because the white space is missing.

```
$ echohello
sh: echohello not found
$ _
```

Capitalization is also extremely important. The UNIX system understands that lowercase letters are different from uppercase letters. The names of most UNIX commands are written in lowercase. If you type in the wrong case, the system will not understand your command.

```
$ Echo Hello
sh: Echo not found
$ _
```

3.3 FILES AND DIRECTORIES

A *file* is a named collection of information. You will use numerous files in your interactions with the UNIX system. The computer term "file" is extremely well chosen. A computer file is completely analogous to a paper file stored in a filing cabinet. Computer files have names, they have lengths, they can get bigger and smaller, they can be created and discarded, and they can be examined.

It is impossible to exaggerate the importance of files in the UNIX system. Every time you run a program, you are accessing a file. Most of the programs you run then access more files—often files that you have mentioned on the command line.

Though there may be thousands of files in a UNIX system, only a few of the files are visible at one time. In the UNIX system, files are clustered into groups called *directories*. Each directory has a name; for example, the full name of the directory that contains many of my files is '/usr1/kc'. Throughout this book the names of files and directories are surrounded by single quotes as in '/usr1/kc'. Most other quoted items in this book are surrounded by double quotes. The filesystem is discussed in detail in

Chapter 5, and the utility programs for managing files are discussed in Chapter 6.

One of the reasons for the login process is to establish your initial environment. One element of your environment is the name of your *current directory*. When you first log in, the system makes the current directory your *home directory*. Each user usually has his own home directory. If your account has just been created for you, then your home directory is probably empty except for a few administrative files.

It is easy to confuse your home directory and your working (current) directory. Your home directory is created when your account is created, and it typically contains many of your files. Naturally, the home directory is where you start out after you log in. The current directory is where you are right now. Since you can move from one directory to another, your current directory can change, but your home directory is fixed in place (unless it is moved or renamed by the system administrator).

The pwd (print working directory) command prints the name of the current directory. Since different files are available in different directories, you should always be aware of the name of the current directory.

```
$ pwd
/usr1/kc
$ _
```

On my system, the pathname '/usr1/kc' is displayed on my terminal when I run the pwd command just after logging in. On your system, the name of your own home directory will be displayed. The organization of the UNIX filesystem and the use of pathnames (e.g., '/usr1/kc') are discussed in the next chapter. The remainder of this chapter only requires you to understand that files are grouped into units called directories.

Besides knowing the name of the current directory, you often want to know what files are in the current directory. The ls (list) command is used to list the files in a directory.

```
$ ls
alphasrch
betatest
csrc
fontinfo
hacks
m2src
pfiles
src
unixbook
$ _
```

A list of the files in the current directory will be printed. If your account has just been created, it will contain only a few (none on some systems) administrative files.

There are certain standard directories on most UNIX systems. The directory '/bin' usually contains many of the programs that you use. When you supply the name of a directory as an argument to the ls command, all of the files in that directory are listed. Enter the command

```
$ ls /bin
```

to see a list of the files in the '/bin' directory. (Since there are over 100 files in most '/bin' directories, the output part of the previous command isn't shown.)

The UNIX system allows you to change your context so that any accessible directory becomes the current directory.

```
$ cd /bin
$ _
```

Now try the pwd command to verify that you are in a new directory.

```
$ pwd
/bin
$ _
```

Now that you are in the '/bin' directory, you can use the ls command to list all of the files in '/bin'. Remember that when you were in your home directory, you had to use the argument '/bin' with the ls command to get this same list of files.

As you can see, the operation of some commands varies according to what directory you are in. Many people are very confused by the rather changeable UNIX system environment. Operations that work in one directory often either don't work or produce different results in another. You should always be aware of the name of the current directory. Once you understand the UNIX system directory structure, you will see that directories are an asset, not an impediment.

3.4 UNIX SYSTEM DIALOGUES

Users engage in dialogues with the UNIX system. Typically the user enters a command, and then the UNIX system replies. For simple commands, the reply usually occurs in a second or so. Complicated commands can take much longer, and even simple commands can take forever when a UNIX system is seriously overloaded. We will discuss the dialogue rules in some detail, because the dialogue is central to working effectively with the UNIX system.

Entering a UNIX system command is analogous to submitting a job on certain other computer systems. When you enter a command, you ask the computer to do something for you. For now, you can imagine that the phrase "entering a command" means that the computer runs a program for you. As you learn more about the UNIX system, you will realize that entering a command often involves more than just running a program, and you will begin to understand how the UNIX system environment makes the whole greater than the sum of its parts.

As a beginner, you should enter just one command on a line. Later chapters will show you how to enter several commands on one line or to run several commands at once. You enter a line of input by typing a string of characters and then hitting the carriage-return key. The carriage return specifies the end of a line of input, and when you are entering commands, it usually specifies the end of a command entry and tells the UNIX system to execute the command.

One difference between the computer and human listeners is that the computer virtually ignores your sentence (command) until you hit return. It is easier to talk to human listeners, because they give you feedback as you talk. Another difference between computers and human listeners is that the computer is extremely picky about what you say (type). People will usually understand what you are saying even if your grammar or pronunciation is poor, but the dumb computer is stopped cold by the simplest typo. You have to be careful as you type your commands, or you will spend most of your time reentering them.

Once you hit the return key, the UNIX system suddenly becomes interested in what you have typed. The UNIX system immediately attempts to figure out what you want. The first word of the command is usually the command name, and a program called the shell attempts to locate that particular command. Let's suppose that you want to run the echo program but by mistake you enter the Echo. We saw above that you get a message similar to *sh:Echo not found*, because there is no command named *Echo*.

If the command is located, then it starts to run, and the shell goes to sleep, waiting for the command to finish. Each particular command has its own format for telling you about errors in your input. For example, you might want to list the files in the '/bin' directory but by mistake you enter the word '/bum'.

```
$ ls /bum
/bum: not found
$ _
```

When you make a mistake in entering the argument to a command, it is the command itself that prints an error message. In the example above, it is ls that complains about the missing '/bum' directory. Although an attempt has been made to make the UNIX system error messages uniform, you will certainly encounter some misleading messages. Your only consolation is that the UNIX system is better than some systems at flagging your erroneous input.

It is important to understand that the characters you type are not sent directly from the keyboard to the screen. Instead, the characters are sent first to the UNIX system and then back to your screen. This rather complicated arrangement is for flexibility. The UNIX system gets each character before it is printed on your screen, so that it can perform any necessary transformations. As an example, the UNIX system can translate a tab character into an appropriate number of space characters. Or the UNIX system can refrain from returning characters to you at certain times, such as when you are entering a private password.

As you type in your line of input, the UNIX system is spending most of its time attending to other matters. However, two special characters are attended to immediately: the *erase* character and the *kill* character. The erase character erases the already entered characters (backing up) one at a time, and the kill character erases the whole line so you can start over.

You can specify which key on your keyboard should be used for the erase character and which should be used for the kill character. For historical reasons, many UNIX systems initially assign the erase character to the number symbol (#) and the kill character to the commercial "at" sign (@). These characters are used because they are present on most terminals and they are seldom used otherwise. If your terminal has more suitable characters, the erase and kill should be reassigned using the `stty` command. On many terminals the Control-H key or the rubout key is used instead of the number symbol as the erase character, and the Control-U key is often used in place of the commercial at sign as the kill character. (A control character is entered by holding down the CTRL button and then hitting the specified character.) On some systems the only way to correct errors during the entry of your login name and password is to use the number symbol and the commercial at because the reassignment doesn't occur until near the end of the internal login procedure.

Here is an example of using the erase character (assigned in this case to the default number symbol):

```
$ qgi###wgo##ho
td       tty10    Jul 5     7:03
kc       tty18    Jul 5     8:18
$ _
```

If you follow the character sequence shown, you will see that the user actually specified the who command; the first false start was *qgi*, and the next was *wgo*.

Here is an example of using the kill character (assigned in this example to the commercial at sign) to erase a mangled input line so that it can be completely retyped:

```
$ echohello@
echo hello
hello
$ _
```

The exact appearance of a line following the entry of the kill character varies from system to system. On some systems, the kill character erases the input line if you are using a display terminal. This is very hard to show in a book. On other systems, the kill character automatically advances you to the next line (as shown in the example above), and on some older systems the kill character logically erases the line, but there is no acknowledgment on the screen.

While you are typing a line you can use the erase character to erase portions of the line or the kill character to erase the whole line and start over. However, once you strike the return key, your input is interpreted as a command.

Many commands perform one function and then stop. For example, a program to type a file will type the file and then be finished. Other commands work *interactively*. One example of an interactive command is a text editor. The text editor interactively accepts commands from the user using a dialogue similar to the UNIX system command dialogue that we are describing in this chapter.

While you are executing an interactive program, only the commands of that program are directly available. When the interactive program terminates, you return to command level and a prompt is printed to tell you that the UNIX system is ready to accept your commands. You always have to remember the context while using a computer. Once you become familiar with the system, this context switching will become a reflex. When things don't work as you expect, you should explicitly think about the context of the situation. Perhaps you are entering editor commands while you are in the UNIX system command mode, or perhaps you are entering UNIX commands while you are in the editor.

Occasionally you will run a program that you want to stop before it is finished. In the UNIX system you stop a running program by striking the *interrupt* character. The interrupt character is similar to the erase and kill characters in that it leads to immediate action by the system. The interrupt character is usually assigned to the delete key (often labeled "DEL") or to Control-C. The interrupt character can be assigned to any key on your terminal using the stty command.

Because certain programs must not be halted during critical sections of their operation, the UNIX system allows programs to disable the interrupt function. If a program has disabled the interrupt function, then the interrupt key will have no effect. For example, the text editor disables interrupts during most of its operation because you don't want to lose the file you are working on by accidentally striking the interrupt key. (Those of you who understand the internal working of computer hardware should be careful not to confuse the unix system interrupt function with hardware interrupts.)

3.5 LOGGING OFF

It is much easier to log off (also called logging out) than to log on. When you are finished using the system, you should log off. Logging out informs the system that you are not going to place any further demands on the system. In a system where you are billed by the minute, it is very important to log off as soon as you finish your work. In a system where computer time is "free," logging off is simply a courtesy to the other computer users.

You can log off by running the exit command. Another way to log off is to strike a Control-D at the beginning of a line. The Control-D is the unix system's end of file character. Typing an end of file character tells the unix system that there are no further commands to process. If you are connected to the system by a dial-up line, an alternate way to log off is to hang up the phone.

3.6 THE UNIX SYSTEM MANUAL

One of the major reference documents for anyone who is using the unix system is the *Unix Programmer's Manual* (UPM). (Some editions use the title *Unix User's Manual*.) The UPM contains information about most of the commands that are available on your system. Make sure that you have the manual that is appropriate for the version of the unix system you are using. Obsolete manuals are frequently more readily available than the latest version.

This book is not a replacement for the UPM. The UPM contains specific information for your system, and it contains specific information for many obscure commands and features that aren't discussed in this book. The strength and the weakness of the UPM are that it is specific. In contrast, this book attempts to present general information that pertains to all unix systems. Another function of this book is to distinguish the common and useful programs from the obscure. Naturally the UPM gives equal treatment to all programs.

The UPM is designed by and for people who are familiar with the basic operation and services of the unix system. If you are a novice user, you might find that some of the descriptions in the manual are too terse to be very helpful. As you become a more advanced user, you might find that the terse style of the manual makes it easier to use than a verbose manual.

Most simple commands are described adequately in the manual. For example, the reference for the `pwd` command in my manual states clearly:

```
Pwd prints the pathname of the working (current) directory.
```

However, the manual entries for many of the more complicated commands are much less useful for a novice. Some of the more complicated commands are described in separate documents, often in reprints of papers published in academic journals. These accounts are usually adequate descriptions for computer scientists, but sometimes they are indecipherable to casual users.

The UPM is traditionally divided into eight sections. The first section describes most of the commands that are available on the system. Sections 2 through 8 describe aspects of the system that programmers are interested in. For most nonprogrammers, Sections 2 through 8 are mere curiosities (except for Section 6—Games). In most modern UNIX systems, Section 1 of the manual is in its own volume.

Section 1 of the manual contains an alphabetized list of citations for the UNIX system commands. There should be a citation in Section 1 for most commands that are available at your installation. Commands that are unique to your installation, such as graphics commands at a graphics laboratory, are often described in a locally distributed addendum to the manual.

Closely related commands are occasionally discussed in a single citation. In my UPM, the `mv` (move), `cp` (copy), and `ln` (link) commands are all discussed in a single citation, because they all shuffle files. If you can't remember the exact name of a command, you should try looking up any related word in the permuted index. For example, you could look up the word "move" in the permuted index in order to discover that the `cp` citation describes how to *copy, link, or move files*. The permuted index in the UPM is similar to the keyword in context index used by some abstracting services and scholarly journals.

Each citation in Section 1 of the UPM follows a uniform format. The top of the citation shows the name and a brief description followed by a synopsis of the command. For the `ls` command the top of the citation looks like

```
NAME
ls - list contents of directories
SYNOPSIS
ls [ -ltasdriu ] [ names ]
```

The synopsis gives you an indication of how you would enter the command. The synopsis for `ls` indicates that you enter the word "ls" optionally followed by a list of options (one or more of the characters "ltasdriu" preceded by a hyphen) followed by a list of names of directories or files. Square brackets in the synopsis indicate that the bracketed quantity is optional. The example above shows that both the options and the names are optional for the ls command.

The description of the command usually follows the synopsis. For the ls command, the description is a little more than a page long. The description of a command usually describes the basic operation of the command and how you can alter the basic operation by using various options. For example, the ls command has options that allow you to display additional information along with the list of file names.

After the description are several brief paragraphs: the FILES paragraph names any files that are used by the program, the SEE ALSO paragraph lists related commands whose citations might contain useful information, the BUGS paragraph might contain some useful caveats, and the DIAGNOSTICS paragraph might help you to decipher error messages. Any or all of these four paragraphs may be omitted, and additional paragraphs may be present. The entire citation for most commands is about a page long.

The citations in Sections 2 through 8 of the manual follow a similar format that should be understandable by anyone who needs to use these sections. They will not be discussed here. Remember that as a novice you will usually use Section 1 of the manual. Beware that Sections 2 through 8 occasionally contain citations with the same names as citations in Section 1. Many versions of UNIX contain the man command to print citations from the UPM.

My book, *The UNIX Command Reference Guide*, follows the format pioneered by the UPM. However, I have organized the book topically, so that it is easier to find information, and I have tried to provide more examples and more tips for each command. In addition, my version of the manual focuses solely on the most often used commands. My manual isn't detailed enough for the most demanding user, but it has been shown to be a useful reference for many, especially for casual users or those who are first learning.

CHAPTER 4

Entering Commands Using the Shell

Computers can perform operations at great speed, but they have no sense of value. The computer cannot distinguish between useful work and idle cycling. Since computers have no initiative, they must be told exactly what they should do. Occasionally someone writes a program that makes it appear that a computer has initiative, but in reality the computer is a sloth.

People have developed *command languages* to make it easier to control a computer. Most command languages are designed so that there are easy commands to specify common operations. Commands specify exactly what programs the computer should execute.

Computers do not have an innate ability to decipher the commands you type at the terminal; there must be a *command interpreter* that performs this function. The standard UNIX command interpreter is called the *shell*. To use the UNIX system effectively, you have to know how to enter shell commands.

The shell provides a wealth of features that make it possible to specify very powerful commands. Although it is possible to survive with only a slight knowledge of the shell, your work will be more rewarding and efficient if you learn to use the shell efficiently. For those of you who want to learn more about the shell, Chapters 11 and 12 discuss shell programming and other advanced features. This chapter presents the shell at a level that can benefit all UNIX users.

4.1   UNIX SYSTEM SHELLS

Today the two most common shells are Steven Bourne's *Bourne Shell* (the program is called sh) and Bill Joy's *C Shell* (the program is called csh). Bourne's shell features a powerful command programming language; Joy's shell is known for its interactive features. The Bourne shell is available on virtually all post-Version 6 UNIX systems, so it is the most "standard" UNIX shell. Joy's shell was originally written for BSD UNIX distributions, but variants are available on many systems. Since the complete C shell relies on some of Berkeley's kernel modifications, implementations of it on other UNIX systems are often slightly different.

In most areas, these two shell programs are very similar. Their standard features, syntax, and notation are extremely close, because both designs were heavily influenced by the obsolete Version 6 shell. However, the areas of difference are deep. Both shells contain many of the features of a programming language, but these features are totally incompatible. Another incompatibility is that the C shell has features for interactive command entry, such as job control, aliases, and a history mechanism, that are not found in the Bourne shell.

Many advisers recommend the csh for interactive use and the Bourne shell for writing shell command scripts. The obvious disadvantage of this method is that one must learn two separate systems where ideally one system should suffice. However, most people prefer the C shell amenities for interactive use, and the Bourne shell is the best choice for writing portable shell scripts, because it is the most widely available.

To complicate matters further, several more recent shells are emerging. As an alternative to the Bourne shell/C shell dilemma, Dave Korn wrote his *Korn Shell* (the program is called ksh). The Korn shell is compatible with the Bourne shell, but it contains additional components that make it superior even to the C shell in its interactive capabilities. In addition, the Korn shell is extremely efficient. If it becomes widely available, the Korn shell could become the next "standard" UNIX shell.

However, another candidate for the "next" standard UNIX shell is the Version 8 shell from the UNIX System Research group at Bell Laboratories. The Research shell tries to attain the functionality of the Bourne, Korn, and Joy shells within a traditional UNIX framework that emphasizes general-purpose tools and deemphasizes large programs.

In this book I am emphasizing the features of the Bourne shell because of its universal appeal. Most of the shell dialogues shown in this book are based on the Bourne shell, as signified by the use of the currency symbol ($) as the standard prompt. Nearly all examples of Bourne shell usage in this book (except for the shell programming examples in Chapters 11 and 12) will also work on the C shell, and all of them will work on the Korn shell.

4.2 SIMPLE SHELL COMMANDS

A *simple command* is a sequence of (one or more) words separated by blanks or tabs. The first word of the command is the command's *name*. Subsequent words are the command's *arguments*. (You should remember from Chapter 3 that arguments are used to pass additional information to a command.) The simplest simple command is a single word. For example, the pwd (print working directory) command prints the name of the current directory.

You can enter several commands on one line by separating the commands with semicolons. This feature is useful when you know in advance the sequence of programs that you are going to run. If you want to know the name of the current directory and what files it contains, you might run the pwd program followed by the ls program:

```
$ pwd ; ls
/usr1/kc
book        eg        junk        mbox
$ _
```

When you enter two commands on a single line, separated by a semicolon, the shell runs the programs in quick succession. In the example above, pwd runs first, and then ls runs.

The spaces surrounding the semicolon may be omitted.

```
$ pwd;ls
/usr1/kc
book        eg        junk        mbox
$ _
```

4.3 COMMAND ARGUMENTS

In Chapter 3 we mentioned arguments to commands. Arguments are used to pass additional information to a program. It would be silly to write a program that performed some function (e.g., displaying a file on your terminal) for only one particular file. Instead, programs are written to provide general services.

The ls command that we used in the first example in this chapter didn't require any arguments, since we wanted to use its standard function. You can modify the operation of ls by supplying an argument specifying a long format listing. A long listing prints more information about each file. Arguments that alter the operation of a command are often called *flags* or *options*. (On some other operating systems the options are called switches or controls.) Options are almost always preceded by a hyphen. You can get a long format list of your files by using the option argument l with ls.

```
$ ls -l
drwxrwxrwx    2 kc    staff    320  Nov 19 16:04 book
drwxrwxrwx    2 kc    staff    512  Oct 25 15:32 eg
-rw-rw----    1 kc    staff     17  Nov 13 21:17 junk
-rw-rw-r--    1 kc    staff   2890  May 29  1985 mbox
$ _
```

The name of the command and the argument must be separated by one or more spaces or tabs. (If you omit the white space then you will get an error message similar to "sh: ls-l: not found.")

You should still see the same list of files, but more information will be printed for each file. (The ls command and its options are discussed further in Chapters 5 and 6.) Although it is customary to insert a hyphen in front of option arguments, their format is controlled by the individual commands, not by the shell. (A few commands ignore the custom.)

Arguments to commands often specify file names. The cat program (cat is derived from the word concatenate, which means to combine) can be used to display a file on your terminal. You specify the file by using an argument or arguments. (Other uses of cat are discussed in Section 8.2.) The simplest use of cat is to print a single file on the terminal.

```
$ cat /etc/motd
NOTICE - The system will be down
from 17:00 to 19:00 tomorrow
for routine maintenance.
Remember, monthly users meeting
this Weds at 5 pm.
$ _
```

The file '/etc/motd' contains your system administrator's message of the day. You can display the file at any time using the cat command.

When you enter the command cat /etc/motd, the shell performs a variety of functions. The command consists of two words, cat and /etc/motd. First the shell makes sure that there is a command named cat. Then the shell performs a series of interpretations on the words following the command name. Following the interpretations (more on that in Section 4.6), the total list of words in the command is passed to the program, and the program is started.

Ordinarily, arguments don't contain spaces or tabs, because spaces and tabs are used to separate one argument from the next. However, a *quoted word* can contain spaces or tabs. For example "the end" is a single argument consisting of the seven characters "t" through "d" (including one space). Quoting is discussed in Section 11.5.

The shell knows nothing about the particular arguments that specific programs need. In the example given above, the shell doesn't make sure that the word */etc/motd* references a file. However, the cat program expects that its arguments do in fact reference files, and it is an error to supply an argument to cat that doesn't reference a file. The shell is responsible for passing the argument list to the program, but each program is responsible for making sure that the arguments are reasonable.

4.4 BACKGROUND PROCESSES

Sometimes you need to run programs that take a long time to finish. If the program doesn't require input from the terminal, then you can run it unattended. The shell has a special feature that enables you to start a program and then let it run unattended while you continue to enter shell commands. The program that is running unattended is said to be running in the *background,* whereas the subsequent commands that you enter are running in the *foreground*. The background processes and the foreground process are running simultaneously. You direct the shell to run a program in the background by entering an ampersand following the command. After you strike return, the shell will immediately prompt you to enter another command.

Suppose you want to run a time-consuming program called acctxx. Presumably the acctxx program takes a long time to run, so you might prefer to do something else while it is working. The exact function of acctxx is not important for this example.

```
$ acctxx &
15388
$ _
```

The number printed after the command is the *process id* number (pid) of the background process. It is printed by the shell so that you have a unique way to reference acctxx.

If acctxx produces output that is sent to the terminal, then there will be ample evidence that acctxx is really running. However, if acctxx places its output in a file, then you might prefer to see some evidence that it is actually running. For that you should use the ps program, which will print a list of your processes on your terminal.

```
$ ps
PID    TTY    TIME    CMD
15388  53     0:14    acctxx
15390  053    0:04    ps
$ _
```

Notice that two programs are running. Here the acctxx program and the ps program are running simultaneously. From the ordinary output of the ps command, there is no way to distinguish the background process from the foreground process. (On the Berkeley or Version 7 system, ps will also print information about your login shell.)

You shouldn't run a program in the background if it requires input from the terminal, because both the background program and the shell will be fighting for access to the terminal. It is possible to run a background process that sends voluminous output to the terminal, but it is very awkward because the output is interspersed with the normal foreground output messages.

This brings up a very interesting point. While you are entering a command, the shell is clearly running in the foreground. What happens to the shell while your command is running? In the UNIX system it is possible for a program to go to sleep while waiting for a certain event. When you enter a normal foreground command, the shell sleeps during the execution of the command. When the command completes, the shell wakes up and prompts you for another command. The sleeping shell and the executing command don't fight over the terminal, because the shell sleeps while the command executes. (Incidentally, the terms sleep, wait, and wake up are all standard terms. UNIX jargon is often quite descriptive.)

Here is another way to start the acctxx program in the background and then run ps command in the foreground.

```
$ actxx & ps
15790
    PID    TTY    TIME    CMD
  15790    53    0:03    acctxx
  15791    53    0:03    ps
$ _
```

After ps finishes, the shell prompts you for a command. acctxx will still be running in the background. There is usually a limit (often 20) to the number of background processes that you can have running simultaneously.

4.5 THE STANDARD OUTPUT AND THE STANDARD INPUT

The computer terminal is the basic communication device between the computer and the users. The UNIX system makes it very easy for programs to access the computer terminal, because most utility programs need to produce output on the terminal, and many read input from the terminal. When a program types something on your terminal, the program is (usually) performing output operations to what is called the *standard output*. When you type at your terminal, a program is (usually) reading your typed characters from what is called the *standard input* (see Fig. 4.1). The standard input and the standard output are UNIX system conventions that simplify programs. (The qualifier "usually" is used above in definitions of the standard input and output because it is possible to access the terminal without using the standard input and output. However, the great majority of programs do use the standard input and output connections when they access the terminal.) For example, programs such as ps, ls, who, date, and echo use the standard output to deliver their information to you. Interactive programs (e.g., the shell and the editor) read your commands from the standard input and write their responses on the standard output.

4.5.1 Output Redirection.

The standard input and output are normally attached to the computer terminal. However, since the standard input and output are controlled by the shell, it is possible for the standard input and output to be reassigned by the shell. The shell's ability to reassign the standard input and output is one of the UNIX system's most important features (see Fig. 4.2).

Let's suppose that you want to save the output of the ps command in a file. If you enter the command as shown above, the process status program will write its information on the standard output—your terminal. However, the UNIX notation for output redirection lets you place the ps program's output into a file.

```
$ ps > posterity
$ _
```

The process status program will still write its information to the standard output, but because of the special notation > posterity, the shell will

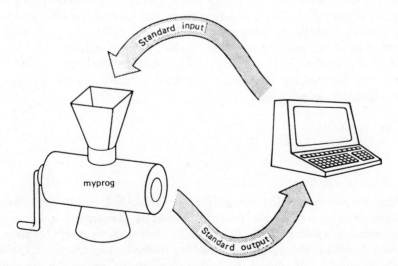

Figure 4.1. The Standard I/O Connections. A program's standard input and output are usually assigned to the terminal.

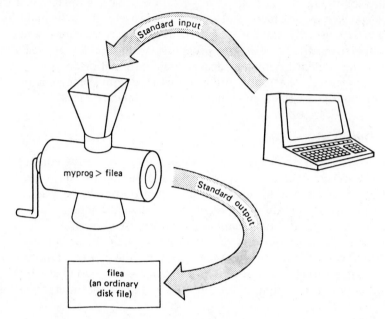

Figure 4.2.   Output Redirection. A program's output can be reassigned to an ordinary file. In this example the UNIX command `myprog > filea` causes the output of the `myprog` command to be sent to the ordinary disk file named 'filea'.

connect the standard output to the ordinary file named 'posterity'. You won't see the output on your screen unless you display the contents of the file named 'posterity'. (Note that the spaces surrounding the > are optional, and also note that the `ps` program doesn't behave differently from usual; it simply delivers its message as usual to the standard output. The output redirection is performed by the shell, not by the individual programs.)

You can see that the file named 'posterity' actually contains the output of `ps` using the `cat` program.

```
$ cat posterity
    PID    TTY    TIME    CMD
  16004    53    0:03     ps
$ _
```

Normal output redirection completely overwrites the output file. In the example given above, the file 'posterity' would be overwritten, and any previous contents would be lost. Occasionally, you want to direct output to a file, but you want the output to be added to the end of the file. The following command will append the output of `ps` to the end of the file named 'ps.logfile'.

```
$ ps >> ps.logfile
$ _
```

You could achieve the same results with the following series of commands, but it is much simpler to enter the command as shown above.

```
$ ps > temp1
$ cat ps.logfile temp1 > temp2
$ mv temp2 ps.logfile
$ rm temp1
$ _
```

4.5.2 Input Redirection.

The standard input can also be redirected (see Fig. 4.3). Thus far, the only program we have encountered that reads information from the standard input is the shell. The other programs we have used—ls, who, ps, date, echo, and pwd—all produce output without reading from the standard input. The shell normally reads commands from the standard input; that is, the shell reads commands that you type at the terminal. Since the standard input can be redirected, it is possible to have the shell acquire its commands from an ordinary file. The commands in a file can be executed by a shell by using input redirection, as shown in the following dialogue.

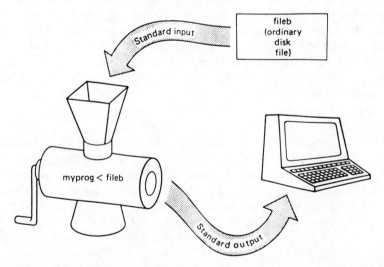

Figure 4.3. Input Redirection. A program's input can be reassigned by the shell. In this example the UNIX command myprog < fileb causes the myprog command to acquire input from the file named 'fileb'.

```
$ cat whoops
who
ps
$ sh < whoops
gilbert   tty17    Dec  1 15:41
gilbert   ttyh1    Dec  1 15:31
kc        ttyh3    Dec  1 15:28
  PID TT STAT   TIME COMMAND
  954 p0 S     0:00 sh
  956 p0 R     0:01 ps
$ _
```

In the dialogue shown above, the cat command is used to display the contents of the 'whoops' file, and then a shell program sh is invoked to execute the commands in the 'whoops' file by making that file the shell's standard input. (The file 'whoops' can be created using a text editor; see Chapter 9.)

The file 'whoops' contains two familiar shell commands you could enter at the terminal. If you often need to run these two commands, rather than type the commands each time, it might be easier to put the commands in a file and let the shell read the commands from the file. Obviously the example shown here isn't a compelling argument for shell command scripts; rather, it is a demonstration of input redirection.

To understand what happened in the above dialogue we have to back up a little bit. At the conclusion of the login process a shell is automatically created to read your commands interactively from the terminal. This shell is called your *login* shell. At any time you can enter the command sh to execute another copy of the shell. When you do this you will have two shells running, your original login shell and the new shell, which is often called a *subshell*. Unless you explicitly specify I/O redirection, any subshells that you create will read their input from the terminal, and send their output to the terminal, just like other commands. In the above dialogue, we created a subshell, but because of input redirection its input was connected to the 'whoops' file. Since we didn't specify any output redirection, its output was connected, as usual, to the terminal.

The first command in 'whoops' is who, so the subshell runs the who command, which prints a list of the active users. (Notice that the user named "gilbert" is logged on twice.) Next the subshell runs the ps command, which prints a list of your active processes. Notice that sh and ps are listed because both are active. who is not listed because it has finished by the time ps starts to run. When the subshell reaches the end of the 'whoops' file, it exits and returns control to the login shell. (Other methods for executing a shell command file are discussed in Section 11.1. However, these alternate methods reflect specific capabilities that are built into the shell rather than the general ability to redirect input and output.)

It is also possible to redirect the standard input and standard output simultaneously. When this happens, as shown in Figure 4.4, the only role of the control terminal is to enter the command line that starts the process. Once the program starts to execute, neither its input nor its output is attached to the terminal.

4.5.3 Pipes.

A *pipe* connects the standard output of one program to the standard input of another, as depicted in Figure 4.5. A pipe is different from I/O redirection. Output redirection writes the output of a program onto a file, and input redirection causes a program to read its input from a file, whereas a pipe diverts the output of one program directly to the input of another program.

Although I/O redirection and pipelines are separate UNIX facilities, it is possible to use both in one command. You can pipe the output of one program to the input of another while simultaneously redirecting the input of the first (or the output of the second) to a file. This type of connection is shown in Figure 4.6.

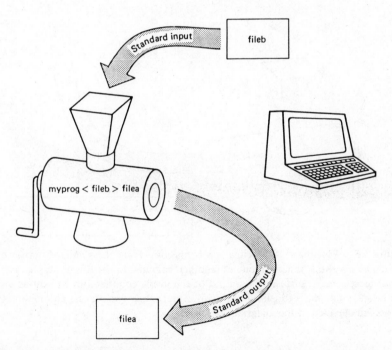

Figure 4.4. Simultaneous input and output redirection. Both the input and the output can be reassigned simultaneously, as in this example. The command myprog < fileb > filea causes the output to be routed to 'filea' and the input to come from 'fileb'.

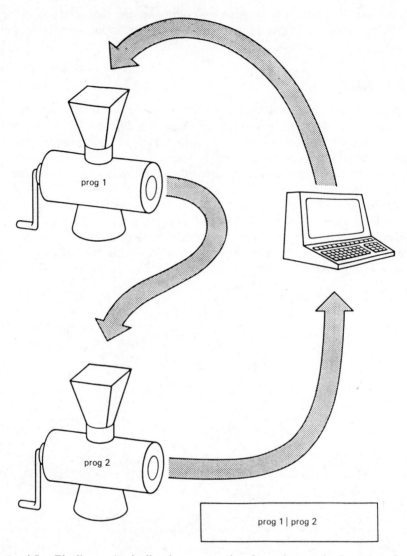

Figure 4.5. Pipelines. A pipeline is a connection from the standard output of one command to the standard input of another command. In this example, the command prog1 | prog2 causes the output of the prog1 command to be sent as input to the prog2 command. Pipelines can involve more than two stages, although only two stages are depicted in this diagram.

Let's suppose we want to know how many files are in my home directory ('/usr1/kc'). Perhaps the most obvious method would be to run the ls command and count the number of files that are listed on the terminal. For a directory with only a handful of files, this might work, but for a crowded

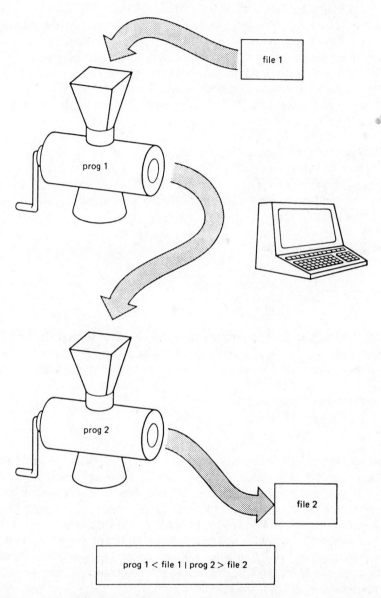

Figure 4.6.   I/O redirection and pipelines. It is possible to combine input and output redirection with pipelines. In this example, the command prog1 < file1 | prog2 > file2 assigns the input of prog1 to 'file1', pipes the output of prog1 to prog2, and then routes the output of prog2 to 'file2'.

directory, the simple method is too much finger pointing and squinting. Fortunately, there is a command for counting words (and lines and characters) called wc (see Section 8.5). Using ls we can generate a list of files in the '/usr1/kc' directory, and using wc we can count the number of words in a list. It seems we have the basic tools for discovering how many files are in my home directory, but how can we combine these tools to work together? As with most work in the UNIX system, there are at least two reasonable methods. Let's explore both methods.

The first method uses the I/O redirection technique of the previous section, and the second method uses a pipeline.

I/O Redirection Technique. Redirect the output of ls so that the list of files is saved in a temporary file. Then use wc to count the number of lines in the temporary file. (The -l option makes wc count lines.) Finally, remove the temporary file. These actions are performed by the following three commands.

```
$ ls /usr1/kc > tempfile
$ wc -l tempfile
8
$ rm tempfile
$ _
```

Pipeline Technique. Pipe the output of ls to wc. The special shell notation for a pipeline connection is a vertical bar (|) or a caret (^) in other systems. The following command pipes the output of ls to the input of wc:

```
$ ls /usr1/kc | wc -l
7
$ _
```

As you see, the pipeline method is simpler. It also gives the correct answer. Although the I/O redirection method works, it has some unpleasant side effects. If you don't have permission to create files in the current directory, you won't be able to execute the ls /usr1/kc > tempfile command because the command creates and writes to 'tempfile'. Another problem is that the shell has to create 'tempfile' and redirect the standard output to it before the ls program can run. 'tempfile' will be one of the files in the list if the current directory is '/usr1/kc'. Therefore the count of files may be one too large (as shown in the first example).

Pipelines make many procedures conceptually easier. Since each program in a pipeline can concentrate on one aspect of a task, it is possible to write coherent, unified programs. It would be very awkward to write the ls program so that it could perform all conceivable operations (searches, counts, sorts, transformations, selections) on its output. The ls program concentrates on listing files, and the wc program concentrates on counting. In the UNIX system you can create a new function by using pipelines to connect existing tools.

Many of the text file utilities (Chapter 8) can be used in a pipeline with ls to augment the capabilities of the ls command. It would not be reasonable to build all of these capabilities into the ls program, but they are all available in the UNIX system via the pipe mechanism. Only commands that can read input from the terminal can be on the receiving end of a pipe. For example, if ls is part of a pipeline, then it is always the first element. Since ls does not acquire information from the standard input, there is no way to deliver information to ls via a pipe.

wc is a typical example of a text manipulation program that can perform its processing either on files named as arguments (the command wc -l tempfile in the first dialogue in this section) or on text supplied via the standard input (the command ls | wc -l in the second dialogue). This flexibility is one of the most powerful features of the UNIX system.

4.6   METACHARACTERS AND FILENAME GENERATION

Most of the command line arguments you supply to programs are filenames. It is very common to name files so that related files have related names. For example, C language program filenames conventionally end with the suffix ".c". All of the chapters of a book might be stored in a series of files named 'chap1', 'chap2', and so on. If you wanted to perform some operation on all of the C language programs in a directory, it would be very tedious to type in all of the names as arguments on a command line.

To avoid tedium, the UNIX system allows you to specify sets of filenames automatically. When you enter the arguments to a command, the shell examines your arguments to see if you are using the *filename generation* shorthand. You control filename generation facility by specifying a *model* for the filenames. The shell compares your model to all of the filenames in the current directory. If any of the filenames match the model, then the alphabetized list of matching filenames is delivered to the program. If none of the filenames in the directory matches the model, then the result depends on which shell you are using. The Berkeley C shell will usually print a warning message, but the Bourne shell will just deliver the unchanged model to the program.

A model consists of ordinary characters and *metacharacters*. The ordinary characters stand for themselves, whereas the metacharacters have special meanings. A model that consists entirely of ordinary characters (e.g., "myfile") doesn't invoke filename generation.

You need to learn about the filename generation process, because it can occur every time you enter a command. The least you can safely know is that filename generation occurs and that you should not use the metacharacters "*", "?", and the square brackets in your filenames. As a next step you should master the metacharacters "*" and "?" because they are simple to use, and you should know how to turn off the special meanings of the metacharacters. If you want to master the UNIX system, then learn about character classes.

I am using the term model because it lends an intuitive perception to the confusing topic of filename generation. (In some other operating systems, the phrase wild card is used to refer to the special characters that control the filename generation process.)

The following metacharacters are used to control filename generation:

```
*  Matches any character string
?  Matches any single character
[  Introduces a character class
]  Terminates a character class
-  Indicates a character range in a character class
```

The asterisk and question mark metacharacters are very easy to use. An asterisk will match any string of characters, including the null string. Thus the model `*.c` will match the filename '.c' or 'a.c' or 'aaaaaaaa.c' but not the filename 'a.ca'.

A question mark will match any single character. Thus the model `??.c` will match the file name 'ab.c' or '77.c' but not 'a.c' or 'abc.c' or 'bc.cc'.

Square brackets and hyphens are used to form models for a set of characters; the model will match any character from the set. The characters in the group are enclosed by the brackets. The model `abc[aeiou]` will match any file name that starts with the letters "abc" and ends with a single vowel. The hyphen can be used inside a pair of square brackets to indicate a range of characters. The model `def[0-9]` will match any file name whose first three characters are "def" and whose fourth and final character is a numeral. The range is inclusive (both zero and 9 are included in the example above) and is defined by the numerical sequence of the character set.

The hyphen loses its role as a metacharacter when it is used outside of the square brackets. Conversely, the asterisk and the question mark lose their power as metacharacters when they are used within the square brackets. In the model `-[*?]abc`, only the square brackets are active metacharacters. Thus the model `-[*?]abc` matches exactly two file names: '-*abc' and '-?abc'. (Note, it is best to avoid creating filenames that contain dashes, asterisks, etc.)

Sometimes the power of the shell is a valuable asset and you want to use its special features such as metacharacters, I/O redirection, pipelines, and background execution. However, at other times the special shell characters used to control these functions are needed for more mundane operations. If you explicitly want any one of the special shell characters to lose its power, you can escape it by preceding it with a backslash character.

```
$ ls *\*
dark*    death*   tel*
$ _
```

If the current directory also contained a file named 'death*logo', the ls command in the dialogue above wouldn't list it because 'death*logo' doesn't end with an asterisk. However, multiple metacharacters can be used in a model.

```
$ ls *\**
dark*      death*      death*logo tel*      *tled
$ _
```

Another way to remove the power from special shell characters is *quoting*. When there is only one special character that needs to be escaped, it is easier to escape it with a backslash, but when there are several, then quoting is usually easier. Quoting is discussed more thoroughly in Section 11.5.

One oddity in the filename generation process concerns filenames that begin with a period. When the shell compares the model strings to the filenames, any leading period in a filename must be matched explicitly. So if you have a file named '.invisible', the model *visible will not match. The model .*visible will match the filename '.invisible'. The model name .* will match all of the filenames that begin with a period.

Another aspect of filename generation that many people find confusing is the fact that slash characters in a pathname must be matched explicitly. A pathname is a path from directory to directory that leads to a file. The name '/etc/motd' mentioned earlier is a simple pathname that leads from the '/etc' directory to the file 'motd'. Pathnames will be discussed in detail in Section 5.4.

The metacharacters are used only to generate filenames within a directory. The model /etc*.c will not match the files with the ".c" suffix in the '/etc' directory. However, the model /etc/*.c will match those files. This restriction on explicitly matching the slash characters in a pathname is basically sensible because the current directory is the default environment unless you explicitly state otherwise.

Let's suppose that the current directory contains the following files:

```
ch1     ch2     ch3     ch4
33.doc  abc     ab.c    ch3.a
```

The command ls ch* will list the following files: 'ch1', 'ch2', 'ch3', 'ch3.a', and 'ch4'. Notice that the list is alphabetized, because file name generation occurs alphabetically.

The command ls *3* will list the following files: '33.doc', 'ch3', and 'ch3.a'. Notice that the asterisk can stand for a sequence of zero or more characters.

The command `ls ch?` will list the following files: 'ch1', 'ch2', 'ch3', and 'ch4'. Since a question mark always matches exactly one character, 'ch3.a' is omitted. The command `ls ch[2-9]` will list the following files: 'ch2', 'ch3', and 'ch4'. The file 'ch1' is omitted because "1" isn't in the range "2 − 9", and 'ch3.a' is omitted because of the trailing ".a".

Here's one for the masters. The command `ls ch[0-15]` will list the file 'ch1'. Although the character class appears to include the numerals zero to 15, it actually contains just three characters: "0", "1", and "5". You should remember that a character class is formed from a group of characters. The sequence "15" looks like the number 15, but in a character class it is simply two characters, a 1 and a 5.

4.7 CONCLUSIONS

Using the UNIX system effectively is equivalent to understanding the basic operation of the shell. You should know how to run a normal foreground process and how to run a background process. You should also understand the idea of command line arguments and options. I/O redirection and pipelines are essential for everyone—why use the UNIX system without using its strongest features? Everyone should at least be aware of filename generation. Learn to use filename generation if you want to get the most out of the UNIX system.

These few topics introduce you to just a small fraction of the power of the shell. However, for people who use the shell as an interactive command interpreter, the topics presented in this chapter are enough to use the UNIX system productively. The shell is one of the most impressive features of the UNIX system, so those of you who want to know more about the shell should read Chapters 11 and 12.

CHAPTER 5

The UNIX Filesystem

Ordinary files are named collections of information stored on a mass storage device such as a computer disk or tape. A *filesystem* is the organizational framework for the files. On many computer systems, files are "organized" by lumping them together into one big heap. As long as there are only a few dozen files, a heap works fine. Unfortunately, a simple filesystem is inappropriate for a multiuser computer system with large modern disks that can store several hundred thousand files.

Several ideas contributed to the development of the UNIX filesystem. The most important was convenience. The UNIX system needed a filesystem that encouraged users to group their files logically. Files are housed in *directories*, and in the UNIX system you are encouraged to create directories as necessary.

Organizing files into more manageable groups is a good first step, but it doesn't solve the problem. If you have several hundred users with several directories each plus dozens of directories for system information, then you are right back in an unmanageable situation. The key idea of the UNIX filesystem is that it is *hierarchical*, like a family tree. Directories can contain both files and (sub)directories.

Another concern for the filesystem of a multiuser computer is who can access each file. Thus in the UNIX system, each file has an access permission that governs who can access (and in what way) each file. Without file security, few people would put private information in a computer, and nobody could vouch for the safety of the operating system's files and tables. Access modes are a necessary nuisance of shared computer systems.

One of the novel features of the UNIX system is the association of the I/O hardware of the computer with *special files*. Access to I/O hardware itself mimics access to ordinary disk files. Each I/O device (printer, terminal, disk, etc.) is associated with at least one special file. A program can access a special file in order to actually access the I/O hardware. Although this sounds complicated, it is actually a great simplification compared to most other computer systems.

All of these aspects of the unix filesystem are discussed in the remainder of this chapter. You should have a working knowledge of these ideas in order to use the unix system effectively. A few advanced filesystem topics are presented in Chapter 23. Some of the data structures that underlie the unix filesystem are discussed in Section 25.8.

5.1 ORDINARY FILES

An ordinary file is used to store information. An ordinary file might contain a program that you can execute, the text of a document, the records of a company, or any other type of information that can be stored in a computer. During a session with the unix system you will encounter dozens of ordinary files.

Ordinary files are a vital part of a computer system, because they allow information to be stored permanently. Without long-term information storage, the information-processing ability of computers would not be very useful. Besides ordinary files, unix systems contain directory files and special files. System V has special files called *named pipes*, and Berkeley contains *symbolic links* and *sockets*. (Named pipes are also called *fifo* files; see Section 23.4. Symbolic links are discussed in Section 23.5, and sockets are discussed in Section 25.14.) Ordinary files are the only file type that is used for long-term storage of general information.

In Version 7 and System V, filenames can be only 14 characters long. The Berkeley unix system allows filenames to be up to 255 characters long. You can use whatever characters you want for filenames, although filenames that contain unprintable characters, space characters, tabs, and shell metacharacters are very difficult to use and should be avoided. Since every unix directory has the filenames '.' and '..' built in, you cannot ever use these names for your own files. Although two files in the same directory may not share the same name, it is possible for one file to have several names. (See ln command; Section 6.4.)

The unix system does not impose any naming conventions on files. However, many unix programs expect files to be named with certain suffixes. For example, files with the suffix ".sh" (such as 'bakup.sh') are usually shell programs, files with the suffix ".bas" (such as 'aster.bas') are usually BASIC programs, and files with the suffix ".c" (such as 'xrefer.c') are usually C-language source files. Files that contain executable programs (such as 'who') customarily have no suffixes.

There are two types of ordinary file: text files and binary files. *Text files* (on most systems) contain only ASCII (American Standard Code for Information Interchange) characters, whereas *binary files* may contain all 256 possible values for each byte. (Text files on some mainframes, and in many countries outside of the United States, often use coding systems other than ASCII.) Let's first discuss text files.

About 100 ASCII characters are recognized by common terminals and printers. Most terminals can display the following printing characters:

```
ABCDEFGHIJKLMNOPQRSTUVWXYZ
abcdefghijklmnopqrstuvwxyz
0123456789
! @ # $ % ^ & * ( ) + = ~ ' _ -
{ } [ ] : ; " ' < > , . ? / \ |
```

In addition to the printable characters shown above, the ASCII character set defines codes for the space character, the horizontal and vertical tab characters, the new-line character, the form-feed character, a whole host of control characters, and certain international characters.

One example of an ordinary text file is the message-of-the-day file ('/etc/motd') that is printed at your terminal each time you log onto the system. You can display the message-of-the-day file on your terminal using the cat command

```
$ cat /etc/motd
NOTICE - The system will be down
from 17:00 to 19:00 tomorrow
for routine maintenance.
Remember, monthly users meeting
this Weds at 5 pm.
$ _
```

The UNIX utility cat is often used to display text files on your terminal. (See Section 8.2.)

Files that contain codes that are not part of the ASCII character set are called binary files. Since binary files use the full range of possible values for the bytes in the file, binary files are a slightly more efficient way to store information. A binary file cannot be typed directly on your terminal because most of the 256 possible values for each byte are not printable ASCII characters.

You can inspect the contents of a binary file by using the octal dump (od) program. (See Section 6.10.) od takes the values in a file and converts them into printable characters.

```
$ od -x /bin/ls
0000000   010b 0000 3800 0000 0800 0000 a864 0000
0000020   093c 0000 0000 0000 0000 0000 0000 0000
0000040   0000 0000 0000 0000 0000 0000 0000 0000
*
0002000   0f00 3d11 5ed0 c15a 5a04 d050 5950 59d0
0002020   d558 1389 1102 d1fa 6859 0319 04c2 d059
0002040   ef59 37de 0000 efdd 37d8 0000 58dd 6add
^C
$ _
```

Virtually every command that you enter references ordinary files. Four commands are especially important for controlling your collection of ordinary files: mv (move), cp (copy), ln (link), and rm (remove). These four commands are discussed in Chapter 6.

5.2   DIRECTORY FILES

Directories are files that contain lists of files. The UNIX operating system maintains the directory system. Executing programs can read directory files, but the operating system prevents programs from writing directly to directory files to guarantee the integrity of the filesystem. Executing programs can add an entry to the list of files in a directory by asking the system to create a file, or remove an entry from a directory by asking the system to delete a file.

Each user has a special directory called the *home directory*. When you log onto the system, you are placed in your home directory. During the course of your session with the UNIX system, you are free to move from one directory to another using the cd command (see Section 6.1).

```
$ cd /bin
$ pwd
/bin
$ _
```

The argument to cd ('/bin' in the dialogue above) specifies the directory you want to move to. The directory you are in is called the *current directory* or the *working directory*, and its name can be printed by the pwd (print working directory) command. The default destination directory for *cd* is your home directory, so you can always return to your home directory easily.

```
$ cd
$ pwd
/usr1/kc
$ _
```

(On older systems the cd command is usually named chdir, and you usually have to specify the name of your home directory to return to it.) cd and pwd are discussed in Section 6.1.

The mkdir (make directory) command is used to create a directory, and the rmdir command is used to remove a directory. Directories are created empty except for the standard files '.' and '..'. (The standard entries '.' and '..' are discussed below.) You can only remove a directory that is empty (except for the files '.' and '..'). mkdir and rmdir are discussed in 6.6.

5.3   THE HIERARCHICAL FILESYSTEM

Files in the UNIX system are grouped into directories, and the directories are organized into a hierarchy. The top of the hierarchy is a special directory called the *root directory*. The root directory contains a variety of system-related files, and it usually contains standard directories such as '/bin', '/usr', '/dev', '/etc' and '/tmp', and '/lib'. A typical but very simplified view of a filesystem hierarchy is shown in Figure 5.1.

The advantage of a hierarchical filesystem is organization. Let's use the corporate analogy. In a corporation you could allow every worker to report directly to the president. This type of organization works well for a small Ma and Pa grocery, but it would be disastrous for a huge organization such as General Motors. Similarly, in the UNIX system it is a great advantage to organize the system by loosening the connection between files and the root directory.

The UNIX filesystem is often called *tree structured,* because diagrams of it resemble an upside-down tree. The *current subtree* is that part of the filesystem that is at a lower level in the hierarchy than the current directory. If the '/usr' directory is the current directory, then all of the '/usr' subdirectories, and so forth, will be the current subtree (Fig. 5.2). Most UNIX commands work with files in the current directory unless you specify another directory. A few UNIX commands work with the current subtree.

5.4   PATHNAMES

The files in the current directory are directly accessible; they can be referenced by simply entering their name. Files that are not in the current

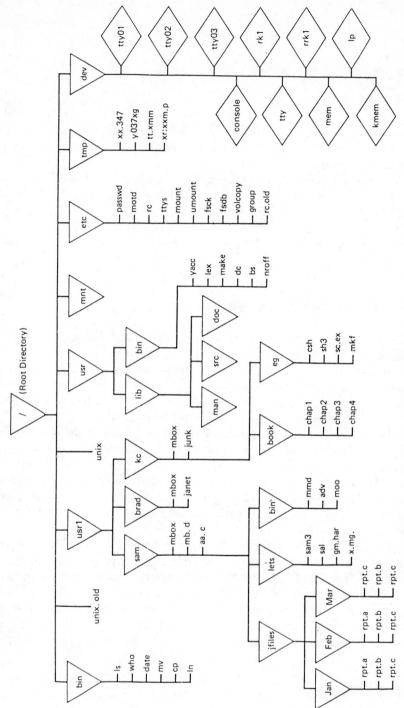

Figure 5.1. Simplified diagram of a typical UNIX filesystem. In this diagram, directory files are shown in triangles, special files are shown in diamonds. Ordinary files are shown without borders.

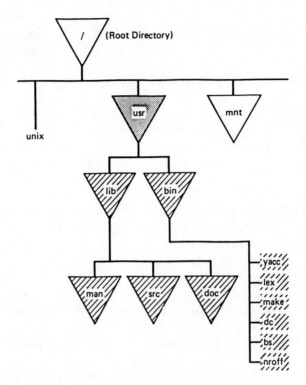

Figure 5.2. The current directory and the current subtree. In this diagram, the current directory is '/usr' (shown shaded). The current subtree consists of all of the directories and files below '/usr' in the filesystem hierarchy (shown hatched).

directory must be referenced using a *pathname*. A pathname specifies a path through the filesystem that leads to the desired file.

The most important thing to remember about paths through the filesystem is that they can start only in one of two places: your current directory or the root directory. Pathnames that start with the ''/'' (slash) character are absolute pathnames, specifying a path starting in the root directory. All other pathnames are relative pathnames, and they specify a path starting in your current directory.

Every directory contains entries for the names '.' (called dot) and '..' (called dotdot). These two entries are the glue that holds the filesystem together. The entry '.' is a pseudonym for the name of the current directory. Programs that want to read the current directory file can use the name '.' rather than scrounge around to determine the name that was given to the directory when it was created.

The name '..' is a pseudonym for the parent directory of the current directory. The entry '..' in each directory allows you to specify a pathname that ascends the filesystem. Notice that all of the other entries in a pathname specify files that are at a lower level in the filesystem hierarchy. You should be comfortable with the ideas behind the names '.' and '..', because you will use these names very often in your interactions with the UNIX system.

A few simple rules apply to all pathnames.

- If the pathname starts with a slash, then the path starts in the root directory. All other paths start in the current directory.
- A pathname is either a list of names separated by slashes or a single name. The initial names in the list (if there are any) are directories. The final name in the list is the target file, which may be a file of any type.
- You can ascend the filesystem hierarchy by specifying the name '..' in a pathname. All other names in a pathname descend the hierarchy.
- No spaces are allowed in a pathname.

Let's show a few examples of pathnames. The pathname '/usr1/kc' is an absolute pathname specifying the file 'kc'. Since the pathname starts with a slash, it is an absolute pathname that starts in the root directory. Obviously the directory 'usr1' is a subdirectory of the root directory (Fig. 5.3). The file 'kc' in the '/usr1' directory is also a directory; it is my home directory.

The pathname 'jfiles/Jan/rpt.a' is a relative pathname, because it doesn't start with a slash. Hence the path starts from the current directory, which is '/usr1/sam' for this example (Fig. 5.4). The directory 'jfiles' is a subdirectory of the current directory, 'Jan' is a subdirectory of 'jfiles', and 'rpt.a' is a file in 'Jan'.

The pathname '../../brad/janet' is harder to understand. The path starts in the current directory, which is '/usr1/kc/eg' for this example (Fig. 5.5). The path leads to the parent of '/usr1/kc/eg', which is '/usr1/kc'. The path then ascends further to '/usr1' and then descends to the directory 'brad'. The target file is 'janet' in the 'brad' directory. An equivalent pathname (one that would reference the same file) is '/usr1/brad/janet'.

Long pathnames are very hard to use. It is usually better to cd (change directory) to the scene of the action.

5.5   FILE TYPES AND MODES

We have already said that a file is a collection of information. This is correct as far as it goes, but there is more to a file than the information it contains. The UNIX system maintains a variety of information that describes each file. The information includes access privileges, the file type, the

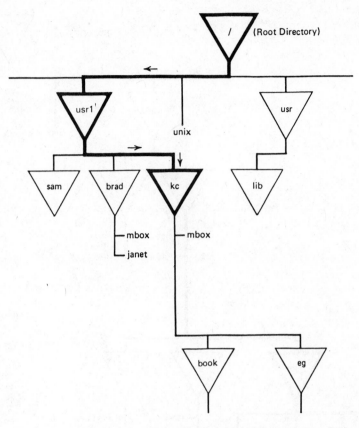

Figure 5.3.   The pathname '/usr1/kc'.

important dates for the file, the size of the file, and the exact location of the file on the disk.

The implications of file types and modes resound throughout the UNIX system. Many operations assume a file of one type or another. For example, the cd command expects its argument to specify a directory. Your only response will be an error message if you attempt to cd to an ordinary file.

```
$ pwd
/bin
$ cd /usr1/kc/mbox
/usr1/kc/mbox:  bad directory
$ pwd
/bin
$ _
```

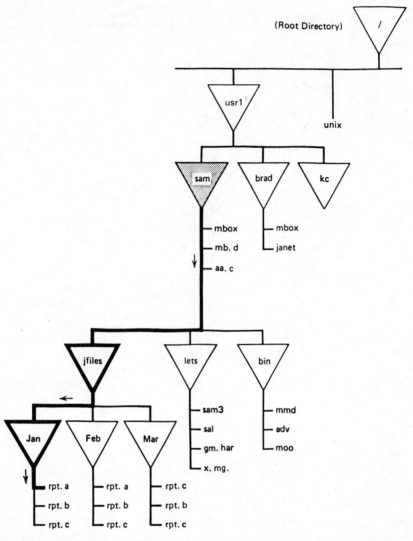

Figure 5.4.   The pathname 'jfiles/Jan/rpt.a'.   In this diagram the current directory is '/usr1/sam'.

The error occurs because '/usr1/kc/mbox' is not a directory but an ordinary file containing electronic mail.   Similarly, the command

```
$ cat /usr1/kc
```

will output gibberish to your terminal, because '/usr1/kc' is a directory, not a text file.

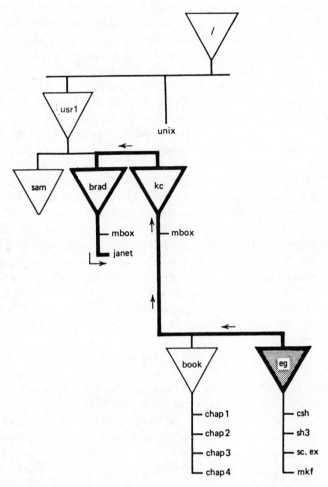

Figure 5.5.   The pathname '../../brad/janet'. In this diagram the current directory is '/usr1/kc/eg'.

Each time you access a file, the system checks your right to perform that access. The privileges are normally set so that you have fairly free reign over your own files and much more limited access to your neighbor's files and probably little or no ability to access most special files or system files. Some of the more cryptic UNIX error messages are simply trying to tell you that you are unable to access a certain file because of the file access protection system.

In the UNIX system there are three operations that can be performed on a file: *reading, writing,* and *executing.* Reading a file means the contents of the file are made available. Writing a file means the contents of the file are changed. For an ordinary file, executing either means loading the file into main memory and performing the machine instructions that are stored in the file or reading shell commands from the file and executing those commands. Execute permission for a directory file means that you can search the directory in the course of resolving a pathname.

Each UNIX file is owned by a particular user, and each file is always associated with a particular group. (In the UNIX system, a group is a set of users who have something in common—groups are typically users from one department, people working together on a project.) The UNIX file access protection scheme depends on two things: the *type* of access that is requested (read, write, or execute), and *who* is doing the access. There is a set of privileges for the file's owner, another set for members of the file's group, and a third set for everyone else. The privileges for a file can be displayed using the ls command. Several examples are shown in Section 6.2.

The owner of a file is able to control the permissions of that file by using the chmod (change mode) command (discussed in Section 6.5). The ownership and the group association can also be changed by using the chown (change owner) and chgrp (change group) commands (also discussed in Section 6.5). The superuser (the system manager uses the superuser privilege to perform operations that are denied to ordinary users) is also able to change the modes of your files, although in most systems this is not likely to happen unless you ask for some help.

Many UNIX files are known by several names. The number of names a file has is called the number of *links,* because each pseudonym is a link from a directory entry to the system's internal bookkeeping records for a file. Directory files always have at least two links because each directory entry contains the pseudonym '.' for itself. Directories that have subdirectories contain more than two links because each subdirectory references the parent directory using the pseudonym '..'. It is also possible to create several names for a given file by using the ln (link) command, as discussed in Section 6.4.

5.6 SPECIAL FILES

Ordinary files are conceptually easy because they contain information, just like a file in a file cabinet. Unfortunately, special files are harder to understand, because they don't contain information. The role of special files isn't information storage; rather, they exist to provide a uniform interface between programs and the computer's I/O hardware.

For each I/O device (terminal, disk, tape, etc.) that is connected to a computer, there is at least one special file. Most of the special files are stored in the directory '/dev'. The names of the special files usually indicate what type of device they are associated with. For example, '/dev/tty4' is a terminal (teletype), '/dev/rp0' is a section of a RP06 disk, and '/dev/lp' is a lineprinter.

When a program writes data to a file such as '/dev/tty4', the operating system accepts the data and sends it to the terminal on communication line 4. When a program reads data from a file such as '/dev/tty4', the operating system is actually acquiring the data from the terminal and passing it along to the program.

A program does not have to know very much about the details of a device to read or write its special file. Special files are an interface between application programs that need to ignore hardware details and the UNIX kernel's internal routines, which exist only to revel in (manage) the details of the computer hardware.

The UNIX system uses special files to access I/O hardware rather than some other mechanism because the UNIX system wants to make the interface to I/O hardware similar to the interface to ordinary files. Therefore, special files appear as entries in directories, they are part of the filesystem, and access to them is controlled by the usual three-tiered protection system.

Special files for terminals are usually owned by the system when they are not being used. During the login process, the ownership of the special file for your terminal is transferred to you. Since you own the special file that connects programs to your terminal, you can control its access modes while you are using it. When you log off, the ownership of your terminal's special file is transferred back to the system.

Special files that provide linkages to disks, tapes, and printers are usually owned by the system, and access to them by ordinary users should be restricted. Special files that provide linkages to graphics displays, laboratory peripherals, and the like are usually owned by the system, and their access modes are often set so that anyone can use them. It is up to you to coordinate your use of these specialized resources with other users so that two people aren't using one resource at one time.

5.7   DIRECTORY ACCESS MODES

Directories have the standard read, write, and execute permissions for owner, group, and other. However, in a directory, these permissions are interpreted differently from ordinary files.

The read permission for a directory means that standard utility programs are allowed to open and read the information in the directory. For example, the `ls` program reads directories to discover their contents. If the read privilege is denied, then it is impossible to discover (until the read privilege is restored) what files are contained in the directory. (However, restricting the read privilege for a directory doesn't prevent reading the files themselves. Only the list of names stored in the directory is inaccessible.)

It is possible to operate in directories where you are denied read permission. As an example, on one of the UNIX systems that I often use, all of the directories containing the operating system source code have the read permission denied. However, since I am very familiar with the organization of these directories, I had no problem examining the source files during the research for this book. Restricting read privileges of directories keeps the uninformed away, but it isn't real protection—it is an annoyance.

The write privilege for a directory means that you are allowed to create or remove files in that directory. You do not need the read privilege to create files or remove files in a directory. Making the write privilege control the creation and deletion rights makes intuitive sense when you consider that creating a file in a given directory means that the system writes the name of the created file into the directory file. Similarly, in deleting a file, the system must erase the entry for the vanishing file from the directory file.

Denying write privilege for a certain directory does not mean that files in that directory cannot be modified. The write privilege on each individual file controls your ability to modify that file.

The execute permission for a directory means that the system will search the directory in the course of resolving a file name. When you specify a pathname in place of a simple filename, each of the directories in the pathname is searched for the name of the next directory in the sequence. If you ask the system to

```
$ cat /usr/bin/source/README
```

then you must have execute (search) permission for the directories 'usr', 'bin', and 'source'. Denying a directory's search permission is real protection against people's using files in that directory. You cannot change directory to a directory where execute permission is denied.

CHAPTER 6

Managing Your Files

The UNIX operating system is a tool for managing information, which is stored in files. This chapter describes the UNIX utility programs that allow you to manage your files. All of these programs perform very simple functions, usually functions that are analogous to the functions you might perform during spring cleaning. Periodically during your interactions with the UNIX system you have to remove old information, make room for new information, adjust the file access privileges for certain files, and occasionally acquire files from other users.

Although there are some areas where information management occurs automatically, in most cases you have to supply the management talent while UNIX supplies the management tools. The unit of information in the UNIX system is the ordinary file. Most operating systems, including the UNIX system, contain programs to display information about files, to create ordinary files, to move ordinary files from one location to another, to rename files, to make copies of files, and to remove files. You need to perform these functions as necessary on your collection of files.

In a multiuser operating system, all files are owned by someone, and it is necessary to have a privilege system so that owners can protect their files from unwanted access by others. Therefore, the UNIX system has programs to control the access rights of files and to change the ownership of files.

The UNIX filesystem is more than a big bunch of files; files are collected in directories, and directories are arranged in a logical hierarchy. The hierarchy makes it easier to organize and arrange your collection of files. Because of this, the UNIX system contains several programs to maintain the directory system. One of the major aspects of your information management task is to decide how you are going to organize your directories. A well-organized set of directories makes it easier to use the UNIX system, especially if you use it for several different functions.

6.1   PWD AND CD—PRINT OR CHANGE THE CURRENT DIRECTORY

The name of the current directory is probably the most basic piece of information about your current environment. The pwd (print working directory) command reveals the name of the current (working) directory.

All files are stored in directories (see Chapter 5). At any given time, just one of these directories is your current directory. When you log onto the system, the current directory is your home directory. You can move from directory to directory using the cd command. After each move it is a good idea to make sure that you have landed in the desired directory.

```
$ pwd
/usr1/kc
$ _
```

Immediately after logging in, you are in your home directory, the directory assigned to you by the system manager. My home directory is '/usr1/kc'. If I execute the pwd command immediately after logging in, then "/usr1/kc" is printed on my terminal, as shown above. If expected files are not present, or if things are not working as you expect, use pwd to make sure you are where you think you are.

The remedy for being in the wrong directory is to change directory to (move to) the correct directory. The cd (change directory) command will change the current working directory to the named directory. That is, your working session moves to the named directory.

```
$ cd /usr1/kc/source
$ pwd
/usr1/kc/source
$ _
```

If you don't specify a directory when you enter the cd command, the new directory will be your home directory.

```
$ pwd
/usr1/kc/source
$ cd
$ pwd
/usr1/kc
$ _
```

The pathname argument to cd may be either an absolute pathname (shown above) or a relative pathname, which is shown in the following dialogue:

```
$ pwd
/usr1/kc/ik/utils
$ cd ../../source
$ pwd
/usr1/kc/source
$ cd junk/programs
$ pwd
/usr1/kc/source/junk/programs
$ _
```

The first cd command makes the current directory the child directory named 'source' of the parent of the current directory's parent. The second cd command makes the current directory the child directory named 'programs' of the child directory named 'junk'. Note that the second cd path starts where the first one finished.

6.2 LS—LIST INFORMATION ABOUT FILES

The ls command is used to list the contents of directories and to print information about files. The ls command uses many options, most of which are not discussed here.

Each argument to the ls command is either the name of an ordinary (or special) file, the name of a directory, or an option (option list). The options are used to control the ordering of the list of files and the information that is printed for each file. For each ordinary (or special) file argument, the requested information is printed. For each directory argument the requested information is printed for all of the files in the directory (unless the "d" option is used).

The following four options are used very frequently:

-l The long-list option is used to print detailed information about each listed file. Without the l option, only the file names are typed.

-t The time-sort option sorts the list of files according to each file's modification date. The most recently modified files are printed first.

The time-sort option is used to show which files have been modified most recently.

-d The directory option is used to force `ls` to simply print the requested information for each directory in the argument list. Normally, all of the directories named in the argument list are searched, and the requested information is printed for all of the files in those directories.

-a Normally when you use the `ls` command, those files whose names begin with a period are omitted from the list. However, when the a option is used, even files whose names begin with a period (such as the standard entries '.' and '..') are printed.

If there are no files or directories named in the arguments, then the contents of the current directory are listed.

```
$ ls
README     megaa.c        megab.c     todo
makefile   megaa.c.orig   megaxy.c    zsrc
$ _
```

Notice that the list of files is alphabetized. You can also use filename generation with `ls` to detail groups of files.

```
$ ls *.c
megaa.c   megab.c  megaxy.c
$ _
```

In this dialogue `ls` lists, in alphabetical order, all of the files in the current directory whose names end in ".c". The -t option can be used to order the files according to modification dates rather than alphabetic ordering.

```
$ ls -t
makefile   megaa.c    todo           README
megaxy.c   megab.c    megaa.c.orig   zsrc
$ _
```

One thing that confuses many UNIX users is the difference between the `ls` command and the `ls *` command. The `ls` command has no arguments, so by default a list of the files in the current directory is produced (see the first dialogue in this section). The `ls *` command uses the metacharacter * to match the names of all files in the current directory. Therefore, this command provides the `ls` process with one argument for every file in the current directory. For ordinary files, the two commands produce the same output, but when subdirectories are present, the first command lists only the subdirectory name, whereas the second command lists the subdirectory's name and its contents (because the subdirectories are explicitly mentioned in the argument list).

```
$ ls *
README      megaa.c       megab.c     todo
makefile    megaa.c.orig  megaxy.c
zsrc:
zeands.c    ikonas.c      zmega.c     ztek.e
$ _
```

A different example showing the difference between ls and ls * is shown in Figure 6.1.

When you need more detailed information about a file, you use the -l (letter 'l') option to ls. Using the long-format option allows you to see the permissions of each file, the number of links, the owner, the group, the size, and the modification time. For special device files, the major and minor device numbers are printed in place of the file size. Figure 6.2 shows some typical outputs of the ls command using the -l option.

Understanding the output of the long-format output of ls is very important, because interacting with the UNIX system involves accessing files. The long-format output of ls is the only way to discover the key information for each file (file type, mode, ownership, and size). The output of the ls command on your system might be somewhat different from the output shown in Figure 6.2, because the format varies slightly from system to system. (On Berkeley systems, the group information isn't shown unless the -g option is used.)

The first field in the long-format listing is the *mode* field. It consists of 10 characters; the first character indicates the file type, and the next nine characters indicate the file access privileges. The coding for the file type is given in the following table:

Code	Meaning
-	Ordinary file
d	Directory file
c	Character special file
b	Block special file
p	Fifo (named pipe) file (System V only)
l	Symbolic link (Berkeley only)
s	Socket (Berkeley only)

The file type is the most basic characteristic of a file. After a short while, you will automatically interpret the first character in a long listing.

In Section 5.5 I discussed the three operations that can be performed on a UNIX file: reading, writing, and executing. I also discussed the three tiers of access privilege: the owner's privileges, the group's privileges, and others' privileges. Since there are three access operations (read, write, and

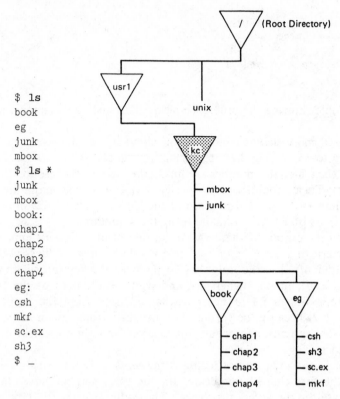

```
$ ls
book
eg
junk
mbox
$ ls *
junk
mbox
book:
chap1
chap2
chap3
chap4
eg:
csh
mkf
sc.ex
sh3
$ _
```

Figure 6.1. Examples of the use of ls. The command ls and the command ls *
act very differently when the current directory contains subdirectories ('book' and
'eg' in this example). Without arguments, the ls command will print a list of the
files in the current directory (the first command shown above). When the ls command receives the name of a directory as an arugment the requested information is
printed for each file in that directory. In this case, the command ls * is equivalent
to the command ls book eg junk mbox because of the shell's expansion of the *
metacharacter into a list of the files in the current directory. Therefore the files in
the directories 'book' and 'eg' appear in the list (the second command shown
above).

execute) and three tiers of protection (owner, group, and others), there are
nine (3 times 3) access permissions associated with each file. The first three
characters of the permissions show the read, write, and execute privileges of
the owner; the second set of three characters shows the read, write, and
execute privileges of members of the group; and the third set of three characters shows the read, write, and execute privileges of all others. If a privilege is *allowed*, the appropriate letter (r, w, or x) is shown. If the privilege
is *denied*, a hyphen is shown. The access privileges for the first example in
Figure 6.2 are shown in the following table:

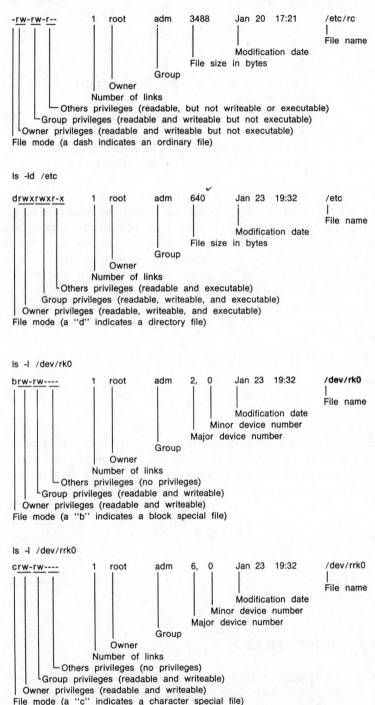

Figure 6.2.   The long-format output of the `ls` command.

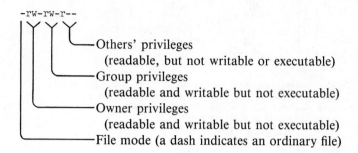

-rw-rw-r--

— Others' privileges
  (readable, but not writable or executable)
— Group privileges
  (readable and writable but not executable)
— Owner privileges
  (readable and writable but not executable)
— File mode (a dash indicates an ordinary file)

If a privilege is denied and you attempt to exercise the privilege, your attempt will be thwarted by the operating system. In many UNIX environments, the read and write privileges associated with files are almost immaterial, because everyone customarily allows everyone else free access. In some other UNIX installations, file access modes are carefully controlled to ensure system integrity.

Occasionally, you need to know the access modes or some other information about a directory file. The simple-minded approach doesn't work.

```
$ ls -l zsrc
-rw-r--r--   1  kc      1804  Feb 13 11:03   zeands.c
-rw-r--r--   1  kc       272  Oct 12 19:54   zikonas.c
-rw-r--r--   1  kc       500  May 14 19:54   zmeg.c
-rw-r--r--   1  kc      2702  Jan  1  7:36   ztek.c
$ _
```

As I mentioned above, using a directory name as an argument to ls will produce a long-format listing of all of the files in the named directory. The d option is needed to suppress ls's normal behavior and force it to simply list the required information for the named directory.

```
$ ls -ld zsrc
drwxr-xr-x   2  kc       512  Dec  7 12:45   zsrc
$ _
```

Another example of the difference between ls -l dirname and ls -ld dirname is shown in Figure 6.3.

6.3 RM—REMOVE FILES

The rm command allows you to delete ordinary files. (The rmdir command is used to remove directories; see Section 6.6.) To remove a file, you must have write permission in the directory containing that file, but you need neither read nor write permission for the file itself. This makes sense, because removing a file actually removes an entry from a directory. Thus it is the

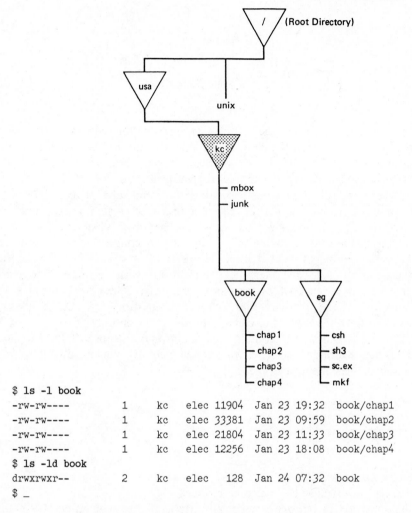

```
$ ls -l book
-rw-rw----        1     kc     elec 11904   Jan 23 19:32   book/chap1
-rw-rw----        1     kc     elec 33381   Jan 23 09:59   book/chap2
-rw-rw----        1     kc     elec 21804   Jan 23 11:33   book/chap3
-rw-rw----        1     kc     elec 12256   Jan 23 18:08   book/chap4
$ ls -ld book
drwxrwxr--        2     kc     elec   128   Jan 24 07:32   book
$ _
```

Figure 6.3. Listing directory contents. When ls is passed the name of a directory, its usual response is to list the requested information for every file in the directory. The first command above shows ls listing in long format all of the files in the directory 'book'. The -d option to ls can prevent it from descending into the named directories to list their contents. In the second command shown above, ls lists in long format the information for the directory 'book' because of the presence of the -d option.

directory's write permission that governs your ability to create or delete files (in that directory).

If you don't have write permission for a file, then rm may, as a precaution, ask you if you really want to remove that file.

```
$ ls -l dnaseq*
-rw-rw-rw-   1 kc       41087  Dec 16 19:40  dnaseq
-r--r--r--   1 kc       47153  Dec  2  8:31  dnaseq.bak
$ rm dnaseq dnaseq.bak
rm: override protection 444 for dnaseq.bak?  y
$ _
```

Notice that rm verifies your request to remove "dnaseq.bak", because its write privilege is denied. Notice also that the file access privilege is displayed in octal notation, rather than the symbolic notation used by ls. The -f (force) option of rm will suppress the verification query.

Be very careful when you use rm, because removed files really are gone. The only way to recover a removed file is to ask the system administrator to recover a copy of the file from a recent backup. Whenever you are in doubt, refrain from removing files. File naming conventions are useful for organizing groups of related files. However, you should be very careful, because using wild-card filename specifications with rm may remove too many files, if unrelated files are named similarly. The command rm * will remove all of the ordinary files in the current directory. Don't use this command unless you want to clean out a directory entirely.

The remove command contains two additional options. If the -i (interactive) flag is present, then rm will interactively ask you if you really want to remove every mentioned file.

```
$ rm -i dnaseq dnaseq.bak
rm: remove dnaseq?  y
rm: remove dnaseq.bak?  y
$ _
```

Replies starting with a "y" or "yes" will cause the file to be removed. Any other reply will cause the file to be retained.

The interactive remove is especially useful if files with untypable names appear in your directory. Any filename containing control characters can be difficult or impossible to type. Weird, unnamable files are occasionally produced by errant programs or by other transient problems. If you want to remove a file with an unprintable name, enter the command rm -i *, and then reply no for each file except the one with the unprintable name.

Another very useful option is -r (recursive), which is used to remove a directory, all of its contents, and all of the files and directories in that directory's subtree. Enter the command rm -r bookdir to remove the directory 'bookdir' and all of its files, subdirectories, etc. The recursive option obliterates the whole tree below the mentioned point. Naturally you should be extremely careful when using the "-r" option. It is safer (slower) to remove ordinary files using rm and then remove directories using rmdir.

The rm options -i, -f, and -r are present in Version 7, System V, and Berkeley UNIX systems. However, these options may not be present on older (or variant) UNIX systems. For example, on most Version 6 UNIX systems, the command `rm -i *` will remove every file in the current directory and then complain that the file '-i' is not found.

6.4 MV, CP, AND LN—MOVE AND COPY FILES

The commands `mv` (move), `cp` (copy), and `ln` (link) allow you to move and copy files. The `mv` command moves a file from one location to another. In most cases the `mv` operation is quite fast because it's simply renaming the file; however, sometimes the file must actually be copied, which takes longer.

```
$ ls chapt*
chapt3
$ mv chapt3 chapt3.save
$ ls chapt*
chapt3.save
$ _
```

The old name is 'chapt3', and the new name is 'chapt3.save'. After the operation there will not be a file named 'chapt3'. The first file ('chapt3') is called the source file, and the second file ('chapt3.save') is called the target or destination.

In general, you can't use `mv` to rename directories. The one exception is when the source and target directory have the same parent. If 'mydir' is a directory, then the command `mv mydir mynewdir` is legal, because the source directory file 'mydir' and the destination directory file 'mynewdir' have the same parent directory. The command `mv mydir ../mynewdir` is illegal, because the source and target don't have the same parent. (Berkeley rules are more lenient than described here.)

If the source file is an ordinary file and the target file is a directory file, then `mv` will move the source file *into* the target directory. If 'wkfile' is an ordinary file and 'mydir' is a subdirectory of the current directory, then the command `mv wkfile mydir` will move 'wkfile' into the 'mydir' directory. You can verify the operation by using the `ls` command.

```
$ ls -d wkfile mydir mydir/wkfile
mydir
ls: mydir/wkfile not found
wkfile
$ mv wkfile mydir
$ ls mydir/wkfile wkfile
mydir/wkfile
ls: wkfile not found
$ _
```

You can have several source files if (and only if) the target file is a directory. The command `mv wkfile1 wkfile2 wkfile3 mydir` will move all three
source files into the 'mydir' directory.

The `cp` (copy) command makes a copy of a file. The main difference
between `mv` and `cp` is that `mv` obliterates the source file, whereas after a `cp`
operation the source file and the target file both exist. However, both `mv`
and `cp` can (and do) overwrite the target file, so be very careful.

```
$ ls chapt4*
chapt4
$ cp chapt4 chapt4.archive
$ ls chapt4*
chapt4
chapt4.archive
$ _
```

Notice that the file 'chapt4' is not changed by the operation.

If the target of a `cp` operation is a directory, then the copy operation will
copy the source file to that directory. The target directory must exist before
the operation. For example, I have a directory named 'bkpdir' where I
keep copies of important files.

```
$ ls chapt4 bkpdir/chapt4
ls: bkpdir/chapt4 not found
chapt4
$ cp chapt4 bkpdir
$ ls: chapt4 bkpdir/chapt4
bkpdir/chapt4
chapt4
$ _
```

`cp`, like `mv`, lets you have several source files when the target file is a directory. The command `cp chapt* bkpdir` will place copies of all of the chapters in the 'bkpdir' directory. You are not allowed to use a directory file as
the source file for a copy operation.

The `ln` (link) command is used to establish pseudonyms for files. In the
UNIX system, it is possible for a file to have several different names.

The difference between ln and cp is this: when you use the copy command, two distinct copies of the file are produced. Changes to one copy of the file will not alter the other copy. However, when you use the ln command, a new name is created which references the original file. No new copies of the actual data in the file are produced by the link command. Think about this for a second. ln creates a new name, but it does not make any new copies of the data. The new name and the old refer to the same thing.

```
$ ln chapt8 introcmds
$ _
```

In the above dialogue, a pseudonym ('introcmds') is created for the 'chapt8' file. The two names are equally valid, and either name can be used to reference the file. There are several reasons for wanting two names for a file. The reason in this case is that we want one naming system that reflects the number of the chapter, 'chapt8', and one system that reflects the contents of the chapter, 'introcmds'.

You can discover the number of links that a file has from the second column of the long format ls listing.

```
$ ls -l chapt8 introcmds
-rw-rw-rw-   2  kc      17935  Dec 12 18:07  chapt8
-rw-rw-rw-   2  kc      17935  Dec 12 18:07  introcmds
$ _
```

You can tell that the two names are actually links to just one file by using the i-node option -i of the ls command. (An *i-node* is an entry in a data table that the system uses to define the characteristics of a single file; see Section 25.8.) If two names reference the same file, then both names will be associated with the same i-node number.

```
$ ls -i chapt8 introcmds
1321   chapt8
1321   introcmds
$ _
```

If the names are actually links to one file, as in this case, then the i-node numbers (displayed in the first column) will be identical. If the names refer to different files, then the i-node numbers will be different.

Another place where pseudonyms (links) are important is in the directory hierarchy. When a directory is created, the system links the name '..' to the parent directory, and it links the name '.' to the current directory. The whole directory hierarchy is maintained by the UNIX kernel by making links between directory files. You cannot use the ln command to change the linking that binds the filesystem together; those links are made automatically when the system creates directories.

6.5   CHMOD, CHOWN, AND CHGRP—CHANGE FILE MODES AND OWNERSHIP

The chmod (change mode), chown (change owner), and chgrp (change group) commands are used to control the access rights to files and ownership of files. The ability to fine-tune the filesystem for flexible and protected access to files is one of the strengths of the UNIX system. All of these commands are usable only by the owner of a file (or by the superuser).

The three operations that can be performed on a file are reading, writing, and execution. There are three levels of privilege associated with each file—the owner's privileges, the group's privileges, and others' privileges. For each level of privilege, each of the three basic operations may be either allowed or denied. (The set id modes and the sticky mode can also be allowed or denied, but they are not discussed here, because they are system programming attributes. See Sections 23.2 and 23.3.)

You are allowed to determine the modes (access privileges) of the files that you own. For example, you can make a file unreadable and unwritable to anyone but yourself.

```
$ ls -l swampdata
-rw-rw-rw-  1  kc     3109  May 13 11:51  swampdata
$ chmod go-rw swampdata
$ ls -l  swampdata
-rw-------  1  kc     3109  May 13 11:51  swampdata
$ _
```

A symbolic mode control word ("go-rw" in the example above) consists of three parts: who, operator, permission. In the example, the who part was "go", to indicate group and others; the op was "-", to remove permission, and the permission part was "rw", to indicate read and write. The characters used in constructing the symbolic mode control word are summarized in Figure 6.4.

The command chmod a=rw myfile will make 'myfile' readable and writable for all: owner, members of the file's group, and everybody else. The command chmod g+x newdoo will add the group execute permission for the file 'newdoo'. The command chmod o-rwx newdoo will make 'newdoo' inaccessible to others.

The commands chown and chgrp change the owner and group associated with a file. These commands are usually used when one user inherits another user's files or when one user gets copies of files from another user. The command chown kc * will transfer ownership of all of the files in the

Who		Operator	
u	User (owner)	-	Remove permission
g	Group	+	Add permission
o	Owner	=	Assign permission
a	All (ugo)		

Permissions

r	Read
w	Write
x	Execute
s	Set user (or group) id mode
t	Save text (sticky) mode
u	User's current permissions
g	Group's current permissions
o	Other's current permissions

Figure 6.4.   Table of chmod **options.**

current directory to the user named "kc". The name of the new owner must be either a valid login name or a user identification number. The login names and the corresponding numbers are found in the '/etc/passwd' file.

The command chgrp staff corelist will associate the group "staff" with the file named 'corelist'. The groups mentioned in the chgrp command can either be group names or numbers from the '/etc/group' file. Some systems make very little use of the UNIX group feature.

On System V the owner of a file may change its owner or its group. However, on Berkeley systems only the superuser may change the ownership of a file. Berkeley systems allow the owner of a file to change its group, but the owner must belong to the new group.

6.6   MKDIR AND RMDIR—CREATE AND REMOVE DIRECTORIES

The mkdir (make directory) command is used to create directories. When the system creates a directory, it automatically inserts entries for the names '.' and '..'. The name '.' is a pseudonym for the directory, and the name '..' is a pseudonym for its parent directory. All directories contain these entries, and ordinary users are prohibited from removing these entries. A directory that contains only the entries for '.' and '..' is considered empty.

The command mkdir morestuff will create a directory named 'morestuff', which will be a subdirectory of the current directory. If you enter the command ls morestuff, you will discover that 'morestuff' doesn't contain any ordinary files. The command `ls -a morestuff` will reveal that 'morestuff' contains two entries, '.' and '..'. The `i` and `d` options to `ls` can help you to understand how links glue the filesystem together.

```
$ ls -id . morestuff/.. morestuff morestuff/.
1801    .
1321    morestuff
1321    morestuff/.
1801    morestuff/..
$ _
```

(See the description of `ls` in Section 6.2 for more information on the options `a` and `d` and the `ln` description in Section 6.4 for more information on the `i` option.)

If you want to remove a directory, you first must remove all of its contents. If the directory 'morestuff' contains just ordinary files, then the command `rm morestuff/*` will empty it, provided you own all of the files in 'morestuff' and have write permission on the directory itself. If 'morestuff' contains subdirectories, emptying it will require more work. Once 'morestuff' is empty the command `rmdir morestuff` will actually remove the directory.

6.7   FIND—SEARCH FOR A FILE

The `find` command is an aid for locating misplaced files. `find` examines a filesystem subtree looking for files that match a set of criteria. `find` is one of those curious UNIX programs that is useful for, and used by, beginners and black belts alike. Programmers and system administrators often use `find` almost as if it were a programming language, invoking one option after another to search for a file based on complicated criteria. Instead of explaining `find` in all its glory, I am going to present a few of its capabilities—capabilities that most UNIX users will find useful.

Probably the most common use of `find` is to find a file whose name (or part of whose name) is known. This capability is useful, because it is easy to misplace a file when you are using several directories and subdirectories. Remember that `find`, unlike most programs, will search through an entire file system subtree. That means that `find` will start in one directory, then search its subdirectories, and so on. Here is a simple example of using `find` to find all files named *checklist* in the current subtree. (The current subtree is the current directory, all of its subdirectories and files, and so on.)

```
$ find . -name checklist -a -print
./m2book/checklist
./m2book/rev1/checklist
./yaccsrc/checklist
$ _
```

Let's examine each argument to **find**. The first argument specifies the subtree to be searched. In this case, it is a ., which means start the search in the current directory. Any directory name could have been supplied in place of the . (such as '/usr1/kc' or '/bin'). The second argument is *-name*, which tells **find** to search for files named in the following argument, and the following argument is *checklist,* the target name. Instead of specifying the name explicitly, shell matching characters (which would need to be quoted) could have been used to specify a group of names. The last argument is *-print,* which tells **find** to print the names of all found files. This is probably the most common thing for **find** to do, and *-print* is the most common last argument for **find** (just as . is the most common first argument).

Let's graduate to a more complicated example. This one is similar to the first, because it looks for files, but in this case the file names start with a *z* and end with a digit. The search is confined to the '/usr' subtree.

```
$ find /usr -name 'z*[0-9]' -print
/usr/lib/terminfo/z/z19
/usr/lib/terminfo/z/zen30
/usr/lib/terminfo/z/z30
$ _
```

Another common use of **find** is to search for files that are larger (or smaller) than a certain size. Instead of the *-name* option, the *-size* option is used. But other than that, the syntax is similar to the first two examples. Following the *-size* is a number that represents the size of file in blocks (512 bytes). A plus sign in front of the number means files larger than that many blocks, and a minus sign in front means files smaller than that many blocks. Here is an example that shows both types.

```
$ find / -size +250 -print
/xenix
$ find /bin -size -4 -print
/bin/false
/bin/true
/bin/whodo
/bin/diff3
/bin/dirname
$ _
```

The dialogue shown above indicates that the only file on my Xenix system that is larger than 250 blocks is the '/xenix' file (the file containing the operating system code), and there are only five files in the '/bin' subtree that are less than 4 blocks long. If you don't place a plus or a minus sign in front of the size specification, you will find files that are exactly that many blocks large.

The last use of find that I am going to mention here is to find files that have been recently modified. For this, find recognizes the *-mtime* option. The option must be followed by a signed number, to find files that have been modified within that many days. The following command searches for files in the '/etc' subtree that have been modified within the last 24 hours.

```
$ find /etc -mtime -1 -print
/etc
/etc/utmp
/etc/wtmp
/etc/mnttab
$ _
```

UNIX veterans will recognize these as system administration files that are often updated by the system, so it makes sense that they have changed recently. If you use a + number with -mtime, find finds files older than that many days, which is useful when you want to clear out old files.

Many other uses of find, including many that are much more complicated than those shown, are possible. You should refer to a manual for more information, or to the *UNIX Command Reference Guide* for more advanced examples.

System administrators often use find to search for dangerous or wasteful uses of the filesystem. find takes a long time to search through a large subtree; it is best to make the subtree as small as possible. You should probably run find during the wee hours of the morning if you are routinely searching through an entire large filesystem.

6.8   FILE—DEDUCE FILE TYPES

The file command attempts to determine what type of information is stored in the files named as arguments. Whereas the ls command prints hard facts about files, the file command makes an educated guess concerning the files' contents. The most important use of the file command is probably to determine whether the file contains text or binary information. Text files can be typed on your terminal; binary files cannot. (Attempting to type a binary file on your terminal may make your terminal freeze, because some of the binary values in the file are probably interpreted as control codes by either your terminal or modem.)

If a file contains binary information, the file program will attempt to determine whether the information is an executable program or binary data. If the file contains text, file will attempt to discern the language. On most systems, the file program knows about languages such as the shell, C, nroff/troff, FORTRAN, and assembler as well as English. Naturally, since it is only a guess, the classification determined for each file may be wrong.

```
$ file *
Readme: ascii text
makefile: ascii text
megaa.c: c program text
megaa.c.orig: c program text
megaxy.c.: c program text
todo: English text
zsrc: directory
$ _
```

6.9 DU—DISPLAY DISK USAGE

You can use the du (disk usage) command to see how much disk storage your files are occupying. du prints the storage consumed in each branch of the specified subtree, followed by the total for the entire subtree.

```
$ du
728      ./originals
31       ./rev1/mycu
3        ./rev1/m4
37       ./rev1/demo
309      ./rev1
253      ./jan
1286     .
$ _
```

The summary shows the number of blocks of disk storage used in every directory in the current subtree. (As mentioned above during the discussion of find, the current subtree consists of all files in the current directory, all files in any subdirectories, and so on.) You can also specify which subtree should be examined.

```
$ du /etc
16      /etc/fstab.d
24      /etc/priv
14      /etc/test
1828    /etc
$ _
```

The summary details disk usage in the '/etc' subtree.

One of the maxims of the UNIX system is "users' disk storage require-ments expand to fill the available space." Periodic removal of old files is necessary to keep your storage charges down and to keep free space on the system. People often use du when they are cleaning their directories in order to concentrate on the directories that consume the most space.

The df (disk free) command can be used to see how much free space exists on a particular storage volume. (See Section 24.5.) System managers often run df periodically to keep track of free space. When the free space diminishes to a certain point, most administrators ask the users to prune their directories.

df in combination with find is an even more powerful storage manage-ment tool. You can use df to locate users who are consuming excessive space, and then you can use find to locate large (or large and not recently used) files in those users' subtrees.

6.10   OD—DUMP FILES

Occasionally you want to know exactly what binary codes are contained in a file. The od (octal dump) program is used to produce octal, decimal, ASCII, and hexadecimal format dumps of a file. The various formats can be produced together or separately.

The term "dump" originated many years ago when program debugging was usually performed by producing a printout of all of the values in mem-ory following a program failure. Since the quantity of information was large and the programmer's deciphering job was unpleasant, the printout was called a dump. Today much debugging is done more intelligently, although "dumps" are still used. Most program failure "dumps" are examined today with the help of programs that make interpreting the infor-mation much easier. Whenever a UNIX system program fails inexplicably, a dump is performed into the file named 'core' in the working directory of the program, and the mysterious message "core dumped" is produced.

The octal dump program can also be used to search for control charac-ters embedded in text files. For example, suppose you want to know whether a certain file contains tab characters. If you were to cat the file onto your screen, the UNIX terminal handler or your terminal would auto-matically expand the tabs into the correct number of spaces. However, if you use the od program to dump the file, you can examine the output for the notation "\t", which indicates a tab. During a dump in ASCII format, printable characters are displayed normally, and unprintable control characters are printed in octal except for a few very standard characters, which are represented as follows:

Backspace	\b	Carriage Return	\r
Tab	\t	Null	\0
New Line	\n	Form Feed	\f

Here is how od is used to dump a file called "spices" in ASCII character (the -c flag) format.

```
$ cat spices
thyme    nutmeg
sage     cumin
salt     pepper
$ od -c spices
000000   t  h  y  m  e \t  n  u  t  m  e  g \n  s  a  g
000020   e \t  c  u  m  i  n \n  s  a  l  t \t  p  e  p
000040   p  e  r \n
000044
$ _
```

od can dump special or directory files as well as ordinary files. The superuser can use od to examine the information stored on a disk by entering the command od /dev/rrp0. od also allows you to examine a file starting in the middle by specifying an offset. The disk could be examined starting at byte 1024 by using the command od /dev/rrp0 +1024. The argument +1024 indicates that you should start dumping 1024 bytes past the start of the file. The same offset could be specified in terms of blocks (in this case a block is 512 bytes) by entering the command od /dev/rrp0 +2b. The b stands for blocks.

CHAPTER 7

"What's Going On" Utilities

One of the strengths of the UNIX operating system is its large set of utility programs. Different installations will have different sets of utility programs; therefore, there is no way that this book can be a complete guide to all of the utilities on all of the systems. Instead I attempt to discuss and show examples of the most useful utilities.

This chapter focuses on the utilities that allow you to observe and control your interactions with the UNIX system. Utilities for text files are covered in Chapter 8, and the utilities for file management are covered in Chapter 6. Utilities for programmers are covered in Chapter 17, and utilities for the system manager are covered in Chapter 24.

The idea of these chapters is to describe a set of programs that form a useful and powerful nucleus of UNIX knowledge. Anyone who seriously uses the UNIX system will be very familiar with most of these programs; less serious users will probably use at least half of them. Large, complicated programs (e.g., the shell, vi) are discussed individually elsewhere in this book (the shell—Chapters 4, 11, 12; vi—Chapters 9, 10). For specific information on the operation of a particular program you should consult your UNIX manual, or the *UNIX Command Reference Guide*.

One of the things that novices often find confusing is that the UNIX environment is variable. As an example, consider the fact that two different users would usually have different home directories and different access rights to files. They might have different types of terminals, and they might need to use very different sets of programs. One of the strengths of the UNIX system is its ability to support many environments. The utilities in the "What's Going On" category help you understand the current environment.

7.1 PASSWD—CHANGE LOGIN PASSWORD

The passwd command is used to change your login password. Some people change their passwords periodically (some system managers insist) to maintain security. The passwd command first prompts you to enter your current password, and then it twice asks you to enter your new password. None of your responses are echoed to the screen to enhance password security.

```
$ passwd
Old password:
New password:
Retype new password:
$ _
```

The new password is entered twice to make sure that you entered it correctly, without typos. Imagine the confusion that would result if you entered your new password incorrectly, and the system accepted it.

A good password contains both uppercase and lowercase letters, does not appear in the dictionary, and is longer than 5 or 6 letters. If your password is too skimpy, the system might ask you to choose another. If you forget your password, the system administrator can remove your old password and give you another one. System V UNIX systems can be administered so that passwords age periodically. You will be forced to choose a new password the first time you log in after your password expires.

7.2 DATE AND WHO—DISPLAY THE DATE AND TIME, AND LIST THE LOGGED-ON USERS

The date command prints the current date and time.

```
$ date
Sun Dec 15 22:30:48  EST  1985
$ _
```

In addition, the superuser can invoke the date command to set the date.

The who command prints a list of the people who are currently using the system.

```
$ who
nuucp     tty01    Dec 15 22:24
gilbert   tty17    Dec 15 15:34
dan       ttyh0    Dec 15 17:37
kc        ttyh3    Dec 15 21:02
$ _
```

When you run who, your login name should be in the list. The second column names the terminal connection that each user is using, and the third column is the time that each user logged onto the system. People who are logged on at multiple terminals will be listed multiple times in the who output.

Some of the older systems were adept at difficult philosophical questions such as "who are you," "who am i" ("whoami" on some systems), and "who is god." Perhaps your system still knows the answers.

On Berkeley systems, several additional commands exist for finding out who is logged on. The simplest of these is the users command, which simply prints a list of the users, without displaying "tty" connections or logon times. If you are using a system connected to a local area network, the rwho will tell you who is logged on to all of the machines in the network. You can use the w command to find out what everybody on your machine is doing. w can just print its best notion of what someone is doing. Most dedicated game enthusiasts know how to play a game in such a way that the w command shows them doing useful work. Many people believe that w is best left as a systems administration command; few users have legitimate needs for the detailed information that is displayed. Some systems also have the whodo command, which is an alternate list of who is doing what.

A related Berkeley command is finger. The finger command will print out most of the password file information about a user, including the full name, telephone numbers, office numbers, etc. Simply entering the command finger will finger all of the logged-on users, or you can supply a user name to limit the display to that individual.

7.3 MAIL—SEND ELECTRONIC MAIL TO OTHER UNIX USERS

One of the earliest, most exciting UNIX facilities is electronic mail. Originally the mail program could send mail to other users on your own machine, but with the development and widespread use of uucp, it is now possible at many sites to use mail to send messages to people on UNIX systems throughout the world.

Unfortunately the original mail program has the poorest user interface of any of the widely used nonprogrammer's utilities. mail's first problem is that it ignores the UNIX dictum to "do one thing well." Instead, mail performs two different functions, reading the mail and sending mail. Although mail is but one program, it may be helpful to imagine it as two—one for sending mail and one for reading mail. mail's second problem is that, like ed, it uses one-character command names, and the error messages are cryptic.

Let's first talk about sending mail. For recipients on your own machine, the first thing you need to do is find out their login names. Login names are cataloged in the '/etc/passwd' file, and login names of the logged-in users are displayed using the who command.

For long messages, it's best to prepare the message in advance using a text editor and then use the shell's capability for input redirection to attach the standard input of mail to the message file. Thus if 'reina.7' is a file containing a message to send to Reina (whose login name is rsb), the following dialogue shows how you can send her the message.

```
$ mail rsb < reina.7
$ _
```

In this example, mail knows that you are *sending* mail because of the user name specified on the command line. (mail is one of a small group of programs whose command line arguments aren't file names.) Of course you can place as many recipient names as you wish on the command line. Many people routinely send a copy of all their outgoing mail to themselves, as a simple error check. If you have a typo in one of the recipient names, mail will complain and save a copy of the message in a file called 'dead.letter'.

Short messages can be entered interactively. Beware that mail swallows each of your input lines as you type, so you cannot go back and fix a mistake on the previous line. However, the UNIX system's ordinary erase and kill characters work normally, so you can fix mistakes on the current line. When your message is complete, strike the EOF character (^D) to terminate the message. A shell prompt will appear, meaning all went well, or mail will complain and save the letter in 'dead.letter'.

```
$ mail e mike
Meeting tomorrow on documentation standards,
3pm in O'Flanagans Bar. (Bring Quarters)
^D
$ _
```

For recipients on distant machines things are more complicated. You need to discover the recipient's login name, the recipient's machine name, and the network route from your machine to the recipient's. Yes, that's a big job.

Your system administrator will know the names of the machines to which your machine is directly connected, and the administrator should be able to help you form addresses for distant machines. One of the easiest ways to discover the address of a distant site is to receive mail from that site. The routing information in the message header should enable you to construct a return address, since most mail routes are bidirectional. (For more information on pathnames, see Section 20.1.)

Reading your mail is an interactive process. When you start `mail` without mentioning any recipients on the command line, the `mail` program assumes that you want to read your mail. If none has arrived, `mail` will tell you so and exit. However, if there is some mail, `mail` will print the first message and wait for you to indicate what should be done with the message. Several commands are available:

d Delete the message.

s Save a copy of the message in a file named 'mbox'.

s *filename*
   The message will be saved in the named file.

w The same as the s command, except the message header lines will not be saved.

p Print the message again.

<CR> or +
   Advance to the next message.

q or ^D
   All undeleted, unsaved mail will be returned to the system mailbox, and `mail` will quit.

x All mail will be returned to the system mailbox, and `mail` will quit. Thus x is an undelete.

!*command*
   The given shell command will run, then control will return to `mail`.

* A help message will be produced. (Use ? on Berkeley or Version 7 systems.)

m *users*
   The message will be mailed to the named users, or to yourself by default.

Berkeley `mail`, written by Kurt Shoens, is much more elaborate than the System V/Version 7 `mail` described above, but it is similar. Whereas System V `mail` prints each message and asks you for its disposition, Berkeley `mail` prints a list of message headers and allows you perform any operation (delete, print, save, etc.) on any message, or group of messages, in any order. Berkeley `mail` also has many more operations, and you can key in full command names, such as `print`, if you prefer them to single-character commands. Because there are more options, Berkeley `mail` is slightly harder to use. However, you can limit yourself to the Berkeley analogs of the commands mentioned above, and Berkeley `mail` will function almost identically to System V `mail`. Berkeley `mail` is often available on System V by using the name `mailx`. Some System V variants, such as Xenix System V, supply Berkeley `mail` instead of the traditional Version 7 `mail`.

Berkeley `mail` also has many more options for sending mail, making it relatively easy to compose messages inside of `mail` instead of preparing messages beforehand with a separate program. As Berkeley `mail` collects lines in an outgoing message, it specially handles each line starting with a ˜ (tilde). Various so-called "tilde escapes" are available to manage files, execute UNIX commands, print the currently entered message, or even my favorite, ˜v, which invokes an editor (`vi` is the default) to edit the current message. These features can be ignored; just be certain that none of your lines of text start with a ˜. See the Berkeley *Mail Reference Manual* or the Berkeley manual pages for more information.

Another important part of Berkeley's mail and networking software is Eric Allman's `sendmail`, an internetwork mail-routing facility. `sendmail` understands most of the common network address syntaxes, and it knows how to manipulate addresses as necessary as mail is forwarded from one network to another and how to access various networks. `sendmail` considerably simplifies the process of specifying network addresses. `sendmail` is not a program that ordinary users access. Instead, users still use `mail` or some other front-end program, and then that program uses `sendmail` as necessary to take care of message routing.

7.4 WRITE—SEND MESSAGES TO LOGGED-ON USERS

The `write` command is used to establish typed communication between two logged-on users. Using a telephone, an intercom, or two tin cans and a string is usually a better way to communicate. Since someone may unexpectedly write to you someday, you should prepare by learning how to use the `write` command.

When someone writes to you, the message "Message from harry on tty33" (or similar) will appear on your terminal. You should respond by stopping whatever task you are engaged in and running the `write` command

```
$ write harry
```

Once both parties have executed the `write` command, anything that either party types will appear on both terminals. Therefore, it is best if only one person types at a time. The person who initiates the conversation usually types a few lines and then by convention types a line containing a single "o" which stands for over. The other person is now free to respond with a few lines and then type "o" for over. The conversation continues until someone types a line containing "oo" for over and out. You can terminate the conversation by striking the EOF (Control-D) character. If both people type simultaneously, the outputs are intermixed, and it is almost impossible to sort it all out. The following dialogue shows Kari's terminal following a conversation between Kari and Sally, the system administrator. Kari starts the `write` conversation, because she is having trouble with a printer.

```
$ write sally
Message from sally on tty9.
Hi Sally, is the fast line printer working today?
o
No, the printhead burned out.
It will be fixed by Friday.
o
Ok, thanks.
oo
oo
^D
$ _
```

In the above dialogue, the line "Message from sally on tty9" is printed on Kari's terminal when Sally, responding to Kari's `write sally` command, issues the command `write kari`. If Sally were not at her terminal, then Kari would not receive Sally's reply. In this case, after waiting a short time, Kari would strike Control-D to abandon her attempt to `write` to Sally.

On Berkeley UNIX systems an alternative user-to-user communication program, `talk`, is available. It is more powerful than `write`. Using `talk` is similar to using `write`. One party starts the conversation by entering the command `talk username`, a message is printed on the recipients terminal that indicates a conversation has been requested, and then the recipient replies.

`talk` has several advantages over `write`. An important advantage in some environments is that `talk` works over a network. Thus users on different machines can have a conversation. Although a username can be a simple login name of someone on your own machine, it can also be of the form *host!user, host.user, host:user,* or *user@host.*

`talk`'s other advantage is convenience. `talk` divides the screen into two windows. Whatever you type is shown in the top window, while messages from the recipient are simultaneously shown in the bottom window. With `talk`, everything you type is immediately displayed on both screens, unlike `write`, which displays your messages on the other terminal only when you strike return. Thus a conversation with `talk` is more like a verbal conversation. One party can interrupt another, and both people can talk (type) at once. `write`'s o and oo conventions are less necessary with `talk`. Either party can end a conversation by striking the interrupt character (often ^C), unlike `write`, where both parties must strike the EOF (^D) character.

7.5 MAN—PRINT MANUAL ENTRIES

The man command is used to display entries from the UNIX manual on your
terminal.

```
$ man pwd
PWD(1)                  Unix Manual                  PWD(1)

NAME
    pwd - print the name of the working directory
SYNOPSIS
    pwd
DESCRIPTION
The pwd command prints the full pathname of the
    current directory.


$ _
```

The man command is useful even if you have an up-to-date printed manual on your desk, because the on-line manual entries are often updated to
reflect local modifications. Also, many installations augment the standard
UNIX distribution with programs from many sources, and these commands
are often described *only* in the on-line manual.

On Version 7 and early System V UNIX systems the man command must
reformat the original text each time it reproduces the manual entry. (The
man command is not included in later versions of System V.) If you will
need to see the output again in the near future, you might want to save the
output in a file.

```
$ man stty > stty.man
$ _
```

On the Berkeley UNIX system, the manual entries are already formatted,
so much less work is required each time you access the on-line manual.
Entries are only reformatted when the original manual entry is changed.
This Berkeley enhancement consumes about three extra megabytes of disk
space, because each entry is stored twice.

On many systems the -t flag will direct man to produce a printed copy of
the manual. This option works only on systems that have access to a suitable typesetter or page printer.

Besides its admirable improvements to the system's on-line manual printing system, the Berkeley version of the UNIX system also has a command
called apropos that tries to discover the names of commands that might be
related to what you want to do. For example, suppose you want to move a
file from one directory to another but you can't recall what name the UNIX
system uses for the file movement command. The command apropos move

lists about 20 manual entries that are related to movements, among them the mv command. apropos doesn't actually print the manual citations, but based on its one-line summaries, you can decide which manual entries to consult.

7.6 ECHO—REPEAT COMMAND LINE ARGUMENTS

The echo command repeats its arguments. When the arguments are simple words, the echo command is useful for printing messages on the terminal, especially when it is used in shell program files.

```
$ echo tum de dum dum dumnnn
tum de dum dum dumnnn
$ _
```

The echo command can also be used to show the current value of shell variables, or to help you understand other aspects of the shell's argument list generation procedure. Arguments that you supply to programs are scanned by the shell to discover whether you have used any of the shell's special characters. The special characters are used to control various substitutions that the shell performs. For example, the shell maintains a system of variables. The word $PATH is a reference to a shell variable named $PATH which codes the current search string. (Shell variables are discussed in Section 11.2, and the search string is discussed in Section 11.4.) You can discover the current value of the $PATH variable by using the echo command.

```
$ echo $PATH
:/bin:/usr/bin:/usr/local/bin:/usr1/kc/bin:/graphics/bin
$ _
```

Filename generation (discussed in Section 4.6) is another form of argument substitution that the shell performs. The shell metacharacters ?, *, and [provide mechanisms for generating lists of files. You can use the echo command to discover what argument lists are passed to programs when you specify arguments containing the shell metacharacters.

```
$ ls
c1      c2      c3      c3.1
$ echo c?
c1 c2 c3
$ echo d?
d?
$ _
```

As shown in the dialogue above, the user's current directory contains four files. The first echo command uses the shell ? metacharacter. When the c? pattern is expanded by the shell, it becomes "c1 c2 c3", as shown in the output of the first echo command. In the second echo command, the shell attempts to expand the d? pattern. In the Bourne shell, when the expansion fails (because there aren't any two-character file names beginning with d), the original pattern is passed to echo, as shown by the output of the second echo command. In the C shell, an error message is usually printed when an expansion fails. Filename generation is a powerful technique for focusing the attention of certain commands on groups of appropriately named files—use the echo command when you want to know exactly what argument lists are being generated.

7.7 PS—LIST INFORMATION ABOUT PROCESSES

The ps command prints a list of your processes. The ps command is often used by systems programmers to determine what is happening on an entire system. You are most likely to need the ps program to determine the process identification (pid) numbers of errant processes so that you can kill them. (For a real surprise, try the ps program during a bout with the learn program. You may be surprised by the number of processes you are running.)

For a list of all of your processes you can use ps without options.

```
$ ps
   PID   TT  STAT  TIME   COMMAND
  26344  H3  S     0:14   -sh
  29313  H3  R     0:01   -ps
$ _
```

The command name, process identification number, controlling tty name, and the cumulative execution time of all of your processes are displayed. You should expect to see information detailing the ps command, the process for your interactive shell, and any background processes that are running for you. (On Berkeley systems, the interactive shell will be omitted from the list.)

If you are executing a process in the background, you can use the ps command to monitor that process. For example, if the process identification number of a background process is 2150, then you can restrict the ps display to that one process.

```
$ ps 2150
  PID  TT  STAT  TIME   COMMAND
  2150  H3  R     0:43   tu58 -s9600
$ _
```

As process 2150 progresses, you can repeatedly use the ps command to watch the cumulative execution time increase. At some point, process 2150 will complete, and then the command ps will print a message similar to "2150: no such process."

7.8 KILL—ABORT BACKGROUND PROCESSES

When a program is running in the foreground, you can usually stop it by striking the interrupt character (usually Control-C or DEL). However, you cannot stop a background process by striking the interrupt character. Instead, the UNIX system has a special command called kill for killing your own background processes. Only the superuser can kill other people's processes.

When you start a command running in the background, the shell automatically prints its process identification number. You can kill a background process by entering the kill command followed by the pid. For example, you can kill process 1284 using the following command.

```
$ kill 1284
$ _
```

If you have forgotten the process ID number, use the ps command. Process 1284 will be killed only if it exists and if it is your process.

Processes are killed by sending them a *signal*. *Signals* are simply conditions that a process examines each time its time slice comes around. Signals always arrive during a process's waiting (for a time slice) period. Some of the common signals are SIGHUP (the modem connection has been broken), SIGINTR (the user has struck the interrupt key), SIGQUIT (the process should stop and produce a coredump file as a debugging aid), SIGKILL (signal 9, the surest kill), and SIGTERM (the default termination signal sent by kill).

Processes can control what happens when certain signals arrive. The three possibilities are to ignore the signal, to perform the default activity, or to perform a specified routine in the program. Interactive programs, such as vi or the shell, usually manage signals carefully, to preserve your work. Noninteractive programs often do not manage signals. Most signals will, in the absence of deliberate handling by a process, cause that process to abort.

Processes that catch or ignore the ordinary kill signal can definitely be killed (unless it is stuck in an I/O device driver) by sending signal number 9.

```
$ kill -9 1284
$ _
```

Using the -9 option with kill is the surest way to stop a command, but you should use it only as a last resort, because programs that catch the ordinary kill signal usually do so for a good reason.

A process that is sleeping or waiting for some event will not react immediately when a signal arrives. Processes that are waiting for events that will never happen can never die. The point of this discussion is that the kill program kills only reasonable processes; really aberrant processes live on.

When you log off the system, any processes that are still running in the background will be sent the SIGHUP signal, which will terminate them unless you have the nohup command or unless the process has arranged to ignore the SIGHUP signal. When things get uncontrollable, hang up (log off), and start from the beginning.

7.9   NOHUP—RUN PROGRAMS WHILE LOGGED OFF

The nohup command allows you to run a command that will continue to run after you hang up or log off the system. This is very useful for large jobs, such as big text-processing commands, sorts of very large files, and major program recompilations. Usually you use nohup to start a background job.

In the following example there is a shell command file called 'nroffbook' that formats and prints a book manuscript.

```
$ nohup nroffbook &
13972
Sending output to 'nohup.out'
$ _
```

You can log off the system immediately after entering the command, and the work will proceed in your absence. If you don't use nohup, the processing will cease when you log off. As noted in the above dialogue, any output of the command that nohup executes will be sent to the file 'nohup.out' unless you use output redirection to send it to some other file.

7.10 NICE—RUN PROCESSES AT LOW PRIORITY

The `nice` command is usually used to reduce the priority of a command. You should use `nice` whenever you are doing major processing and you want to reduce the demands on the system. Programs started by `nice` may take significantly longer than programs run at the usual priority. `nice` is often used in conjunction with background tasks, often with tasks that are run using nohup.

nice essentially reduces the size of the time slice allocated to a process, but the process is bound to consume some CPU time under all conditions. Unfortunately, there is no method in the UNIX system for running a job that executes only when the system has absolutely nothing else to do. Very demanding jobs that can wait till the wee hours of the morning or the weekend should be run at those times in order to completely minimize interference with the normal processing on the system.

The following dialogue shows how to run a large job (the same one as in the previous section) in the background at reduced priority.

```
$ nice nroffbook &
14920
$ _
```

If you want to log off while the processing is proceeding, then you can combine nohup with `nice`.

```
$ nice nohup nroffbook &
15072
Sending output to 'nohup.out'
$ _
```

7.11 TIME—TIME PROCESSES

The `time` command is used to time processes. You might want to time a process in order to compare two different methods, or you might just want to know how long something takes. For example, you might want to time the print job mentioned in the previous sections.

```
$ time nroffbook
338.8  213.7  26.5
$ _
```

After the `nroffbook` command completes, the `time` command prints three key timing statistics. The first number is the total elapsed time for executing the command, the second is the user time spent executing the command, and the third is the time spent by the system on behalf of the command.

On most systems, the total elapsed time is measured differently from the user time and the system time. Thus it is possible for the sum of user and system time to exceed elapsed time. Ordinarily the sum of user and system time is much less than total elapsed time, because the system spends some time performing other peoples' work. In the example above, user time plus system time is about 70% of total time. This is indicative of a lightly loaded system.

The reported times can vary depending on load conditions. Timing a command several times in quick succession is likely to generate consistent data; timing a command at several different times of the day may generate less consistent data because of load variations. The ratio of system time to execution time indicates the relative importance of system calls during the execution of the process. (See Section 15.6.)

7.12   STTY AND TTY—MANAGE YOUR TERMINAL HANDLER

The tty command is used to print UNIX's name for the communications port that your terminal is using. If you use a single hardwired terminal, your communication port will remain the same, but if you use dial-up ports, your communication port may vary. One common situation where knowing your terminal's name is important is restoring order when one of your jobs hangs. You can use the ps command to find out what jobs are running on a given terminal and then use kill to remove those jobs.

You also might want to know the name of your communication line for system administration purposes. For example, names are important if lines are being reconfigured or repaired.

```
$ tty
/dev/tty30
$ _
```

The dialogue above indicates that the communications line is accessed by the '/dev/tty30' character special file.

```
$ ls -l /dev/tty30
crw--w--w-  1 kc  staff   1,   0 Jan 20 23:31 /dev/tty30
$ _
```

The tty command is also used in shell programs to determine whether the standard input is a terminal. The exit status of tty is true if the standard input is a terminal; it is false otherwise. (See Section 11.7.)

The stty (set terminal options) command allows you to control the way the system treats your terminal. stty is very important because there are many different types of terminals and because users have different preferences, habits, and expectations. On some systems there is a program that automatically adapts the system to your terminal based on the value of the $TERM variable. On other systems you should include the appropriate stty command in the file '.profile' ('.login' for csh users) to set the modes appropriately at the beginning of each session.

The part of the UNIX system that performs the conversions to adapt to a particular type of terminal is called the terminal handler (also called the tty handler). The terminal handler doesn't manage the higher-level aspects of the dialogue, such as managing windowing or performing cursor addressing. Rather, it is concerned with low-level issues like terminal-dependent delays, tab expansion, and the control characters you used for input editing and control.

This section discusses some of the options that can be enabled in the tty handler using the stty command. A complete discussion of all of the possibilities is beyond the scope of this book, partly because there are so many options and partly because some options are dependent on system, version, and hardware.

The stty command (without options) displays the settings of a few key modes.

```
$ stty
speed 2400 baud; tabs
erase = #, kill = @, intr = ^?
$ _
```

The output indicates that the communication speed is 2400 baud, that the tabs option is set, the erase character is the number symbols, the kill character is the at sign, and the interrupt character is the DEL key (indicated cryptically by the "^?" notation). The tabs option indicates that the system believes that I have a terminal capable of handling tabs (more on that in a few paragraphs). The erase, kill, and interrupt characters are discussed in Section 3.4.

The erase character is used to erase the previously entered character, and the kill character is used to erase the entire line. Because the standard UNIX system erase and kill characters are hard to type (not reachable from the home row), many people reassign them. Frequently the Control-H character is used for erase, and the Control-U character is used for kill. You can reassign erase and kill by using the command

```
$ stty erase \^h kill \^u
$ _
```

The notation of a caret followed by a letter indicates a control character to stty; the backslash is used to escape the caret, because the caret has a special meaning to some versions of the shell. (On Berkeley systems you can specify Control-H by typing Control-V, then Control-H. The Control-V is a Berkeley tty feature that quotes the following character, even special characters.)

We can verify that the assignments have actually changed by using the stty command.

```
$ stty
speed 2400 baud; tabs
erase = ^h, kill = ^u, intr = ^?
$ _
```

Striking the interrupt character sends an interrupt signal to the currently executing foreground processes. Some programs, such as the shell and the editor, choose to ignore the interrupt, but most other programs, such as cat and grep, exit when they receive the interrupt. Many people prefer to use Control-C as the interrupt key rather than the default DEL key.

```
$ stty intr \^c
$ _
```

You could use the stty command to verify the reassignment.

The handling of tabs varies from one terminal to another. Some terminals recognize and expand the tab character; other terminals ignore it. The -tabs option informs the terminal handler that you are using a terminal that doesn't know how to expand tabs.

```
$ stty -tabs
$ _
```

The UNIX terminal handler will expand tab characters into spaces so that output appears correct on your terminal.

The tabs setting informs the system that your terminal expands tab characters; thus they will pass directly through the terminal handler to be expanded by your terminal.

```
$ stty tabs
$ _
```

You should use the tabs setting on terminals that expand tabs, because it slightly increases the output speed when a tab is encountered.

It is possible, although very difficult, to use the UNIX system with a terminal that doesn't produce lowercase letters. The lcase option informs the terminal handler that you are using a terminal that only supports uppercase.

```
$ stty lcase
$ _
```

When you are using an uppercase terminal, all input is automatically translated from upper- to lowercase, and all output is automatically translated from lower- to uppercase. In the uppercase mode, if you enter a backslash followed by a letter, then an uppercase letter is generated. For example, the input \JOHN \DOE is translated to *John Doe* when you are in uppercase mode. The same convention is used for output; the word *Susan* will be printed \SUSAN.

The -lcase option will return you to the normal mode where uppercase and lowercase letters are acceptable.

```
$ stty -lcase
$ _
```

You may inadvertently get into the uppercase only mode if the terminal's shift lock key is depressed during login. During the login process the system attempts to determine the type of terminal and make the proper settings. If you enter your login name in all uppercase letters, then the system assumes that you are using an uppercase terminal, and you have to use the stty -lcase command to revert to normal mode (or you have to log out and then back in).

You can also use stty to change the baud rate for communication between the terminal and the computer. (The baud rate is a measure of the speed at which characters are passed between a terminal and a computer. As a rough estimate, the baud rate divided by 10 is the number of characters that can be transferred in a second.) Once you tell the UNIX system about a new baud rate, you must be able to change your terminal's rate to match.

The common baud rates are acceptable stty options.

```
$ stty 1200
xx_e
```

The example shown above sets the communication speed to 1200 baud. The *xx_e* is the standard currency symbol prompt, printed by the system at 1200 baud but received (incorrectly) by the terminal at the original speed.

You can use stty to change the settings of a terminal other than the one you are using interactively. On Version 7 and System V UNIX systems, the stty command changes the settings of the standard *input*, while on Berkeley UNIX systems, stty changes the settings of the standard *output*. (In the dialogues below, the Version 7, System V usage is shown. Change the < to a > on Berkeley systems.) For instance, if you want a display of the settings of 'tty33', you can use the command

```
$ stty < /dev/tty33
speed 9600 baud; evenp hupcl
brkint -inpck icrnl onlcr cr0 nl0 tab0 bs0 vt0 ff0
echo echoe echok
$ _
```

(You usually need superuser privilege to open terminal special files other than one where you are logged in.) Similarly, you can use the following command to set the baud rate to 9600 on 'tty33'.

```
$ stty 9600 < /dev/tty33
$ _
```

This method for setting the baud rate is useful for controlling communication channels for special devices such as receive-only printers. The major caveat is that terminal settings persist only as long as some process keeps the line open. Processes where people are logged in are kept open by the login shell, thus stty-induced changes stick during your login session (or until overridden by a subsequent stty command). However, lines used, for example, by a printer may not remain opened by a process when nothing is being printed. Thus the duration during which a stty mode will stay effective depends on what software is using a line.

stty contains many other options you can use to adapt the system to individual terminals. You really have to know a lot about terminals, computers, and serial communication to use most of the options of the stty command. On many systems the system administrator will place the appropriate commands into your login script, and you won't need to use the stty command.

CHAPTER 8

Text File Utilities

Many UNIX users use the system because of its excellent text-processing facilities. It is not surprising that many programmers love the UNIX system, because much of the work of programming is manipulating text. Secretaries, scientists, and businessmen as well have found that the UNIX system's text facilities can increase their productivity.

Naturally, the UNIX system contains programs to type files on the terminal or to print files on a printer. The UNIX system also contains programs to sort files; to search through files for text patterns; to count lines, words, and columns in files; and to check for spelling errors in document files. These programs are described in this chapter.

The UNIX system also contains a variety of much more sophisticated programs for working with text files. The first section of this chapter is a guide to the UNIX system's sophisticated text manipulation programs. All of these programs are covered elsewhere in this book.

8.1 TEXT UTILITIES

Text files are often created by using a text editor such as vi. A text editor allows a user to enter and change text in a file. Many UNIX systems have several text editors, including EMACS, ed, the Rand editor, and vi. vi is described in Chapter 9, and some of its advanced features are described in Chapter 10. ed is described in Appendix III.

The UNIX system contains programs that can format a file of text. Formatting smooths out the margins, inserts titles and footnotes, adjusts the spacing, aligns columns of tabular data, and handles all of the special

102

characters in mathematical equations. The UNIX system formatting programs nroff, troff, eqn, tbl, and the -ms and -mm macro packages, pic and refer are described in *The UNIX Text Processing System*.

The UNIX system also contains utilities that can help you write programs that recognize command languages and grammars. These recognizers are useful if you are writing a text formatter or a programming language translator or a variety of other programs that perform various actions based on text. The UNIX system programs to assist you in writing recognizers, named lex and yacc, are described in Chapter 19.

Text files are often derived from other text files, and there may be several versions of a text file. To help you maintain groups of text files, the UNIX system contains the make program, which keeps track of dependencies in a group of files, and the Source Code Control System (SCCS), which keeps track of different versions of a file. make and SCCS are described in Chapter 18.

The UNIX system contains two programmable text manipulation programs: awk and sed. The awk programming language is a simple language that combines standard modern programming language features with special features for text pattern matching and text manipulation. The sed editor is a text editor designed expressly for following editing scripts. Its command syntax is close to that of ex or ed. awk is described in Chapter 13, and sed is described in Chapter 14.

8.2 CAT—CATENATE (TYPE OR COMBINE) FILES

The cat (concatenate) program is one of the UNIX system's most versatile text manipulation programs. The standard use of the cat program is to type text files on your terminal.

```
$ cat /etc/motd
System will be down all
weekend for equipment
installation.
$ _
```

Since cat is an abbreviation for concatenate, it is reasonable to expect cat to concatenate files.

```
$ cat /etc/greeting
Welcome to RNA UNIX 4.2
$ cat /etc/greeting /etc/motd
Welcome to RNA UNIX 4.2
System will be down all
weekend for equipment
installation.
$ _
```

The ability of cat to concatenate files is also useful in the following way:

```
$ cat chapt1 chapt2 chapt3 chapt4 chapt5 > book
$ _
```

This command concatenates five chapters of a book into a single file called 'book' using output redirection. The command could have been entered more elegantly.

```
$ cat chapt[12345] > book
$ _
```

This works because file name generation occurs alphabetically. (Numbers are alphabetized as you would expect, 1, 2, etc.) If there were only five numbered chapters in the directory, the command could also have been entered as

```
$ cat chapt? > book
$ _
```

or it could have been entered as

```
$ cat chapt* > book
$ _
```

However, you should note that the command

```
$ cat chapt3 chapt1 > newchapters
$ _
```

is not equivalent to the command

```
$ cat chapt[31] > newchapters
$ _
```

The second case relies on the shell's filename generation process to generate the argument list for the cat program. Filename generation always produces an alphabetized list, so if you are relying on filename generation when

you are concatenating files, remember the alphabetization. You can use the
echo command to see the difference.

```
$ echo chapt3 chapt1
chapt3 chapt1
$ echo chapt[31]
chapt1 chapt3
$ _
```

Another use of the cat command is to create empty files.

```
$ cat /dev/null > empty
$ ls -l empty
-rw-rw-rw-     1   kc   0  Jan 7 13:01  empty
$ _
```

The UNIX "bit bucket" is a special file named '/dev/null'. If you direct
output to the null device, it is discarded. If you read input from the null
device, you immediately encounter an end of file. Therefore, performing a
cat of the null device will produce a zero-length output (which was directed
above to the file named 'empty').

Another way to create an empty file for Bourne shell users is the following.

```
$ > naught
$ ls -l naught
-rw-rw-rw-     1   kc   0  Jan 7 13:01  naught
$ _
```

When you enter a command that consists solely of an output redirection,
the shell creates the named file.

Another use of the cat program is to place a few lines of text in a file
without the bother of using a text editor. If you execute cat without arguments, it reads from the standard input until an end of file is encountered.

```
$ cat > msgforbob
Victor from IBM called.
New machine will arrive on
Tuesday. He will try to
call you tomorrow.
^D
$ _
```

Since cat is not an editor, you cannot back up a few lines and fix errors,
but for simple one- or two-line inputs, this command is useful. When you
strike Control-D, cat receives the end-of-file indication and closes the output file and exits.

Many UNIX text-processing programs read their input from the standard input if you don't explicitly mention input files in the command line. When used intentionally, this is a powerful technique, but when you accidentally fail to mention input files, most programs are willing to sit there all day waiting for input from the terminal while you sit there all day waiting for them to complete their chores.

8.3   PR—TITLE AND PAGINATE FILES

The `pr` command is used to paginate and title text files. The most common use of the `pr` command is to prepare a text file for printing on a lineprinter. `pr` is also used to produce several columns of output, compress files by replacing spaces with tabs, expand tabs into spaces, number the lines in a file, and perform other simple reformatting tasks.

If you don't supply any command line options, `pr` will supply a five-line header and a five-line trailer at the beginning and end of each page. The third line of the header will contain the filename, date, and page number. The number of lines in the file will be rounded up to exactly fill the last page. By default pages are 66 lines long, but with the five-line header and five-line trailer, there will be only 56 lines of the input file on each page.

The following example shows `pr` used to paginate the '/etc/motd' file on my Xenix System V machine. To make the example short enough to show in this book format, the output is fed to the Berkeley `head` filter which discards everything but the first 10 lines. The `pr` output is also fed to the `wc` (word count) program just to convince you that the output is exactly 66 lines.

```
$ cat /etc/motd
            Welcome to XENIX System V
            for personal computers
              Brought to you by
           The Santa Cruz Operation
$ pr /etc/motd | wc
      66     23     220
```

```
$ pr /etc/motd | head


Jun 24 20:50 1987  /etc/motd Page 1


        Welcome to XENIX System V
         for personal computers
          Brought to you by
        The Santa Cruz Operation

$ _
```

You can replace the filename in the page header with any text you want using the -h option. Following the -h should be the text you want in each page header (quoted if it is more than one word). You can completely omit page headers and footers by using the -t option, which allows you to put 66 lines of text on each page.

You can produce multiple-column output with the *-n* (where *n* is any number) option. Normally the output will completely fill the first column on a page before flowing over to the next column. If instead you want all of the columns on a line filled before starting on the next line, simply tell pr that the page is just one line long, using the -1 option. Here is an example.

```
$ ls ../gplot/mail
gplot1
gplot2
gplot3
gplot4
gplot5
gplot6
$ ls ../gplot/mail | pr -t -11 -3
gplot1          gplot2          gplot3
gplot4          gplot5          gplot6
$ _
```

In the above example, the pr command uses the *-t* option to suppress headers and footers, the *-11* (letter *ell*, numeral *one*) to make pages one line long, and the *-3* option to produce three-column output.

8.4 LP AND LPR—PRINT FILES

The lp and lpr commands print files on the system lineprinter. Systems with several lineprinters may offer several versions of these commands, or command line options may be used to select a specific printer. lp is available on System V, and lpr is available on Berkeley systems. On my system, the lpr is for the main lineprinter, and vpr, dpr, and npr are for other printers.

It isn't possible to share a printer among several users simultaneously. Instead, the printer is assigned to a single user for the duration of a print request. The main role of the lpr command is to synchronize requests for the lineprinter. If the lineprinter is busy when you enter the lpr command, your files will be placed in a queue and then printed when the printer is free. lpr will return control to you as soon as the print files are placed in the queue.

The lpr command normally prints a banner page before and after the file, but the file contents are not changed. lpr does not insert blank lines at the top and bottom of pages or number pages or perform any of the other actions of the pr command. If you want to paginate or title contents of the file, you should use the pr command first. (Figure 8.1 depicts the difference between lpr, pr, and cat.)

```
$ ls -l /bin /usr | pr | lpr
$ _
```

Perhaps the most common use of lpr is to print a file or group of files as in this example.

```
$ lpr chapt1.pr chapt2.pr chapt3.pr
$ _
```

8.5   WC—COUNT LINES, WORDS, AND CHARACTERS

The wc (word count) program will tally a count of characters, words, and lines in a text file.

```
$ wc chapt?
   408    2007   12093   chapt1
   684    7921   32313   chapt2
  1071   11040   45818   chapt3
   509    7210   29398   chapt4
   606    7680   30910   chapt5
  3278   35858  150532   total
$ _
```

Flag arguments -c, -w, and -l can be used to direct wc to count only characters, words, or lines, respectively. The default, as shown above, is to count all three.

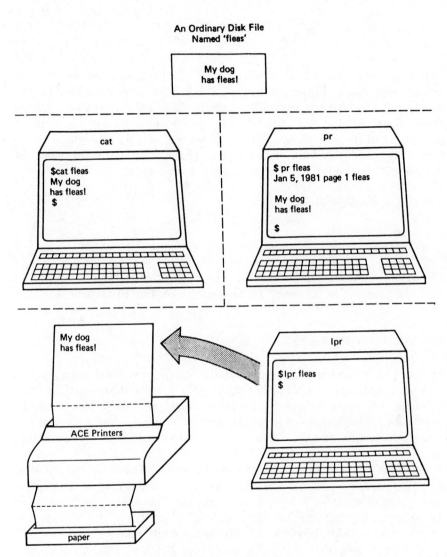

Figure 8.1. Cat, pr, and lpr.

8.6 DIFF—COMPARE FILES

The diff program shows which lines are different in two text files. The output of diff consists of a line that resembles an editor command followed by the affected lines from the two files. Lines from the first file are preceded by a <, and lines from the second file are preceded with a >.

The diff command produces three types of editor pseudocommand lines:

```
n1 a n3, n4
n1, n2 c n3, n4
n1, n2 d n3
```

Line numbers n1 and n2 refer to lines in the first file, and line numbers n3 and n4 refer to lines in the second file. The first of these editor pseudocommands indicates that the second file contains lines (n3 through n4) that are absent from the first file after n1, the second indicates that the lines n1 through n2 in the first file are different from the lines n3 through n4 in the second file, and the third indicates that the first file contains lines (n1 through n2) that are missing from the second file after n3.

```
$ diff arlinote arlinote2
10a11
>Susan - 586-1234
$ _
```

The output indicates that the two files will be identical if the line "Susan − 586-1234" (line 11 in 'arlinote2') is appended after line 10 of 'arlinote'.

8.7 SORT—SORT FILES

The sort command is used to sort and/or merge text files. sort outputs the rearranged lines in a file according to your command line specifications; ordinarily the input file is not changed. Unless you make other arrangements, the sorted output will appear on the terminal. Naturally you can redirect the output to a file if you want a permanent copy of the sorted output.

Each line of the input can contain several fields. The fields are delimited by a field separator, which is usually a tab or space but may be assigned to some other character. The portion of the input line that sort examines to determine an ordering for the file is called the *sort key*. The sort key can be one or more fields, or parts of fields, or the entire line.

As an example, let's sort a file containing a list of people's telephone numbers and initials. To sort a file, you must have a file with a regular structure, and you must know the details of that structure. In our example, let's suppose that each line of the file contains a person's initials, a tab character, and that person's telephone number, in that order. For simplicity let's consider a short file named 'telnos' containing only three lines.

```
$ cat telnos
kc      362-4993
gmk     245-3209
arm     333-3903
$ _
```

Here is how you can sort the file by field one, the people's initials.

```
$ sort +0 -1 telnos > namesorted
$ cat namesorted
arm     333-3903
gmk     245-3209
kc      362-4993
$ _
```

The arguments +0 and -1 inform the sort program that we want to restrict the sort key to the first field; the +0 indicates that the sort key starts at the beginning of the line, and the -1 indicates that the sort key stops at the end of the first field. If we wanted the file sorted according to the telephone numbers, we could use the following command.

```
$ sort +1 telnos
arm      243-3209
gmk      333-3903
kc       362-4993
$ _
```

The +1 argument informs the sort program that we want to restrict the sort key to start after the first field.

Of course, much more sophisticated sorting can be accomplished.

8.8   GREP—SEARCH FOR TEXT PATTERNS IN FILES

The grep program (and its relatives fgrep and egrep) searches for text patterns in files. Whenever the text pattern is recognized on a line, that line of the file is typed on the standard output. You can think of the grep program as performing a horizontal slice through a file based on a text-matching criterion. One common bit of UNIX trivia is the derivation of the the word grep—it comes from the phrase "global regular expression print," which is the ed editor command that performs the same function as grep.

The first argument to the grep command is the text pattern, and the following arguments specify the files that should be examined. The text pattern for grep can use most of the regular expression syntax of the ed text editor. (Regular expressions are discussed in Appendix III.) The text patterns for egrep can be more complicated, and the text patterns for fgrep are limited to fixed strings. The biggest advantage of fgrep over grep and egrep is its ability to search for many different strings simultaneously. grep and egrep can search for a group of strings only if the group can be specified by a regular expression.

Suppose you want a long format list of the subdirectories of the root directory. If you enter the command ls -1 /, you will produce the desired list intertwined with a list of all of the ordinary files contained in the root directory. The grep command can be used to filter out all of the unwanted information. If no files are supplied as arguments to grep, then it reads from the standard input. Thus grep can be used in a pipeline as follows:

```
$ ls -1 / | grep '^d'
drwxrwxr-x   4   bin    3136   Sep 17 11:28   /bin
drwxr-xr-x   9   root   3648   Sep 16 17:24   /dev
drwxrwxr-x   4   root   2496   Sep 17 18:40   /etc
drwxrwxr-x   5   bin     752   Jul  1 11:24   /lib
drwxrwxr-x   6   root    160   Aug 26 13:37   /mnt
drwxr-xr-x  12   mal     528   Sep  2 15:48   /source
drwxrwxrwx   2   root    896   Sep 17 19:27   /tmp
drwxrwxr-x  26   root    416   Jul 27 12:57   /usr
$ _
```

The text pattern for grep is quoted because it contains a caret, a meaningful character to the shell. The regular expression ^d matches all lines that begin with the letter ''d'' (because in a regular expression, the ^ anchors a match to the beginning of a line). Thus only directories are listed, since directory lines in a long listing start with a ''d'' whereas ordinary file lines start with a ''-''.

The standard use of grep is to find all occurrences of some word in a document. I have a bad habit of typing ''teh'' when I mean ''the''.

```
$ grep teh chapt*
chapt3: In one of teh drosophila experiments James
chapt3: until teh ether is evaporated
chapt5: another day. Then teh result can be explained
$ _
```

Of course I could do the search using the editor, but it is easier to use grep to identify those files that contain errors before using the editor to fix the errors.

8.9 CUT AND PASTE—REARRANGE COLUMNS OF FILES

cut and paste are used to manipulate vertical slices of files. cut and paste are most useful for files that contain *tabular* data. The cut program is used to cut a vertical section from a file, whereas the paste program merges several vertical sections into one file. Both cut and paste manipulate input files and produce their output on the standard output (the terminal). Usually you will want to redirect their output to a file. These programs are available in System V, but they are not standard utilities in Version 7 or Berkeley UNIX systems.

To use cut and paste, you have to know how the columns (fields) of the files are separated. The easiest field separator is a tab, although other characters can be used.

Let's suppose that we need to separate the initials from the telephone numbers in the 'telnos' file described above. As you remember, the 'telnos' file contained a few phone numbers:

```
$ cat telnos
kc      362-4993
gmk     245-3209
arm     333-3903
$ _
```

The -f option of cut tells it which field you want to cut.

```
$ cut -f1 telnos > initials
$ cat initials
kc
gmk
arm
$ _
```

We can use the paste command to combine vertical slices. Let's create a new file called 'newtelnos' where the numbers come before the initials on each line. paste will automatically separate the two columns with a tab character.

```
$ cut -f1 telnos > names
$ cut -f2 telnos > numbers
$ paste numbers names > newtelnos
$ cat newtelnos
362-4993    kc
245-3209    gmk
333-3903    arm
$ rm names numbers
$ _
```

8.10   SPELL—FIND SPELLING ERRORS

The UNIX spell program checks a text file for possible spelling errors. spell uses an online dictionary of common words. Each word in the input text is looked up in the dictionary. spell is rarely fooled by prefixes, suffixes, and inflections, and spell is able to ignore most nroff/troff formatting commands.

If "frequent" is in the dictionary, then spell will accept "frequents", "frequently", "frequenting", and other variants. Because some words don't follow the normal rules for prefixes and suffixes, there is a separate dictionary listing all of the exceptions. Words from this dictionary (called the stop list) must be matched exactly.

There are many possible spelling errors, including usage errors, that spell is incapable of finding. spell also complains about many correct words, because its dictionary can't possibly contain every word, especially proper names and technical terms. spell is a valuable proofreading aid, but it is not a substitute for careful proofreading.

```
$ spell chapt5
arthropod
Darwin
Mendel
teh
vicorously
$ _
```

spell will find hundreds of problems in a moderately large document, so you should usually collect the words in a file using output redirection.

If no files are mentioned on the command line, then spell reads from the standard input. This is useful for checking spellings interactively or for using spell in a pipeline.

8.11   CRYPT—ENCODE FILES

The crypt program reads the standard input, encodes it, and writes to the standard output. Encryption is more secure than using the file protection mechanism, because the superuser can access any file, but the superuser cannot decrypt files (unless he or she happens to be a competent cryptographer). An encrypted file can be decoded only if you know the password or if you are very good at cryptanalysis and you have substantial computer time to devote to the decoding.

```
$ crypt xyZZy321 < chaptn.doc > chaptn.cry
$ rm chaptn.doc
$ _
```

In the example the file 'chaptn.doc' is encrypted using the password "xyZZy321". The result is placed in the file 'chaptn.cry'. The rm command deletes the original copy of the document, leaving only the encrypted copy on the system. Note that crypt doesn't remove the original file for you and you should never redirect crypt's output to its input file. You should also note the use of I/O redirection to attach crypt's input and output to the desired files. Unlike most UNIX programs, crypt won't process files that are named on the command line. Thus I/O redirection is necessary when you use crypt.

Instead of supplying the password as an argument to crypt, you can enter it interactively.

```
$ crypt < chaptn.doc > chaptn.cry
Password:
$ rm chaptn.doc
$ _
```

Echoing is turned off during your response, just as it is when you enter your login password. Interactive password is considered to be better practice than placing the password on the command line. crypt is one of the relatively few programs that need to read input from the controlling terminal, not from the standard input.

The original file can be recovered using the same password:

```
$ crypt xyZZy321 < chaptn.cry > chaptn.new
$ _
```

The file 'chaptn.new' should be identical to the file 'chaptn.doc'. It is good practice to recover your original text from the encrypted version before deleting the original file, just as a check that you correctly keyed in the password.

crypt is not available in most versions of the UNIX system exported from the United States because of restrictions on the export of cryptanalysis software. This seems to make little sense, because the algorithm used by crypt is well known and simple enough that its implementation holds no secrets.

8.12   TEE—DUPLICATE OUTPUT

The tee program reads the standard input and diverts it to the standard output and to one or more named files. It is analogous to the tee pipefitting that plumbers use to split one pipe into two. tee is usually used

when you want to divert a program's output to a file and also see it on your
terminal.

```
$ spell chapt5 | tee errwords
arthropod
Darwin
Mendel
teh
vicorously
$ cat errwords
arthropod
Darwin
Mendel
teh
vicorously
$ _
```

tee can also be used to collect intermediate results in a pipeline. If you
want to print a five-column titled document showing the contents of a directory, you might use the following command

```
$ ls | pr -5 | lpr
$ _
```

You could save the two intermediate stages of the pipeline by inserting
the tee command in the the pipeline:

```
$ ls | tee /tmp/lsfile | pr -5 | tee /tmp/lsprfile | lpr
$ _
```

The file '/tmp/lsfile' will contain the original output of the ls command,
and the file '/tmp/lsprfile' will contain the five-column titled version of the
the ls output. tee's output files were placed in the '/tmp' directory rather
than in the current directory so that they wouldn't be listed by ls.

8.13   TAIL—PRINT THE END OF A FILE

The tail program is used to print the end of a file. This allows you to see
the end of a large file without sitting through a tedious display of the entire
file.

```
$ tail grt_uk_novel
''So,'' remarked Inspector Savitsky, ''there remains but one suspect.
As we have all agreed, the evidence rules out the family members,
the maids, and the cook. Only James, the butler, knew the safe
contained ten thousand dollars on the night of the third.''
    ''But it didn't! It was empty,'' blurted out James.
    ''Exactly!'' triumphed Savitsky. ''And only the murderer could
have found out it was empty. Sergeant, take him away!''
$ _
```

You can control just how much of the end of the file is printed.

```
$ tail -132 grt_uk_novel | wc
   132   1056   8448
$ _
```

As you see in this example, a number preceded by a hyphen tells `tail` to start that many lines from the end of the file. Beware that there is a limit to how far `tail` can read back from the end of the file. Alternatively, a number preceded by a + tells `tail` to skip that many lines from the beginning and then print the rest.

```
$ tail +66 chapt3 > chapt3.end
$ _
```

`tail` can also be used in pipelines.

```
$ ls /usr/bin | tail -5
uustat
uux
xget
xsend
yacc
$ _
```

Berkeley contains a program called head that is similar to `tail`, except that head prints the beginning of a file. By default, head will print the first 10 lines, but the *-n* option tells head to print *n* lines. On System V (or Berkeley), the first few lines of input can be printed using sed, as shown below.   (P.T.O.)

```
$ ls | head -5
aped.t
chadmin.t
chawk.t
chbench.t
chcunix.t
$ ls | sed -e 5q
aped.t
chadmin.t
chawk.t
chbench.t
chcunix.t
$ _
```

sed is discussed in Chapter 14.

CHAPTER 9

Text Editing with Vi

`vi` is a text-editing program that was originally conceived of as a programmer's editor. University of California at Berkeley graduate student Bill Joy enhanced `ed`, the original UNIX text editor, to create `vi`. Although it contains some features that are used only when you are writing programs, `vi`'s flexibility and power are often useful.

`vi` is actually the full-screen, display-oriented persona of a family of text editors. The other members of the family are `edit`, a simple line-oriented editor; `ex`, a powerful line-oriented editor; and `view`, a browsing (no changes) editor. A *display editor* such as `vi` uses the screen of your display terminal to portray a portion of the document. A *line editor* shows you the lines in your document, but the lines displayed on your screen may not be in the same order as those in your document. Most people find visual editing more convenient than line editing, and the focus of these two `vi` chapters is on visual mode commands.

You needn't master `vi` to use it successfully. In fact, enough basic `vi` is presented in this chapter for realistic use. However, if you are planning to work with it extensively, you should learn most of the more advanced features discussed in Chapter 10. If you already know `vi`, you can skip this chapter and possibly Chapter 10. Appendix I lists most `vi` commands, and Appendix II lists the `vi` option settings.

The original `vi` document is *An Introduction to Display Editing with Vi* by William Joy, with revisions by Mark Horton. A related document is *Ex Reference Manual* also by William Joy, and also containing revisions by Mark Horton. The `ex` manual describes the line-oriented command set of `vi`. People who want to master line editing can read any of the original UNIX `ed` documents or the `ed` material in Appendix III.

9.1   UNIX TEXT EDITORS

Throughout the UNIX system's history there have been several common programs for editing text. The UNIX system's first text editor was ed. ed is a
powerful program, but it is best used by programmers or other technically
inclined people. Because it was the original text editor, ed has had a major
impact on the entire UNIX system. Many UNIX programs contain a syntax or
command language that has many similarities to ed's. Some examples are
sed (a stream editor), lex (a programmer's utility), awk (a programmable
text manipulation language), grep (a text searching program), and the
edit/ex/vi family of text editors. Because of ed's enduring legacy, most
serious UNIX users learn its use. However, both System V and Berkeley contain the vi program.

   Another common UNIX text editor is EMACS. First developed at MIT by
Richard Stallman, EMACS is a flexible and powerful text-editing program.
Most versions of EMACS support windowing, so that several documents
can be displayed and edited simultaneously. EMACS can be programmed
to behave one way for one user and another way for someone else. This is
EMACS' strength and weakness—there are many versions, all slightly
different, and then once customized the many versions become a dense for-
est of different editors. If you want to program your editor so that it
behaves as you think an editor should, then EMACS is for you. Many versions of EMACS are available for the UNIX system, including Warren
Montgomery's version, Jove (Jonathan's Own Version of EMACS),
Gosling's EMACS, and GNU EMACS (a recent version produced by
Stallman for his GNU project).

   Some text editors are touted as "modeless," meaning that all commands
are accessible at all times. EMACS is a good example. You don't need to
go into a text entry mode to enter text; you just need to start typing. The
drawback is that all of EMACS' commands are control sequences, which
some people find hard to type. Bill Joy had more freedom to design vi's
command structure because of its different modes of operation. (Perhaps
more importantly, vi was based on the ed text editor, which has always had
two basic modes of operation.) vi has, by my count, five modes of operation if you don't count the shell escape as a separate mode.

9.2   CHECKING YOUR TERMINAL TYPE

vi is called a visual (or screen-oriented) editor, because it portrays, on your
terminal's screen, a picture of part of the file being edited. Because there
are a multitude of different terminals, each with its own control codes, vi
must know what model of terminal you are using. It is possible to start vi
and then specify the terminal, but it is much better to specify the terminal
type in your login script so that you can use vi conveniently.

vi learns the name of your terminal from the $TERM environment variable. (Setting $TERM is discussed in Section 9.3. Environment variables are discussed in Section 11.2.) Ordinarily the system administrator makes sure that $TERM is set correctly when your account is created. On personal UNIX systems, the $TERM variable may be set correctly during the standard procedure for creating a user account. You can check to see if $TERM is set correctly by entering the command

```
$ echo $TERM
vt100
$ _
```

In the example shown above, the word vt100 is the name of the terminal. If the answer had been a blank line, or if the answer had been wrong, then you would have to go through the procedure specified below to tell the UNIX system the name of your terminal. If the $TERM variable is set correctly, skip the following section and proceed to Section 9.4.

9.3 SETTING THE TERMINAL TYPE

Each time you log into the UNIX system, your shell executes a *login* script. If your standard shell is the Bourne or Korn shell, the login script is a file in your home directory named '.profile', and if you are using the C shell, the login script filename is '.login'. For your convenience, you should put the commands to set $TERM in your login script so that the terminal type is set correctly each time you log in. You can do that with vi once you learn to use it, but for now you can set $TERM using simple UNIX commands.

Each model of terminal has been assigned a short name. Like your login name, terminal's names are generally in lowercase, they never contain spaces, and they don't usually contain punctuation. Typically a terminal's UNIX name consists of a few identifying characters followed by a model number. The easiest way to find the UNIX name for your terminal is to ask your system administrator.

Here is the command to tell the UNIX system that your terminal is an adm3a:

```
$ TERM=adm3a ; export TERM
$ _
```

If you are using the Berkeley csh command interpreter, the command would be

```
% setenv TERM adm3a
% _
```

Once you have learned to use **vi**, you can use **vi** to place the command in your login script.

9.4   STARTING VI

Once the name of your terminal is stored in the $TERM environment variable, you can start **vi**. Enter the shell command **vi**. The screen should clear, **vi** will print the message ''new file'' at the bottom of the screen, and the cursor will be left flashing at the top left corner of the screen. This event is portrayed in the following pictures:

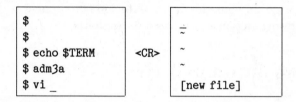

The picture on the left shows a portrayal of a miniterminal (5 short lines) before a <CR> has been struck to tell the system to execute the **vi** command. The screen on the right portrays the screen once **vi** has started. The <CR> between the screens indicates that a carriage return was struck to advance from the situation on the left to the situation on the right. The _ in each screen symbolizes the cursor. The tildes (˜) below the cursor on the right screen are **vi**'s indication that there is no text on those lines.

If your result is a garbled screen, or if **vi** prints a warning message and then prompts you with a :, your $TERM variable is set incorrectly. Section 9.3 shows how to set $TERM correctly.

Another possibility is that $TERM is set, but it is set to something other than the terminal that you are using. If the terminal **vi** thinks you have used very different control codes from what you actually have, then the screen will display a hash of control codes. This problem is easy to diagnose, and the fix is obvious: get $TERM set correctly. However, there are only a few families of terminals, and within a family the members usually have similar control sequences. This makes it possible for the name of your terminal to be slightly wrong, so that **vi** won't send an improper code except in some obscure situation. This problem is subtle, but the remedy is, as before, obvious: get the $TERM environment variable set correctly.

The hard part of portraying **vi** in a book is that most commands have an effect, but the command characters themselves aren't directly displayed. Another problem is that most commands are carried out as you enter each keystroke. This is very different from your line-at-a-time interactions with the shell. You must be very careful while entering vi commands, because the keyboard is live—each keystroke is acted on immediately, and there is no way to take back an erroneous keypress (although there is an "undo" command). This immediacy of execution coupled with vi's refusal to echo your keystrokes on the screen makes for an interesting dialogue. You must (correctly) remember your keystrokes to deduce what went wrong when some command produces an unexpected result.

Of course you could proceed to edit text, but instead let's show how you depart from vi. The command to quit vi is ZZ (capital Z struck twice).

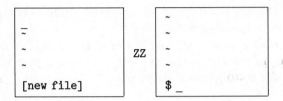

The diagram above, like all vi diagrams in this book, is read from left to right. The text between the screens indicates the keys that are struck to move from the situation shown on the left to the one shown on the right. In the diagram above, vi is running in the left picture, and the ZZ command is entered, causing the user to return to the shell command level of the UNIX system, as portrayed in the right-hand picture. Notice that the ZZ isn't displayed on the screen. You can observe that you have returned to the shell by the characteristic shell prompt in the lower left-hand corner of the screen.

In the following section you will learn several vi commands for moving from one place to another in a file. For that exercise you need to have a file for practicing. Here's how to make one using vi. Carefully perform these simple steps:

1. Enter the shell command

    $ vi ex1

    The screen should clear, and the cursor will move to the upper left-hand corner of the screen.
2. Enter the vi command a (append) to enter text entry mode. There will be no response on the screen. Type the a only once, and remember that there won't be any visual feedback.
3. Type the following list of words, one per line. While you are entering a word, you can use the backspace key to fix a typo, but don't bother to fix mistakes on any previous line. Remember that for the following section you need only a list of words; it doesn't matter if the words are

spelled correctly. At the end of each word hit return (enter) to advance
to the next line.

```
John
has
seen
some
mice
and
men.
```

4. Strike the ESC key to return to **vi** command mode. (Text entry will be
explained in more detail in Section 9.6.)

5. Strike ZZ to save your work and return to the shell. **vi** should print a
message giving the size of the 'ex1' file, and then a shell prompt should
appear on the bottom left of the screen.

Just as a check, you might want to display your newly created file using
the UNIX **cat** command (see Section 8.2).

```
$ cat ex1
John
has
seen
some
mice
and
men.
$ _
```

Now you are ready to learn how to move from one place in a file to
another.

9.5   MOVING FROM HERE TO THERE

Now you are ready to use the 'ex1' file that you created in the previous section to learn the **vi** cursor movement commands.

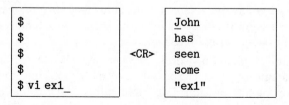

Note that the 'ex1' file is too large to fit on the screen of these little diagrams, but it will certainly fit onto the screen of your terminal. On our diagram screen, the name of the file is shown on the bottom row, whereas the name and file length would be shown on a full-size screen.

Since most files are too large to be displayed on your terminal screen, vi actually presents a window that shows just a part of the file. For the miniscreen in our vi diagrams, the active part of the window is only four lines tall. Thus just four lines of this seven-line file are visible. When vi is used with a normal 24-line terminal connected directly to a computer, the entire 24 lines are normally used. However, when your connection is via a telephone link, vi attempts to compensate for the slower communication speed by using a smaller window. This can improve the speed of screen updates, although the smaller viewing region is a drawback. When you edit the example file on your terminal, the entire file will probably be visible.

On some terminals, vi uses the terminal's arrow keys to move around in the file. However, some terminals don't have arrow keys, and even some that include arrow keys don't use them with vi. Therefore vi has adopted the convention of using the hjkl keys for moving the cursor. Notice that on a standard keyboard layout, the hjkl keys are next to each other. The h key moves one character left, j moves one line down, k moves one line up, and l moves one character right. Here is a picture of that region on the keyboard.

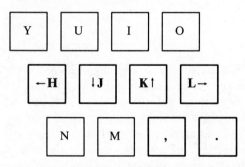

The hjkl keys shown above work on any terminal, and they are easy to use because you don't need to take your hands away from the main part of the keyboard. On some terminals the arrow keys will work, and you can use them if you prefer.

Here is an example showing simple cursor movement:

```
John          John          John
has           has           has
seen     j    seen    llk    seen
some          some          some
"ex1"         "ex1"         "ex1"
```

Many commands can be performed repeatedly by supplying *numeric prefixes*. For example, the command 4j will move the cursor down four lines.

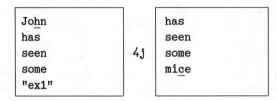

On these miniscreens, moving down four lines causes the screen to scroll up one line, so that the line containing the cursor will be visible. Because your screen is larger, no scroll is necessary in this case.

Another way to move around is the G command. You can go to a specific line by typing the line number followed by G. Typing the command G without a numeric prefix will move to the end of the file. Note that the line number is not echoed on the screen as it is typed.

```
has        some       has
seen       mice       seen
some    G  and     3G some
mice       men.       mice
```

Another way to navigate in a text file is to use vi's page-forward command and its page-backward command. These commands move through a file in larger chunks, making them very useful for browsing. However, these commands are easier to demonstrate with a large file. So if you are still editing the 'ex1' file, use the ZZ command to exit from vi. On most systems, there is a large dictionary of words in a file called '/usr/dict/words'. (If you don't have a copy of '/usr/dict/words' on your system, ask your system administrator for the name of a largish file to use for this exercise.) To make sure that you don't accidentally modify your practice file, you should use vi's -R "read-only" command line option. The read-only option makes it impossible to accidently modify the file.

Starting from a shell prompt, execute the following command.

```
$ vi -R /usr/dict/words
```

As usual, the screen will clear, and the first few lines of the '/usr/dict/words' file will appear on your screen. The commands to move forward and backward by screen-size chunks are control characters. You must hold down the *Ctrl* key and then strike the given letter. For example, the ^F command (the caret F notation means control F.) scrolls forward one screen, and ^B scrolls back one screen. Variants on these commands are ^D to scroll down about a half screen, and ^U to scroll up about a half screen.

10th			4th			6th
1st	^F		5th	^D		7th
2nd			6th			8th
3rd			7th			9th
"words"						

Two additional commands for moving around in a text file are w, to move forward one word, and b, to move backward one word.

4th			4th			4th
7th	w		7th	ww		7th
8th			8th			8th
9th			9th			9th

vi considers '4th' to be two words, the '4' and the 'th'. That's why the first w command shown above moves the cursor from the '4' to the 'th' instead of all the way to the following line. The W (capital W) command also moves forward one word, but for W a word is delimited by white space. Thus the W command often moves the cursor farther than the w command.

The commands e and E move to the end of a word. Similarly to the w and W commands, the e command considers words to end at any boundary between letters and digits or digits and punctuation. The E command considers a word to be any text delimited by white space.

Table 9.1 summarizes the movement commands that have been presented in this section.

9.6   ADDING AND INSERTING TEXT

Although moving from one place to another in a document is an important part of text editing, actually adding (and deleting—see next section) text is really the heart of the matter. In this section we are going to show commands that are used to enter and leave vi's visual text entry mode.

To understand what happens when you insert text into a document, you must understand that the vi editor has several distinct modes, including a visual command mode (several of its commands were discussed above) and a visual text entry mode. In command entry mode, you can move the cursor, delete text, scroll through your document, etc. Everything that you type in command mode is interpreted as a command, including the commands that lead into text entry mode. (The two vi modes mentioned above

TABLE 9.1   Basic vi Commands

Cursor Movement Commands

h	Left
j	Down
k	Up
l	Right
G	Goto a Line
^F	Forward screenful
^B	Back screenful
^D	Down half screenful
^U	Up half screenful
w	Forward one word
b	Backward one word

Text Entry Commands

a	Append text following current cursor position
i	Insert text before the current cursor position
o	Open up a new line following the current line, and add text there
O	Open up a new line in front of the current line, and add text there
\<ESC\>	Return to visual command mode

Text Deletion Commands

x	Delete character
dw	Delete word
db	Delete word backward
dd	Delete line
d$	Delete to end of line
d^	Delete to beginning of line
u	Undo last change
U	Restore Line

File Manipulation Commands

:w\<CR\>	Write workspace to original file
:w file\<CR\>	Write workspace to named file
:e file\<CR\>	Start editing a new file
:r file\<CR\>	Read contents of a file to the workspace
:q\<CR\>	Quit (a warning is printed if a modified file hasn't been saved)
:q!\<CR\>	Quit (no warning)
ZZ	Save workspace and quit

---

aren't its only modes. There are also a line-oriented command mode similar to the ed editor and an open line-editing mode that lets you (somewhat) conveniently edit a single line. These two vi modes are used little by most people, and they aren't discussed here.)

Although there are several ways to get into visual text entry mode, there is only one way out, the escape key (often labeled ESC). In the diagrams that follow, the escape key will be indicated using the <ESC> notation. When you see <ESC>, it means that you strike the escape key (without the angle brackets). (If you need to type <ESC> on a terminal that doesn't have an escape key, try ^[, which is control left square bracket.)

One simple way to add text to a document is with vi's append command. From visual mode, striking the a key places you into visual append mode. From that point forward, everything you type will be added to the document as text, until you strike the escape key. Here is a simple example.

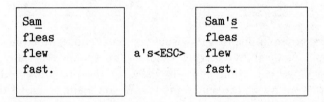

In the command illustrated above—a's<ESC>—the a is used to enter visual append mode, the apostrophe and the *s* are the added text, and the <ESC> is the terminator for visual text entry mode. Notice that the appended text was placed after the position of the cursor.

A similar command allows you to insert text in front of the cursor. The i key puts you in text entry mode. Then everything you type will be inserted into the file in front of the cursor position, until you strike <ESC> to return to visual command mode.

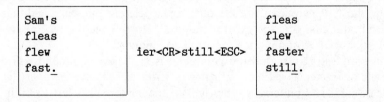

In this example, the added text is the letters er followed by a carriage return followed by the word still. Note that the screen scrolls up as necessary.

Both a and i modify text starting at the current position in the current line. However, sometimes you want to open up a new line and start there, for which you would use the o command.

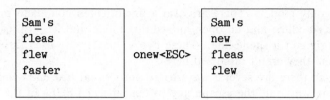

The o (lowercase) opens up the line following the current line, but there is also an 0 (uppercase) command to open up the preceding line, as shown in the following.

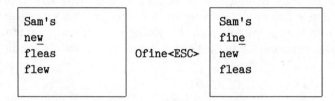

Whenever you are in one of vi's visual text entry modes, the only way back to command mode is by entering <ESC>. You should especially note that the cursor movement commands discussed in the preceding section don't work while you are in text entry mode. If you want to move the cursor, you must first return to command mode, and then you can use any visual mode command. When in doubt, strike the escape key. If you are already in visual command mode, the terminal's bell will sound after about a second, but if you are in text entry mode, you will be returned to visual command mode.

9.7   DELETING TEXT

Some people can enter text once, correctly, and be done with it. Unfortunately, most of us need to revise our work, deleting the worst, adding new material, and changing the existing material. In this section we are going to cover several of vi's many text deletion commands.

The simplest vi text deletion command is x. The x command will delete text one character at a time. When you strike x, whatever is over the cursor is deleted, and material to the right of the cursor shifts left to fill in.

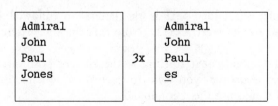

Remember, you can type a number before a command to make the command repeat that many times. When you place a number before a command, vi considers that a single command. If you actually enter the command several times, each is considered a separate command. Thus xxx is three commands, whereas 3x is just one command.

The difference between one command and several is important when you use vi's u (undo) command. By striking u, you can undo the last deletion, change, text addition, etc. (More sophisticated methods of recovering deletions are discussed in Chapter 10.)

```
Admiral                         _                              ral
John              kkk4x3x       John             u            John
Paul                            Paul                          Paul
es                              es                            es
```

Notice that there are two deletions—first four characters and then three characters. When vi executes the u command, it merely undoes the most recent change; thus in the example above only the last three letters are recovered.

A variant undo command is executed when U (uppercase) is struck. Unlike u, which undoes the last change, the U command undoes all the recent changes on the current line. (*Recent* means since you last moved to the line. Once you move away from the line, the U command won't work.) Here is the example from above, redone using the U command.

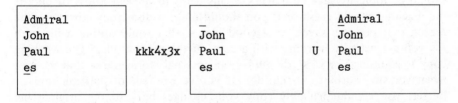

```
Admiral                         _                              Admiral
John              kkk4x3x       John             U            John
Paul                            Paul                          Paul
es                              es                            es
```

vi's general-purpose text deletion operator is d. The d command can be used to delete any unit of text. For example, the command dw will delete the following word, db will delete the previous word, d$ will delete to the end of the line, d^ will delete to the beginning of the line, and dd will delete the entire line. Several other modifiers are available to instruct the d command how much to delete. In my work, I use dw (delete word) and dd (delete line) more frequently than the other variants.

```
┌─────────────────┐          ┌─────────────────┐          ┌─────────────────┐
│ Admiral         │          │                 │          │                 │
│ ‾               │          │ John            │          │ es              │
│ John            │          │ ‾               │          │ ~               │
│ Paul            │   dwj    │ Paul            │   2dd    │                 │
│                 │          │ es              │          │ ~               │
│ es              │          │                 │          │                 │
│                 │          │                 │          │                 │
└─────────────────┘          └─────────────────┘          └─────────────────┘
```

9.8 MANAGING FILES

One way to tell vi which file you want to edit is to supply that filename as an argument when you start vi. Thus the UNIX shell command

```
$ vi ch8.t
```

tells the system that you want to use vi to edit the file 'ch8.t'. (If the file doesn't exist, it will be created, and vi will print the *New file* message.) When you are done with your editing, you can use vi's ZZ command to save the changes and then exit from vi. This method is fine if all you want to do is edit a single file and then do something else, but it is clumsy if your needs are more complicated. vi contains several other file manipulation possibilities you should know about.

9.8.1 Saving without Exiting.

If you are working with a single file for an extended period of time, you should periodically save your work. This helps to prevent a loss of data if the machine should crash or if you should make a disastrous mistake. The reason that periodic saves are a good idea is that while editing a file with vi, you are actually working with a copy of the original file. The working copy is contained in vi's edit *buffer*, an internal storage area that vi uses when you are working on the file. If you've worked for half an hour or longer, you should probably copy your changes back to the original file using the :w (write) command. When you invoke the :w command, the command itself is displayed on the bottom of the screen, and then when the update is complete, the size of your file is printed on the bottom line of the screen.

All vi commands that require the : prefix are more like ordinary UNIX shell commands than the vi commands that have been discussed above. Unlike other vi commands, the : commands are echoed on the bottom of the screen, they must be completed with a carriage return, and you can use the backspace or rubout key to correct typing errors.

The following dialogue shows the :w command in action. Not shown in the following dialogue is the beginning of the editing session, when vi was invoked to edit a file named 'f1'. vi remembers the name of the file being edited, and when you issue a :w command without explicitly specifying a filename, you will write the edit buffer to the original file. Unlike some editors, vi will not keep a copy of your original file under a different name. Once you perform the write operation, your original file will be replaced with the updated copy.

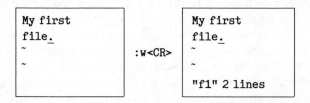

The :w command also allows you to specify a filename when you write the file. This allows you to make copies of your text in several different files.

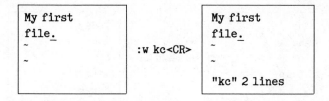

9.8.2 Quitting without Saving.

Occasionally while editing you make a mess of the file. Your mistake might be an accidental deletion, an addition that you don't like, or some other change that is too pervasive to repair with the undo command or with a few moments of judicious reediting. In these cases it is sometimes better to abandon the file without updating the original copy. The :q! command quits an editing session without saving the work. The exclamation point in the command says to vi, "Yes, I know what I'm doing," so vi won't question your action or print a warning message. Without the exclamation point, vi will warn you if the file has been modified (since it was last saved) and refuse to quit.

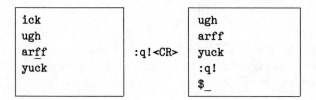

You should be very careful when you quit without saving your work. As a safety precaution, you might save your work in a file with a different name, so that you have the original copy and the copy that you are abandoning.

9.8.3 Editing a Different File.

It isn't necessary to leave vi to start working on a completely different file. All you need to do is to save your work (:w) and then tell vi that you want to edit a new file using the :e command. You must supply the name of the new file following the :e. If the file doesn't exist, it will be created; otherwise it will be read in to the edit buffer so that it can be edited.

If you haven't saved your previous work, the :e command will cause vi to print an error message, because the new file will overwrite the file you have been working on. If you really want to start working on a new file without saving the changes to your previous file, you must use the :e! command to tell vi that you are purposefully abandoning your unsaved work.

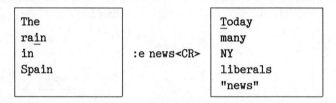

9.8.4 Adding One File to Another.

The last file manipulation command in this section lets you take one file and insert it into the file that you are working on. Unlike the :e command, which starts a new editing session, the :r takes the text from a UNIX file and merges it into the file that you are editing. The text is added following the current line. One use of the :r is to add boiler plate text to a document.

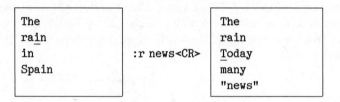

Notice that the new text is added after the current line of the file. If you were to move the cursor down to the end of the added text, you would then see the lines *in* and *Spain*, which are the lines that originally followed the line *rain*.

9.9 VI'S COMMAND SYNTAX

At first glance, the vi command set appears to be a hopeless jumble. There are 128 separate codes in the ASCII character set, and vi has assigned a specific meaning to about 100 of them. Although few people master all 100 commands, many people know most of them. The goal of this section is not to teach any particular commands, but rather to help you understand how it is organized.

The overriding goal in the design of the vi commands was to make them mnemonic. With just a few exceptions, each command letter or symbol is reminiscent of the command name. a for append, i for insert, <ESC> to escape from text entry mode. Some of the exceptions have other organizing principles; for example, the hjkl keys have a layout on the keyboard that makes them easy to remember, and the < shift operator looks like what it does.

Another principle is that for most lowercase commands there is an upper-case variant. For example, the w command moves forward one word, but W moves forward one larger word. Another example is that both a and A lead into into text entry mode; a adds text after the cursor position, and A adds text at the end of the current line. Once you have learned the lower-case commands, it is easy to remember their upper-case variants.

Many vi commands accept numeric prefixes. For most commands, a numeric prefix means repeat the command that many times. For example, if you type 50j you will move the cursor down 50 lines. A few commands interpret the numeric prefix uniquely. For example, the unadorned G command goes to the end of the file, whereas 50G goes to line 50. (It would be pointless to go to the end of the file 50 times!) You should be careful, because not all commands accept a numeric prefix. For example, the intra-line search commands (f and variations) can be repeated with a prefix, but the full-search command (/ and variations) cannot be repeated. Even stranger are commands where the ordinary form (e.g., d) can be repeated but the uppercase variant (D) can't. Commands that accept a numeric prefix are marked in Appendix I with a bullet.

There are six vi commands that are called *operators*. These six commands must be followed by a suffix that indicates a region of text to work on. The suffix can be any of the cursor movement commands, text search commands, or the "goto marked place" command (Sections 1, 2, and 3 of Appendix I). But again you must be careful. The <, > and ! operators can only take a suffix that indicates a range of lines, whereas the c, y, and d operators can take any suffix. One important thing to know about operators is that each can be doubled when you want to operate on whole lines. For example, the command dd will delete the current line, cc will change the current line, and yy will yank the current line.

CHAPTER 10

===

Advanced Vi Editing

Although vi has hundreds of commands, one can get by with just a handful. In Chapter 9, I presented my personal selection of introductory commands, the commands I usually show to someone starting to learn vi. In this chapter I am going to present a second handful, a group of commands that will enable you to perform sophisticated text editing with vi. Appendix I summarizes most visual mode commands. Section 10.5 summarizes the most useful vi option settings; a more complete list is in Appendix II.

10.1 ESCAPING TO THE SHELL

Interruptions are a fact of life. The phone rings, and you need to look up a telephone number stored on the system. A co-worker wants to see the latest draft of an important business letter. Or perhaps lunchtime is approaching, and you want the computer to display the time.

Of course you could save your vi file, exit from vi, and then attend to the interruption. However, it is usually easier to escape temporarily to a UNIX shell, do what needs to be done, and then resume your vi session where you left off.

There are two ways to escape to the UNIX command interpreter from within vi. The first method is used if you simply want to run a single UNIX command, such as the date command. From the vi visual command mode, enter :! followed by the UNIX command, followed by a carriage return. vi takes the UNIX command and hands it to a shell (command interpreter), the shell executes the command, and then vi continues.

```
Flying                    Flying                    Roseland.
Roaches                   Roaches                   :!ls
Tonight at      :!ls      Tonight at      <CR>      ch1   ch1a
Roseland.                 Roseland.                 ch2   ch3
                          :!ls_                     [Hit <CR>]_
```

In the example pictured above, the `ls` command is executed from within `vi`. When `ls` has finished listing the four files in the current directory, `vi` regains control, prompting the user to strike return to continue. When the carriage return is entered, `vi` erases the screen, redraws the display of the file being edited, and returns the cursor to the original position.

The second method of escaping to a shell from within `vi` is used when you are likely to want to execute several commands. From visual mode the command `:sh<CR>` starts a new shell that can be used as long as you want.

```
Flying                    Flying                    Roaches
Roaches                   Roaches                   Tonight at
Tonight at      :sh       Tonight at      <CR>      Roseland
Roseland                  Roseland                  :sh
                          :sh_                       $_
```

The shell prompt in the right-hand frame indicates that a shell is running, waiting for commands. You can enter as many UNIX shell commands as you want, and then you can resume your original editing session by terminating the shell, either by entering the command **exit** or by striking ^D at the beginning of a line.

One common mistake in this situation is to attempt to resume the original `vi` editing session by entering the `vi` shell command. The problem with this is that you will be starting a fresh `vi` session, not resuming the original `vi` session. Because the UNIX system has multitasking, you can have multiple `vi` programs running concurrently. Sometimes you want to let one `vi` session lie dormant while temporarily using another `vi` session to do something else, but usually you want to run just one copy of `vi`. If you become confused about how many copies of `vi` are running, use the `ps` command.

10.2   SEARCHING FOR TEXT

`vi` has several ways to search for text patterns in your file. `vi` has a single-character search for moving from one place on a line to another, and it has a more sophisticated search command for locating a text pattern anywhere in the file.

The single-character search is a speedy way to maneuver on a line. The f command followed by a character will move the cursor to the next occurrence of that character on the current line. For example, fa will move the cursor to the right to the next *a* on the line. The F command will search backward (left) from the cursor position, and the last f or F search can be repeated using the ; command (or it can be repeated in the reverse direction using the , command).

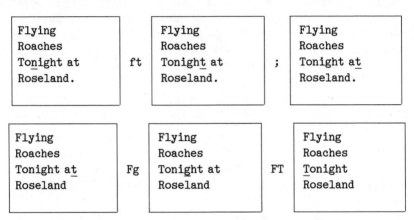

The general text search capability of **vi** is invoked by the / command. After you type the /, the cursor will move to the bottom line of the screen (just as with : commands), then / you enter the search target and then a carriage return. **vi** then moves the cursor forward (down) to the target or beeps to indicate that the target isn't found.

You can direct the search to start from the current location and proceed toward the top of the file by using the ? command instead of the / command. The last search can be repeated by using the n (next occurrence) command, or it can be repeated in the opposite direction by using the N command.

```
Roaches                    Roaches                    Roaches
Tonight at                 Tonight at                 Tonight at
Roseland        ?Ro<CR>    Roseland        n          Roseland
Ballroom.                  Ballroom.                  Ballroom.
                           ?Ro                        ?
```

Notice that the n command performs a reverse search if the previous search was a reverse search. In the dialogue shown above, the N command would have performed a forward search.

If the search target isn't found between the cursor location and the end of the file, vi restarts the search from the top of the file and searches down to the current location. (See the wrapscan setting in Section 10.5 to see how this behavior can be modified.) In long files you can save time by searching in the correct direction, and if there are multiple search targets, it is of course important to search in the correct direction.

Besides the literal searches described above, vi also can perform searches using a pattern matching language. This lets you find text that meets some criteria. For example, you might search for the word *The* only if it appears at the beginning of a line, or you could search for a word in its capitalized or uncapitalized form. You can avoid this capability by avoiding the characters *, [, ^, $, \, and . (period) in your target strings, or you can set the *nomagic* mode to disable these characters (see Section 10.5). Another way to make a special character lose its meaning inside a search target is to precede it with a backslash, and you must use a backslash in front of a literal / in a forward search (and you must use a backslash in front of a literal ? in a reverse search). Table 10.1 summarizes the usage of the magic characters. There are examples of editor search strings in Appendix III.

10.3 FINE-TUNING YOUR SCREEN DISPLAY

Sometimes you want the current line to appear at a given point on the screen. Perhaps you want the first line of a paragraph to rest on the top line of the screen, or you might want one line in a list to appear in mid-screen so that you can see what comes before and after. vi's z command lets you position your screen exactly as you wish. The z command requires one of three suffixes that specifies where (on the screen) the current line should be displayed.

z<CR>   Move the current line to the top of the screen.

z.   Move the current line to the middle of the screen.

z–   Move the current line to the bottom of the screen.

TABLE 10.1   vi's Pattern-Matching Characters

---

^ A *caret* anchors a search target to the beginning of a line. Thus the pattern ^the will match the letters the at the beginning of a line. The caret is only magic when used as the first character of a target (or when used in a *character set*).

$ A *currency symbol* anchors a search target to the end of a line. Thus the pattern PP$ will match the letters PP only when they occur at the end of a line.

. A *period* matches any character. Thus the pattern b.d will match bed, bid, bad, etc.

[A *left square bracket* introduces a *character set*. The end of the set is indicated by a right bracket. A character set matches any *one* of the characters in the set; e.g., [aeiou] matches any single vowel. A hyphen may separate two characters to indicate that range of characters; e.g., [0–9] indicates any one of the numerals. A caret as the first character of a character set means "the character set consists of all characters not explicitly mentioned." Thus the character set [^A–Z] matches anything other than a capital letter.

* An *asterisk* matches zero or more repetitions of the previous single-character matching expression. The asterisk is often used after a period, to match anything, or after a character set, to match any number of occurrences of that set. Thus the pattern [aeiou][aeiou]* will match any sequence of one or more vowels.

\< The pair of characters *backslash, less-than* anchors a pattern to the beginning of a word. For example, the pattern \<S will match any word that starts with a capital *S*. This pattern is present in vi but not in ed.

\> The pair of characters *backslash, greater-than* anchors a pattern to the end of a word. For example, the pattern <ing> will match *ing* only when it occurs at the end of a word. Another example is the pattern \<the\>, which will match the letters *the* only when used as a complete word. This pattern is present in vi but not in ed.

\ A *backslash* is used to escape the next character.

```
┌──────────────┐        ┌──────────────┐        ┌──────────────┐
│ Roaches      │        │ Ballroom.    │        │ Roaches      │
│ Tonight at   │        │ Come see     │        │ Tonight at   │
│ Roseland     │ z<CR>  │ a thriller.  │   z-   │ Roseland     │
│ Ballroom     │        │ Wow!         │        │ Ballroom.    │
│              │        │              │        │              │
└──────────────┘        └──────────────┘        └──────────────┘
```

Another way to move your window to exactly where you want it is with the ^E and ^Y commands. The ^E command moves the window down 1 line (the text on the screen moves up 1 line). ^E is similar to the ^D command that scrolls down a half screenful, except ^E moves just one line. The ^Y command is the opposite. It moves the window up one line (the text moves down on the screen). The ^Y command is a relative of the ^U command that moves up a half screenful. Of course both the ^E and ^Y commands accept a numeric prefix to direct them to scroll just that many lines.

```
┌──────────────┐        ┌──────────────┐        ┌──────────────┐
│ Roaches      │        │ Ballroom.    │        │ Tonight at   │
│ Tonight at   │        │ Come see     │        │ Roseland     │
│ Roseland     │ ^E^E^E │ a thriller.  │  2^Y   │ Ballroom.    │
│ Ballroom.    │        │ Wow!         │        │ Come see     │
│              │        │              │        │              │
└──────────────┘        └──────────────┘        └──────────────┘
```

You can move the cursor to the top of the screen with the H (home) command, to the middle line using the M (middle) command, or to the bottom line using the L (last) command. If the cursor is on the bottom line, it's easier to use the H command to move to the top than to strike 22 k commands or enter the command 22k.

vi tries to keep the screen display up-to-date, which means that on some terminals it has to redraw a large part of the screen whenever a line is deleted. Fortunately, most newer display terminals are more sophisticated, and vi can insert or delete lines without redrawing from the cursor to the bottom of the screen. On terminals without appropriate commands, vi often places an @ on the left end of a blank line to indicate that the display is not quite up-to-date, especially when it is operating at speeds of 1200 baud or less. The @ isn't part of the file; it merely means that particular line of the screen should be disregarded. At some point, vi may close up the gap, or you can force a screen update by entering the ^R command. vi lets you choose when you want the screen update, so that your typing isn't disrupted by massive screen redraws. If your screen begins to appear sloppy because of several @ lines, use the ^R command. (vi also places an @ in the left margin when a line that is longer than the screen width could be partially displayed only at the bottom of the screen. Such lines aren't cleared up by the ^R command.)

```
┌─────────────┐        ┌─────────────┐        ┌─────────────┐
│ The         │        │ The         │        │ The         │
│ oft         │        │ @           │        │ Jones       │
│ belittled   │  2dd   │ @           │  ^R    │ Antibody    │
│ Jones       │        │ Jones       │        │ has proven  │
│             │        │             │        │             │
└─────────────┘        └─────────────┘        └─────────────┘
```

Occasionally your editing screen is disrupted without vi's knowledge. For example, you might receive a broadcast message, or transmission line (phone line) problems might cause a display irregularity. In any case, you can tell vi to completely redraw the screen by entering the ^L command. The ^L command is a more powerful but slightly slower screen update command than ^R.

10.4   MORE WAYS TO MODIFY TEXT

In Chapter 9 I presented the basic commands for appending and inserting text (the a and i commands) and for opening lines (the o and 0 commands). vi has several similar commands that are very useful for more specialized situations.

You often need to change one letter to another. One approach is to use the x command to delete the incorrect character, then use the i command to go into insert mode, then enter the replacement character, and then hit <ESC> to get out of insert mode.

That process can be simplified using the r (replace) command. Following the r you must type a single replacement character. The letter at the cursor position will be replaced by the replacement character. The easiest way to split a long line in two is to move the cursor to a space and then enter the command r<CR> to replace the space with a line separator.

```
┌─────────────┐          ┌─────────────┐            ┌─────────────┐
│ The arc     │          │ The art     │            │ The art     │
│ of third    │          │ of third    │            │ of          │
│ century     │  fcrt    │ century     │  jbhr<CR>  │ third       │
│ guitar      │          │ guitar      │            │ guitar      │
│             │          │             │            │             │
└─────────────┘          └─────────────┘            └─────────────┘
```

The first command shown above moves the cursor to the *c* (the fc command) and then replaces the *c* with a *t* (the rt command). The second command moves the cursor to the blank on the second line (the jbh command) and then replaces that blank with a line separator (the r<CR> command).

A slightly more powerful command is the s command. The s command replaces the text over the cursor with whatever is typed in. An <ESC> terminates the input. The s command is often used to form the plural of a word or to perform other simple chores where one letter is replaced by a few letters.

In the dialogue shown above, the line containing the word *units* is deleted (the dd command), the cursor is moved up to the *y* on the previous line (the kfy command), and then the text *ies* is substituted for the *y* (the sies<ESC> command).

An even more powerful change command is the c command. The c command, like the d command, is an operator. It requires a suffix that indicates how much text should be changed. For example, the command cw will change a word, cb will change the preceding word, c$ will change to the end of the line, c^ will change to the beginning of the line, and cc will change the entire line. Numeric prefixes can make the change affect that many text objects. (I use cw and cc most often.) After the change command is initiated, you type in replacement text, and then you hit the <ESC> key to terminate the change.

In the dialogue shown above, the cursor is moved to the beginning of the word *units* (the b command), and then the word is changed to *members* (the cwmembers<ESC>). (In this particular situation, the change command could have been cc, because the entire line is changed.)

The uppercase variant of the r (replace single character) command is R, which replaces indefinitely. After entering the R command you just type, and whatever you type replaces what was there before. Unlike an insertion, in which text is pushed out of the way as you type fresh text, during a replace the new text overwrites the old. You terminate the R replacement by striking <ESC>.

Lines can be joined using the J command. Put the cursor on a line, and then strike J. The following line will be glued onto the first, and the cursor will be placed between the two parts. If you want to delete the (vi inserted) space, you can immediately strike the x command. Any trailing white space on the top line, or leading white space on the bottom line, will be lost.

```
┌─────────────────┐         ┌─────────────────┐
│ One             │         │ One_Two         │
│ Two             │         │ Three           │
│ Three           │    J    │ Four            │
│ Four            │         │ Five            │
│                 │         │                 │
└─────────────────┘         └─────────────────┘
```

When you are in text entry mode, a control character can be entered into the document using the ^V (Control-V) prefix. For example, you can enter a form-feed into a document by striking ^V^L when you are in insert mode. (^L is the ASCII code for a form-feed.)

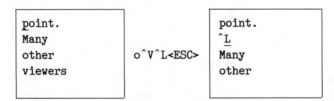

```
┌─────────────────┐                    ┌─────────────────┐
│ point.          │                    │ point.          │
│ Many            │                    │ ^L              │
│ other           │  o^V^L<ESC>        │ Many            │
│ viewers         │                    │ other           │
│                 │                    │                 │
└─────────────────┘                    └─────────────────┘
```

The ^V prefix is also useful when you are setting up macros or abbreviations. Note that ^V isn't a command. Striking ^V while in command mode has no effect. It is only used in text insert mode.

10.5   SELECTING YOUR PREFERENCES

vi has a limited ability to adapt to your needs and preferences. Many of its features are controlled by internal options that can be enabled and disabled using the set command. You can see a list of the settings that differ from the defaults by entering the command :set<CR>, or you can see the complete list of settings by entering the command :set all<CR>. Also note that many of the setting names have abbreviations.

Many of vi's settings are either on or off. For those settings, the mode is enabled with the command :set modename<CR> or unset by prefixing a no to the mode name, :set nomodename<CR>. The other options have values, which are set using the command

```
:set modename=modeval<CR>
```

The following list explains some of the more common options. You should consult Appendix II for more information about all vi options.

autoindent is often used for editing programs and other work that often contains leading white space. When autoindent is set, each newly appended line has the same amount of white space as the preceding line.

You can add additional white space to the beginning of a line, thus causing all following lines to be similarly indented. Striking ^D at the beginning of a line will cause the indentation level to retreat to the left. The
special input character sequence ^^D (a caret followed by a Control-D)
will reset the indent to zero for a single line, and the special input
sequence 0^D (a zero followed by a Control-D) will reset the indent to
zero. (The default is noautoindent, and the abbreviation is ai.)

ignorecase causes vi to ignore case distinctions in searches and substitutions. (The default is noignorecase, and the abbreviation is ic.)

list causes vi to display tabs and end-of-line markers explicitly: tabs are
shown as ^I, and end-of-line markers as $. list mode is useful in cases
where the distinction between a tab and an equivalent number of spaces
is important, and it is the easiest way to discover white space dangling at
the end of lines. (The default is nolist, and the abbreviation is li.)

magic mode enables the vi regular expression characters. When nomagic
mode is turned on, only ^ and $ are magic. nomagic mode is often more
convenient than using a backslash to escape the special characters. (The
default is magic.)

number mode makes vi display the line number at the beginning of each
line. (The default is nonumber, and the abbreviation is nu.)

shell contains the name of the shell to use for the :! and :sh commands.
The value of this option is taken, if possible, from the shell environment
variable $SHELL when vi starts to run. Setting shell to '/bin/csh' will
make the C Shell your default shell. (The abbreviation is sh.)

shiftwidth specifies the width of vi's software tab stop. This value is used
by the shift commands and when autoindent mode is on. (The default
is 8, and the abbreviation is sw.)

term is the name of the terminal. This setting may only be changed from
ex line-editing mode. The value of the term option is taken, if possible,
from the $TERM shell environment variable when vi starts to execute.
The following commands change to line-editing mode, set term for a
C.Itoh 500 terminal, and then change back to visual editing.

```
Q
:set term=cit500<CR>
:vi<CR>
```

wrapscan mode affects vi's text search strategy. Setting wrapscan forces vi
to search the entire file (circularly) before giving up. When nowrapscan
mode is set, searches proceed from the current location to the end (or
beginning) of the file and then stop. (The default is wrapscan, and the
abbreviation is ws.)

wrapmargin sets the boundary at which vi automatically inserts a new line
when you are entering text. When you get within wrapmargin characters

of the right screen column during a text insertion, vi will attempt to break your line at a space character and continue on the next line. This mode is very useful when you are entering ordinary text, because you don't need to strike the return key every line. However, some people find the wrapmargin-induced cursor movement disconcerting. Another inconvenience is that the new lines inserted by wrapmargin mode occasionally make it hard to use the delete key to erase the last few input characters (because the erase can't back up to the previous line). You can disable wrapmargin by setting it to zero. When enabled, wrapmargin is often set to 8 so that vi will wrap your lines when you get to about eight characters from the right edge of the screen. (The default is 0, and the abbreviation is wm.) The following command sets the wrapmargin to eight.

```
:set wm=8<CR>
```

Although any of these option settings (except for term, which can only be set outside of visual mode) can be changed while in visual mode, you might want to place your customary options into an '.exrc' startup file so that they will be engaged each time you use the editor. Each time vi starts to execute, it reads and executes the commands stored in the '.exrc' file. The '.exrc' file can be in your home directory or your current directory or both. Alternatively you can place a :set command in the shell environment variable $EXINIT. Most people set environment variables in their login session startup file, either '.profile' for Bourne shell users or '.login' for c shell users.

10.6 MARKING TEXT

vi has numerous ways to identify lines of text. As in ed, you can identify a line with a text pattern or with line numbers. Line numbers are easy to use if you set the number option (see Section 10.5). You can always find out what line you are on using the ^G command.

```
cheese                    cheese
fruit                     fruit
grapes         ^G         grapes
flowers                   flowers
                          line 6 of 12
```

Notice in this example that the top line visible on the screen is actually the fifth line of the document.

Another method for identifying lines is the m (mark) command. vi can remember up to 26 marked lines, each identified by one of the letters a through z. For example, you can mark the current line with the label a using the ma command. There is no visible feedback when you enter the mark command.

Marks can make it easy to move from one place in the file to another, or they can mark a region of text so it can be deleted or moved. When a mark is placed, the particular marked *line* can be referenced using the ' (single quote) command, or the particular marked *character location* can be referenced using the ` command (a reverse single quote, or accent *grave*). Both the single quote and the reverse single quote must be followed with a letter indicating the given mark. By itself, the command 'a will move to the line marked as a.

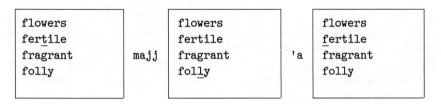

The ' command shown above interprets the given location as a *line* location, and returns to the beginning of that line. A similar feature, the ` command, interprets the given location as a *character* position and moves to that position.

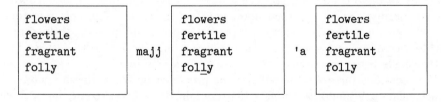

Marks are often used with operators, such as the d (delete) operator, which deletes regions of text. In Chapter 9 I mentioned some of the variants of the d command, including d$, dw, and d^. In all of these commands the d is followed by an indicator of the region of text to be deleted. This feature also works with the ' indicator. Thus d'a will delete from the current line to the line marked a (in either direction), inclusive. The command d`a will delete from the current cursor position to the character position marked a, inclusive.

flowers		flowers		flowers
fertile		fertile		file
fragrant	mzlll	fragrant	d`z	fragrant
folly		folly		folly

The marks in a file last only for your current editing session. When you start a new session, all the marks are unset. Marks also disappear when you change the line they are on.

10.7   MOVING BLOCKS OF TEXT

Editing text with a computer is more efficient than working with a type-writer, because the revisions are easier. Some revisions are local—fixing the spelling of a word, revising a sentence, or adding or deleting snippets of text. However, the greatest benefit of text processing is making those much harder global changes, moving paragraphs from one place to another, or moving text from one file to another.

vi's text movement capability works with several internal *buffers*. To move text from one place in a file to another (or even from one file to another; see Section 10.8), you yank the text into a buffer, move to the destination, and then pull the text out of the buffer and put it back in the text. You can't see what's in a vi buffer without pulling the text out, but since vi has an undo command, you can always put the contents of a buffer into your file, look at it, and then undo your modification. The best rule for working with buffers is "keep it simple." Although it's possible to load up a dozen buffers and keep track mentally (or on paper) of what's in each, it's usually better to use just one or two buffers at a time.

vi contains three sets of buffers: the *unnamed* buffer (it doesn't have a nicer name), 9 numbered buffers that contain the 9 most recent, line dele-tions, and 26 buffers identified by a through z. The easiest way to move a chunk of text from one place in a file to another is to use the unnamed buffer. (Note, the unnamed buffer can't be used to move text from one file to another. Its contents are discarded when you edit a new file.) There are two ways to put something into the unnamed buffer; you can perform a deletion, or you can use the yank command. If you want to move text from one place to another, the easiest way is to delete it from one place, move to the destination, and then put the text back. However, you must be careful. Once you make a deletion, the text is in the unnamed buffer, but it vanishes from the unnamed buffer when you make another deletion. Thus a common mistake is to delete something that you want to recover, then delete something trivial, thereby making it harder (but usually not impossi-ble) to retrieve the original text.

Any of the text deletion commands—x, dw, d\$, dd, etc.—will place the deleted text into the unnamed buffer. The text in the unnamed buffer can be placed back into the text using the p command, which places the buffer text after the cursor, or using the P command to place the text before the cursor. If the deletion was a sequence of characters, the text is pulled back relative to the current cursor location in the file. If the deletion was of a group of lines, the text is pulled back relative to the current line, and the position of the cursor within the line doesn't matter. These two situations are shown in the following two examples.

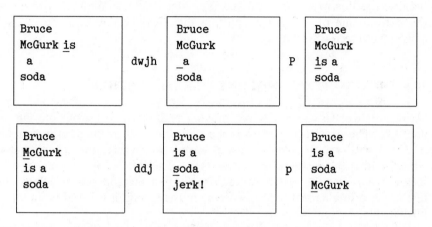

In the first example, a word is deleted on one line (dw) and then put back (P) on the following line. Since the original deletion wasn't a full line (or group of lines), the put-back text was inserted in front of the cursor. In the second example above, the deleted line (dd) is put back (p) following the current line, and the position of the cursor within that line is irrelevant.

Yanking text into the unnamed buffer is somewhat safer than deleting the text, because whatever is yanked into the unnamed buffer (right or wrong) remains in its original place in the document. The y (yank) command is similar to the d (delete) command. Following the y, there must be an indication of how much text to yank. The suffixes w, \$, ^, 'a, `b, and y mean word, to end of line, to beginning of line, to the line marked a, to the character position marked b, and full line, respectively. When you yank text, the cursor position is unchanged. As with the delete and put commands, when the yank command affects more than a few lines, a summary message appears on the bottom line of the screen.

Bruce		Bruce		McGurk
McGurk		McGurk		is a
is a	yyjj	is a	p	soda
soda		soda		McGurk

Notice that in this example the cursor must be moved down one more line (jj) than in the previous example to get to the line containing *soda,* because the line *McGurk* is yanked (yy), not deleted. With the cursor on the bottom line of the screen, putting the *McGurk* line into the text (p) causes the screen to scroll up.

10.8   MOVING TEXT FROM ONE FILE TO ANOTHER

There are two basic methods for moving regions of text from one file to another. The overall procedure is the same for both methods: the first file is edited with **vi**, the desired text is saved somewhere, the second file is edited, and then the saved text is inserted. The difference between the two methods is where the text is saved. In the first method shown below, the text is saved in a named buffer, whereas in the second it is saved in an intermediate file.

Since the last section talked about buffers, let's start with that technique. Once you understand moving text with the unnamed buffer, it's easy to extend your understanding to moving text from one file to another. First we need to talk about named buffers. Whenever a delete or yank command is prefixed with a " command, the indicated text is deleted or yanked into the named buffer. Thus the command "fdw will delete a word (dw) into the f buffer (the "f part). vi has 26 named buffers, but use of more than two or three at once is error-prone. Similarly, whenever the put command is prefixed with the " command, the extracted text will come from the named buffer. Thus, the command "fp will put the contents of the f buffer into the text.

Be careful not to confuse the "x prefix, which references buffer x, with the goto mark commands (`x references the character position of mark x). For example, the command "ay'a yanks (the y part) from the current line to the line marked a (the 'a part) into the buffer named a (the "a part).

Whenever you start to edit a new file, vi clears the unnamed buffer. Thus, it cannot be used to transfer text from one file to another. However, the named buffers aren't touched when you switch from one file to another, so they are ideal for moving text from one file to another. You should be careful here, because the named buffers are maintained only during your current session with vi. The named buffers are preserved when you switch from editing one file to another during one session, but their contents are lost if you exit from vi and then restart vi to start another editing session.

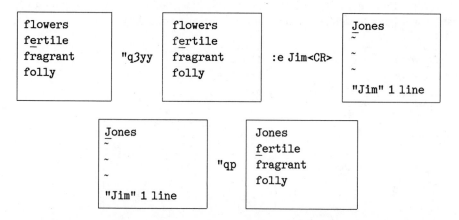

All five panels shown above form a complete sequence. The first command, "q3yy, tells vi to yank three lines (3yy) into the buffer named q ("q). The second command, :e Jim<CR>, tells vi to switch to the file named 'Jim'. As you can see from the screen's status line, the file 'Jim' has just one line. In the final command, "qp, the q buffer is put into 'Jim'.

Besides the buffers identified by letters, there are 9 buffers identified by the digits 1 through 9. These buffers hold the last 9 substantial deletions. If you mistakenly delete a line or more, you can get it back by putting the correct numbered buffer back into the text. How do you know which one? If you need to retrieve the next-to-last deletion, simply enter the command "2p. If you are unsure, perhaps the best way is to start with the last deletion ("1p), and then strike the . command repeatedly until the desired text appears. The . command normally repeats the last change to the buffer, but when you are putting the numbered buffers into the text, the . command puts each in turn back into the text.

The second method for moving text from one file to another uses an intermediate file to contain the text. If you are familiar with ed, this technique will seem natural, because ed uses the same method for moving text. If you don't feel confident of your ability with buffers, use this method.

The vi write command will write the entire workspace to a file by default, but by supplying line addresses you can write a portion of the workspace to a file. The simplest line addresses are line numbers, which can be obtained by the ^G command (to learn the number of the current line) or by turning on the line numbers option (See the number setting in Section 10.5). In either case, a command of the form :n1,n2w filename<CR> will write lines n1 through n2 to the named file. Once the text to be transferred has been copied to an intermediate file, you can edit the second document file and use the read-file command (see Section 9.8) to load in the intermediate file.

The following panels show how an intermediate file can be used to transfer text from one file to another. The write command shown assumes that the first line on the screen is actually the first line of the file. In practice, you will have to determine line numbers as discussed above.

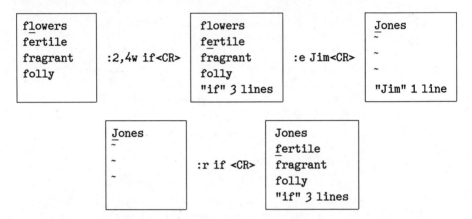

The first command in these five panels, :2,4w if<CR>, tells vi to write lines 2 through 4 to an intermediate file named 'if'. The message on the screen's status line confirms the write and mentions the fact that three lines were written. In the next command, :e Jim<CR>, the file named 'Jim' is edited. The final command, :r if<CR>, uses the vi read command to read in the intermediate file. The intermediate file will remain in your directory until it is removed, so you should plan to perform frequent housecleaning if you commonly use intermediate files to transfer text from one document to another.

vi will complain if you attempt to use the :w command to overwrite an existing file. If you really want to overwrite an existing file, use the :w! variant to tell vi that you know what you are doing and you really want to overwrite the file.

10.9   VI MACROS

A *macro* is one thing (usually small) that is expanded into something else (usually large). vi macros let you expand one or two keystrokes into a more complicated chain of keystrokes. vi has four flavors of macros that will be discussed below: buffer macros, maps, insert-mode maps, and abbreviations.

Buffer macros allow you to place a series of vi commands into one of vi's 26 named buffers. To create a buffer macro, you type the desired vi command into your document and then delete that text into a named buffer. To use a buffer macro, you enter the command @b to execute the macro stored in buffer *b*, where *b* is any of the letters of the alphabet. Here is an example.

As a typical task consider the job of entering the troff command to italicize a given word. Any word in a troff document can be presented in italics (underline in nroff) by preceding it with the code \f2 and following it with \fP. If you have a document that needs to have keywords italicized, it will save time to automate the process. But first let's see how the task would be done manually. First you would move the cursor to the beginning of the word, then you would use the i command to enter insert mode, then you would type \f2, then you would escape from insert mode, then you would move to the end of the word, and then you would go into append mode to add the text \fP, and finally you would return to command mode. A simple series of commands for a vi expert, but a grand total of 11 keystrokes.

To create an italicizing macro in vi, open up a blank line in your input file, and type the following 13 characters:

```
i \ f 2 ^V <ESC> E a \ f P ^V <ESC>
```

(A ^V stands for Ctrl-V, and <ESC> is the escape key.) The i enters insert mode, the \f2 is the inserted text, the ^V allows a literal escape code to be entered into the buffer, the escape terminates insert mode, the E moves to the end of the word, the a command appends \fP to the end of the word, and the ^V and escape terminate the append mode.

On your screen it will look like this when it is completely typed, because vi displays the escape code on screen as ^[.

```
i\f2^[Ea\fP^[
```

To put that text into a named buffer, you move the cursor to the beginning of the line and enter the vi command

```
"iD
```

which deletes the entire line (without the trailing linefeed) into the buffer named i. Then to insert italics codes around a word, you move the cursor to the word's beginning and type the command @i. The troff italics codes should quickly bracket the given word.

Maps allow you to assign a given command string to a given key on the keyboard. You enter a map using the :map *lhs rhs* <CR> command, or you can see a complete list of the current maps by entering the command :map<CR>. The *lhs* must be a single keystroke, the character sequence produced by a function key, or the notation *#n* to mean function key *n* (0 − 9). Remember that ^V can be used to quote the next character, so that control characters, escapes, or carriage returns, etc., can appear in the *rhs*. (Note that you can put a ˆV itself into the *rhs* by typing it twice. This lets you quote spaces or tabs.)

On a model VT100 terminal, function key one (labeled PF1) sends the three-character sequence <ESC>OP. You can assign it the italicizing macro described above by typing any of the three following **vi** commands:

```
:map #1 i\f2ˆV<ESC>Ea\fPˆV<ESC><CR>
:map ˆV<ESC>OP i\f2ˆV<ESC>Ea\fPˆV<ESC><CR>
:map <PF1> i\f2ˆV<ESC>Ea\fPˆV<ESC><CR>
```

The *lhs* of the third command was formed by striking the <PF1> key, whereas the *lhs* of the second was formed by typing in the exact character code manually. On your screen these three commands will look like the following:

```
:map #1 i\f2ˆ[Ea\fPˆ[
:map ˆ[OP i\f2ˆV<ESC>Ea\fPˆ[
:map ˆ[OP i\f2ˆV<ESC>Ea\fPˆ[
```

You can use any of the above commands; they all produce the same result. In an '.exrc' **vi** startup file, the *#n* notation is preferred because it will work on any terminal's function keys. During an editing session, simply hitting the given function key is probably the simplest. You can assign a macro to any key, including the common **vi** command keys.

If your terminal doesn't have function keys you have two choices: you can assign a macro to an ordinary key (including control keys), or you can assign a macro to a function key using the *#n* notation and then activate that macro by entering the two-character sequence *#n*. (On terminals with function keys, the *#n* notation can be used to enter a map, but it can't be used to activate a map.)

Given any one of the map definitions shown above, you can enter the troff codes to italicize a word by moving the cursor to the beginning of the word and then hitting the first function key.

A map can be disabled with the :unmap command, and **vi** will print a list of the current maps if you use the :map command.

Maps are also possible during insert mode, although the command used is map! instead of map. An ordinary map is not active while you are in text-insert mode, and a text-insert mode map isn't active while you are in visual-command mode, although it is active while in line-oriented command mode. Like ordinary maps, insert-mode maps should be assigned to a single keystroke or to a function key.

Let's set up two insert-mode maps to make it easier to enter text containing troff italicizing commands. The plan will be to hit a function key to enter the start-italics code (\f2), then type in the word or phrase to be italicized, and then hit another function key to enter the code that cancels italics. Here are the two `vi` commands that you would type to set up the two insert-mode maps:

```
:map! #1 \f2<CR>
:map! #2 \fP<CR>
```

Pressing the given function keys while in insert mode will make the replacement text appear in your document.

Abbreviations are `vi`'s fourth type of macro. An abbreviation is a word that, when it is recognized during insert mode, is replaced by some other character sequence. For example, you could make "ux" an abbreviation for "The Unix(tm) Operating System" using the following command:

```
:ab ux The Unix(tm) Operating System<CR>
```

When *ux* is typed as a word, it is replaced by the full phrase. However, typing a word such as *flux* will not trigger the replacement, and if the word *ux* already exists in the document, it won't be replaced. You can cancel an abbreviation using the `:una` command. For example, the command `:una ux` will cancel the `ux` abbreviation. Use the `:abb` command to a list of the current abbreviations.

You must avoid using the abbreviation in the replacement text. For example, the following abbreviation is a disaster—whenever you type "Unix" the system will repeatedly try to substitute the whole phrase each time it encounters the word "Unix" inside the phrase.

```
:ab Unix The Unix(tm) Operating System<CR>
```

Avoid self-referential abbreviations.

10.10   FILTERING THE BUFFER

`vi` allows you to filter a portion of the edit buffer. Text from the edit buffer is routed into a UNIX pipeline, it is transformed by the filters in the pipeline, and then the output of the pipeline replaces the original text. The operation of a `vi` filter is shown schematically in Figure 10.1.

Filters have numerous applications. Programmers sometimes filter their work through cb, a C language-formatting program. You can enter commands using `vi` and then send them to a command processor such as the shell or the bc arithmetic program. If you want to include the output of a UNIX command in a document, you can filter a single line of the buffer into that command. The `sort` command is often used to rearrange the order of part of the edit buffer.

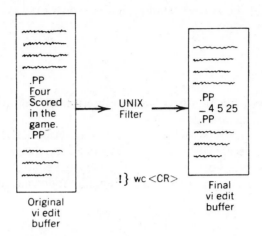

Figure 10.1. Filtering part of the vi edit buffer. In this example, a paragraph is being filtered by the wc command. The fork system call.

There are two approaches to filtering the vi edit buffer. You can use commands in visual-command mode, or you can use ordinary line-editing commands. In either case, the exclamation point is the command character. In visual-command mode, you enter the ! operator followed by a suffix that selects a region of text. The suffixes must select whole lines; for example, suffixes such as w (word) are not accepted. (See Section 9.7.) The usual visual-mode filter commands are !! to send one line into the pipeline, !} to send the remainder of the paragraph into the pipeline, !'a to send from the current line to the line marked *a* into the pipeline, !]] to send the remainder of the section into the pipeline, and !G to send the remainder of the edit buffer into the pipeline.

In line-editing mode you enter the command

```
:n1,n2 ! command
```

Lines *n1* through *n2* will be sent to the pipeline, and its output will then replace those lines. For example, you might suspect that one of the words on the current input line is misspelled. In visual mode you can enter the command !!spell<CR>. The output of the spell program, a list of possibly misspelled words from the current line (see Section 8.10), will replace the current line. Carefully examine the output for misspellings, then enter the command u to undo the buffer change, and then fix any incorrectly spelled words. This style of interaction with vi is more dangerous than any presented so far, because you don't really want to discard your original text and replace it with a list of incorrectly spelled words. Timely use of the undo command is essential. Don't be too adventurous until you are confident of your abilities. (A safer approach would be to enter the command yyP to duplicate the current line, then the command !!spell<CR> to spell the current line, and then finally the command dd as many times as necessary to delete the list of misspelled words.)

The same technique can be used to check the spelling of an entire paragraph, or an entire document. Occasionally you might want to pipe all (or part) of a document to wc for a word count, etc.

You can also use vi buffer filters with commands that don't read the standard input. For example, you might want to include today's date in a document. Open up a blank line, type the vi command !!date<CR>, and the date will appear on the given line. This technique is often used with ls, who, etc. to include their output in a file.

10.11   LINE-EDITING COMMANDS

vi has multiple personalities—a feature or a fault, depending on your preference. The easiest vi personality to use is visual mode, and most of the commands discussed in this chapter and in Chapter 9 are visual-mode commands. In addition, vi has a line-editing command set similar to the command set of ed (but somewhat more powerful). The line-editing command set is harder to learn than the visual command set, but it is much more powerful.

As shown in many of the examples in this chapter (and Chapter 9), you can temporarily dip into the line-editing command set by prefixing a line-editing command with a : (colon). When you enter such a command, the cursor immediately drops down to the bottom line of the screen (the status/command line), where you enter the remainder of the command. When you dip into the line-editing command set, you are immediately returned to visual mode when the command is completed.

If you are going to perform a sequence of line-editing commands, you can use the Q command to move from visual mode to the ex line-editing mode. You can also invoke the ex line-editing part of the editor directly from the shell, by entering the ex command. Once you have moved from visual mode to line-editing mode, the screen will scroll upward as lines are displayed on the screen, much as if you were using ed. One difference is that vi customarily prompts with a : in line-editing mode, whereas ed customarily doesn't print a prompt when it is waiting for a command. While in line-editing mode in vi, you can prefix your commands with a : as if you were in visual mode. The redundant : is allowed in line-editing mode, because old habits die hard. When you are through entering line-editing commands, the command vi<CR> will return you to visual editing mode.

Other than the file reading and writing commands, the ex line-editing commands aren't discussed extensively in this book. ed is discussed in Appendix III. There are several other references for learning the powerful ex line-editing commands. The ex commands are just an extension of ed, so learning ed will teach you most of ex. The ultimate reference for ex is *Ex Reference Manual* by William Joy with revisions by Mark Horton.

10.12   OPEN-LINE EDITING

Besides the ability to work on a full screen, vi can perform most of its commands on a single line. This feature is useful on primitive terminals that don't have cursor addressing capability, and it can even be used reasonably on a printer terminal. If you start vi without first setting the $TERM environment variable, it will complain that it doesn't know what terminal you are using and proceed to enter ex line-editing command mode. You won't be able to enter visual mode until you tell vi what kind of terminal you are using, but you can enter open-line-editing mode immediately, because vi doesn't need to know anything about your terminal to use open-line mode. Open-line editing looks very similar to line-editing mode, because you see only one line at a time. The difference is that in open mode you can still use all of vi's visual commands, including the cursor movement commands and search commands. It's as if you are using vi on a one-line screen.

Open-line editing can be invoked from line-editing mode by entering the command open<CR>. In open-line mode, your cursor will always be on the bottom line of the screen (or on the only line of the printer). All of the vi visual commands will work, although only one line at a time will be visible. For example, if you enter the j command to move down one line, the screen will scroll up to make room, and then the next line will be displayed. When you enter the k command, the screen will also scroll up, and then the preceding line will be displayed. Thus the commands work, but the screen display is a record of your previous line selections, not a window into the file.

While in open-line mode, you can use the : prefix to escape temporarily to line-editing mode. You can return to simple line-editing mode from open-line mode using the Q command.

TABLE 10.2 More vi Commands

Shell Escapes

:!cmd<CR>	Escape to perform one command
:sh<CR>	Start a subshell. You may enter commands, then exit from the subshell to return to vi

Text Searches

fc	Intraline search forward for char c
Fc	Intraline search reverse for char c
;	Repeat last intraline search
,	Repeat last intraline search in opposite direction
/pat<CR>	Forward search for pattern pat
?pat<CR>	Reverse search for pattern pat
n	Repeat last search
N	Repeat last search in opposite direction

Window Movement

z<CR>	Current line to top of screen
z.	Current line to middle of screen
z-	Current line to bottom of screen
^Y	Scroll down one line
^E	Scroll up one line
H	Move cursor to top line of screen
M	Move cursor to middle line of screen
L	Move cursor to lowest line of screen

Text Entry

r	Replace character under cursor
s	Substitute the following text entry for character under cursor. <ESC> terminates text entry mode
c	Change the given object. Suffixes w, b, c, $, and ^ have the usual meanings. <ESC> terminates text entry mode

Marked Text

ma	Mark text with mark named a
'a	Go to line marked a
`a	Go to character position marked a
^G	Report current line number

Buffers

y	Yank text into buffer. (Delete also saves text in a buffer.)
p	Pull back text from buffer, and place it after current line or character position
P	Pull back text from buffer, and place it before current line or character position
"a	A prefix to yank, delete, or put to indicate that buffer named a should be used

---

CHAPTER 11

The Shell Programming Language

The shell is probably the most important UNIX utility program; unfortunately, it is also one of the most poorly understood and one of the most poorly documented utilities. The UNIX shell is both an interactive command interpreter and a command level programming language interpreter. This duality is one of the most powerful aspects of the UNIX system, but it also can be a barrier to understanding the shell.

Some computer systems have simple and effective interactive command interpreters, but they lack the ability to program sophisticated command sequences. Other computers have elaborate command level programming languages but no provisions for simply running a program. The UNIX system combines the two abilities in the shell.

We have already discussed the shell (Chapter 4), and you should have already used the shell interactively. Most interactive users exercise only a few of the shell's capabilities. Typical interactive use of the shell involves entering simple commands (`ls`), using the shell's filename generation facilities (`ls *.doc`), specifying I/O redirection (`ls > myfile`), and specifying pipelines (`ls | wc -1`). These techniques are powerful and extremely useful, but they are only a small part of the shell's capabilities.

There is a very important difference between controlling a task interactively, and creating a program to perform a task automatically. When you control a task interactively, you can use your intellect to react to the situation as it develops. Programs have no intellect. Their reactions must be determined in advance and coded into the program. Anyone who has written a large program knows that anticipating all of the possible circumstances is very difficult.

Let's use an example to clarify the difference between interactive and automatic procedures. Suppose you want to examine a file on your terminal and you recall that the name of the file is 'groc.lst' or perhaps 'grocery.l' or something similar to that, and you remember it is in your 'data.lsts' directory or perhaps in your current directory or maybe in your 'groc.proj' directory. Interactively, it is easy to browse through the directories and locate the file and then use the cat program to display the file on your terminal. Writing a program to find and display the 'gro...' file is more difficult. What is a sufficient criterion for locating the file? What should the program do if zero (or several) candidates are located? A program to locate and print 'gro...' would have to include answers to these and other questions.

The interactive procedure is a simple sequence of commands, whereas a program to produce the same effect is a logical structure. Experience shows that sophisticated control structures for repeating sequences of instructions and for testing certain conditions make it easier to write good programs. The UNIX shell contains these control structures. Experience has also shown that it is very useful to have items (called variables) whose value can change during the course of a program. The UNIX shell contains variables.

One of the major differences between Version 6 of the UNIX system and later versions (Version 7, System V, Berkeley) is the shell. The Version 6 shell is a good interactive command interpreter, but it is a weak programming language. For Version 7 of the UNIX system, S. R. Bourne created the Bourne shell. It combines all the interactive features from the Version 6 shell with a powerful programming language. Today the Bourne shell is available on all UNIX systems, although on Berkeley UNIX systems an alternative shell, Bill Joy's C shell, is also available.

Choosing an interactive shell is really a matter of personal taste and local availability. Many people prefer the C Shell for interactive use, and Dave Korn's ksh has excellent interactive features. There are also several window environments and several more display-oriented shells. However, for writing shell language scripts, the Bourne shell is widely regarded as the best choice, mostly because it is the only shell that is universally available.

The first third of this chapter is useful for most UNIX users. You should read the remainder of the chapter if you intend to write shell programs or if you really want to know more about the shell. Read Chapter 12 if you want to see some examples of shell programs. Most UNIX users don't write complicated shell programs, and most users don't need to understand the shell at the level that is presented starting in Section 11.19.

11.1 EXECUTING A SHELL PROGRAM

Any command or sequence of UNIX commands stored in a text file is called a *shell program, command file,* or script. Usually the term command file is used when the file contains a simple sequence of commands, and the term shell program sometimes identifies a file containing a more complicated arrangement of commands (often using the shell's conditional commands and other advanced features). There are three ways to get the shell to execute a command file. The first method is very simple. Since the shell normally reads commands interactively from the standard input, you can use input redirection to get the shell to read commands from a file.

In the example below, the text file named 'lsdir' contains commands that will print a list of the subdirectories of the current directory. The shell can easily be persuaded to execute the commands in the 'lsdir' text file using I/O redirection. (The name of the shell program is sh.)

```
$ cat lsdir
if [ $# = 0 ]
then
  dir=.
else
  dir=$1
fi
find $dir -type d -print
$ sh < lsdir
.
./bin
./bkpdir
./corr
./zsrc
$ _
```

Any program that normally reads input from the standard input, such as the shell, can instead read input from a file by using input redirection. Because the shell often reads commands from files (rather than interactively), a special capability is built into the shell. If the shell is invoked with the name of a file as an argument, then the shell will read commands from that file.

```
$ sh lsdir
.
./bin
./bkpdir
./corr
./zsrc
$ _
```

Many commands are built so that you can specify a file name as a command line argument or use input redirection. However, not all commands allow both forms of expression. The advantage of specifying a file as a command line argument is that you can pass arguments to the shell script.

```
$ sh lsdir /bin /etc
/bin
/bin/old
/etc
/etc/priv
/etc/test
$ _
```

The 'lsdir' shell script can access the "/bin" and the "/etc" arguments. As you will see later, arguments to shell programs can be very useful.

The third method is even more refined. The UNIX text editor usually creates files with the execution privileges turned off, because most text files contain letters and documents. Whenever the shell encounters a text file that has the execution privileges turned on, the shell assumes that it contains a shell program script. You can turn the execution privileges of the file 'lsdir' on by using the change-mode command (see Section 6.5). Once the execution privileges are turned on, you can execute the commands in a file by simply typing the name of the file.

```
$ ls -l lsdir
-rw-rw-rw-   1   kc    130    Dec 2 11:15 lsdir
$ lsdir
sh lsdir  cannot execute
$ chmod a+x lsdir
$ ls -l lsdir
-rwxrwxrwx   1   kc    130    Dec 2 11:15 lsdir
$ lsdir
.
./bin
./bkpdir
./corr
./zsrc
$ _
```

As you can see, the shell will balk if you try to execute a file that doesn't have the execute privilege turned on.

One advantage of this third method is that you can execute a shell program by merely entering its name as a command. You don't have to treat shell programs differently from any other programs. Another advantage is that the shell will search for executable commands in all of the usual directories (often '/bin', '/usr/bin', etc.), but when you explicitly tell the shell to read commands from a command file (e.g., sh lsdir or sh < lsdir), the command file must reside in the current directory (or be specified using a pathname).

You can pass arguments to shell programs the same way you pass arguments to ordinary programs.

```
$ lsdir /usr/lib
/usr/lib/font
/usr/lib/tmac
/usr/lib/learn
$ _
```

Shell programs that are going to be used frequently should be made executable and placed in a standard executables directory (such as '/bin' or '/usr/bin') so that users can execute them easily.

11.2 SHELL VARIABLES

A programming language uses *variables* to store values. The name "variable" suggests that the stored values can change during the course of execution. Shell variables can store strings of text. Numbers are stored in shell variables as text strings rather than in a binary format, which would be more appropriate for a more computationally oriented (number-crunching) language.

A variable can be assigned a value by entering an assignment command; as shown below.

```
$ ux=u.UNIX
$ echo $ux
u.UNIX
$ _
```

The assignment command listed above assigns the value "u.UNIX" to the shell variable named "ux". The name of a shell variable must start with a letter, and it may contain letters, digits, and underscores.

When you assign a value or a mode to a variable, you use the name of the variable. However, when you use the value stored in a variable, you have to place a currency symbol before the name of the variable. The currency symbol informs the shell that the following name refers to a variable. The echo command can be used to display the values of variables, as shown above.

Since $ux is a variable, its value can be changed by using another assignment statement.

```
$ echo $ux
u.UNIX
$ ux=UNIX
$ echo $ux
UNIX
$ _
```

If you want to assign a value that contains internal spaces or tabs or new lines, then you need to quote the value.

```
$ hero="John Paul Jones"
$ echo $hero
John Paul Jones
$ _
```

The shell has a very cavalier attitude toward variables that haven't been assigned a value. It's not an error to refer to a variable that has not been assigned a value. The result is merely the *null* string; which is a string that doesn't contain any text.

```
$ echo $pn butter is yummy
butter is yummy
$ pn=peanut
$ echo $pn butter is yummy
peanut butter is yummy
$ _
```

The *readonly* command allows you to mark a variable so that its value cannot be changed.

```
$ flower=tulip
$ readonly flower
$ flower=rose
sh: flower: is readonly
$ echo $flower
tulip
$ _
```

Use `readonly` wisely, as it persists until the shell exits. Without arguments, the `readonly` command is used to list the variables that are "readonly."

```
$ readonly
flower
$ _
```

The variables you create are local to the current shell unless you export them. Local variables can be used in expressions that are interpreted by the current shell (during parameter substitution), but they cannot be accessed by name by a process that is started by the shell. The `export` command can transform a local variable into a global variable, thereby making it available to all processes that are started by the shell. Exported variables are often called *environment* variables, because their names and values are placed into the environment of each process that the shell executes.

The following command exports the variable named "ux".

```
$ export ux
$ _
```

The export designation sticks until the shell terminates. You can get a list of the current exportable variables by entering the `export` command without arguments.

```
$ export
ux
HOME
PATH
TERM
$ _
```

Here is a longer example showing how the `export` command lets you pass the value of a variable from your login (interactive) shell to a command script executed by a subshell.

```
$ cat foodilike
echo $pn butter is yummy
$ $pn=peanut
$ sh foodilike
butter is yummy
$ export pn
$ sh foodilike
peanut butter is yummy
$ _
```

At the beginning of the above dialogue, the `$pn` variable is a local variable. Thus when the `foodilke` script is interpreted the first time, it is unable to access `$pn` by name. In the middle of the dialogue the `$pn` variable is exported. Consequently, when the *foodilike* script is executed the second time, `$pn` is accessible, and its value is displayed by the `echo` command.

You should use curly braces to surround the name of a variable when the name is immediately followed by characters that are not part of the name.

```
$ echo ${ux}tm
UNIXtm
$ _
```

Another way to separate variable names from surrounding characters is by using double quotes.

```
$ echo "$ux"tm
UNIXtm
$ _
```

See Section 11.5 for an explanation of quoting to understand why this works.

The following shell variables are automatically set by the shell:

$? The variable $? contains the exit value (see Section 11.7) returned by the last executed command.

$$ The variable $$ contains the process id number of the shell.

$!   The variable $! contains the process id number of the last background process that the shell invoked.

$#   The variable $# contains the number of arguments (positional parameters) to the shell (see Section 11.10).

"$*"   A single word, consisting of the shell's entire argument list. Equivalent to "$1 $2 $3 $4 ...". The number of arguments is not maintained because null arguments are lost and arguments containing spaces or tabs become multiple arguments. It is used to pass the entire argument list to a program.

"$@"   The shell's entire argument list, maintained as individual words. Equivalent to "$1" "$2" "$3" "$4" .... When you use "$@" the number of arguments is preserved: null arguments remain, and arguments containing spaces or tables remain a single word. It is used to pass the entire argument list to a program.

$-   The variable $- contains the flags that were passed to the shell when it was invoked or flags that were set using the set command.

These automatic variables can be used the same way as user-created variables. For example, the following prints the process id number of the shell.

```
$ echo $$
13927
$ _
```

The pid number can be verified using the ps command.

11.3   USING SHELL VARIABLES INTERACTIVELY

Besides their obvious value in shell programs, shell variables can also be very useful interactively. Suppose that there is a certain directory (we'll use '/usr/td/c/mon/src/doc') containing some files you are using, but for some good reason you decide to remain in your current directory and reference the files in the '/usr/td/c/mon/src/doc' directory using absolute pathnames. It is clumsy to enter commands that reference the '/usr/td/c/mon/src/doc' directory, because they are so hard to type. You can simplify matters by storing the directory name in a variable and typing the variable name instead of the full directory name.

```
$ docdir=/usr/td/c/mon/src/doc
$ echo $docdir
/usr/td/c/mon/src/doc
$ ls $docdir
mon.doc1   mon.doc2   sema.txt   tmonprint
$ ls -i $docdr/*.txt
13801   /usr/td/c/mon/src/doc/sema.txt
$ _
```

If you need to run a program called 'tmonprint' that resides in the $docdir directory, you can create a new variable to store the absolute pathname of 'tmonprint'. You could enter the command

```
$ tmonprint=/usr/td/c/mon/src/doc/tmonprint
$ _
```

to create the $tmonprint variable, or you could use the slightly shorter command

```
$ tmonprint=$docdir/tmonprint
$ _
```

Now the command

```
$ tmonprint $docdir/sema.txt
$ _
```

will run the '/usr/td/c/mon/src/doc/tmonprint' program with the argument "/usr/td/c/mon/src/doc/sema.txt". Shell variables are a convenient shorthand for simplifying common interactive tasks.

11.4   THE SEARCH STRING

When you enter a command, the first thing the shell does is search for the program. But where does it look? Many UNIX system installations contain thousands of directories, and it would be too time-consuming to look everywhere. To focus the search, the UNIX shell contains a *search string*. The search string is a list of directories where the shell looks for your commands.

Most search strings include the current directory, the '/bin' directory, and the '/usr/bin' directory. In the UNIX system, it is customary to store most of the frequently used commands in '/bin' and '/usr/bin'. In Berkeley UNIX systems, the commands are also stored in '/usr/ucb' and '/usr/local/bin'. (Directories containing executable files are conventionally named 'bin', because most executable programs are stored in binary files.)

The search string can be modified so that additional directories are searched whenever you enter a command. If the command is not found in any of the directories in the search string, then the shell prints a message complaining that the program was not located. Each user has his or her own search string. Thus, different users may have access to different sets of commands.

The search string is stored in a variable named $PATH. You can display your current search string by using the echo command.

```
$ echo $PATH
:/bin:/usr/bin
$ _
```

This above search string specifies searches of the current directory, then the '/bin' directory, and finally the '/usr/bin' directory. The directories in the search string are separated by colons. Any null directories (2 colons in a row or a leading or trailing colon) in the search string are taken to mean the current directory. The order of the directories in a search string is important. The shell will execute a command as soon as it is found. When different commands with the same name exist in several directories, the order of the search string decides which will be executed.

The search string that specifies searches through '/bin' and then '/usr/bin', but not the current directory, is

```
/bin:/usr/bin
```

If you wanted to look in '/bin' first, and then in the current directory, and then finally in '/usr/bin', the search string would be

```
/bin::/usr/bin
```

Since the search string is just a shell variable, you can set it interactively.

```
$ PATH=:/bin:/usr/bin:/usr1/kc/bin
$ _
```

This creates a search string containing all of the usual directories plus the directory '/usr1/kc/bin'. Changes to the search string take effect immediately.

If your login directory contains a file called '.profile', then the shell commands in that directory will be executed when you log in. The commands in '.profile' are usually used to adjust the terminal handler to your terminal, initialize environment variables such as $PATH, and execute any commands you want executed. If you want a unique search string, you should place the appropriate command in your '.profile' file.

It is important to search as few places as possible and to search them in the optimal order. People with very long search strings often have much poorer response time, because the shell must search dozens of directories each time a command is entered. In a related matter, it is important to keep the sizes of directories manageable. It takes much less time to search for an executable program in a directory containing just a few files than in a swollen directory that contains hundreds of files. The time the shell spends searching for commands is significant, and careful control of your search string and directory sizes can minimize that time.

Search strings are very important when a group of people all need access to a body of programs. For example, if a group of people all use a set of teletext programs, then all of the teletext programs should be put in a directory (perhaps '/usr/teletext/bin'). Everyone who uses the programs should modify his or her search string to include the teletext directory. If instead the teletext programs were placed in '/bin' or '/usr/bin', then every user on the system would constantly be penalized, because it would take longer to search through the standard directories, and it would take longer to execute each command. This is an example of the system manager's ability to create a more productive atmosphere.

11.5   QUOTING

Unfortunately, most of the special characters used by the shell are also used by other programs. There just aren't enough characters and symbols to go around. When you enter commands interactively or when you place commands in a file and execute the file, the shell is the first program to acquire the information. If a command contains any of the shell's special characters, you can expect the shell to alter the command unless it is quoted.

Some of the special characters we have already encountered are > and < to symbolize input/output redirection, | to symbolize a pipeline, and $ to indicate a shell variable. When you want to send these symbols to a program, they must be quoted. Without quotes, the special symbols will be gobbled up by the shell.

There are three methods of quoting in the UNIX shell:

- The backslash (\) quotes the immediately following character.
- Characters enclosed by single quote marks (') are quoted. No interpretations occur. Even new lines lose their role as command terminators within single quotes. Thus an argument that is surrounded by single quotes can contain embedded newlines.
- Characters enclosed by double quote marks (") are quoted except for backslash, accent grave, double quote, and currency symbol. Command and parameter variable substitution occur within double quotes.

When a single character has to be quoted, it is usually easiest to use a backslash. When a group of characters must be quoted and you don't want any interpretations to occur, it is easiest to use the single quotes—the strongest form of quoting in the UNIX shell. The double quote marks are a weaker form of quoting. Command and parameter substitution occur within double quote marks. Therefore, the characters that control command and parameter substitution (`, $) need to be quoted if you want to suppress these substitutions. Backslash and, of course, the double quote are also special within double quotes. Words within double or single quotes are seen by the shell as a single argument.

```
$ echo '$HOME'
$HOME
$ echo \$HOME
$HOME
$ echo "$HOME"
/usr1/kc
$ echo $HOME
/usr1/kc
$ _
```

In the first two commands, the $ is strongly quoted, so its shell meaning "here is a variable" is suppressed. In the third command, the weaker " quotes are used. Within " quotes variables are active, so the value of the $HOME variable is printed.

Here is an example where the double quotes are strong enough to change the meaning of the enclosed characters.

```
$ echo Howdy | wc
1 1 6
$ echo Howdy \| wc
Howdy | wc
$ echo 'Howdy | wc'
Howdy | wc
$ echo "Howdy | wc"
Howdy | wc
$ _
```

In the first command, the echo program pipes its output to the wc program. In the second, third, and fourth commands, the pipe character is quoted, which suppresses its meaning, so it and the word "wc" are simply echoed by echo.

However, you should note that there is a subtle difference between the second command and the third and fourth. In the second command, the \ quotes the following | character; thus, echo receives *three* arguments. In the third and fourth commands, the quotes have an effect on the spaces and on the |; thus in these cases, echo receives just *one* argument. The echo command will echo however many arguments it receives, but certain other commands are very sensitive to how many arguments they receive.

Here is another example of quoting spaces.

```
$ echo   one    two    three
one two three
$ echo "   one    two    three"
    one    two    three
$ _
```

In the first command, the multiple spaces separating the arguments are just field separators. The shell passes three arguments (with no spaces) to echo. In the second command, all the spaces are quoted. The shell passes a single argument to echo, containing embedded spaces. The difference is visible in the output. Quoting is also used with variables.

```
$ macedonian=Alexander the Great
sh: the not found
$ echo $macedonian
Alexander
$ _
```

In this example $macedonian is assigned the value "Alexander" and then the shell reports an error in locating the program called "the." Instead, you could enter any of the following commands.

```
$ macedonian='Alexander the Great'
$ macedonian="Alexander the Great"
$ macedonian=Alexander\ the\ Great
$ echo $macedonian
Alexander the Great
$ _
```

All three commands assign the value "Alexander the Great" to the shell variable $macedonian.

11.6 STANDARD VARIABLES

The meanings of a handful of shell variables have been standardized over time. These variables are no different from any other variables, except that their widespread use makes them more famous. The set command, when invoked without arguments, will print a list of the current variables. (The set command, which is discussed fully in the following section, is also used for several other tasks.)

```
$ set
HOME=/usr1/kc
PATH=:/usr1/kc/bin:/bin:/usr/bin
IFS=

PS1=$
PS2=>
TERM=vt100
$ _
```

These variables are created during the login process, and they are an important part of your UNIX environment. Any variable created by you would also appear in the list. (Note: the automatic variables $$, $?, $!, $#, and $- are not listed by the set command.) Let's discuss each variable individually:

- The $HOME variable contains the name of your home directory.
- The $PATH variable contains the name of the search string that the shell uses when it searches for your commands. The search string is discussed in Section 11.4.
- The $IFS variable contains the internal field separators—usually space, tab, and new line. The internal field separators separate the words of commands.
- $PS1 and $PS2 are the primary and secondary prompt strings used by the shell. $PS1 is the normal prompt used by the shell, and $PS2 is used for additional input to complete obviously incomplete commands.
- The $TERM variable contains the model name of your terminal. Some commands such as vi need to know what type of terminal you are using in order to produce correct output.

When an interactive Bourne shell first starts executing, it reads and executes the commands in the file '.profile' in your home directory. Typically the commands in '.profile' adjust the system's treatment of your terminal using the stty command and adjust some of these variables to suit your preferences. For example, if the '.profile' file contains the assignment

```
PS1="Yes boss -> "
```

the system will address you with the "Yes boss ->" prompt rather than the standard prompt. Of course, you can also reassign $PS1 (or any of the parameters) interactively.

11.7   SIMPLE CONDITIONALS

The ability to make a decision is the hallmark of intelligence. Decisions imply a choice among options: a selection of one path in preference to others. When a decision is made in a program, one sequence of commands is executed, and the other possible sequences are ignored. The structures that enact decisions in a programming language are called *conditionals*.

The *primitives* of a system are the lowest-level operations built into the system. In computer-programming languages such as BASIC and FORTRAN, the primitives are operations on binary quantities. The sequence of calculations in a BASIC or FORTRAN program is based on the results of the primitive operations. The primitives of the shell command programming language are the UNIX utility programs. Therefore, in the shell command programming language, the control flow is based on the success or failure of the executing programs.

When a UNIX program executes successfully, it usually returns a zero exit status. By convention, if an executing program encounters serious problems, it returns a nonzero exit status. The particular number often indicates the exact difficulty that the program encountered. If I enter the following command on my system, the exit status of ls will be zero.

```
$ ls -d /usr1/kc
/usr1/kc
$ _
```

However, if you enter the same command on your system, the shell will probably print "/usr1/kc: not found" (because there is no '/usr1/kc' directory on your system), and the exit status of ls will be a small number, often 1 or 2.

The shell's built-in $? variable contains the exit status of the last command executed by the shell. You can echo the $? variable if you want to see the exit status of a command.

```
$ ls -d /usr1/kc
/usr1/kc
$ echo $?
0
$ ls -d /usr1/nobody
/usr1/nobody not found
$ echo $?
2
$ _
```

The exit status of a pipeline is the exit status of the last command in the pipeline. The exit status returned by a command (or pipeline) can be used to control the flow of execution in a shell program.

Most systems contain the special programs true and false. The only function of the program true is to return a true (zero) exit status. Similarly, the only function of the false program is to return a false (nonzero) exit status.

The Bourne shell has several conditional operators. The simplest conditional is the double-ampersand (&&) operator. When two commands are separated by a double ampersand, the second command will execute only if the first command returns a zero exit status.

```
$ ls -d /usr1/kc > /dev/null && echo FOUND
FOUND
$ _
```

On my system, the message "FOUND" is printed because the exit status of ls is true. The result would probably be the opposite on your system, because a '/usr1/kc' directory doesn't exist on most systems. (Note that the test program is a better way to determine the existence of files. See Section 11.21.)

The opposite of the double ampersand is the double bar operator (||). When two commands are separated by the double bar operator, the second command will execute only if the first command returns a nonzero exit status.

```
$ ls -d /usr/xyz || echo No /usr/xyz
ls: /usr/xyz: not found
No /usr/xyz
$ _
```

The first message in this dialogue is from ls, while the second is from echo.

11.8   SIMPLE COMMANDS, PIPELINES, LISTS

We have already defined a simple command to be a command and its arguments. There are two other command types in the UNIX shell: pipelines and lists. You need to understand pipelines and lists, because they are used in shell control structures.

A *pipeline* is a simple command or group of simple commands connected by pipe fittings (|). Each of the following lines is a pipeline:

```
ls -l /bin /usr/bin
who | wc -l
a| b| c| d
ps
```

In the UNIX system, a *list* is a sequence of pipelines; therefore, the four pipelines just mentioned form one list. In the list shown above, the list elements (the pipelines) are on separate lines. (In UNIX jargon, we say that the pipelines are separated by the new line character.) The following list is equivalent to the first:

```
ls -l /bin /usr/bin ; who|wc -l;a|b|c|d ; ps
```

In this list the elements are separated by semicolons. The following characters can be used to separate the elements of a list.

    ;   (or the new line character) to indicate sequential execution
    &&   to indicate conditional (true) execution of the following pipeline
    | | to indicate conditional (false) execution of the following pipeline
    &   to indicate background (asynchronous) execution of the preceding pipeline

The list is a basic structure in the UNIX system shell. A list can be as simple as a single command or as complicated as you choose to make it. The value returned by a list is the exit status of the last pipeline in the list. It is important to understand the differences between a command, a pipeline, and a list:

- A *simple command* executes one program.
- A *pipeline* is a sequence of simple commands joined by pipe fittings. The simplest pipeline is a simple command.
- A *list* is a sequence of pipelines. The simplest list is a single pipeline (which may be a simple command).

11.9   THE IF CONDITIONAL

The double-ampersand conditional and the double-bar conditional are useful for creating very simple conditional structures. However, the shell has many more sophisticated conditionals. One of the most important Bourne shell features is the *if conditional*, which is a greatly improved version of the Version 6 if conditional. The syntax of the if conditional is

```
if  condition
   then list
elif condition
   then list
else
   list
fi
```

The words **if**, **then**, **elif**, **else**, and **fi** are keywords. Keywords are words
that the shell (or any programming language) uses to indicate built-in structures such as the if conditional statement. The keyword that marks the end
of each **if** conditional is **fi**, which is *if* spelled backwards. The *conditions*
and *lists* are lists of UNIX commands. The "elif ... then ... " part is
optional, the "else" part is optional, and there can be as many "elif ...
then ... " parts as necessary. Therefore the simplest **if** conditional is

```
if condition
    then list
fi
```

The UNIX shell's **if** conditional behaves similarly to the if statement in
many programming languages. Let's use a simple example to show how the
if works. Imagine there are four programs—winter, spring, summer, and
fall—that return a true exit status during their season and false otherwise.
Also imagine a set of programs that prints the chores that should be performed during each season. Our shell program to print chore reminders is

```
$ cat chores
if winter
   then
      snowremoval
      weatherstrip
elif spring
   then
      startgarden
      mowlawn
elif summer
   then
      tendgarden
      painthouse
      mowlawn
      waterlawn
```

```
elif fall
  then
    harvest
    mowlawn
else
    echo Something is wrong.
    echo Check the 4 season programs.
fi
$ _
```

If you execute the chores shell program during the spring season, the spring command will be true, and the startgarden and mowlawn programs will be executed. During the fall season, the fall command will return a true status, and the harvest and mowlawn commands will be executed. If none of the season programs exit with a true status, then the "else" part of the conditional will be executed, causing an error message to be printed.

Now let's show a more realistic example. Suppose some continuously running program writes a diagnostic to an errorfile each time it encounters errors during an operation. Another program runs once each hour to log the errors. If the errorfile exists, then this second program should copy the errorfile to a lineprinter at headquarters; if the errorfile doesn't exist (because no errors occurred), then the second program should send an "all is well" message. The following shell command file would perform this simple task:

```
$ cat errmonitor
date > /dev/lp-to-hdq
if test -r errfile
  then
    cat errorfile > /dev/lp-to-hdq
    rm errorfile
else
    echo "No errors this hour" > /dev/lp-to-hdq
fi
$ _
```

Notice that date, cat, and echo redirect their output to the lineprinter-to-headquarters device.

11.10 SHELL PROGRAM ARGUMENTS

We have already seen the importance of writing programs that perform general functions. Most programs that perform general functions can be directed to perform more specific functions by supplying them with command line arguments.

```
$ ls
corr   corr.c   corr.c.1   corr.doe
$ _
```

If you want a more specific list, such as a list of all of the files in the '/usr1/kc/bin' directory, you have to enter a more specific command.

```
$ ls /usr1/kc/bin
checkit   mycw   printit.qms
$ _
```

The argument */usr1/kc/bin* is used by the `ls` program to direct its attention to the '/usr1/kc/bin' directory.

In shell programs, the command line arguments are made available in a series of numbered variables. `$1` is the variable that contains the first command line argument, `$2` contains the second argument, etc. The numbered variables are often called positional parameters, because `$1` refers to the argument in the first position, etc. The special variable name `$0` always refers to the zeroth argument, which is the name of the executing shell program. An additional feature is the special name `$#`, which refers to the number of arguments to the command (see Section 11.2).

Consider a few simple examples of the use of positional parameters. Suppose you need a program that acquires four arguments and then echoes those arguments in the reverse order. Here is how it would be used:

```
$ rev-4 20 30 40 50
50   40   30   20
$ _
```

`rev-4` checks the number of arguments and prints an error message if there are too few or too many. If the number of arguments is OK, then the arguments are printed in the reverse order.

```
$ cat rev-4
if test $# = 4
        then echo $4 $3 $2 $1
else echo $0 usage: arg1 arg2 arg3 arg4
fi
$ _
```

In this simple shell program, we use the `test` command (Section 11.21) to see if the automatic variable `$#` indicates that the program was executed with four arguments, and we use the positional parameters `$1`, `$2`, `$3`, and `$4` to represent the actual arguments. As a convenience, most versions of the UNIX system use a `[` as a synonym for the `test` command. On these systems the example immediately above could have been written equivalently as follows:

```
$ cat rev-4a
if [ $# = 4 ]
        then echo $4 $3 $2 $1
else echo $0 usage: arg1 arg2 arg3 arg4
fi
$ _
```

The square brackets are often used to make things more readable, but the `test` program is actually performing the operations in either case. (Note that the UNIX `expr` command can also be used to perform arithmetic comparisons. See Section 11.21.) The `for` conditional (see Section 11.16) provides a more flexible method for working with positional parameters.

11.11   THE WHILE AND UNTIL CONDITIONAL LOOPS

The `while` and `until` conditionals allow you to repeat a group of commands. Let's first examine the `while` conditional. Its syntax is

```
while condition
    do list
done
```

The keywords here are *while*, *do*, and *done*. First the *condition* list is executed. If it returns a true exit status, then the *do* list is executed and the operation restarts from the beginning. If the *condition* list returns a false exit status, then the conditional is complete.

Suppose you must write a shell program that waits for a certain file to be removed. (Some other program is responsible for removing the file.) The *while* command can wait for a condition to become true. Since we want other UNIX users to get some processing time, we should delay a few seconds between tests rather than test continuously. The following shell program waits for a file named 'lockfile' to vanish:

```
$ cat waitlock
while test -r lockfile
    do sleep 5
done
$ _
```

This program tests to see if the file named 'lockfile' is readable. If it is, then the command "sleep 5" suspends execution for five seconds. When 'lockfile' is removed, the test fails and the command completes.

Notice that the 'waitlock' shell program separates the command lists by placing them on separate lines. We could also enter the program on a single line and use semicolons to separate the lists.

```
$ cat waitlock1
while test -r lockfile ; do sleep 5 ; done
$ _
```

The until conditional is a variant of the while structure. Whereas the while structure repeats while the condition returns a true value, the until structure repeats while the condition returns a false value. The syntax of the until structure is:

```
until condition
do
    list
done
```

The only new keyword is until.

Suppose you have to write a shell program that waits until a certain file is created. One method would be to use the while structure and negate the test:

```
$ cat waitgo
while test ! -r proceedfile ; do sleep 1 ; done
$ _
```

The exclamation point argument to the test program negates the readability test so that the test returns a true indication if the file is not readable. (The exclamation point is not a special character for the Bourne Shell, but it is for the C shell. On the C shell the ! argument to the test command must be quoted.) Another method uses the until structure:

```
$ cat waitgo1
until test -r proceedfile ; do sleep 1 ; done
$ _
```

With this method the loop will continue until the test command returns a true value (until the file 'proceedfile' is created).

11.12 STRUCTURED COMMANDS

Conditional structures such as while and until are executed by the shell almost as if they were a single command. The entire structure is scanned by the shell before any part of it is executed. Try entering the following line interactively on your system:

```
$ until test -r stopfile ; do
> _
```

The command is obviously incomplete, so the shell prompts you for further input (usually with a "`>`"). Complete the command as follows:

```
$ until test -r stopfile ; do
> sleep 2 ; echo Hello ; done &
$ _
```

The final ampersand indicates that the entire until command should run in the background. The command will type "Hello" every two seconds until you create the stopfile. Since your command is running in the background, the shell should be ready to accept another command. When you tire of seeing the greeting on your terminal, type the following command to create a file called 'stopfile':

```
Hello
Hello
Hello
> stopfile
$ _
```

Since it might take you longer than two seconds to enter the command, you will probably be interrupted in midstroke by a greeting or two. Just remember that the system is keeping track of the characters you are typing even while it (the system) is periodically typing the "Hello" greeting. As soon as you successfully create 'stopfile', the background greeting process will terminate. (You should remove 'stopfile' so that your directory doesn't become cluttered.)

The Bourne shell has two ways to bracket a group of statements, with parentheses or with curly braces. When statements are surrounded by parentheses, these statements will be executed by a subshell. However, when shell statements are surrounded by curly braces, the statements will be executed by a group by the current shell. Both of these capabilities are useful interactively and in shell programs.

Having a group of statements executed by a subshell is sometimes useful interactively. Changes to the environment, such as a change from one directory to another, won't persist in the original shell.

```
$ pwd
/usr1/kc/src/mega
$ (
> cd/usr/sys/io
> pwd
> ls -l * | lpr
> file * | lpr
> )
/usr/sys/io
$ pwd
/usr1/kc/src/mega
$ _
```

Similar uses of parenthesized command lists are common in shell scripts.

One of the most common uses of curly-bracketed command lists is when you want to execute more than one statement as a result of a || or && conditional.

```
$ pwd
/usr1/kc/src/mega
$ test -d /usr/lib/ikonas && {
> echo Ikonas directory present
> cd /usr/lib/ikonas
> ls -l | lpr
> }
Ikonas directory present
$ pwd
/usr/lib/ikonas
$ _
```

(The -d option of test directs it to determine if the named file is a directory; see Section 11.21.) In this example of a curly-bracketed command list, the shell's working directory is changed by the cd command. Such lists are more commonly managed by subshells; the intent in this example is to demonstrate the difference between the Bourne shell's two types of command lists.

All Bourne shell conditionals are structured commands. In a structure, all of the alternative processing paths are part of the structure; control flow is local to the structure. The opposite of a structure is the goto construct. In a goto statement, the alternative processing paths are not part of the statement; control flows to a nonlocal statement.

Modern programming languages favor control structures over the goto construct. Goto's are shunned because their nonlocal control transfers can lead to incomprehensible programs. The Bourne shell doesn't include the goto statement, because it would violate the convention of processing one command (or structured command) at a time.

11.13   COMMAND SUBSTITUTION

The shell allows you to take the standard output of a command and use it within a shell procedure. When a command is surrounded by accents grave (also called backquotes), that command is executed by the shell, and the resulting text is substituted in place of the command. For example, you could deposit the current date and time into a variable called now by executing the following command:

```
$ now=`date`
$ _
```

It might help to think of this process in two stages. In the first stage, the date program is executed and the resulting text is substituted. Conceptually, this leaves us with the shell command *now = "Tue Jun 30 22:48:46 EDT 1987"*. This command is executed causing the text to be stored in the variable $now.

```
$ echo $now
Tue Jun 30 22:48:46 EDT 1987
$ _
```

Command substitution is often used with the expr command to give the shell simple arithmetic abilities. (The expr command can perform arithmetic operations on its arguments. See Section 11.21.)

```
$ frames=`expr 5 + 13`
$ echo $frames
18
$ _
```

Many of the operators you use in expressions (parentheses, asterisks, ampersands, etc.) are special characters to the shell, and you have to be very careful to escape them (see Section 11.5). If a shell variable is assigned a numeric value, then the value can be increased by 1 by using command substitution:

```
$ count=10
$ echo $count
10
$ count=`expr $count + 1`
$ echo $count
11
$ _
```

The expr command will receive the arguments 10, +, and 1. The result is 11, which is stored in the shell variable $count.

Now that we can do arithmetic on variables, we can rewrite the reverse arguments program (mentioned in Section 11.10) to reverse any number of arguments.

```
$ cat revargs
count=$#
cmd=echo
while test $count -gt 0
do
    cmd="$cmd \$$count"
    count=`expr $count - 1`
done
eval $cmd
$ revargs 3 2 1
1 2 3
$ revargs 2 4 6 8 1 3 5 7
7 5 3 1 8 6 4 2
$ _
```

This program is a bit difficult, because it uses many of the facilities of the shell. The program consists of a while conditional loop that executes once for each argument, starting at the final argument and sequencing down to the first argument. The argument being processed is indicated by the variable $count; its initial value is the number of the last argument, and then its value is decreased by 1 each time through the loop.

Each trip through the loop adds some text to the variable $cmd. Initially the variable $cmd contains the text "echo". If the program were invoked with four arguments, after the first trip through the loop, the variable $cmd would contain "echo $4", after the second trip the variable would contain "echo $4 $3", and so on. The loop terminates when the variable $count is decremented to zero.

The word "\$$count" in the first statement of the do list deserves some attention. The goal is to create a text string consisting of a currency symbol followed by the current value of the $count variable. Since the currency symbol is a special symbol to the shell, it has to be escaped with a backslash. This explains the first backslash and the first currency symbol. The second currency symbol is just the start of the reference to the variable $count.

The hardest part of the program is the line beginning with the word eval. eval is a special command that provides an extra layer of substitutions on its arguments and then executes the arguments. At the completion of the loop the shell variable $cmd contains the text of an echo command to output the reversed list of arguments. For the four-argument case, the shell variable $cmd could contain the text "echo $4 $3 $2 $1". The eval causes this text to be reevaluated and executed, resulting in the output of the arguments in reverse order.

11.14 SHELL SUBSTITUTIONS

Thus far we have discussed all of the substitutions the shell performs. Let's summarize all of the substitutions in the order in which they occur. The order becomes very important in situations where one word undergoes several substitutions.

> *Command substitution.* All the commands that are surrounded by accents grave are executed, and the resulting text is substituted in place of the command, as discussed in Section 11.13.
>
> *Parameter (or variable) substitution.* All the words in the program that begin with a "$" are replaced, as discussed in Section 11.2.
>
> *Blank interpretation.* The results of the preceding substitutions are scanned for field separators. The usual field separators are blanks, tabs, and new lines. Any word that contains a field separator is divided into multiple words. Field separators in quoted words are ignored, and null words (except for explicitly quoted null words) are discarded.
>
> *File name generation.* The shell examines each word for the metacharacters "*", "?", and "[". If any of the words contain these metacharacters, that word is replaced by an alphabetically sorted list of filenames that match the pattern or by the original word if there are no matches. Filename generation is discussed in Section 4.6.

Much of the shell's power lies in its ability to perform text substitutions. However, the technique is confusing for people who are used to programming languages such as FORTRAN and BASIC, which are oriented toward numbers. The substitutions that occur in the shell are more similar to the general text-handling capabilities that are built into programming languages such as LISP and SNOBOL.

11.15 HERE DOCUMENTS

A *here document* is used to temporarily redirect the standard input within a shell program. The notation for a here document resembles standard input redirection:

```
cmd args < <symbol
   The here document
   . . .
symbol
```

The start of the here document is indicated by the "< <" notation. The following symbol is remembered and is used to indicate the end of the here document. The symbol can be a special character, such as !, or a unique word that is unlikely to occur within the here document, such as CGLOWDATDUFF. The here document can be as long as necessary. A line containing only the symbol indicates the end of the here document. The shell makes the here document available to the command as the standard input.

Consider the problem of handling errors in a large shell program that runs during the wee hours of the morning. You could have the shell program write an error message to a file and give someone the responsibility of looking at the file every day. A better method would be to send mail to the responsible person so that the notification is automatic.

If the following command were included in the error-handling section of the shell program, then the named person ("opsmanager" in this case) would get mail describing the problem:

```
mail opsmanager < <!
************ PROBLEMS AGAIN ****************
The midnight error has struck again!
The tdata file was missing - all processing stopped.
!
```

An alternative solution would be to put the message in a separate file and then use ordinary input redirection. The here document enables you to keep everything in one file.

11.16   THE FOR STRUCTURE

The UNIX shell contains a for structure, which allows a group of commands to be executed once for each word in a list of words. The general form of the for structure is

```
for name in word1 word2 ...
do
    do-list
done
```

The do-list will be executed once for each word in the list of words (word1, word2, etc.). The current word in the list will be assigned to the shell variable $name. The keywords are for, in, and the familiar do and done.

The following example shows a silly use of the for structure.

```
$ cat fruits
for fruits in apples pears oranges mangos
do
     echo $fruit are fruits
done
$ fruits
apples are fruits
pears are fruits
oranges are fruits
mangos are fruits
$ _
```

This form of the for structure is often used to perform some function for each file in a group of files or for each directory in a group of directories.

The for structure can also be used without the keyword "in" followed by the list of words.

```
for name
do
     do-list
done
```

In this form the do-list is executed once for each positional parameter (argument) of the shell. This is the simplest method for sequencing through the arguments to a shell program.

We can use the second form of the for structure to rewrite the reverse argument's shell program.

```
$ cat revargs1
list=""
for arg
do
    list="$arg $list"
done
echo $list
$ revargs1 spot likes jane
jane likes spot
$ _
```

In this shell program the for structure sequences through the arguments to the shell, placing each argument in front of the previous arguments stored in the variable $list. The reversed list is printed in the last line of the program.

11.17   THE CASE STRUCTURE

The shell's case structure is a multiway branch based on pattern matching. The general form of the case structure is

```
case word in
    pattern1) pat1-list ;;
    pattern2) pat2-list ;;
    ...
esac
```

The word is compared with all of the patterns. The first match causes the corresponding pattern list to be executed, and execution of the structure is complete. The patterns can be composed of the usual shell metacharacters: * to match any sequence of characters, ? to match any single character, and square brackets to delimit a class of characters. Several distinct words can be included in one pattern by using the vertical bar to indicate alternation. The usual meaning of the vertical bar (pipe connection) is suppressed during a case statement.

The following shell program attempts to determine the breed of an animal.

```
$ cat breeds
for breed
do
  case $breed in
    arabian|palomino|clydesdale) echo $breed is a horse ;;
    jersey|guernsey|holstein) echo $breed is a cow ;;
    husky|shepherd|setter|labrador) echo $breed is a dog ;;
    siamese|persian|angora) echo $breed is a cat ;;
    *) echo $breed is not in our catalog ;;
  esac
done
$ _
```

The order of the patterns is important. If more than one match is possible, only the first encountered will be executed. Notice that the final pattern is *, which will match everything. Since only one of the pattern lists can be executed on one pass through the case structure, the * catch-all won't be reached if the argument matches any of the other patterns.

```
$ breeds husky holstein terrier
husky is a dog
holstein is a cow
terrier is not in our catalog
$ _
```

The case structure is often used in conjunction with the for structure.

11.18   BREAK AND CONTINUE

The shell's break and continue statements are used to alter the action of
for loops, while loops, and until loops.   The break statement causes the
shell to break out of the enclosing loop, and the continue statement causes
the shell to branch to the beginning of the enclosing loop and start another
iteration.

As a first example, let's rewrite one of the argument reverse shell programs. You might recall that the original version used a while loop.

```
$ cat revargs
count=$#
cmd=echo
while test $count -gt 0
do
    cmd="$cmd \$$count"
    count=`expr $count - 1`
done
eval $cmd
$ _
```

The program could be written equivalently using a break statement.

```
$ cat revargs1
count=$#
cmd=echo
while true
  do
    cmd="$cmd \$$count"
    count=`expr $count - 1`
    if test $count -eq 0
      then break
    fi
  done
eval $cmd
$ _
```

In this program a break statement offers little advantage, because there is only one loop exit criterion and only one exit point. The break is the only clean solution when a loop has several exit points or when the exit criterion is quite involved.

We could also rewrite this problem using a continue statement.

```
$ cat revargs2
count=$#
cmd=echo
while true
do
    cmd="$cmd \$$count"
    count=`expr $count - 1`
    if test $count -gt 0
      then continue
    fi
    eval $cmd
    exit
done
$ _
```

The last two statements of the loop (eval $cmd and exit) are executed only once, at the conclusion of the processing. They are skipped on all of the initial passes through the loop, because of the continue statement. The exit statement terminates processing in a shell program.

11.19   THE SET COMMAND

The set command is used for several purposes. In Section 11.2 the set command was used to print a list of the current variables. When arguments are supplied to set, two other tasks can be performed: you can control the settings of the shell's internal options, or you can load values into the shell's positional parameters. For example, the command

```
$ set -v
$ _
```

causes the shell to turn verbose mode on. In verbose mode all shell input lines will be printed as they are read. This is very useful for debugging shell scripts. Verbose mode can be turned off by the command

```
$ set +v
set +v
$ _
```

(Notice how the command to turn off verbose mode is itself echoed to the screen before it is executed, when verbose mode is in effect.)

Another useful flag is **x**, which makes the shell display commands as they are executed. Setting this option lets you see exactly what the shell is doing. The **x** flag is a valuable aid for debugging shell scripts.

Most of the flag arguments that can be controlled using the **set** command can also be supplied as command line arguments when you are invoking the shell to execute a series of commands in a file.

```
$ cat lsdir
if [ $# = 0 ]
then
  dir=.
else
  dir=$1
fi
find $dir -type d -print
$ sh -x lsdir
+ [ 0 = 0 ]
dir=.
+ find . -type d -print
.
./bin
./bin/obin
./tbin
./xsrc
$ _
```

The shell command shown above executes the commands in 'lsdir' with the **x** flag set. The effect is the same as if the command **set -x** were the first command in 'lsdir'. The lines that start with a + are the result of supplying the **-x** flag.

The **set** command accepts the following option flags. The flags are set when preceded by a hyphen; they will be unset when preceded by a plus.

-e is used in shell scripts to cause an immediate exit if a command fails. This option must be used with extreme caution, because many UNIX programs don't properly set their exit status and thus may appear to fail when everything is fine.

-k causes all keyword arguments (i.e., arguments that look like an assignment) to be placed into the environment of the given command. When this option is set, it is hard to pass an argument to a program that contains an embedded equals sign, but this option does make the notation for passing environment variables more attractive. This option is often set in an interactive shell to make it easier to run shell scripts that make heavy use of environment variables.

-n tells the shell to read commands without executing them. It is useful when you want to test the syntax of a shell script without actually running it. -n is often used together with -v for syntactic debugging.

-t makes the shell exit after executing one command.

-u makes it an error to reference an unset variable. Ordinarily an unset variable expands to nothing.

-v tells the shell to print its input as it is read. Note that the shell reads structured commands (loops, conditionals) in a single gulp. This option is useful as a debugging tool to trace shell scripts.

-x tells the shell to print each command, preceded by a +, as it is executed. This option is probably the most commonly used shell script debugging tool.

- tells the shell to disable the -v and -x debugging flags.

-- is an option no-op. None of the flag options will be changed, and subsequent words in the argument list will not be interpreted as possible set options. It is useful when some of the following arguments may have leading hyphens. If arguments with leading hyphens aren't preceded with the -- option, the set command will interpret those arguments as its own options, and havoc will ensue.

Once the option arguments have been attended to, set takes the remaining arguments and assigns them to the positional parameters $1, $2, etc. If this feature of set is used (i.e., the *args* are present) in a shell script, then the original values of the positional parameters will be lost. Otherwise, set can be used to change the flags without affecting the positional parameters.

Keep in mind that set is commonly used for three distinct purposes: it automatically manages the options and arguments when the shell is invoked, it lets you change the shell options as needed, and it lets you take a multiword line and place those words into the positional parameters.

Many shell scripts have debugging facilities that are activated by command line options. Here is the prototype for such a script. Its command line options -U, -V, and -X control the shell's corresponding options.

```
$ cat opts
#
# skeleton script
#    to set sh debugging options from command line flags
#
while test $# -gt 0
do
    case $1 in
    -U)
        set -u
        shift
        ;;
    -V)
        set -v
        shift
        ;;
    -X)
        set -x
        shift
        ;;
    #
    # other option handling goes here
    #
    esac
done
#
echo The body of the shell script goes here.
#
$ opts
The body of the shell script goes here.
$ opts -X
+ shift
+ test 0 -gt 0
+ echo The body of the shell script goes here.
The body of the shell script goes here.
$ _
```

(The test program is discussed in Section 11.21, while is discussed in Section 11.11, and case is discussed in Section 11.17.) The # in a shell script introduces comments. The shell will ignore the #, and everything following up to the end of the line. A # can be the first thing on a line, as in this example, or it can occur in midline.

The preceding script could be written more compactly as follows:

```
$ cat opts
#
# skeleton script
#    to set sh debugging options from command line flags
#
while test $# -gt 0
do
    case $1 in
    -U| -V| -X)
        set `echo $1 | tr UVX uvx`
        shift
        ;;
    #
    # other option handling goes here
    #
    esac
done
#
echo The body of the shell script goes here.
#
$ _
```

The **tr** (translate) command in this script is used to translate the uppercase
script option arguments into lowercase arguments for **set**.

set is a flexible way to separate a line of input into separate words:

```
$ date
Mon Aug 11 22:40:08 EDT 1986
$ set -- `date`
$ echo $1 $2 $3
Mon Aug 11
$ year=$6
$ echo $year
1986
$ ls -l /etc/motd
-rw-r--r-- 1   root   staff   270 Aug 11 00:00 /etc/motd
$ set -- `ls -l /etc/motd`
$ echo $9 : $5 $1
/etc/motd : 270 -rw-r--r--
$ _
```

Once you have used **set** in a shell program to parse a line into individual
words, the program's original arguments are unavailable. In a shell script,
this technique must be performed after argument processing, unless the
arguments can be ignored.

In case you don't understand the necessity of the -- option of **set**, here
is the last part of the previous example repeated without using the --
option.

```
$ ls -l /etc/motd
-rw-r--r-- 1   root    staff   270 Aug 11 00:00 /etc/motd
$ set `ls -l /etc/motd`
sh: -rw-r--r--: bad option(s)
$ _
```

The problem occurs because the set command interprets the *-rw-r--r--* argument as a request to set a shell option. When the special -- argument is present, the shell treats all following arguments simply as arguments—not as requests to set flags.

Some shell scripts use the following technique to duplicate the facility provided by the -- option. Because X doesn't start with a hyphen, the set program interprets it, and all following words, as words rather than as set options.

```
$ set X `ls -l /etc/motd`
$ shift   #moves args to their usual position
$ echo $9 : $5 $1
/etc/motd : 270 -rw-r--r--
$ _
```

Variable assignments that are made before (to the left of) the command name are automatically exported into the environment of that command. This feature can be extended to variable assignments that occur following the command name by setting the -k flag.

```
$ cat myname
echo My name is $name and my argument is $1
$ echo $-
sim
$ name=george myname john
My name is george and my argument is john
$ myname name=george john
My name is and my argument is name=george
$ set -k
$ echo $-
sikm
$ name=george myname john
My name is george and my argument is john
$ myname name=george john
My name is george and my argument is john
$ _
```

11.20   SHELL FUNCTIONS

The Bourne shell is touted here and elsewhere as a powerful programming language. It is, but as critics have pointed out, the original Bourne shell lacks one of the major components of modern programming languages— functions. A function is a bundle of statements that are collected together and executed as a group. For example, a group of statements that performs a useful operation, such as computing the trigonometric sine of a number, is usually programmed as a function. Then the sine function can be invoked whenever a trigonometric sine must be calculated.

Some people have argued that functions in a shell program can be provided by other shell programs, but this has several drawbacks. One disadvantage is efficiency, because in the UNIX system there is a considerable speed penalty each time a shell program is invoked. Another problem is more practical: Where are all these "functions" to be stored? It would be impractical to create a directory to hold each program's functions, and it would be equally impractical to clutter the existing executables directories with shell function files.

The obvious omission of functions from the Bourne shell programming language has been rectified starting with Release V.2 of UNIX System V. Unfortunately, Berkeley UNIX systems use an older version of the Bourne shell, and shell functions are not always available on Berkeley systems. Shell functions are present in the Korn shell, so it is technically and legally possible on a Berkeley system to use a Bourne-compatible shell that contains shell functions.

Shell functions have a very simple syntax.

```
name()
{
    statements
}
```

It is possible to pass arguments to shell functions using the familiar UNIX notation. Within a shell function, the values of the arguments can be accessed using the notation $1, $2, and so on, just like the arguments for a shell script. Note that within a shell function the arguments to the shell script itself are not available. There is only one pool of variables in a shell script. Within a shell function, you can access the variables of the surrounding shell script, and the surrounding script can access any variables created within a shell function. A shell function can return an exit status using the **return** keyword. The value 0 signifies success, and any other value denotes a failure.

Here is an example shell program that contains two shell functions. The first shell function, called *errexit*, is used to exit from the program when an error is encountered. The reason for using a shell function is to make it easy to perform a standard set of chores before actually exiting. In this example program, `errexit` deletes temporary files, logs the error in a log file, and prints a message. The other shell function is called *ok*. It reads in a line from the standard input and returns a true or false indication, depending on whether the user types a *y* or an *n*.

The body of the shell program simply asks if you want to test the `errexit` function. It will be invoked if the response is *y*, and it will be skipped if the response is *n*.

```
$ cat fna
# demonstrate a simple shell function
TMP=/tmp
PIDLOG=${TMP}/pidlog$$
DATEFILE=${TMP}/date$$
ERRLOG=${TMP}/demolog
#
#shell function to clean up and exit
errexit() {
    echo $1
    date >> $ERRLOG
    echo $1 >> $ERRLOG
    rm -f $PIDLOG $DATEFILE
    exit
}
#
#shell function to read a y/n response and set fn exit
status
ok() {
    while true
    do
        read ans
        case $ans in
            [yY]*)    return 0 ;;
            [nN]*)    return 1 ;;
            *)    echo Please answer y or n ;;
        esac
    done
}
#
echo $$ > $PIDLOG
date > $DATEFILE
#
# test error exit
echo Test errexit function [y/n]?
ok && errexit "Testing the errexit function"
#
echo Normal Termination
echo Please remove $PIDLOG and $DATEFILE
```

```
$ fna
Test errexit function [y/n]?
y
Testing the errexit function
$ fna
Test errexit function [y/n]?
maybe
Please answer y or n
n
Normal Termination
Please remove /tmp/pidlog297 and /tmp/date297
$ _
```

These shell functions illustrate several of the capabilities discussed above. Note that the **errexit** function accesses its parameter using the **$1** notation, and also notice that it accesses several shell variables that were defined in the outer level of the script. Notice also that the **ok** function returns status information using the **return** statement. To return values other than an exit status, a shell function typically uses the **echo** statement.

Although these simple example shell functions are called from only one place in the script, in more practical shell scripts, shell functions are often called from many locations in the script.

11.21   THE TEST AND EXPR COMMANDS

test and **expr** are commands that are commonly used in shell scripts. **test** performs various tests for equality, and it can determine if certain files exist. The **test** command is built into some versions of the Bourne shell. The **expr** command is a simple arithmetic program. It is often used to perform arithmetic operations with shell variables, such as assigning a variable the value that results from a calculation.

The **test** program performs three different types of tests: it can test files for certain characteristics, it can perform string comparisons, and it can make numeric comparisons. **test** indicates the success or failure of its testing by its exit status. Thus it is almost always used as part of a conditional statement. Each flag and operator must be passed as a separate command line argument.

When **test** is passed a command line flag from the table below followed by a filename, it performs a file access test.

f	Ordinary file	r	Readable	w	Writable
d	Directory file	s	Size > 0		

On System V the following tests are also available:

c	Character special	b	Block special	p	Pipe (fifo)
u	Set user id	g	Set group id	k	Sticky bit
		x	Executable		

-t [*n*] tests to see if file descriptor *n* (assumed to have the value one if *n* isn't supplied) refers to a terminal.

The name [is a recognized synonym for test. When the [alias is used, the last argument to test must be a]. Some people find the [] form of test more readable, but in either case the test program is doing the work.

```
$ if test -r /etc/motd
> then
> echo Readable
> fi
Readable
$ [ -d /bin ] && echo /bin is a directory
/bin is a directory
$ _
```

The test program can compare strings for equality or inequality, or it can look for zero length strings.

-z *s1*	True if string *s1* has zero length.
s1	True if string *s1* is non-null.
-n *s1*	True if string *s1* has length greater than zero.
s1 = *s2*	True if the two strings are equal.
s1 != *s2*	True if the two strings are not equal.

```
$ [ $HOME = `pwd` ] || echo we are not home now
we are not home now
$ _
```

test can perform numeric comparisons of integers using the *n1 -op n2* command line syntax. *op* must be one of the following:

eq	Equal	gt	Greater Than	ge	Greater or Equal
ne	Not Equal	lt	Less Than	le	Less or Equal

Here is an example of performing a numeric comparisons, performed in a directory that contains about 80 files.

```
$ [ 40 -lt `ls | wc -l` ] && echo too many files here
too many files here
$ _
```

test also allows you to combine tests using the following boolean operators.

!   NOT   -a   AND   -o   OR

The precedence of OR is lower than AND. Parentheses (which must be escaped from the shell) may be used for grouping.

The expr command evaluates command line expressions. Each of expr's arguments should be either a number or an operator. Numbers should be integer values; most versions of expr cannot handle floating point values or exponential notation. Negative numbers are allowed; simply precede a number with a minus (hyphen), which is the expr command's only unary operator. All other operators are binary operators. Note that many of the expr operators that appear in the following list are special characters to the shell. They must be quoted, so that they are passed to the expr command rather than interpreted by the shell. Note also that each element of the expression must be a separate argument. You cannot simply place single quotes around the entire expression, because that would reduce it to a single argument.

expr's binary operators all follow the *expr op expr* syntax. Parentheses can be used for grouping, but each parenthesis must be a separate argument, and each must be escaped from the shell. In the following list, the operators are listed in order of decreasing precedence.

:   The colon is a text-matching operator. The colon operator compares its left operand, which must be a simple text string, with its right operand, which may be a regular expression. The regular expression may contain all of the ed regular expression metacharacters: . to match any single character; $ to anchor a pattern to the end of the string; [*list*] to match any single character in the list; and * to match zero or more occurances of the previous single character expression. Unlike ed, expr regular expressions are always anchored on the left, much as if the first character of the regular expression were ed's ^. The result normally is the length of the match, or zero if there is no match. If part of the regular expression is enclosed in \(and \), then that part of the expression will be printed if there is a match.

* / %   Multiplication, division, and remainder.

+ -   Addition and subtraction.

= > > =   Comparison operators. If both the left and right operands are integer

!= < < =   numeric, a numeric comparison is performed. Otherwise a string comparison is performed. The result of a comparison is one if it succeeds, and zero otherwise.

    &   Returns the left operand if both operands are nonnull and non-zero. Otherwise the result is zero.

    | Returns the left operand if it is neither null nor zero. Otherwise the result is the right operand.

Note that both & and | work somewhat differently from logical operators in other languages.

Probably the most common use of expr is to perform simple arithmetic calculations.

```
$ expr \( 5 \* 9 \) % 4
1
$ count=4
$ while test $count -gt
> do
>     echo $count
>     count=`expr $count - 1`
> done
4
3
2
1
$ _
```

Another common use of expr is to compare strings, or to extract part of a string.

```
$ tty
/dev/tty12
$ expr `tty` : "/dev/tty\(..\)"
12
$ _
```

CHAPTER 12

A Few Shell Programs

One of the most interesting features of UNIX is the shell. The shell is a powerful interactive command interpreter entwined within a sophisticated, high-level programming language. The primitive operations in the shell programming language are the UNIX commands. Hence the entire power of the UNIX operating system can be harnessed in a shell program.

Programmers are usually trained to work with conventional programming languages. However, shell programming requires a different mind-set. Because the shell is so important to the UNIX system, we next consider a few examples of shell programs. All of these examples are designed to work on the Bourne shell, which is available on all modern UNIX systems.

Simple shell programs can be written by nonprogrammers, but sophisticated shell programming—in fact, all programming—is still a job for experts. The first section of this chapter examines some of the issues you should consider when you are considering the shell language for a given application. Simple shell programs are commonly used UNIX commands conveniently stored in a file. One example is shown in Section 12.2. Other shell programs are conceptually simple but involve more commands, such as the examples shown in the last sections of this chapter.

12.1 WHEN DO YOU USE THE SHELL PROGRAMMING LANGUAGE?

There are no firm rules for deciding when to use the shell programming language to write a program. When program execution speed is important, more efficient languages should be used because there is a large execution speed penalty for using the high-level features of the shell. But even when execution speed is important, the shell is often a good *prototyping* language. Write your application first using the shell to get the kinks out, and then rewrite the final version in another language for greater speed.

The shell programming language should be used when the problem solution involves operations that are available as standard UNIX commands. There are UNIX commands to search through files, sort files, transform files, create files, move files, and so on. If the problem can be expressed in terms of the operations that are already part of the UNIX tool chest, then a strong case can be made to use the shell programming language.

Once you become fluent in shell programming, you begin to view problems in terms of their potential for shell language solutions. Many problems that don't appear at first to be amenable to shell language solutions can be performed elegantly by the shell.

Another way to evaluate the suitability of the shell programming language is to examine the basic data involved in the problem. If the basic data are lines of text or files, the shell may represent a good solution. If the basic data are numbers or single characters, the shell may not be a good solution.

The final criterion we mention in relation to using a shell program is program development cost. It is expensive to develop a program in a compiled language such as C or FORTRAN. Interactive languages such as the shell make it easier to test and experiment, so for programs that are going to be used only once or twice, it may be much cheaper to put up with the slow execution speed of shell programs in order to take advantage of the easy development of shell programs.

12.2   HOW MANY USERS?

Although the who command will tell you who is on the system, it won't tell you how many. However, the who command combined with wc, the word count program, will work nicely.

```
$ cat > nusers
who | wc -l
^D
$ chmod a+x nusers
$ who
nuucp      tty01    Dec 15 22:24
gilbert    tty17    Dec 15 15:34
dan        ttyh0    Dec 15 17:37
kc         ttyh3    Dec 15 21:02
$ nusers
4
$ _
```

The -1 option to wc specifies that wc should count only lines; normally wc counts lines, words, and characters. If you want to be fancier, you can embed the summary in a message.

```
$ cat > nusers
echo `who | wc-l` users on the system
^D
$ nusers
4 users on the system
$ _
```

Why would you want a one-line summary of the number of users? Many systems keep track of system usage for management purposes. For example, a graph of daily usage would provide a visual display that might help in designing a load-balancing rate structure. Here is a variant of nusers that will keep a log of system usage in files named 'Sun', 'Mon', etc. Given a day's worth of info, a separate program can be used to produce the actual graph.

```
$ cat logusers
while true
do
    set -- `date`
    day=$1
    who | wc >> /usr/adm/$day
    sleep 600
$ _
```

The $day shell variable contains the name of the day. The name of the day is obtained using the set command to set the positional parameters to the output of the date command. The first word of date's output, hence the first positional parameter, is the day name. Notice in the fourth line that >> style output appends the number of users information onto the usage file. sleep 600 is a ten-minute (10 × 60 sec) delay.

As written above, there is one thing missing from `loguser`. For the first week, everything will be fine, but when the eighth day arrives, the new data will be tacked onto the end of the previous instead of truncating the old data and starting fresh. Cleaning up the old files could be handled by `cron`, but instead, let's show how it would be handled in this program.

```
$ cat logusers
lastday=never
while true
do
    set -- `date`
    day=$1
    if [ $day != $lastday ]
    then
        > /usr/adm/$day
    fi
    who | wc -l  >>  /usr/adm/$day
    lastday=$day
    sleep 600
done
$ _
```

In this version of `logusers`, the shell variable `$day` contains the day of the week, and `$lastday` contains the day that `logusers` last updated the usage file. The line `> /usr/adm/$day` clears out the usage file each time the day changes. The `>` output redirection symbol usually follows a command to redirect the command's output. Without a command, the `>` symbol tells the shell to create an empty file with the given name. This version of `logusers` could be run in the background to provide continual monitoring of system usage. Notice that `logusers` must run continuously. If it were started fresh every ten minutes (by `cron`), all of the state information stored in `$day` and `$lastday` would be lost.

How would you solve this problem using the C language? A C solution to this problem would be difficult because you would have to be able to decipher the contents of the file '/etc/utmp' (the file where logins are recorded) to find out how many people are using the system. Since the `who` command already knows how to examine '/etc/utmp', this is an example of a problem that is solved easily using existing UNIX tools but is fairly hard to solve using C.

12.3 LISTING SUBDIRECTORIES

The UNIX operating system contains the `ls` command to list all of the files in a directory, but it lacks the built-in capability to list all of the directory files in a directory. Whenever you are poking around in an unfamiliar part of the filesystem, you are likely to want to know the names of the subdirectories of the current directory.

Section 8.8 explained that the command

```
ls -l / | grep '^d'
```

will list all of the directory files in the root directory, because in a long-format listing, all the lines describing directories start with the character "d". (In the grep pattern, the caret anchors a match to the beginning of a line; thus, the pattern ^d matches all lines that start with the character d.) We can extend this simple command line so that we can list the subdirectories of any directory, not just the root directory, by using shell program arguments. The trick is to use a positional parameter in place of the name of the root directory, to make this a more general solution:

```
$ cat > lsdir
ls -l $1 | grep '^d'
^D
$ chmod a+x lsdir
$ lsdir /
drwxrwxr-x   4   bin    3136   Sep  17  11:28   /bin
drwxr-xr-x   9   root   3648   Sep  16  17:24   /dev
drwxrwxr-x   4   root   2496   Sep  17  18:40   /etc
drwxrwxr-x   5   bin     752   Jul   1  11:24   /lib
drwxrwxr-x   6   root    160   Aug  26  13:37   /mnt
drwxr-xr-x  12   mal     528   Sep   2  15:48   /source
drwxrwxrwx   2   root    896   Sep  17  19:27   /tmp
drwxrwxr-x  26   root    416   Jul  27  12:57   /usr
$ _
```

If no arguments are supplied, then the positional parameter $1 will be unset and the ls program won't receive any directory names as arguments, so the files in the current directory will be listed. This is very nice behavior. The command lsdir will list the subdirectories of the current directory just as the command ls (without arguments) will list the files in the current directory.

Obviously, the lsdir command expects just one argument. If you enter the following command, only the subdirectories of '/etc' will be listed.

```
$ lsdir /etc /lib
drwxr-xr-x  2  ops   512  Oct 19 14.01  /etc/priv
$ _
```

Probably the easiest fix is to change $1 to "$@". Then ls will get all of the arguments instead of just the first. However, let's explore an alternative method that shows how shell arguments can be managed individually.

```
$ cat lsdir2
for i
do
    ls -l $i | grep 'ˆd'
done
$ _
```

This improved version will work with one or more arguments, but what happens when no arguments are supplied? With no arguments, the for loop will never execute, and no output will be generated. To correct this deficiency, we need to put a test at the beginning of the file 'lsdir' to make sure that there is at least one argument. Here is one way to do it.

```
$ cat lsdir3
if test $# = 0
    then lsdir3 .
else
    for i
    do
        ls -l $i | grep 'ˆd'
    done
fi
$ _
```

lsdir3 checks to make sure that there is at least one argument. If there is at least one argument, then the for loop is executed, but if there are no arguments, then the command lsdir3 is executed to list the subdirectories of the current directory. Notice that lsdir3 is calling itself—a technique known as recursion. Shell programs are allowed to execute other shell programs (nesting) or to execute themselves recursively. Here is another way to modify lsdir to handle zero arguments.

```
$ cat lsdir4
if [ $# = 0 ]
then
  args=.
else
  args="$@"
fi
for i in $args
do
    ls -l $i | grep 'ˆd'
done
$ _
```

What other techniques could be used to perform this same function, listing subdirectories? The UNIX program named test can test files to see if they are directories.

```
$ cat lsdir5
for i in $1/*
do
    if test -d $i
        then echo $i
    fi
done
$ lsdir5 /etc
/etc/priv
$ _
```

The -d option of test means "test to see if the named file is a directory." The names of all of the files that pass the test will be printed using the echo command. Using this alternative technique for identifying directories, we can create a version that handles zero, one, or more arguments.

```
$ cat lsdir6
if test $# = 0
then
  args=.
else
  args="$@"
fi
for i in $args
do
  for j in $i/*
  do
    if test -d $j
        then echo $j
    fi
  done
done
$ _
```

Can you think of any alternative methods for generating a list of the subdirectories of a given directory? Are these methods more or less efficient than the method we have shown? Which of the two approaches we have shown is more efficient, and which approach is more general and flexible? How hard would it be to write a C program to list subdirectories?

12.4 LISTING FILES IN THE CURRENT SUBTREE

Everyone who uses UNIX occasionally misplaces a file. Perhaps you can't remember the exact name of the file, or you put it in some unknown directory. In any case, the file is missing, and you want to find it. Perhaps the easiest way to find a file is just to list all of the files in the current filesystem subtree. (The current subtree consists of the current directory and all of its subdirectories, their sub-subdirectories, etc.) Very often you will know that the file is in a certain part of the filesystem but you won't know exactly where. (Typically the file is in some unknown subdirectory of your home directory.)

The find command is used to find files. You can use arguments to find files with certain names, to find files that have been modified more recently than a certain date, to find files with certain privileges, and so on. If you don't use any of the special options, then find will find all of the files in the subtree.

The simplest form of the find command is

```
find . -print
```

This will print the names of all of the files in the current subtree. The dot indicates that the search should start in the current directory (remember that dot is always the name of the current directory), and the option "-print" indicates that the filenames should be printed. (See your UNIX system manual for a complete explanation of the find command, and all of its options.) You could memorize the syntax for the find command or you could put the command in a shell command file that we will call 'lstree'. Whenever you want a list of all of the files in the current subtree, you can enter the command

```
lstree
```

instead of the command

```
find . -print
```

Many shell programs are this simple; they are just a useful command placed in a file.

A variant on this problem is the problem of listing all of the directories in the current subtree. As a first solution, let's use the find command. The find command contains a test for directories. The command

```
find . -type d -print
```

will find and print all of the directories in the current subtree. The argument "-type" indicates that we are trying to find certain types of file—directories in this case as indicated by the "d" argument. We could place this command in a file and enter the name of the file whenever we want a list of the directories in the current subtree.

Let's show another way to solve this problem. We can use the shell's for loop to perform tests on each file in a directory. The command

```
for i in *
do
        if test -d $i
                then echo $i
        fi
done
```

will test all of the files in the current directory and print the names of all of the files that prove to be directories. To list all of the directories in the current subtree, we need to use recursion. Recursion is a technique by which a routine calls itself. We can modify the command listed above so that it descends into each directory and then calls itself to list the files in that directory, and descend still further, and so on. We will put the following commands in the file 'lstree1':

```
$ cat lstree1
if test $# = 0
then dirname=.
else dirname=$1
fi
for i in $dirname/*
do
        if test -d $i
        then
                echo
                lstree1 $i
        fi
done
$ _
```

The argument 'lstree1' is used to keep track of the pathname leading to the directory being examined. When 'lstree1' is invoked without arguments, then the variable $dirname acquires the value "."; otherwise $dirname acquires the value of the first argument to 'lstree1'.

Let's look at yet another method. Instead of a for loop to generate a list of all of the files in the current directory, we can use the ls command in combination with the read command. This time we will store the program in the 'lstree2' file.

```
$ cat lstree2
if test $# = 0
then dirname=.
else dirname=$1
fi
ls $dirname | (
        while read i
        do
                if test -d $dirname/$i
                then
                        echo $dirname/$i
                        lstree2 $dirname/$i
                fi
        done
)
$ _
```

This program is similar to the previous one except that the for loop is replaced with the ls command. In this version, we generate a list of the files in the current directory using the ls command. The list of files is piped to the list of commands enclosed in parentheses. The read command reads lines from the pipe and places them in the variable $i. The end of the program is the same as 'lstree1'.

It is left to the reader to evaluate these three approaches.

12.5   MANAGING A BACKGROUND PROCESS

Many UNIX sites run customized programs in the background. The following shell script is modeled on an actual shell script that was used to manage a set of background tasks. The purpose of the shell script is to make it easy to start, stop, and monitor the background tasks.

In this example, the background task is a process called *tu* that manages a specialized communication protocol on a given serial communication line. Each time the protocol is started, the tu process must be supplied with several arguments. Instead of memorizing the arguments, they are coded into the shell script, so the person running the shell script needs to know only which tu process (0, 1, or 2) to start or stop.

The first half of the following script sets shell variables to their default values and processes the command line arguments; the second half does the useful work. When a new communication process is started, the old one must first be killed. If the -v option is supplied, extra information is printed as the script executes; if the -s option is supplied, the existing process will be killed, but a new one will not be executed; and if the -l option is supplied, the status of the existing processes will be displayed. By default, the tu process number 0 will be managed, but the arguments *-1* or *-2* can be supplied to manage the other two communication lines.

```
$ cat tustart
# restart the tu background process
# -l -- just list; -v -- verbose
# -0|1|2 -- start tu0, tu1 or tu2
# -s -- stop but do not restart
TU=/usr/local/bin/tu
LIB=/usr/local/tu/dk
baud=9600        port=/dev/ttyi9
dk=0 verbose=n   stop=n
for i            # process command line
do
     case $i in
          -l) ps -edaf | egrep '(PID|tu)' ; exit ;;
          -v) verbose=y ;;
          -s) stop=y ;;
          -0) ;; # the default
          -1) baud=9600 port=/dev/ttyia dk=1 ;;
          -2) baud=4800 port=/dev/ttyib dk=2 ;;
           *) echo Unknown option: $i
                echo usage: $0 '[-l] [-v] [-s] [-0|1|2]'
                exit
                ;;
     esac
done
set -- ""  # erase command line arguments
set -- `ps -edaf | grep tu | grep $port`
[ x$2 != x ] && {     # kill old (if it exists)
     [ $verbose = y ] && echo killing $2
     kill -9 $2
}
[ $stop = y ] && exit
$TU -s $baud -p $port $LIB$dk &
[ $verbose = y ] && ps -f -p$!
$ _
```

The for loop processes each argument, and the case statement executes the appropriate code for each argument. Any unrecognized argument forces the script to exit, after printing an error message. The most interesting case in the case statement processes the *-l* option. The action for that statement is to pipe the ps command into the egrep command. The pattern for egrep is *'(PID|tu)'*, which selects any line that contains *PID*, or *tu*. The first selects the ps title line and the second selects any lines pertaining to the *tu* process.

The main action of the program follows the for loop. Three major jobs are performed: (1) the pid number of the existing tu process is determined;

(2) the existing tu process (if any) is killed; and (3) the new tu process is started. The third step is skipped if the -s option is supplied, and the second and third steps are verbosely documented if the -v option is supplied.

The pid number of the existing tu process is determined by piping the output of ps to a pair of grep processes. The first grep rules out all processes that don't have the text *tu*, and the second grep narrows it further to the tu process for the given communication line. A single grep won't do, because it will select itself, as shown below.

```
$ sleep 500 &
460
$ ps -f
     UID   PID  PPID  C   STIME TTY   TIME COMMAND
      kc    30     1  0 20:23:25 01   0:09 -sh
      kc   460   458  0 23:16:21 01   0:00 sleep 500
      kc   461   458 16 23:16:40 01   0:00 ps -f
$ ps -f | grep sleep
      kc   460   458  0 23:16:21 01   0:00 sleep 500
      kc   462   458  5 23:16:47 01   0:00 grep sleep
$ ps -f | grep sleep | grep 500
      kc   460   458  0 23:16:21 01   0:00 sleep 500
$ _
```

The first set command in the tustart script clears the positional parameters, and the second sets the positional parameters to the output of the ps command for the selected line. If a tu process is already running on the given communication line, the positional parameter $2 will have its pid number. Otherwise the $2 parameter will be empty.

The next job is to kill the tu process, if any, that is already running. The test program (called by its pseudonym ∕) tests the $2 parameter to see if it is nonempty. If so, the given process is killed. Another approach would be to kill $2 without performing the test. If $2 were empty, the kill program would complain, but the complaint could be suppressed using output redirection. The line that reads

```
[ $stop = y ] && exit
```

will make the script exit if the -*s* option is supplied. Otherwise, the last two lines of the script are executed. The first of these starts a new tu process in the background, with the required parameters, and the second of these runs ps to print information about the new tu process (if $verbose is set).

CHAPTER 13

Awk

awk is a programmable filter for text files. Like grep, awk can search for patterns in a text file. Like sed, awk can replace one text pattern with another. Like expr, awk has arithmetic capabilities. And like the shell or C, awk is programmable. These characteristics make awk a valuable tool for manipulating text files.

awk is an appropriate tool for jobs too complicated for the standard filters. If speed is essential, awk is an inappropriate production language, but even for jobs where speed is essential, awk is useful for prototyping. Although awk and the shell are both programmable, they are specialized for different applications. awk is best at manipulating text files, whereas the shell is best at managing UNIX commands.

awk is suitable for very simple chores, such as extracting one of the words printed by the date command, or more complex chores, such as serving as a simple data base manager or statistics package. Here is an example of a simple awk application, a program that prints the day of the month.

```
$ cat dayofmonth
date | awk '{ print $3 }'
$ date
Tue Mar 25 20:15:43 EST 1986
$ dayofmonth
25
$ _
```

More complicated awk programs will be shown later in this chapter.

awk was developed by Alfred V. Aho, Peter J. Weinberger, and Brian W. Kernighan. They also wrote the manual for awk, *Awk—A Pattern Scanning and Processing Language.* Brian Kernighan has pointed out that "naming a language after its authors ... shows a certain poverty of imagination." Although awk's name lacks the conciseness and mystique of some of UNIX's more renowned names (e.g. C), nonetheless it is a fitting name for a useful UNIX tool.

13.1 SIMPLE SCRIPTS

An awk script (also called a program) consists of two parts, *patterns* and *actions*. The patterns are similar to ed's regular expressions, and the actions bear some resemblance to the C language. In an awk program, there are patterns followed by actions, with curly braces surrounding each action. An action is performed if the pattern matches something in the current input line. If the pattern part of the program is absent, the action is performed for each line in the file. If the action is absent, then the default action is to print the line. A few simple examples should make some of these ideas clear.

One easy chore is to write an awk script that mimics UNIX's grep command. The goal is to print each line of a file that matches the given pattern. Later in the chapter, I'll show how you can generalize this to handle multiple arguments and specify the pattern on the command line. However, for now let me show an awk program that simply looks for the text pattern "paris" in its standard input. Each line containing the pattern is output.

```
$ cat findparis
awk /paris/
$ echo an american in georgia | findparis
$ echo an american in paris | findparis
an american in paris
$ _
```

The awk program shown above consists of a single pattern, /paris/. Since there is no action specified for the pattern, the default action—print the entire line each time there is a match—is performed.

Here is an equivalent program, with the action clearly spelled out.

```
$ cat findparis
awk '/paris/ { print }'
$ echo an american in georgia | findparis
$ echo an american in paris | findparis
an american in paris
$ _
```

The quotes surrounding the awk script are necessary, because the script contains blanks. Either single or double quotes would suffice in this example.

The print statement in the 'findparis' program doesn't have any parameters, so the entire line is printed. It is also possible to print constants, words from the input line, and so forth, by supplying them as arguments to print. An example of print with arguments appears in the next example.

In an awk program, the words $1, $2, and so forth, refer to the words of the current input line. This is similar to their meanings in a shell program, but different enough to cause problems, especially when an awk command is a part of a shell program using positional parameters. So if the current input line in an awk script is *The rain in Spain,* then $1 in the awk script has the value *The*, $2 has the value *rain,* etc. The special variable $0 contains the entire current input line.

Although it hasn't been mentioned so far, an awk program can be supplied in two ways. What has been shown above is supplying the awk program as the first argument on the command line, as in

```
$ date | awk '{ print $3 }'
25
$ _
```

It is also possible to place the awk program in a separate file.

```
$ cat prarg3.awk
{ print $3 }
$ date | awk -f prarg3.awk
25
$ _
```

The -f flag argument tells awk that the following argument is the name of the file containing the awk program. In either form of the command, filenames can be mentioned on the tail end of the command line if you want awk to read its input from named files instead of from the standard input.

Here is an awk script that computes the average position of a series of x, y, z points. The input contains x, y, z positions on each line; the desired output should contain the average of the positions. A final version, to be shown soon, will simply print the final result, but in this first-cut version, we will produce all of the intermediate answers. Here is a first-cut awk script to average a series of x, y, z coordinates.

```
$ cat ave
awk '{
        n = n + 1
        X = X + $1
        Y = Y + $2
        Z = Z + $3
        print X/n, Y/n, Z/n
        }'
$ cat test
1 2 3
4 5 6
7 8 9
0 1 2
$ ave < test
1 2 3
2.5 3.5 4.5
4 5 6
3 4 5
$ _
```

This awk script must be quoted using the powerful single (') quotes to prevent the shell's parameter substitution from occurring. The words $1, $2, and $3 in this program are awk variables, not shell positional parameters, so they must be quoted. Even a one-line awk script containing $1 etc. must be quoted with single quotes to suppress parameter substitution.

Besides its use of the field variables $1, $2, and $3, this program illustrates the fact that variables in awk programs are created automatically simply by mentioning their name. In this program the variables are named n, X, Y, and Z. In awk you can count on a variable to start out initialized to zero or blank, although it is possible to initialize variables explicitly. In a language designed for larger projects, awk's relaxed attitude toward variable declarations would be a fault, but in a language designed for short projects awk's lack of rigor seems acceptable. You should also notice that the default pattern is missing for the action in this script, so the action is performed for every line of the input.

Our average program would be more useful if the average position were printed only after all of the input had been exhausted. As a first attempt, the program is useful; in fact, an overly verbose first attempt is usually better than a silent, mysterious first attempt. However, consider the overhead of running this program with an input of 10,000 lines. The resulting output would clutter the screen for hours!

awk has the built-in patterns BEGIN and END that are ideal for specifying actions that should be performed before or after the data are read. BEGIN and END must be the first and last patterns, respectively, if they are present. In the following variation on the program from above, the BEGIN pattern is used to explicitly (but somewhat needlessly) initialize all of the variables, and the END pattern is used to print the result. Although the initialization is, in a strict sense, not necessary, I think it is useful as a form of documentation. It draws the reader's attention to the assumed initial values of the variables.

```
$ cat ave2
awk '
BEGIN  { n = 0 ; X = 0 ; Y = 0 ; Z = 0 }
       {
       n = n + 1
       X = X + $1
       Y = Y + $2
       Z = Z + $3
       }
END    { print X/n, Y/n, Z/n }'
$ cat test
1 2 3
4 5 6
7 8 9
0 1 2
$ ave2 < test
3 4 5
$ _
```

This awk program has three actions—two that have patterns and one that, because it doesn't have a pattern, is executed for every line of the input. (Notice that if the input file for this program is empty, then n will have the value 0 when the END pattern is encountered. This will lead to a "divide by 0" message, which can in this case be ignored. In Section 13.2 the if statement is introduced; it could easily solve this problem.)

awk patterns are more flexible than simple ed-style regular expressions. One extra feature was shown above, the special patterns BEGIN and END. Another feature is related to the built-in awk variable NR (number of records), the input line counter. The pattern NR == 5 will just print line 5. More complicated patterns using NR are possible, such as those in the following script. The 'hcut1' program prints lines numbered between 5 and 10.

```
$ cat hcut1
awk 'NR >= 5 && NR <= 10'
$ _
```

This version of the program relies on a logical expression to determine which lines are output. It is also possible to use more of an ed style of pattern. The ed command 5,10 prints lines 5 through 10. The awk analog of this is the following.

```
$ cat hcut2
awk 'NR == 5, NR == 10'
$ _
```

In this example, the awk program consists of a single pattern without an action, meaning the input will be printed for every line matched by the pattern. The pattern in this example contains two logical expressions separated by a comma. The comma is critical; it means execute the action for every line from the first line matched by the first expression, until the first line matched by the second expression. The first line matched by the pattern is line 5 and the last is 10, so the range of lines from 5 to 10 is printed.

Obviously this program is much too specialized. It would be more useful if it accepted a command line specification of which lines to print. This requirement leads directly into confusing territory; the shell uses the notation $1 to indicate the first positional parameter, and awk uses the same symbol to refer to the first word on the current input line. If we are to supply input parameters to 'hcut', we need to let the shell perform its parameter substitution. One way to do this is to leave the shell positional parameters outside the protection of the single quotes. I have arbitrarily decided that if no line numbers are supplied as parameters, the entire input should be printed, and if just one line number is supplied, then just that line should be printed.

```
$ cat hcut3
case $# in
        0) first=1 ; last=1000000000 ;;
        1) first=$1 ; last=$1 ;;
        2) first=$1 ; last=$2 ;;
esac
awk 'NR == '$first', NR == '$last
$ cat numtree
1
22
333
4444
55555
666666
$ hcut3 3 4 < numtree
333
4444
```

```
$ cat aas
a
bb
ccc
dd
e
$ hcut3 3 < aas
ccc
$ _
```

Remember that the built-in shell variable $# is the number of parameters that have been supplied to the script. This shell script gets its input from the standard input.

When a program is used once and then thrown away, anything that works is probably good enough. However, a program that is used more frequently needs more attention. hcut is a potentially useful program, but as written above it doesn't follow UNIX conventions. Wherever possible, programs (especially filters) should read their input either from the standard input or from named files. As written above, hcut doesn't do the latter. Also, program options are traditionally marked by placing a hyphen in front of the option key. The version of hcut shown above doesn't follow this convention. All these faults are remedied in the following version of hcut.

```
$ cat hcut4
first=1
last=1000000000
files=""
setfirst=no
for i
do
        case $i in
        -[0-9]*)
                if [ $setfirst = yes ]
                then
                        last=`echo $i | sed s/.//`
                else
                        first=`echo $i | sed s/.//`
                        setfirst=yes
                fi ;;
        *) files="$files $i" ;;
        esac
done
awk 'NR == '$first', NR == '$last $files
```

```
$ time hcut4 -3 -5 /etc/ttys
13tty01
16tty02
16tty03
        4.6 real        0.8 user        1.4 sys
$ _
```

Notice that the `awk` command line is passed a list of files in the `$files` shell variable. If this list is empty, `awk` will read from the standard input.

Although this version of `hcut` has the interface common to all UNIX tools, it has become too slow. In some programs the overhead of calling the stream editor to delete the leading hyphen from a single argument might be acceptable, but in `hcut` it is too much.

Here is an alternate version. It is more subtle than the version shown above, because `awk` is used to process the flag arguments instead of `sed`. Since `awk` is being called anyway, the additional overhead is low. In the shell case statement, the arguments representing line numbers (e.g., -5) are left alone. When these strings are passed to the `awk` script, they look like negative numbers. Hence the extra minus signs in the `awk` script, which turn them back into positive quantities.

```
$ cat hcut5
first=-1
last=-1000000000
files=""
donefirst=no
for i
do
        case $i in
        -[0-9]*)
                if [ $donefirst = yes ]
                then
                        last=$i
                else
                        first=$i
                        donefirst=yes
                fi ;;
        *) files="$files $i" ;;
        esac
done
awk 'BEGIN { start = - '$first' ; stop = - '$last' }
    NR == start, NR == stop' $files
```

```
$ time hcut5 -3 -5 /etc/ttys
13tty01
16tty02
16tty03
        2.4 real          0.7 user          0.8 sys
$ _
```

The decrease in elapsed time from 4.6 seconds to 2.4 seconds is significant, so when you are using awk anyway, you may want it to do double duty processing the arguments.

13.2   FLOW OF CONTROL STATEMENTS

The awk scripts shown above exhibit some intelligence, but much more powerful scripts are possible using awk's flow of control primitives. Like many common programming languages, awk has if statements, while loops, and for loops. As in C, curly braces can be used to group statements together.

The test expression in an if statement and the limit expressions in a while or for loop are formed using relational operators. awk has the usual assortment: >, >=, <, <=, ==, and !=. These comparison operators perform a numeric test if the data items are obviously numeric, and a string comparison otherwise. awk also has operators for comparing fixed strings with regular expressions: ~ and !~. The ~ operator succeeds if a string matches the given regular expression; !~ succeeds when a regular expression pattern match fails. The relational operators can be combined using && (and) and || (or), and parentheses can be used for grouping. (See Section 13.4.)

Here is a simple example that uses the if statement. It comes from a computer graphics system for making line drawings. In this system a line drawing consists of just two elements: lines and points. The lines can be visible or dark; thus one would draw a dashed line by alternating dark and visible segments. In the display file, dark vectors are represented by x, y, z coordinates followed by a zero; visible vectors contain x, y, z coordinates followed by a 1; and points are represented by x, y, z coordinates followed by a 2. The coordinates are the end points of the vectors. The starting point of each is the end point of the previous vector, with the starting point of the first vector assumed to be zero. When paper copies are made of these line drawings, the points are often much harder to see than on the interactive display; thus it became necessary to convert point commands in the display list into something more visible. Here is a simple awk program that converts all of the point commands in a display list into vector commands to draw a triangle centered at the point's location.

```
$ cat tri.awk
awk '
            {
                    if ($4 != "2")
                            print $0
                    else {
                          print $1, $2+12, $3, "0"
                          print $1+10, $2-6, $3, "1"
                          print $1-10, $2-6, $3, "1"
                          print $1, $2+12, $3, "1"
                          print $1, $2, $3, "0"
                    }
            }' $*
$ cat sdata
200 200 18 0
200 -200 18 1
-100 -200 18 1
-100 200 18 1
200 200 18 1
50 0 18 2
$ tri.awk sdata
200 200 18 0
200 -200 18 1
-100 -200 18 1
-100 200 18 1
200 200 18 1
50 12 18 0
60 -6 18 1
40 -6 18 1
50 12 18 1
50 0 18 0
$ _
```

Notice that the four statements in the else part of the if are enclosed in braces so that they are executed as a group.

A while loop executes as long as the given condition is satisfied. The following example produces a line-by-line average of a file. The program adds all of the numbers on a line and prints their average. (NF is an awk built-in variable whose value is the number of fields in the current line. See Section 13.4.)

```
$ cat aveline
awk '
            {
                if (NF > 0) {
                    sum = 0
                    n = 1
                    while (n <= NF) {
                        sum = sum + $n
                        n = n + 1
                    }
                    print sum/NF
                }
                else
                    print
        }' $*
$ cat hits
11 3 44 10
13 -7
20 30

18 -18
$ aveline hits
17
3
25

0
$ _
```

There are two types of for loops in awk. In this section I will discuss the
more traditional form, and in the following section I will discuss the for
loop that sequences through the indices of an associative array.

A traditional for loop steps an index through a predictable sequence of
values. Usually there are three separate conditions that must be specified:
the starting value, the final value, and the increment. awk for loops follow
the mysterious syntax pioneered by C. The word for is followed by three
expressions: the first initializes the control variable, the second is a test
whose failure signals the end of the loop, and the third is an expression that
is performed at the end of each trip through the loop. The expressions are
separated by semicolons, and any or all may be absent. Any introductory
book on C can provide more information on the first form of awk for
loops—they are the same as C for loops.

Here is an awk program that uses a for loop to print a table of the first
10 values of 'N!' (N factorial). Unlike the previous awk programs, this one
doesn't read any input. The special BEGIN pattern takes over before any
input is read, and the exit statement at the end terminates the program.

Thus awk is more than a programmable filter; it is a rudimentary stand-alone programming language.

```
$ cat nfact
awk '
BEGIN {
                prev=1
                print "n  nfact"
                for(i=1; i<=10; i++) {
                        fact = i * prev
                        prev = fact
                        print i, fact
                }
                exit
        }'
$ nfact
n  nfact
1 1
2 2
3 6
4 24
5 120
6 720
7 5040
8 40320
9 362880
10 3628800
$ _
```

The i++ expression in the for loop increments i by 1. It is discussed in Section 13.4.

The break and continue statements are used to alter the operation of awk's looping statements. When break is encountered, the immediately enclosing for or while is terminated, and control resumes at the statement following the loop. When the continue statement is encountered, it causes the next iteration of the loop to start immediately. The effect of continue is that the part of the loop below the continue statement is skipped.

awk's final control flow primitive is next. When next is encountered the next input line is read in, and execution resumes at the first action whose pattern matches the input.

13.3   ARRAYS

Like most programming languages, awk has *arrays*. An array is a list. The list as a whole has a name, and individual elements of the list are accessed using an index. In a traditional programming language, such as C, the indices of an array are numbers. For example, if X is an array of three elements, in C those elements would be X[0], X[1], and X[2]. awk is more flexible; the indices of an array can be any awk data type, including strings. Thus an awk array named scores might have the elements scores["mary"], scores["rich"], scores["redteam"] and scores["champ"]. (The quotes are necessary if your intent is to use constants as the array indices; scores[mary] will evaluate the variable named *mary* and then refer to that item in the scores array.)

Another convenience of awk arrays is that the array elements are created as necessary, while the awk script executes. You don't have to tell awk how big an array you want or what indices you plan to use. Instead, the whole business is taken care of as you actually use the elements of an array. Each time you refer to an array element, it is created, if it doesn't already exist. However, sometimes you need to make sure that awk knows that a given variable is an array.

Here is an example program that removes duplicate or blank lines from a text file. Each time the program reads a line from the file, it compares that line with all of the lines it has read previously. If the line hasn't been encountered before, it is added to the list and then output. If the line has been previously encountered, it is skipped, and the next input line is examined. This filter is a more powerful form of the standard uniq utility, which will remove duplicate lines only if they are adjacent. The drawback of rmdups is that it can only handle files small enough to fit in memory, because eventually the entire input is stored in the awk array. (uniq will handle any size of input file.) Many current UNIX machines support virtual memory, and on those machines rmdups can handle multimegabyte files, if only very slowly.

```
$ cat rmdups
awk '{
     found = 0
     for ( i=1; i<=NR; i++ )
          if ( lines[i] == $0) {
               found = 1
               break
          }
     if ( found != 1 ) {
          lines[NR] = $0
          print
          }
     }' $*
```

```
$ cat dups
Now is
the
time for men and women of
the
principle to unite.
$ rmdups dups
Now is
the
time for men and women of
principle to unite.
$ _
```

Notice that the `lines` array has many holes. There are as many elements in the array as there are lines in the input file, but there are only as many filled elements as there are lines in the output file. For each discarded line, there is an empty element in the `lines` array.

`awk` has a special form of the `for` statement that is used to examine all of the elements of an array. If you have an array such as that in the previous example where the indices are a numeric sequence, then you can use the usual (C-like) form of the `for` statement to examine the entire array. However, when your indices are more eclectic, the alternative form of the `for` statement is useful. The syntax is

```
for ( var in arrayname )
```

The *var* will take on the value of each of the indices in the named array. The order in which the indices will appear is completely arbitrary. The `for` loop in the `rmdups` program shown above could have been replaced with the statement

```
for ( i in lines )
```

and the operation of the program would have been unchanged. (However, in this case, `awk` would need to be warned that `lines` was an array, by including a `BEGIN` pattern whose action simply stuck an empty string into an element of the `lines` array.)

Here is an `awk` script that prints a list of how many times each person is logged on. This script derives its basic input from the `who` command, and an array called `logins` keeps track of how many times each person is logged on. This script relies on the fact that when an array element is created, it is automatically set to zero if it is used in a numeric context. The indices of the `logins` array are the names of the people who are logged in. (The script also uses `awk`'s `print` function, which will be discussed in Section 13.4.)

```
$ cat nlogins
who | awk '{
      logins[$1] = logins[$1] + 1
      }
END   {
      for (i in logins)
      print logins[i], i
      }'
$ nlogins
1 tom
3 dan
1 melissa
1 barbara
2 julie
$ _
```

When the data have been tabulated, the END pattern's action prints the results, in an unpredictable order. If you want a predictable order, you can pipe the output to sort.

It is possible to construct multidimensional arrays in awk by using string concatenation. For example, 5 "." 8 concatenates a 5, a period, and an 8, forming the string 5.8. Such a string is a valid awk array index. Here is an example that uses two-dimensional arrays. The task is to reverse the rows and columns of a matrix.

```
$ cat rev.awk
awk '{
      for(i=1; i<=NF; i++)
            x[NR "." i] = $i
      if (NFIELDS < NF)
            NFIELDS = NF
      }
END  {
      for(i=1;i<=NFIELDS;i++) {
            line = ""
            for(j=1;j<=NR;j++)
                  line = line " " x[j "." i]
            print line
            }
      }'
```

```
$ cat data
92 18 17
28 09 13
47 43 18
$ rev.awk < data
 92 28 47
 18 09 43
 17 13 18
$ _
```

If you find this program confusing, add the line

```
for(i in x) print i, x[i]
```

to the END pattern to see the subscripts and values of the x array.

13.4   OPERATORS, FUNCTIONS, AND BUILT-IN VARIABLES

awk has *operators* for mathematical operations, comparisons, logical operations, and assignments. The precedence of an operator dictates which operation should be performed first, given a choice. For example, the expression 5 + 2 * 3 should be interpreted as "multiply 2 by 3, and then add 5 to the result," because multiplication customarily has precedence over addition. You can use parentheses to alter the normal order of operations. The following list of awk's operators is in order of decreasing precedence.

++ --   The autoincrement and autodecrement operators are a shorthand for adding 1 to (or subtracting 1 from) a numeric variable. Thus the expression x = x-1 is equivalent to x--. To a person used to the C language, this shorthand is clear and concise, but persons used to other languages may find it peculiar.

* / %   These conventional operators signal the operations multiplication, division, and remainder.

+ -   Addition and subtraction. Note that awk has three classes of arithmetic operators, all having higher precedence than awk's other operators.

nothing
When two strings appear side by side, without any separator other than white space, they are concatentated. That's why the statement print 1 2 3 will produce 123 whereas the statement print 1, 2, 3 will produce 1 2 3. Because of the precedence of arithmetic over string concatenation, the statement print 1+1 3 will print 23.

> >= < <= == != ˜ !˜

> These relational operators compare strings or numbers, which-ever is appropriate. The two tilde operators are used to compare a string with a regular expression. The regular expression must be delimited by a pair of slashes. The logical expression $1 == /.ones/ will succeed only if the first field is a slash followed by a period, followed by "ones", followed by a slash. However, the logical expression $1 ˜ /.ones/ will succeed whenever the first field is "Jones" or "jones" or "tones", etc.

!   The exclamation point complements the value of an expression.

&&   A pair of ampersands denotes the logical AND operation.

|| A pair of vertical bars denotes the logical OR operation.

= += -= *= /= %=

> These assignment operators take the value to their right and assign it to the variable on their left. The *op*= forms of the assignment statement are equivalent to *var = var op (expr)*. Thus, the expression x += 10 is equivalent to x = x + 10. The *op*= notation is a gift from C; while C cognoscenti may appreciate its brevity, others often find the compactness too extreme.

awk has several *built-in variables*. We have already encountered NF, the number of fields in a record, and NR, the number of records encountered. Here is a complete list of awk's built-in variables.

FILENAME
> The name of the current file.

NF   The total number of fields in the current input record.

NR   The number of input records that have been encountered. This total is cumulative across multiple files. You can reset NR each time a new file is encountered using the following awk code.

```
FILENAME != prev {
      NR = 1
      prev= FILENAME
      }
```

FS   The input field separator character. The default is white space (a space or a tab). Other common choices are commas, colons, and semicolons. You can assign a value to FS to change the field separator in your awk script, or you can use the -Fc command line argument to set FS to c. If you change FS, you can only set the separator to a single character.

RS   The input record separator. The default is a new line. You can assign any single character to RS in an awk script, although it

cannot be set with a command line option. As a special dispensa-
tion, if RS is empty, a blank line will be used as the record separator.

OFS   The output field separator. The default is a space. The output
field separator is placed after each field printed by the print statement. For example, print a, b will print the value of a followed
by the OFS character followed by the value of b. If the input is
simply echoed, or printed by print $0, then the original FS will be
preserved.

ORS   The output record separator. The default is a new line. It works
the same as OFS.

OFMT   The output format for numbers. The default is %g, which will
print most numbers reasonably. You can change OFMT to any of
the numeric format specifications recognized by the printf subroutine. OFMT applies to numbers printed by the print statement,
not to numbers printed by the printf statement.

awk contains *functions* for performing arithmetic and for managing text
strings. These functions can be used in expressions almost as if they were
variables. In the following descriptions, s is a string-valued argument, and
n is a numeric argument. The function arguments can be constants, variables, or functions.

exp(n)
The exp function calculates the exponential of its argument. Here is
an awk script that prints a small table of the powers of *e*.

```
$ cat exp.awk
awk '
BEGIN  {
        print "i e**i"
        for(i=0;i<10;i++)
               print i, exp(i)
        exit
        }'
```

```
$ exp.awk
i e**i
0 1
1 2.71828
2 7.38906
3 20.0855
4 54.5981
5 148.413
6 403.429
7 1096.63
8 2980.96
9 8103.08
$ _
```

getline

The getline function reads in the next line in the input. Its return value is 0 for end of file and 1 for success. Following a successful getline, the built-in variables NR and NF reflect the latest line of input, and the execution resumes at the statement following getline.

index(s1,s2)

The index function is used to search the s1 string for an occurrence of the s2 string. If s2 is found, its location is returned. If it is not found the value 0 is returned.

```
$ cat index.awk
awk 'BEGIN {
      print "substr", "sub", index("substr", "sub")
      print "sub", "substr", index("sub", "substr")
      print "substr", "str", index("substr", "str")
      exit
      }'
$ index.awk
substr sub 1
sub substr 0
substr str 4
$ _
```

int(n)

The int function returns the integer part of its argument.

length(s)

The length function returns the length of string s.

log(n)

The log function returns the natural logarithm of its argument.

split(s,array,sep)

The split functions divides the string s into fields. Each field will be placed into elements of the array, using the indices 1, 2, etc. If the sep parameter (which must be a single character) is supplied, it is used as the input field separator, instead of using the default FS. This function is useful when you want to separate an input into fields based on several different criteria, when you want to access subfields, etc. Here is a very simple example.

```
$ cat split.awk
awk 'BEGIN {
        v = "This:is:a split demo"
        n = split(v,words,":")
        for(i=1; i<=n; i++)
                print i, words[i]
        exit
        }'
$ split.awk
1 This
2 is
3 a split demo
$ _
```

sprintf(f,arg1,arg2,...)

The sprintf function returns a string formatted according to its arguments. The format string f follows the conventions of the C language printf statement. (See below for a discussion of printf.)

sqrt(n)

The sqrt function returns the square root of its argument.

substr(s,n1,n2)

The substr function is used to extract a string from s. The extraction starts at position n1 and continues to position n2. If n2 isn't given, then the extraction continues to the end of s.

The print statement has several options that let you control the destination of the output. Ordinarily the output from the print statement is directed to the standard output. However, the output can be directed into a named file using a notation similar to the shell's output redirection syntax. The statement print hello > "tmp" will output the word hello into the file named 'tmp'. Note the use of the quotes around the filename. Without them, awk would interpret tmp as a variable, and use its value as the filename.

Here is an awk script that is a blend of UNIX's col and split commands. It takes each column of the input file and writes it to a separate output file. If the input is in a file named 'data', column 1 is output to 'data.1', column 2 is output to 'data.2', etc. A production version of 'col.awk' would allow you to specify the field separator character. This version uses the awk default.

```
$ cat col.awk
awk '{
     for(i=1; i<=NF; i++)
           print $i > FILENAME "." i
     }' $*
$ cat data
1 2 3
4 5 6
7 8 9
10 11 12
$ col.awk data
$ ls data.?
data.1    data.2    data.3
$ cat data.2
2
5
8
11
$ _
```

Other output selection choices are **>>** to append output to a file, and **|** to pipe output to a UNIX process.

awk contains a `printf` statement that is usually used when the standard print statement doesn't provide adequate control of the output format. awk's `printf`, like the C language `printf`, has a format string as the first argument. The remaining arguments are printed according to the instructions in the format string. For example, the following `printf` statement specifies that the variables x and y should be printed in decimal format and that the variable named count should be printed as a string.

```
printf "x %d, y %d %s\n", x, y, count
```

You should examine the description of the `printf` subroutine in the UNIX manual for more information about the format string.

CHAPTER 14

Sed

sed is a noninteractive text editor. It is a good way to perform routine modifications of text files, provided that the modifications can be keyed to textual contents in the files and that the operations can be done while reading forward through the file. For example, sed can delete all lines that contain a given text pattern, replace one pattern with another on certain lines, read one file into another at certain places, or disseminate parts of the input file to output files. sed cannot perform chores such as adding a column of figures in a file, performing sophisticated file reformatting, or storing parts of a file for later use. Those more sophisticated operations are ideal chores for awk, which is more programmable than sed.

sed is similar to ed, but with a twist: it is designed to be controlled by a script, rather than by a person. This difference in philosophy has led to a difference in how sed operates internally. Whereas ed may course through the edit buffer each time a command is entered, sed browses through the command script each time a new line is read from the text input.

There are a few simple concepts that must be mastered to use sed. sed operates *cyclically*. A cycle usually consists of (1) reading a line of input into the pattern space, (2) executing the edit script, which may possibly alter the contents of the pattern space, and (3) copying the pattern space to the output. Note that this is simply the usual cycle; some of the commands in the edit script can produce alternate cycles.

sed, like ed, has an *edit* buffer to hold the text that is being edited. The difference is that the sed edit buffer, called the *pattern space*, typically contains just one line of text, whereas the ed edit buffer contains the entire file. Although there are sed commands that let you stuff more than a single line into the pattern space, conceptually it is a single line buffer that can hold lines containing embedded newlines.

Besides the pattern space, sed contains a *hold* buffer. Several commands exist to swap text back and forth between the pattern space and the hold buffer.

sed accepts the following command line options:

-n Don't output the pattern space at the end of each cycle. When -n is given, output is produced only when one of the print commands is encountered.

-e *script*

The -e argument specifies that the following argument is an editing script. Multiple editing scripts may be specified on a single command line. You can omit the -e flag if there is just a single script specified on the command line, and no scripts in auxiliary files.

-f *scriptfile*

The -f arguments specifies that the following argument is the name of a file that contains an editing script.

sed must be supplied with a script, either on the command line or in a file.

sed addresses lines in the style of ed. An address may be

n An absolute line number *n*. The line counter is not reset each time a new file is processed. Thus if the first file has 20 lines, line 21 is the first line of the second file.

$ The last line of the input.

/*pat*/

A context address matches any line containing the *pat* regular expression. ed style regular expressions are allowed: . will match any single character except a terminal new-line, ^ will match the beginning of the pattern space, $ will match the end of the pattern space, [*abc*] will match any one of the enclosed characters, * will match 0 or more repetitions of the previous single-character regular expression, and anything else will match itself. In sed the \n expression will match a new line embedded in the pattern space.

One of the hardest aspects of sed for experienced ed users is the following. ed-style *relative* addresses, such as +++ or /sam/-- are not allowed. This limitation results from sed's forward-only journey through a file. Relative addresses sometimes need to back up. sed also doesn't allow the character . to name the current line.

Most sed commands accept zero, one, or two addresses. Zero addresses means perform the command on every line, one address means perform the command on all lines that match that address, and two addresses means perform the command on that range of lines. If the second address is less than the first, then the command is performed only on the first line.

Any command may be preceded by a ! so that the command will be executed on lines that don't match the given address. You can surround a group of commands with {} to make them executed as a group. The syntax is one or two addresses followed by the { command, then commands on the following lines, and then a final } to delimit the end of the group.

The following example reads the command script from the terminal.

```
$ sed -n -f /dev/tty /usr/dict/words
3000p
6000p
9000p
12000p
15000p
18000p
21000p
24000p
^D
Brindisi
decreeing
Friday
irritant
Nassau
radioastronomy
Staunton
whosoever
$ _
```

14.1 TEXT MODIFICATION

sed's text modification commands resemble ed's. You can append, insert, or delete lines of text; change one group of lines to another; substitute one text pattern for another; or translate one group of characters into another.

addr a\

text\

text

> The append command places *text* on the output before the next input line is read. All but the last line of text must have a \ at the end to escape the following newline.

addr1,addr2 c\

text\

text\

The change command deletes each addressed pattern space, then out-puts the *text,* and then starts a new cycle. All but the last line of text must have a \ at the end to escape the following new line.

addr1,addr2 d

The delete command deletes the pattern space and then starts a new cycle.

addr1,addr2 D

The variant delete command deletes the initial segment of the pattern space, which extends from the beginning of the pattern space to the first new line, and then starts a new cycle. D is equivalent to d if the pattern space contains just one line.

addr i\

text\

text

The insert command immediately places *text* on the output. All but the last line of text must have a \ at the end of the line to escape the new line.

addr1,addr2 s/*expr*/*repl*/*f*

Substitute *repl* for *expr* on all of the addressed lines. The text of *expr* may contain regular expression characters: . will match any single character except a terminal new line, ˆ will match the beginning of the pattern space, $ will match the end of the pattern space, [*abc*] will match any one of the enclosed characters, * will match 0 or more rep-etitions of the previous single-character regular expression, and any-thing else will match itself. The flags *f* may be: g to make all possible substitutions on the line, rather than just the leftmost; p to print the pattern space if a substitution is made; and w *wfile* to append the pat-tern space to the named file.

addr1,addr2 y/*string1*/*string2*/

Translate each occurrence of a character in *string1* into the corre-sponding character from *string2*. *string1* and *string2* must be the same length.

Note that the append and insert commands allow only one address, whereas delete, change lines, substitute text patterns, and translate allow one or two addresses. You should also notice that the transfer and move commands from ed are not present in sed, because they might entail reverse motion through the file.

The following example shows simple usage of sed editing commands.

```
$ cat remind
Jan today at 4.
Call DEC
add serial line for Brad
Home at five sharp
$ cat script
s/DEC/Dept. Environ. Cons./
/Jan/s/today/tomorrow/
1i\
Werner and Raquel this weekend\
Feed polly for adam
4d
$ sed -f script remind
Werner and Raquel this weekend
Feed polly for adam
Jan tomorrow at 4.
Call Dept. Environ. Cons.
add serial line for Brad
$ sed -e /DEC/d -e s/five/four/ remind
Jan today at 4.
add serial line for Brad
Home at four sharp
$ _
```

14.2   CONTROL FLOW

sed has two kinds of control flow primitives. The more familiar is the branch, which changes the point of execution in the command script. Branches flow to a label, or to the end of the script. sed has unconditional branches, which always branch, and conditional branches, which branch if a substitution has been performed. sed's other form of control flow is changing the ordinary operation of the cycle, either by appending another line of input to the pattern space or by starting another cycle without completing the current cycle.

: *label*
> Make *label* a symbolic name for this location in the script.

addr1,addr2 b *label*
> Branch to the given label, or to the end of the script if *label* is absent.

addr1,addr2 n
> Write the pattern space to the output and then read in the next line of input. Note that the next line of the script to be executed will be the following line, not the first line of the script (which would be executed if a new cycle were executed).

addr1,addr2 **N**

Append the next line of input to the pattern space. The boundary between the previous end of the pattern space and the start of the newly added line will be marked with an embedded new line.

addr q

Quit writes the pattern space to the output, and then halts processing.

addr1,addr2 **t** *label*

Branch to the given *label* if any substitutions have been made since the last **t** or since the last input line. If *label* is missing, the branch will go to the end of the script.

The following script demonstrates some of the flow of control statements.

```
$ cat f1
.CX 3
.DS
Twas Sol and solstice
Ad and Astra
Til Hic saw Sum
In Corporate
.DE
$ cat script
/DS/b fail
/KS/b fail
/EQ/,/EN/p
b
: fail
s/.*/No displays allowed at start/p
q
$ sed -n -f script f1
No displays allowed at start
$ sed -e s/DS/EQ/ -e s/DE/EN/ -n -f script f1
.EQ
Twas Sol and solstice
Ad and Astra
Til Hic saw Sum
In Corporate
.EN
$ _
```

14.3 INPUT AND OUTPUT

The following commands let you control which parts of the input are printed and which parts are copied to other files.

addr1,addr2 p

Print the addressed lines. An explicit print command isn't suppressed by the -n command line flag, which only stops the default output at the end of each cycle.

addr1,addr2 P

Print the initial segment of the pattern space. (The initial segment is from the beginning to the first embedded new line.)

addr1,addr2 r *file*

Read the named *file* and place its contents on the output before reading the next input line. The entire file will be copied to the output each time this command is encountered.

addr1,addr2 w *file*

Append the pattern space to the named file. Each file mentioned in a w command is created before the script starts to execute, and there can be only 10 output files.

addr =

Print the line number on the standard output.

The following script prints the nth line of its input.

```
$ cat line_n
if [ $# -eq 0 ]
then
    echo usage: $0 n [ files ]
    exit -1
fi
n=$1
shift
case $n in
    [0-9] ) ;;
    [0-9][0-9]  ) ;;
    [0-9][0-9][0-9]  ) ;;
    [0-9][0-9][0-9][0-9] ) ;;
    [0-9][0-9][0-9][0-9][0-9] ) ;;
    *)  echo usage: $0 n [ files ]
        echo n must be a number
        exit -1
        ;;
esac
sed -n -e ${n}p $*
$ line_n 3 line_n
        echo usage: $0 n [ files ]
$ _
```

The sed command in this script will completely read all of its input, which might be undesirable when you print an early line of a long file. The script could be updated to make sed exit immediately after printing the desired line.

14.4   THE HOLD SPACE

sed's hold space is its only extra storage space. You can copy text from the hold space to the pattern space and back, but sed's severe storage constraint makes it difficult to write flexible editing scripts.

addr1,addr2 g
:   Load the pattern space with the contents of the hold space. The original contents of the pattern space are lost.

addr1,addr2 G
:   Append the hold space to the end of the pattern space.

addr1,addr2 h
:   Load the hold space with the contents of the pattern space. The original contents of the hold space are lost.

addr1,addr2 H
:   Append the pattern space to the end of the hold space.

addr1,addr2 x
:   Exchange the pattern space and the hold space.

The following script double-spaces a file by printing each input line, copying the empty hold space into the pattern space, and then printing the blank pattern space.

```
$ cat lines
10
20
30
$ sed -n -e 'p
> g
> p' lines
10

20

30

$ _
```

The following script shows a practical application of sed, a script to insert cross-reference numbers into documents. Managing cross-references is difficult when you are writing large documents, because document organization changes during the writing process. If you insert cross-reference numbers into your document early in the process, they will need to be changed if you reorganize your document. However, it's bad to delay too long, because you tend to forget exactly what should be cross-referenced. My solution is to create symbolic names as I write each section in a document and then use a sed filter during final document printing to replace the names with the correct references.

```
$ cat script
s/CUXBASIC/3/g
s/SCMDARGS/CSHONE.2/g
s/SMETA/CSHONE.8/g
s/CSHONE/4/g
$ cat doc
Chapter CUXBASIC covers the fundamental
features of the URC language. However two
important features -- arguments and meta-
arguments -- aren't discussed until
Section SCMDARGS and Section SMETA.
$ sed -f script doc
Chapter 3 covers the fundamental
features of the URC language. However two
important features -- arguments and meta-
arguments -- aren't discussed until
Section 4.2 and Section 4.8.
$ _
```

Notice that two substitutions are made to create section numbers. The first substitution replaces the section name with a chapter name and a section number, and then the second substitution replaces the chapter name with its number. This minimizes the changes to the script when entire chapters are moved.

A related tool allows me to find all of my cross-references that I have not yet inserted into the cross-reference script. It is a simple shell script that turns the input into a list of words, performs the substitutions in the cross-reference script, and then prints any word that contains three or more adjacent capital letters.

```
$ cat capsfind
deroff -w $* | \
sed -n -f sedscript -e '/[A-Z][A-Z][A-Z]/p' | \
sort -u
$ capsfind doc
URC
$ _
```

The output happens not to be a cross-reference; rather, it is a fully capitalized acronym. (`deroff -w` separates the input into words, and `sort -u` sorts and removes duplicates.)

CHAPTER 15

C and the UNIX System

The C programming language and the UNIX operating system are very closely associated. Over 90% of the UNIX kernel and the great majority of the UNIX utility programs are written in C. C is a middle-level programming language. It is much easier to use and much more productive than assembly language, yet it lacks many of the expensive facilities of very high level languages (e.g., Prolog).

C was developed by Dennis M. Ritchie in the early 1970s for work on the early versions of UNIX. C evolved directly from B, a language designed by Ken Thompson. The major difference between B and C is that B data types are limited to native machine words whereas C contains several basic data types: characters (or bytes); short, long, and native integers; and floating point numbers. The typing in C allows it to adjust to a variety of machines.

Ken Thompson's B evolved from BCPL, a systems programming language designed by Martin Richards. BCPL introduced many of the features for which C is famous, including the marriage of pointers and arrays and the terse style of expression. The evolution of BCPL into B into C has transformed a systems programming language into a general-purpose language. C occasionally is called a systems programming language, because it has been used very successfully for systems programming, but in fact C is a general-purpose language.

C is general purpose in part because it lacks many of the features that direct a language to a specific application. C lacks a built-in I/O subsystem, it lacks built-in support for database management, and it lacks dynamic facilities for storage management. When these facilities are needed, they are provided as external subroutines.

In a simple single-user computer system, application programs are either allowed or encouraged to access many computer resources directly. This is not possible in a multiuser computer system such as UNIX. In the UNIX system the *kernel* is responsible for supervising all data transfers between programs and I/O devices and files. *System* calls are the mechanism that programs use to access the services of the operating system. UNIX contains system calls to perform I/O, to work with certain status elements that the system maintains, and to create new processes.

This chapter discusses the interface between the C programming language and the UNIX operating system in a general manner that will be interesting to nonprogrammers who are curious about how programs interface with the system. It also provides a general introduction for programmers who want to become familiar with UNIX. This chapter is not an introduction to programming in C; very little knowledge of C is required to read this chapter. A more pragmatic approach to this material is in Chapter 16, which discusses how the UNIX shell is programmed.

The first section discusses subroutines, and the next few sections discuss some of the more interesting system calls. The final sections discuss the C compiler and a program called `lint`, which can be used to perform tests on a C program.

The result of a compilation of a C source program is an *object* file. An object file contains machine instructions that correspond to the original C source program as well as various other information that makes it possible to combine object files from several compilations to produce a file containing a complete program image that can be executed. In the UNIX system, an executable program image is often called a *binary*. Chapter 17 discusses several UNIX utilities for manipulating object files, profiling, and debugging.

UNIX system calls are documented in Section 2 of the UNIX manual, and the standard subroutines are documented in Section 3 of the manual.

15.1 STANDARD SUBROUTINES

Many features are omitted from the C programming language that are built into other languages. For example, C does not contain any built-in capacity for manipulating character strings. Instead, common string functions are provided in the standard subroutine library. Many people who are accustomed to higher-level programming languages (PL/1 or PASCAL) are surprised that you have to call a subroutine in C to compare two character strings. In PASCAL, you would use the statement

```
IF Str1 = 'Hello' THEN ....
```

to compare the variable "Str1" with the constant-string "Hello". The equivalent in C is

```
if (!strcmp(Str1,"Hello")) ....
```

The standard subroutine `strcmp` isn't built into C; rather, it is supplied in the C subroutine library.

The standard subroutines are used to provide string manipulation functions, common arithmetic functions, a variety of conversions from one representation of numbers to another, and a few common algorithms such as the quick sort. The object versions of the subroutines are stored in the standard subroutine library file 'libc.a' in the '/lib' directory. '/lib/libc.a' is usually searched by the C compiler so that programmers need not make special arrangements to use the standard subroutines.

One of the most interesting C subroutines is `printf`. `printf` is used to display text on the terminal. There are versions of the `printf` subroutine that will output to a file or to a character string. You can output a message in a program by using the subroutine call

```
printf("The world is not safe for democracy.\n");
```

The argument to `printf` in this case is a constant string. (The ''\n'' at the end of the string is C shorthand for a new-line character.) `printf` usually is used to output the value of variables or to print prompts. The first argument to `printf` is a *format* string, and the following arguments (if there are any) are variables or constants whose values are to be output. Normal characters in the format string are just copied to the output while the conversion specifiers in the format string cause one of the following arguments to be converted to a printable form and then output. The conversion specifiers consist of a percent symbol followed by one or more characters that detail the conversion. Using `printf` is much easier than describing it, so let me show some examples.

If x, y and z are integer variables, then their values can be printed in decimal format by using

```
printf("Values of x, y, and z: %d %d %d\n",x,y,z);
```

The `%d` conversion specifier in the format string indicates decimal output conversion of an integer.

If `Strptr` is a pointer to a character string, then the following will print the address of the string (in the octal radix) followed by the contents of the string:

```
printf("Address %o, Contents %s\n",Strptr,Strptr);
```

`Strptr` appears twice as an argument, because it is needed twice—once for the `%o` octal conversion and once for the `%s` string conversion.

When a programmer includes a standard subroutine in a program, the actual computer instructions for executing the subroutine are stored in the executable program file. Thus the size of the executable program depends somewhat on how many subroutines are included in the program. Some subroutines, such as `printf`, are notoriously large and consume a lot of space. However, since the subroutines are contained in the body of the executable program, there is very little time wasted in calling a standard subroutine.

15.2   INPUT/OUTPUT SYSTEM CALLS

Device independence is one of the most important ideas in the Unix system. It means that a program can access a disk file as easily as a terminal or a printer. Disk files and special I/O devices are accessed using a single set of system calls. I/O devices, like ordinary disk files, have names. For example, the name '/dev/lp' refers to a printer.

Even the exceptions to the idea of device independence are handled in a very straightforward manner. Obviously, you cannot randomly access a sequential device such as a terminal, so any attempts to do so will lead to an error. But an error is the correct response in contrast to many systems that do horrible things when a program attempts to manipulate an I/O device in an unexpected way.

From the point of view of a program performing I/O, all I/O system call requests are handled synchronously. A program requesting input is suspended from the point of making the request until the input has been completed. Writing operations are more complicated. When a program wants to transfer a few characters to a terminal, the program will be suspended from the time of making the request until the time the characters are accepted by the kernel and started on their journey. However, synchrony as practiced in Unix doesn't mean that the characters will have arrived at their destination by the time the program resumes execution; it just means that the characters have been swallowed by the Unix kernel and are at least about to start the journey. What synchrony does mean is that I/O requests almost certainly take awhile, and large requests take longer than small requests.

In addition to the system call mechanism for managing I/O, the Unix system also has the standard I/O library. The standard I/O library's main advantage is that it locally buffers I/O requests. Most I/O requests simply add a character to, or remove a character from, one of the standard I/O library's local buffers. The standard I/O library routines automatically fill (flush) the local input (output) buffers when they become empty (full). An example contrasting the standard I/O library with the system call mechanism appears in Section 15.6.

Each I/O connection that is available to a program is identified by a number known as a *file descriptor*. Most UNIX systems allow each program to have between 10 and 20 files open simultaneously. Remember that in UNIX a file can be either a disk file or a terminal or some other I/O device or even a connection to another program.

One UNIX process can create another by executing the fork system call. fork is discussed more in Sections 15.4, and 16.3, and 25.5. The process that executed the fork system call is called the parent, and the created process is called the child. One of the unusual and surprising features of UNIX is that child programs inherit the open files of their parents. Because most of the programs running on a typical UNIX system are direct offspring of the shell, the files it deliberately leaves open for its child processes are universally important. By convention the shell opens three files for the use of its offspring: the standard input, the standard output, and the standard error output.

The first connection that is available is identified by file descriptor zero, and it is usually called the *standard input*. The standard input is usually connected to your terminal's keyboard, although it can just as easily be connected to a disk file. The standard input is the usual source of interactive input to a program.

The second connection that is automatically opened by the shell is identified by file descriptor 1, and it is usually called the *standard output*. The standard output usually is connected to your terminal's screen, although it can also be redirected to a file. The standard output generally is used by programs for their main text output. For example, the ls command writes its list of files on the standard output.

The third connection, identified by file descriptor 2, is called the *standard error output*. It is usually connected to your terminal, and it is the channel that receives most error messages. It is sometimes used so that error messages are directed to a terminal when the main output of a program is directed elsewhere, and it is sometimes used so that error messages are collected in a disk file when programs are run from long shell command files.

If no alternative arrangements are made, then all three standard channels are connected to your terminal. If the shell command line contains a ">", then the standard output is redirected to some other file; if the command line contains a "<", then the standard input is redirected from some other file. The standard error connection can be redirected by using the "2>" notation in a Bourne shell command line.

The three standard connections can be used or ignored by an individual program. They are merely a convenience that allows the powerful I/O redirection facilities of UNIX. A program can write output to your terminal without regard to I/O redirection by opening the file associated with the terminal ('/dev/tty') and performing I/O.

The UNIX system calls for performing I/O include

open
>   Establish a connection with a file that already exists.

creat
>   Create a file and then establish a connection with that file.

pipe
>   Create a connection that can be used in a pipeline between two processes.

dup
>   Create another connection to a file that has at least one existing connection. This lets a process access files via specific file descriptor values.

fcntl
>   Perform any of several control operations on a file.

read
>   Read data from a file.

write
>   Write data into a file.

seek
>   Change the read/write location in a file.

close
>   Sever a connection with a file.

A file descriptor is returned when a program executes an open, create, pipe, or dup system call and by some operations involving the fcntl system call. The returned file descriptor then can be used to perform input and/or output operations on the file using read and write. The read and write system calls simply transfer data between data regions in the process and the file. Uₙₑₓ also includes routines for performing higher-level input and output (printf and scanf) and for performing locally buffered input and output (putchar and getchar). Any files that remain open when a program terminates are automatically closed.

Pipes are established between processes by using the pipe system call in conjunction with system calls for creating processes. This very interesting feature of the uₙₑₓ system is discussed in Section 15.4.

15.3   STATUS SYSTEM CALLS

Most operating systems have a host of features that must be controlled and monitored to fine-tune the performance of the system. Some examples are the priorities of executing programs, the privileges of programs, the protection attributes of files, the environment in which a program executes, and the mounting and unmounting of filesystems.

In many operating systems, the status items are controllable only from the system console via a hard-coded command interpreter. Since the UNIX system does not come with a hard-coded command interpreter, the only way to control and monitor these items is by using an ordinary program. Any executing program can request, for example, that its execution priority be increased or decreased. Any program can decrease its execution priority, but only programs run by the superuser can actually increase their priority. In UNIX, any program can request control of system status functions, but only certain program requests are honored by the kernel.

Controlling the access modes of a file is an example. In UNIX, a program can execute the chmod system call to control the modes (read, write, and execute for owner, group, and other; see Chapter 5) of a file. The following short C program uses the chmod system call to make the file named 'nopeeking' inaccessible (no privileges to anyone) until some future change in mode:

```
#define NOACCESS 0
main()
{
    chmod("nopeeking",NOACCESS);
}
```

The program will change the modes only when run by the owner of the file 'nopeeking' or by the superuser.

The UNIX system calls that control or monitor status items include

time
  Read the date.
stime
  Set the date.
getpid
  Determine the process identification number.
getuid
  Get the user identification number.
getgid
  Get the group identification number.
chown
  Change the ownership of a file.
chmod
  Change the mode of a file.
chdir
  Change the current working directory.
link
  Create a link to a file.

```
unlink
```
Remove a link to a file.
```
mount
```
Mount a filesystem.
```
umount
```
Unmount a filesystem.
```
nice
```
Change priority of a process.
```
stat
```
Get file status.

Several other status-related system calls exist on various versions of UNIX.

15.4 PROCESS CONTROL SYSTEM CALLS

One of the strengths of UNIX is its set of system calls for creating and coordinating processes. Most of these system calls would be superfluous in a system that allowed only one process at a time. The system calls for controlling processes are basic but effective. They include

```
fork
```
Create a new process, by duplicating the current process.
```
exec
```
Change the identity of a process, by overlaying it with a new process.
```
_exit
```
Terminate a process.
```
kill
```
Send a signal to a process.
```
signal
```
Specify an action that should be performed when a particular signal is received.
```
wait
```
Wait for the termination of a child process.
```
brk
```
Change the memory allocation for a process.

In many systems, it is possible to chain programs together so that one program follows another. The equivalent operation in the UNIX system is called an *exec,* and several versions of the exec system call are available for replacing the current process with a new process. The created process is called the *successor,* and the process that called exec is known as the *predecessor* (see Fig. 15.1).

UNIX would be a very weak system if exec were the only system call for creating a process. The exec system call doesn't increase the number of processes but merely replaces one process with another. To increase the number of processes in UNIX, you must use the fork system call. The fork system call creates a new process that is an exact copy of the calling process (except for a few parameters concerning the identity of the process such as the process identification number). The created process is called the *child,* and the process that called fork is called the *parent* (see Fig. 15.2). The parent process is not destroyed by the fork system call. Following the fork, both processes compete for system resources (e.g., execution time).

Probably the most common use of fork is to create a child process that immediately executes the exec system call. The effect of a fork followed in the child by an exec is for the parent process to create a child process with

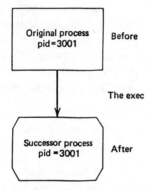

Figure 15.1.   The exec system call is used to change the identity of a process.

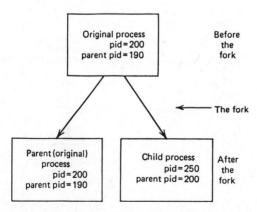

Figure 15.2.   The fork system call. The fork system call is used to duplicate a process. After the fork, the processes are identical except for a few key parameters that describe the process (*pid* is the process identification number).

a new identity (see Fig. 15.3). This is much more interesting than just creating a duplicate.

Often a child process is created to accomplish some specific task, and the parent wants to wait for the task to be completed before continuing. One obvious example is the shell that uses the `fork-exec` pair to execute almost all of the commands you enter. (A few commands are handled internally by the shell.) Unless you follow a command with the ampersand character (to specify background execution), the shell (parent) executes the `wait` system call to wait for the completion (death) of the child process. (This is discussed more in Chapter 16.)

The `kill` system call is used to send signals from one process to another. (Most agree that the name "kill" is poorly chosen.) A signal is a mutually agreed upon value that communicates some piece of information from one process to another. One of the common uses of the `kill` system call is to send the SIGKILL signal to a process. A process that receives SIGKILL terminates itself. About a dozen other standard signals are used in the UNIX system.

Since only one process is actually running at a given instant in time, it is a sure bet that the target process of the `kill` system call is suspended (or occasionally nonexistent). The signal sent by the `kill` system call doesn't

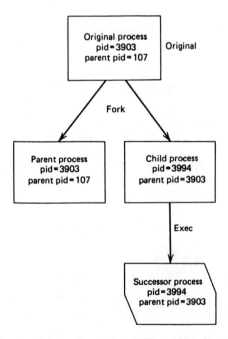

Figure 15.3. Creating a child process with a different identity. In the UNIX system a `fork` often is followed by an `exec` in the child to create a new process with a different identity. This technique is used by the shell to execute your commands.

take effect until the target process is activated. Whenever a process starts executing after a suspension, the kernel automatically checks a list of signals to see if any signals have arrived. If there have been arrivals, then appropriate action is taken. For example, the appropriate action to take following the arrival of the SIGKILL signal is to execute the _exit system call. The system call named signal is used to specify the action that should be taken if a given signal arrives. Taken together the kill-signal pair of system calls allows a simple yet powerful interprocess communication system.

One insidious consequence of the fact that processes respond to signals only when they awake is that processes that are endlessly waiting for something can't be killed. Such processes are common in UNIX systems with buggy device drivers. Although they cause no harm individually, a large accumulation of endlessly waiting processes usually spells doom for the system, because the kernel's process table eventually fills up.

UNIX also includes the _exit system call, which causes the demise of the calling process. _exit is called automatically in response to a variety of signals and at the end of the main module in a C program. The _exit call can be used explicitly anywhere in a program, and it automatically closes all of the process's open files. Although _exit is universally available, most programs actually call the exit subroutine, which performs standard clean-up operations (such as flushing I/O buffers) and then calls _exit.

Let's conclude our discussion of the process control system calls with a discussion of pipes. Pipes are connections between related processes. The first stage in creating a pipe is for a process to execute the pipe system call. Two file descriptors are returned—one for reading and one for writing. Next the process forks to create two processes, and usually the child process execs to change its identity. Throughout forks and execs, the open files established by the pipe system call remain open. After the forking and execing, one of the processes uses the read descriptor, and the other uses the write descriptor (see Fig. 15.4.). Both processes close their unused pipe file descriptor. When the shell establishes a pipe connection between two processes, the shell arranges for the pipe descriptors to have the values zero and 1, which are customarily associated with the standard input and the standard output.

15.5 PASSING ARGUMENTS TO PROGRAMS

An *argument* is information that you specify on a command line to pass additional information to a command. For example, when you enter the command

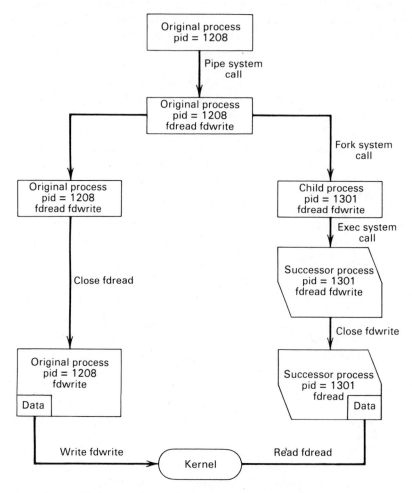

Figure 15.4.   Creating a pipe connection between two processes.

```
$ cc myprog.c
$ _
```

the word "myprog.c" is an argument that tells the C compiler to compile the code contained in the file 'myprog.c'. This section discusses the mechanism that is used in UNIX to pass command line arguments to programs.

One of the most valuable features of UNIX is that arguments for a program can be placed right on the command line. Passing arguments to programs on a command line is not unique to the UNIX system. However, UNIX is unique in the amount of processing done by the shell to generate the arguments, and the arguments are especially easy to use in UNIX. The next few paragraphs discuss how the arguments are actually passed, and then the last few paragraphs in this section present an example of a C program accessing command line arguments.

In the discussion here, we ignore all of the work done by the shell or some other program to generate a list of arguments to be passed to a command. In Section 11.14 we discussed filename generation, parameter substitution, and command substitution. The net effect of all of these chores is the generation of a list of words to be passed to a command.

Let's start this discussion at the point where some program (typically the shell) has an array of character strings (the arguments) and the name of a program to be executed using the **exec** system call. As usual in these matters, the program forks once to create a new process, and then the child process prepares to perform the exec.

Several versions of the **exec** system call allow an array of character strings to be passed to a program. When the **exec** system call containing the array of arguments is executed, the kernel of the operating system acquires the array of arguments from the calling program. Then the successor program is loaded into memory (remember that the calling program is overlaid in a successful exec), and the array of arguments is placed in the memory space of the successor program. (See Fig. 15.5.)

Two parameters are made available to the program—a *count* of the arguments and a *pointer to an array of pointers* to the arguments. The two parameters, like all parameters for C routines, are on the stack, and the actual arguments are in high memory. Be careful not to confuse parameters, which are values that are available for routines, with arguments, which are character strings that are passed to a program.

Once all of this is complete, the program starts to run. It might seem strange to use just two parameters to access virtually any number of command line arguments. The advantage of using two parameters is uniformity; the program doesn't have to know in advance how many arguments it may receive. The main routine of a program has to declare the two parameters. The first is an integer, and the second is a pointer to an array of character strings. Here is a short program that prints out its arguments one on a line:

```
main(argc,argv)/* echo arguments one per line */
int argc;
char *argv[];
{
        int i;
        for(i=0; i<argc; i++)
                printf("%s\n", argv[i]);
}
```

C language programmers will recognize this as a program that prints an array of character strings. If you don't know C, then don't worry about

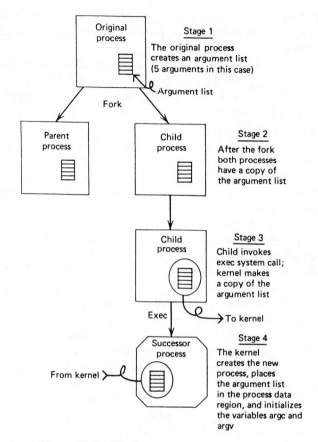

Figure 15.5.   Passing arguments to a program.

the exact syntax of the program. This program is stored in the file 'showargs.c'.

```
$ cc -o showargs showargs.c
$ showargs one two three
showargs
one
two
three
$ showargs
showargs
$ _
```

The compile command shown compiles 'showargs.c' and places the execut-able output in the file 'showargs'. You should notice that the name of the program is always printed before the "true" arguments. This is because the name of a program is considered to be argument number zero. Notice therefore that argc is always at least 1. If you wanted to print only the arguments other than the name of the program, you would have to change the for loop to start at 1 instead of zero.

The two parameters are often named argc (argument count) and argv (argument vector), although these names are strictly optional. The argv parameter is often declared equivalently

```
char **argv;
```

(C experts can explain to you why this is equivalent.) The order of the declarations is important; the argument count must be first.

15.6   THE IMPLEMENTATION OF SYSTEM CALLS

The UNIX call interface has been designed to appear the same as the subroutine interface. Parameters may be passed to a system call and a value can be returned. The basic difference is that the code that is executed during a subroutine is linked into the executable program module, whereas the bulk of the code that is executed during a system call resides in the kernel address space (rather than in the program's address space). Therefore, adding a new system call to a program will have little effect on the size of the program, but adding a new subroutine to a program may increase the size of the program by thousands of bytes.

There is very little time wasted in calling a subroutine. However, executing a system call is a time-consuming process. System calls on many versions of the UNIX system work by means of a *trap* instruction. A trap is an instruction whose effect is somewhat similar to that of a hardware interrupt. The trap leads to a time-consuming change in context, and it often causes the calling process to be suspended or even swapped out.

The bottom line is that system calls are time-consuming and they should be used sparingly. Probably the biggest waste of time occurs when large numbers of bytes are read or written using single-byte transfers. For example, the following simple program counts the number of blanks in a file using single-character read operations:

```
/* count blanks in a file reading char by char */
main(argc,argv)
int argc;
char *argv[];
{
        int fd;
        int count = 0;
        char c;
        if (argc == 1)
                fd = 0;/* stdin */
        else
                fd = open(argv[1], 0);
        if (fd < 0)
                { printf("Cannot open %s.\n", argv[1]); exit(1); }
        while(read(fd, &c, 1) == 1)
                if (c == ' ')
                        count++;
        printf("There are %d blanks in %s.\n", count, argv[1]);

}
```

Written this way, the program executes the read system call to read each character. When I ran the program to count the number of blanks in a file containing about 20,000 characters, it took an average of 33 seconds to run on a lightly loaded PDP 11/70. About 95% of the time was spent executing the 20,000 system calls. If this program were needed only once, then it might be considered acceptable. However, UNIX includes buffered I/O, which is much better for this application. Using the standard buffered I/O routine get in place of read results in the following program:

```
#include <stdio.h>
main(argc,argv) /* count blanks using buffered I/O */
int argc;
char *argv[];
{
        FILE *finp;
        int count = 0;
        int c;
        if (argc == 1)
                finp = stdin;   /* stdin */
        else
                finp = fopen(argv[1], "r");
        if (finp == NULL)
                { printf("Cannot open %s.\n", argv[1]); exit(1); }
        while((c = getc(finp)) != EOF)
                if (c == ' ')
                        count++;
        printf("There are %d blanks in %s.\n", count, argv[1]);

}
```

This version is slightly more complicated, because it uses the standard buffered input package. (See the descriptions of fopen and getc in Section 3 of the UNIX system manual.) However, the slight increase in coding is more than offset by the enormous increase in speed. When this version was run, it required about one second, and it spent only one-third of its time executing system calls. The difference is that this second version executes only about 40 system calls to scan a 20,000-character file.

UNIX does buffer files at the system level, so there is no unreasonable penalty for reading files conveniently, but there is no excuse for needlessly reading or writing large quantities of input a byte at a time using a system call rather than a buffered input or output routine.

15.7 SEPARATE COMPILATION

The C language is designed so that the source code for an entire program can be dispersed into separate files. Placing the source code in separate files is intended to encourage modular design, development, and debugging. Small programs (up to a few hundred lines of code) such as the the echo program or the blank count program shown earlier in this chapter can be stored easily in a single file. Larger programs (several hundred lines and up) are usually stored in multiple files.

A file containing just a few subroutines (typically a few hundred lines of code) is much easier to understand and work on than a massive file containing thousands of lines of code. A program contained in a single file can be partitioned into several files by collecting groups of subroutines or data structures and placing the groups into the separate files. A single logical entity such as a subroutine or a data declaration cannot be split into two files.

Separating a program into several files introduces several new problems. One problem is the need for the subroutines in one file to know about the subroutines and data declarations in the other files. The C language contains a special type of declaration called an external definition. The purpose of an external definition is to reference and describe items that may not be defined in the local file. If the number of references to items in other files is small, then a few external definitions can be placed in the file. However, if the number of references to items in other files is large, it might be best to create a file that contains external definitions for everything in the program and use the include feature of the C compiler to include the file. Files are included by using the include directive. In a C language program the line

```
#include "defs.h"
```

will include the contents of the file 'defs.h' in a program. An example appeared in the previous section, where the file 'stdio.h' was included into the example buffered input program.

Another problem is the need for certain constants and tokens to be known throughout the program. For example, in a program that manipulates lists of items the maximum number of items in the list is a key constant that needs to be known by all of the subroutines. In C, the `define` directive can be used to create a named constant. The line

```
#define LISTLEN 20
```

in a C program will define a constant called "LISTLEN". Wherever the name "LISTLEN" is encountered in a program, the text string constant "20" will be substituted. An include file usually contains all of the definitions that are used throughout a large file. The `define` directive is actually a macro replacement facility. It can have parameters and can be used to generate complicated sequences of C code.

All of the lines in a C program that begin with a number sign (#) are assumed to be directives such as `include` or `define`. All of these directives are processed by a part of the C compiler known as the C *preprocessor*. The C preprocessor also performs other chores such as removing the comments from a program so that the compiler can concentrate on compilation. Occasionally you want to see the output of the C preprocessor to see if it is doing what you want it to do. You can also use this technique to check for a comment that has unwittingly extended past its intended limit. The shell command

```
cc -E myprog.c
```

will run the preprocessor on the file 'myprog.c' and send the result to the standard output.

The normal goal of the C compiler is to compile an entire program to produce an executable module. If you have partitioned a large program into several files, you can perform a complete compilation by mentioning all of the source code files (C language files usually use the .c extension) in the command line.

```
$ cc fileA.c fileB.c fileC.c
fileA.c:
fileB.c:
fileC.c:
$ _
```

If everything works well and no errors are detected, then the executable code will be placed in a file named 'a.out', and the individual object code files will be placed in files with the .o extension.

The object codes for the individual source files are retained to reduce the amount of work in subsequent compilations. If 'fileA.c' is updated but 'fileB.c' and 'fileC.c' are unchanged, then the only object file that is out of date is 'fileA.o'. The object modules 'fileB.o' and 'fileC.o' can be used as is, because the source code they depend on has not been changed. The entire system can be recompiled by performing a partial compilation on 'fileA.c' and then relinking the three object files to produce a new 'a.out' executable file. This will be accomplished by entering the following command.

```
$ cc fileA.c fileB.o fileC.o
$ _
```

One very useful feature of the C compiler is that it knows what suffixes are used on what types of files. Based on the suffix ".c", the C compiler knows that 'fileA.c' is a C language source program that must be compiled, and based on the ".o" suffix, the C compiler knows that 'fileB.o' and 'fileC.o' are object files that need only to be linked (with 'fileA.o') to produce an executable 'a.out' file.

Remembering which files are obsolete and which are not can be very difficult. One solution is to always keep the object files up to date. Whenever a source file is changed, the corresponding object file is immediately recreated. The term *partial compilation* is used to describe a compilation where the goal is to compile just one module, not a complete software system. The "-c" option of the C compiler is used to perform partial compilations.

```
$ cc -c fileA.c
$ _
```

The command shown above produces an up-to-date 'fileA.o'. If the "-c" option were not used, the C compiler would issue an error message when it determined that the source code in 'fileA.c' did not contain a complete program.

The 'a.out' file can be produced from a set of up-to-date object files using the cc command.

```
$ cc fileA.o fileB.o fileC.o
$ _
```

Another way to keep track of which object files are obsolete is to use the UNIX program make, which looks at the dates of all of the files in a software system to determine what needs to be recompiled. See Chapter 18 for more information on the make program.

15.8   LINT—CHECK C PROGRAMS

The C programming language is very lax about checking for certain errors in programs. Many of these problems arise from the fact that when a program is divided into separate modules, the compiler relies on the external definitions for determining the data types in the other modules. If the external definitions are inaccurate, then incorrect code may be generated. Problems also arise from the use of pointers, a technique that tends to obscure the basic type of an object.

In short, the C compiler assumes that the code you have written embodies the operations you want to perform, and if an operation is logically possible, then in most cases the C compiler attempts to produce the corresponding machine instructions. The attitude of most C compilers is that you are smarter than the compiler and whatever you dictate should be attempted.

Fortunately, UNIX also contains a much more suspicious program, called lint. It is used to check C programs for many types of error including objects whose types are defined differently in different files, objects or values that are never used, variables that are apparently used before their value is established, and other dubious practices. lint does not produce object files; it merely produces warnings and comments on your coding practices. Occasionally the warnings produced by lint do not indicate trouble, but in general the warnings mean that something is wrong or nonportable. Many companies are requiring that all software written for them be able to survive analysis by lint with no complaints.

```
$ cat t.c
#include <math.h>
main()
{
    printf("sin of one radian: %f\n", sin(1));
}
$ cc t.c -lm
$ a.out
sin of one radian: 0.000000
$ lint t.c -lm
t.c:
sin, arg. 1 used inconsistently llib-lm(24)  ::  t.c(4)
$ ed t.c
76
/print/
    printf("sin of one radian: %f\n", sin(1));
s/1/1.0/p
    printf("sin of one radian: %f\n", sin(1.0));
w
78
q
$ cc t.c -lm ; a.out
sin of one radian: 0.841471
$ _
```

One problem with using one program to compile a program and another to perform usage checks is the possibility that the two programs will get out of synchronization. Features in the C language that are recognized and working in the compiler may be absent from lint, or vice versa.

However, there are several advantages to performing these checks in a separate program rather than in the compiler. One advantage is that exhaustive analysis can be performed in a separate program—analysis that would be too time-consuming in a compiler. Another advantage is that lint can analyze a software system as a whole, a very desirable feature for a language that encourages separate compilation.

CHAPTER 16

Shell Internals

The internal organization of the UNIX shell, while not as conceptually difficult as the structure of the UNIX kernel, provides an interesting example of UNIX software. The shell is interesting because it exercises the full range of UNIX facilities: process creation, I/O connectivity, signaling, memory allocation, etc.

In the following sections I will outline how the shell performs its most interesting operations. I have tried to separate the various functions so that each can be understood separately. For example, the following command invokes filename generation, output redirection, executing a process, and running a process in the background.

```
$ echo Curr text: *.t > tfiles &
1833
$
```

Each of these facilities is presented in a separate section.

16.1 ARGUMENT LIST GENERATION

The overall intent of the argument list generation process is to provide you with a set of tools that allows you to specify what the computer should do. Experience has shown that simply entering the name of a command is not enough; you need to reference files, use the output of one command in the specification of another, and reuse bits and pieces of previous commands.

Each command you enter is a list of words that is transformed during argument list generation into a possibly different list of words. Although the Bourne shell, the Korn shell, and the C shell all perform argument list generation, the actual transformations made by these three shells are slightly different.

In all shells, argument list generation comprises several distinct phases. The Bourne shell performs command substitution, parameter substitution, blank interpretation, and filename generation. In addition to these four, the C shell and Korn shell offer tilde and alias substitution, and the C shell also offers history substitution.

Each of the substitutions is triggered syntactically by special characters in the command text. For example, command substitution is performed whenever a part of the command text is set off by reverse single quotes. The quoted part of the command is executed as a command in its own right, whose output is then put back into the text of the original command.

```
$ ls | wc -l
      61
$ echo There are 'ls | wc -l' files here.
There are 61 files here.
$ _
```

It is easy to understand parameter substitution. The shell stores the name and the text value for each variable. When the shell is scanning the list of words in a command and it notices a currency symbol, it looks up the word attached to the $ in its list of variables. If the variable exists, its value is put into the command text in place of the original name. If the variable isn't found, then the reference is removed, without any replacement.

Filename generation is probably the most interesting aspect of argument list generation. We often want our commands to work with multiple files, but no one wants to type in a dozen filenames by hand. Filename generation lets you specify a group of files using a pattern-matching language. Of course this works best if you choose filenames consistently.

The original design of the UNIX filesystem was a subtle compromise that allowed programs such as the shell to access the information in directories while protecting the integrity of directory entries. UNIX directory files are similar to ordinary files. A process can read the contents of a directory, provided it has read-access permission. However, to protect the integrity of the filesystem, it is forbidden for any process to write to a directory file. If you want another file added to a directory, you must execute the creat system call, and then the kernel will add the entry to the directory for you. Writing to a directory is simply not allowed (except by the kernel). (Note that the write privilege for a directory file means that you are allowed to create or remove files in that directory. It does not mean that your processes can open the directory file and perform a write.)

UNIX originally had a very simple format for directories. Each directory entry was 16 bytes long, a two-byte I-node number and a 14-byte name. In Berkeley UNIX, the format is enhanced to allow longer filenames, but the same principle applies. It is easy for a program to open a directory file and read its contents. That's how ls works, and that's how the shell performs filename generation. When the shell spots one of the filename generation characters in the text of a command, it opens the appropriate directory file and performs a textual pattern match on each entry. For example, if you specify the pattern *.t, the shell will look at the last two characters of every file in the directory to generate a list of the files whose names end with a period followed by the letter *t*.

Although filename generation is similar in principle to the regular expression syntax of the standard UNIX text editors, it obeys a slightly different set of rules and uses a different set of metacharacters. Nonetheless, from the shell's vantage point, the filename generation process is simply a pattern-matching exercise, aided by easy access to the UNIX directory names.

16.2   INTERNAL COMMANDS

When you enter a command, it is handled in one of three ways, depending on whether the command is a script, a binary executable file, or one of the shell's internal commands. In this section I will discuss how the shell handles some of its internal commands, and in the next I will talk about how the scripts and binary executable files are executed.

The shell has internal commands that enable you to control the shell's operation. For example, you can assign a value to a variable. The shell maintains a list of variables and their values, and each time it encounters an assignment command, it updates its list of variables and values. The shell doesn't have to execute a subprocess to change the value of a variable; the shell itself contains the logic for managing variables.

The commands that are built into the shell would usually be difficult or impossible to provide otherwise. For example, the cd command is internal to the shell. When you enter the cd command, the shell simply invokes the chdir system call to move to another directory. The shell can't run a subprocess to achieve the same result because a subprocess can't change the shell's working directory; it can only change its own. The value of changing the shell's working directory is that child processes inherit the working directory of their parents.

There are two major categories of shell built-in commands. The flow of control commands, such as for, while, and if, is built into the shell, because providing a programming interface is one of the shell's major roles. Similarly, the commands that manage the shell's variables are built in. The second category is commands such as cd, that alter the shell's working environment.

16.3 EXECUTING A SUBPROCESS

Each time you enter a command (unless it is one of the shell's built-in commands), the shell runs a subprocess. The shell's $PATH variable tells the shell where to look for each executable file. For example, if your $PATH is /bin:/usr/bin:/usr/graf and you enter the xplot command, the shell will first look for xplot in '/bin', then in '/usr/bin', and then finally in '/usr/graf'.

The UNIX system call for executing a process is exec. There are several variants of exec, depending on how you want to specify the argument list. The form of exec used by the shell expects its first argument to be an absolute pathname. (There is a form of exec that automatically uses the $PATH environment variable to search for executable files.) When you enter a command name that starts with a /, the shell will use that name directly as the first argument for exec, but otherwise the shell will take each component of $PATH, glue it onto the front of the command name, and then try to exec that file.

When exec succeeds, the original process is overlaid by the new process. Obviously the shell, if it wants to survive, must fork before the exec. Each time the exec fails, the shell simply glues on the next component of the $PATH. If the exec fails in every directory in the search path, the child shell prints an error message and then exits. The parent shell will then awake and issue a prompt for a new command.

> *Repeat forever*
> *Read the command name and form the argument list*
> *fork*
> *If child*
> *   if cmd name starts with /*
> *   exec cmd, arguments, environment*
> *   otherwise*
> *   for each component of $PATH*
> *   glue component onto front of cmd name*
> *   exec cmd, arguments, environment*
> *   Issue "Not Found" error message*
> *   exit*
> *otherwise*
> *   wait for termination of child*

The *Not Found* error message will be printed only if all of the attempted execs fail. Notice how the first successful exec overlays the child shell with the exec'd process. That's why the order of the directories in the $PATH variable is important.

The shell must perform additional work when you attempt to run a shell command script by typing its name. Unlike a binary file, which the kernel loads into memory and executes, a shell script must be executed by a shell interpreter. The kernel can identify binary executable files because they start with a magic number. The magic number is chosen so that it will never occur as the first few characters of a text file.

An attempted exec of a shell command script will fail because the command script doesn't start with a magic numbers. When the shell recognizes that particular exec failure, it spawns a shell to interpret that command script. Thus it is the shell that promotes one of the better features of UNIX its uniform syntax for running programs.

The Berkeley system's handling of command scripts is a slight enhancement of the traditional System V approach outlined above. On Berkeley systems, command scripts may start with a line that reads

```
#! /bin/sh
```

This line looks like a shell comment, so it is compatible with the operation of command scripts on non-Berkeley versions of UNIX. When the kernel encounters a file whose first two bytes are #! (you can think of it as a magic number), it automatically exec's the command interpreter mentioned on the remainder of the line. This is slightly more efficient than fielding an error and letting the shell exec the command interpreter, and it lets the correct command interpreter be loaded for each script. Another important advantage of the Berkeley system is that it makes it easier for applications programs to exec shell scripts without expending the extra effort performed by the shell. Command scripts on Berkeley systems that don't start with #! have their interpreter exec'd by the shell (not the kernel), just the same as on System V.

16.4 BACKGROUND PROCESSES

Each time you enter an ampersand at the end of a command, the shell runs the command in the background without waiting for it to complete before prompting you to enter the next command. At first you might imagine that the shell does this simply by omitting the wait system call mentioned in the previous section. What actually happens is slightly more complicated because of zombie processes.

A zombie, to a UNIX person, is a process that has died but not yet been waited for by the parent. Zombies are dead, but not yet at rest. Zombies are significant because they occupy a slot in the process table, one of the UNIX system's finite resources. The slot is occupied because it contains the exit status information and pid number that will be returned to the parent, should the parent choose to `wait` for the child. Until the parent dies or waits for the child, the slot must be occupied.

The system would quickly run out of process table slots if the shell created a zombie each time it ran a process in the background. To avoid this the shell must be careful to wait for its background progeny. The problem is that the `wait` system call doesn't test to see if any offspring have died; it waits for one to die. `wait` returns immediately only if a not-yet-awaited child exists or if there aren't any children. You can't just call `wait` on the chance that a background process has died; you might be waiting a long time.

The original strategy adopted by the shell to avoid creating zombies is very simple. Each time the shell issues an ordinary foreground command, it `waits` for its demise before continuing. However, instead of simply issuing a single `wait` request and then continuing, the shell is careful to wait for the termination of the specific foreground process it just executed. If `wait` returns with the wrong process id, the shell waits again until the foreground process's process id is returned. Thus the shell `waits` for the background processes while it is waiting for the termination of the foreground process.

An alternate strategy, adopted by the C shell, is to catch the `SIGCHLD` signal. Each time a child process dies, the parent receives a `SIGCHLD` signal. The receipt of `SIGCHLD` means that at least one child has terminated, and it is thus safe to issue a `wait` system call.

Because the shell is constantly issuing `fork` and `exec` system calls, efficiency is important. However, a process that cared less about efficiency has a third method of safely spawning background jobs without creating zombies or being delayed by unexpectedly long waits. The method is to `fork` twice before the `exec`. I will refer to this trio of processes as grandparent, parent, and child. The grandparent `forks` to create the parent, the parent `forks` to create the child, and then the child `execs` the background process. The parent `exits` as soon as the child has been created, and the grandparent `waits` for the parent. Eventually the child dies, but since its parent is already gone, the child doesn't become a zombie. And of course the parent doesn't become a zombie, because it is waited for by the grandparent.

16.5   VARIABLES AND THE ENVIRONMENT

The shell's variables are a list of names and values. There are a few predefined variables, such as $HOME, which contains the name of your home directory. There are also a few variables that the shell maintains, such as $!, the process id number of the most recently spawned background process.

You can create your own variables by executing an assignment command. When the shell encounters a variable assignment, it checks the list of current variables to see if the new variable is in the list. If so, the list is updated with the new value. If the variable is not in the list, the shell allocates a place to store the variable and its value and places them on the list.

Some variables, known as the environment variables, are treated specially. They are passed to each process you run. Thus, environment variables are public, whereas the other variables are private to your shell. The Bourne shell's export internal command lets you mark an ordinary variable as part of the environment.

Processes can find the values for the environmental variables using the getenv subroutine. For example, the $TERM variable is in the environment so that processes can find out what kind of a terminal you are using.

```
$ echo $TERM
kermit
$ cat term.c
char *getenv();
main()
{
        char *term;
        term = getenv("TERM");
        puts(term);
}
$ cc -o term term.c
$ term
kermit
$ _
```

If $TERM were simply an ordinary variable instead of an environment variable, the echo command in the dialogue above would work as shown. Because the value of $TERM is sent as an argument to echo, it doesn't have to fetch the value from its environment. However, the term program, since it gets the value of $TERM from its environment, wouldn't work if $TERM were a local variable.

16.6 INPUT/OUTPUT REDIRECTION

Each process started by the shell can count on three I/O connections—the standard input, the standard output, and the standard error output. Ordinarily these connections are made to your terminal, but the shell's I/O redirection syntax enables you to specify alternate connections.

The most important system call for controlling the specific files associated with file descriptors 0, 1, and 2 (standard input, output, and error, respectively) is dup. The dup system call takes an open file descriptor and creates a duplicate handle for that descriptor using the lowest numbered currently unused file descriptor. dup is one of the earliest UNIX system calls, but it has been overshadowed by the fcntl system call, which can perform all of dup's functions.

If you specify that a command's standard output should be connected to a file named '/tmp/kc', the shell will creat '/tmp/kc', close file descriptor 1, and then attach (using dup or fcntl) the file descriptor returned by creat, thereby attaching the reference to '/tmp/kc' to file descriptor 1, the standard output.

A here document is input for a command that appears in the shell's input stream. Although here documents can be entered interactively, they are usually used in shell scripts so that the input for a command, often the line editor or the mail program, can be embedded in the script. The shell handles here documents by copying them into a temporary file. Once the here document has been placed into the temporary file, the management of the here document is the same as the management of input redirection.

The shell performs its I/O redirection activities after it forks but before it performs the exec to create the new process. Thus the I/O redirection doesn't change the parent process's I/O connections, only the child's.

CHAPTER 17

<hr>

Programmers' Utilities

The UNIX system's programming language compilers (C, FORTRAN, PASCAL, etc.) translate a text file containing a program source into an object file that contains binary information. Since object files contain binary information, not text information, they cannot be manipulated using the standard UNIX utilities for text files, such as the vi editor. Instead, object files are managed with the utilities described in this chapter.

Some UNIX systems have software that allows a programmer to compile programs on a UNIX system for execution on some other system. Such programming systems are called *cross-compilers,* and there is no standard for the format of the files that are produced. The manipulation of executable files produced by cross-compilation systems is not discussed in this chapter and the utilities discussed here cannot be assumed to work on such files.

The first section of this chapter describes various utilities for working with object files, and the last two sections discuss profiling programs and briefly introduce the UNIX debuggers.

17.1 COMPILATION

An *object file* is the result of a compilation of a high-level language program or the result of an assembly language program. All of the object files produced by the standard UNIX compiled languages can have four sections: the header, the program (instructions and data), the relocation information, and the symbol table (Fig. 17.1). The header and the program are always present. The header specifies the sizes of the various sections, and it indicates whether the relocation information and the symbol table are present.

276

The relocation information and the symbol table are useful for combining object files to form executable programs and for debugging executable programs.

The program source code for very short programs is often contained in a single file. It is possible to compile such a program to immediately produce an executable object file. The default executable file name in UNIX is 'a.out'.

```
$ cc myprog.c
$ _
```

The above command compiles the C language program 'myprog.c' using cc (the C compiler) and places the output in the file 'a.out'. If 'myprog.c' contains unresolved references to other program modules or if it contains source code errors, then 'a.out' will not be made executable. When no errors are detected and there are no unresolved references, then 'a.out' is made executable (has its execution privilege enabled). You can have the executable output placed in the file of your choice if you use the -o filename option.

```
$ cc -o myprog myprog.c
$ _
```

In this case, the output is placed in 'myprog' rather than in 'a.out'.

The program source code for large, complicated programs is usually stored in several files to simplify program development and maintenance. A compilation of just one (of several) source code files is called a *partial* compilation. The object file resulting from a partial compilation is named 'file.o' if the source file is named 'file.c'. (Object files are often called ".o" (dot oh) files.)

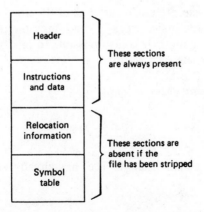

Figure 17.1.   The structure of an object file.

The C compiler option -c instructs the compiler to perform a partial compilation. The major difference between a partial compilation and a complete compilation is that unresolved external references are not considered an error during a partial compilation.

```
$ cc -c fileA.c
$ _
```

The above command produces the object file 'fileA.o'. The result of a partial compilation is never made executable.

A complete compilation of a program stored in several source code files can be performed using any mix of object and source files so long as each separate program module is represented. Thus, a program stored in the source files 'fileA.c', 'fileB.c', and 'fileC.c' could be completely compiled from the C language source files by using the following command:

```
$ cc fileA.c fileB.c fileC.c
fileA.c:
fileB.c:
fileC.c:
$ _
```

The name of each file is printed before it is compiled to make it easier to know where each error occurred.

If all of the source code files have been compiled separately to produce object files, then a complete compilation can also be performed using the following command:

```
$ cc fileA.o fileB.o fileC.o
$ _
```

This command will execute much faster than the previous one because there is much less to do; the major work is combining the object files to produce an executable file (linking). It is also possible to mix object files and source files in a single complete compilation:

```
$ cc fileA.c fileB.o fileC.c
fileA.c
fileC.c
$ _
```

In this example we assume that 'fileB.c' has already been compiled to produce 'fileB.o'.

17.2   SIZE—PRINT OBJECT FILE CHARACTERISTICS

The `size` program prints the size of the program section of an object file. The program section consists of three parts—the *instructions* (often called *text* although there is no relation to text files), the *initialized data,* and the *uninitialized data* (called *bss*). The `size` program prints the sizes of these three parts followed by the sum of these sizes, usually printed in both decimal and octal (or hex).

   The size printed by the `size` program reflects just the size of the program section of an object file, not the size of the entire object file. (The `ls -1` command will reveal the entire size of an object file.)

```
$ size *.o
text    data    bss    dec     hex
2424    604     4      3032    bd8     fileA.o
848     60      4      912     390     fileB.o
2920    436     480    3404    d4c     fileC.o
$ _
```

17.3   STRIP—REMOVE SYMBOL TABLE FROM OBJECT FILE

The `strip` command is used to remove the relocation information and the symbol table from an object file. This results in a significant reduction in size of the file, but it has no effect on your ability to run the program.

```
$ file mdraw
mdraw: pure executable not stripped
$ size mdraw
text    data    bss    dec     hex
34816   5120    19928  59864   e9d8
$ ls -1 mdraw
-rwxr-xr-x   1    kc     49152  Mar 27 16:57  mdraw
$ strip mdraw
$ file mdraw
mdraw: pure executable
$ size mdraw
text    data    bss    dec     hex
34816   5120    19928  59864   e9d8
$ ls -1 mdraw
-rwxr-xr-x   1    kc     40960  Apr 11 20:06  mdraw
$ _
```

The same effect could be achieved during compilation by using the `-s` option of the C compiler:

```
$ cc -s -o myprog myprog.c
$ _
```

Stripped production quality files save space, but they can't be debugged using a symbolic debugger. (You might also want to know that it is somewhat harder for a computer hacker to tamper with a stripped file.) Some executables are stripped to improve system security. The UNIX kernel executable file, '/unix' or '/vmunix', is never stripped, because utilities such as ps need to read its symbol table. There is no point in stripping the result of a partial compilation because a stripped file cannot be combined with other files by ld (the linker) to form an executable program.

17.4   NM—PRINT OBJECT FILE SYMBOL TABLE

The nm (list symbol table names) program examines the symbol tables in the named object files. The object files examined by nm must not have been stripped using the **strip** command. Without any options the nm program prints a list of everything in the symbol table:

```
$ cat deb.c
extern int x, y;
deb(ylen)
int ylen;
{
    while (ylen--)
            putpix (x, y++);
}
$ cc -c deb.c
$ nm deb.o
000000   a   L14
000000   T   _deb
         U   _putpix
         U   _x
         U   _y
$ _
```

This form of nm has little use unless you pipe the output to grep to select certain items or unless you examine very small object files such as the one above. Most programs contain many more symbols than you would expect.

nm prints the symbols one per line. The first field on the line contains the value of the symbol (if it is defined), the second field is a letter that indicates the type of the symbol, and the final field is the name of symbol. In C, and in most other high-level languages, from the compiler's point of view the "value" of a symbol is its address, so the "value" printed by nm is the symbol's address. The type letter is in lowercase for local symbols and in uppercase for external (global) symbols.

The most important type letters are D and B, for initialized and uninitialized data; T, for text; A, for absolute; and U, for undefined. A complete list of the type letters can be found in the UNIX manual.

In the example shown above, L14 is a local label created to manage the while loop, _deb is the entry point for the subroutine, and _putpix, _x, and _y are externals. When the 'deb.o' file is linked to the final program, L14 and _deb will be relocated to their final positions, and references to _putpix, _x, and _y will be resolved.

One of the most useful options for nm is -u, which causes nm to print a list of the undefined symbols:

```
$ nm -u deb.o
_putpix
_x
_y
$ _
```

Undefined symbols are those symbols that were used but never defined in a program. They are to be expected in an unlinked object file, such as 'deb.o'. The program source files are usually a better source of information, but when things become unexplainable, you can try examining the symbols in the object files.

The -g option causes nm to print a list of the externals in the symbol table:

```
$ nm -g deb.o
000000   T   _deb
         U   _putpix
         U   _x
         U   _y
$ _
```

The list of externals includes those that are defined in the file, or referenced in the file.

17.5 AR—ARCHIVE FILES

The UNIX librarian program is called ar (archive). A *library* (alternatively called an archive) is a file that contains a set of files. Although UNIX libraries can contain any type of file, most libraries contain object files.

Object files are frequently combined into libraries to make them easier to reference. For instance, all of the object files for the standard C subroutines and system calls are contained in a single library, '/lib/libc.a'. Other libraries contain subroutines for graphics, mathematical functions, and so on. If a program requires several of the graphics subroutines, it is much easier to mention the graphics library than to mention each graphics subroutine by name.

Many people are confused by the difference between a library and a subdirectory. The similarity is that each can be home for a group of files. The difference is that a directory is a place in the filesystem. You can cd to a directory. A library is an ordinary file into which you have placed the contents of other files. It is analogous to a literary anthology, whereas a subdirectory is analogous to a group of books.

The ar program can be used to print a table of the files in an archive, to add files to an archive, and to extract copies of files in an archive. Let's first create an archive to contain the object files 'fileA.o', 'fileB.o', 'fileC.o'.

```
$ ar rv libfile.a file?.o
a - fileA.o
a - fileB.o
a - fileC.o
ar: creating libfile.a
$ _
```

The options for the ar program (r and v in this case) are not preceded by a hyphen as in most other UNIX programs because ar always requires at least one option. The r option indicates that the specified files should be added to the library 'libfile.a'. The file 'libfile.a' will be created if necessary. Usually the r option is used to add files to an existing library, but it can also be used to create libraries. The v option specifies the verbose mode; a message is printed for each operation performed by ar. It is a good idea to use the verbose option when you are using ar interactively.

Following the execution of the command listed above, the library 'libfile.a' will contain 'fileA.o', 'fileB.o', and 'fileC.o'. The t option of ar prints a table of contents for an archive.

```
$ ar t libfile.a
fileA.o
fileB.o
fileC.o
$ _
```

The order of files in an archive is important because archives are searched sequentially during a compilation. Anything in an archive that is encountered before it has been referenced (i.e., encountered before the compiler knows it is needed) will not be linked into the program, thereby causing an "undefined external" error. The m option of ar moves files within an archive.

```
$ ar mva fileA.o libfile.a fileC.o
m - fileC.o
$ ar t libfile.a
fileA.o
fileC.o
fileB.o
$ _
```

The above command will move (the m option) 'fileC.o' after (the a option) 'fileA.o' in the library 'libfile.a'. (As usual, the v option of ar specifies verbose mode.) Alternatively, 'fileB.o' could be moved to the beginning of the archive by using the following command:

```
$ ar mvb fileA.o libfile.a fileB.o
m - fileB.o
$ ar t libfile.a
fileB.o
fileA.o
fileC.o
$ _
```

This command moves (the m option) 'fileB.o' before (the b option) 'fileA.o' in the library 'libfile.a'.

Probably the most common ar option is r, replace. If 'fileB.c' were changed and recompiled, the copy of 'fileB.o' outside of 'libfile.a' would be different and newer than 'fileB.o' in the library.

```
$ ar rv libfile.a fileB.o
r - fileB.o
$ _
```

The command shown above replaces the outdated version inside the library with the new version. The after and before (a and b) options can be used during a replace to change the ordering; without these options, the ordering is not changed during a replace operation.

Sometimes you want to acquire a copy of a file from an archive. Copying out of an archive is more common with archives containing source code or text than with archives containing object files. The x option extracts a component from an archive.

```
$ ls fileB.o
file B.o not found
$ ar xv libfile.a fileB.o
x - fileB.o
$ ls fileB.o
fileB.o
$ _
```

The archive is not changed by an extraction; the only change occurs outside of the archive in your current directory where the copy of the archive member is created.

17.6   LD—COMBINE OBJECT FILES

ld is the UNIX system's linkage editor program. It is not an editor for text files; it is an editor for object files. ld combines object files, usually to produce an executable output file. Occasionally ld combines files so that they can be used in further linkage editing sessions.

Object files are linked by combining all of the program sections to form one big program section. Then the information in the symbol tables and relocation sections is used to adjust the cross-references. When object files are combined in a library, the individual files are not changed; when object files are combined using ld, the individual sections of the object files are merged into one larger object file with the same four sections (header, program, relocation, symbols).

Most UNIX users do not use the ld program directly. Instead, they use one of the compilers (cc, f77, pc), and the compiler automatically calls the ld program. Compilers generally consist of several passes. The last phase in a full compilation is linkage editing. Linkage editing is not performed during partial compilations.

You can control the operation of the ld program by supplying its options to your compiler. The compiler will pass them along to ld. For example, the -s option for ld causes ld to strip the relocation information and the symbol table from the output file.

```
$ cc -s myprog.c
$ _
```

The command shown above invokes cc with the -s option, but cc understands that -s is actually a link editor (ld) option. In the final phase of compilation, cc passes the -s flag to ld. ld actually strips the output.

Some programs are regularly executed simultaneously by several users. Two examples are the shell and the editor. When one program is being executed simultaneously as several different processes, it is not necessary to keep several copies of the program's instructions. However, it is necessary to keep one copy of the program's data for each executing process.

A program where the instructions (text) can be shared between several processes is called *pure executable*. The linkage editor will create a pure executable program if the option -n is present. The disadvantage of pure programs is memory utilization—they require a little more memory than impure programs. If only one copy of a pure program is executing, some-what more memory is used, but when several copies are running, there is a net savings, because there is only one copy of the text.

```
$ cc -o nprocs nprocs.c
$ file nprocs
nprocs:  executable not stripped
$ cc -n -o nprocs nprocs.c
$ file nprocs
nprocs:  pure executable not stripped
$ _
```

From the program user's point of view, there is no difference between a pure program and an impure program. They execute the same, and it is hard to discover that other people are sharing the program's text. On sys-tems without memory protection and memory mapping, this feature may be absent.

Another frequently useful ld option is -i, which arranges for the pro-gram text and the program data to reside in separate address spaces. On computers that support separate instruction and data address spaces, the -i option usually allows for larger programs.

The ld options discussed above are widely available on many hardware architectures. However, on many systems ld has many additional options, so that programmers can optimize their software for particular machine fea-tures.

17.7   PROF—PROFILE AND OPTIMIZE PROGRAMS

When your newly minted program just drags along, it's time to find out where it spends most of its time. The adage that most programs execute 10% of the code 90% of the time is often correct. prof can help you to find that crucial 10% so that you can concentrate your optimizing efforts where they count.

In a profiled program, a subroutine called monitor keeps track of how many times each routine is called and how much time is spent inside of each routine. When the program terminates, monitor outputs the accumu-lated data to the 'mon.out' file.

The role of prof is to interpret the information in the 'mon.out' file. prof can print a textual display of the information on your text-only

```
$ ls corr mon.out
mon.out
not found corr
$ make corr
cc -p corrmain.o corrsubs.o -o corr
$ nm corr | grep mon
0000028a T _moncontrol
00000186 T _monitor
00000078 T _monstartup
$ corr < cdata1
$ prof corr
  %time  cumsecs  #call   ms/call  name
   39.4  156.79   45129      3.47  _corr
   18.8  231.60  106729      0.70  __innum
   10.6  273.72   46125      0.91  __doprnt
    9.3  310.69   53365      0.69  __doscan
    5.5  332.71                    mcount
    3.1  344.91  160092      0.08  _ungetc
    2.4  354.34       1   9434.93  _main
    2.0  362.23   69204      0.11  _random
    1.4  367.68   15850      0.34  _runcorr
    1.4  373.08      45    120.02  _writechan
    1.2  377.91   53365      0.09  _scanf
    1.1  382.46                    _monstartup
    1.0  386.63   53364      0.08  _store
    1.0  390.42   46080      0.08  _fprintf
             -- more profile data - -
$ ls -l mon.out
-rw-r--r-- 1 kc          10660 Apr  8 21:13 mon.out
$ _
```

Figure 17.2. A prof dialogue. The prof dialogue shown above reveals that the corr program spends most of its time in a subroutine called corr. Optimization of the corr subroutine is the most likely route to a faster program.

terminal, or it can graph the results on a graphics terminal or graphics printer. Various prof options allow you to display the data optimally for your application.

Programs to be profiled must be compiled with the -p compiler option. The compiler then automatically loads in the monitor subroutine and arranges the code for profiling. When the program is run, it executes normally except for a very small time penalty related to the profiling activity. When the program terminates, it automatically produces the mon.out file. A sample prof dialogue is shown in Figure 17.2. prof can also produce graphs of program activity. An example is shown in Figure 17.3.

On Berkeley UNIX systems, a profiler called gprof is also available. It performs a more exhaustive analysis of the execution profile by grouping

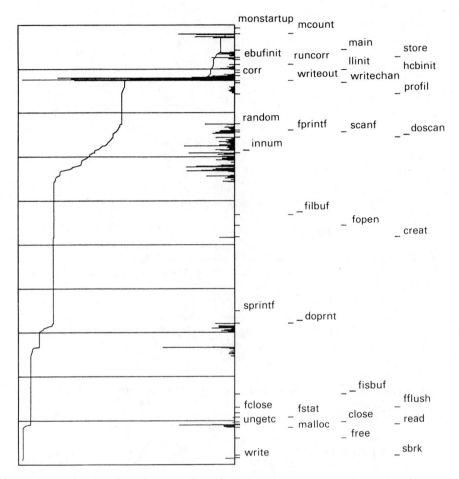

Figure 17.3.   An activity graph produced by prof.

the data for related families of subroutines. gprof also contains more sophisticated controls for controlling what parts of the program are profiled. An example gprof output is shown in Figure 17.4.

gprof's output reveals how often a low-level subroutine is called by each parent, unlike prof, which merely reveals how much time is spent executing each routine. This style of analysis is useful because low-level subroutines are often called from several different parts of a program.

index	%time	self	descendents	called/total called+self called/total	parents name index children
					<spontaneous>
[1]	100.0	0.00	227.91		start [1]
		5.57	222.34	1/1	_main [2]
-----	-----	-----	-----	-----	-----
		5.57	222.34	1/1	start [1]
[2]	100.0	5.57	222.34	1	_main [2]
		3.97	96.32	15850/15850	_runcorr [3]
		3.05	75.95	53365/53365	_scanf [5]
		0.00	34.00	1/1	_writeout [9]
		4.79	0.00	69204/69204	_random [13]
		2.22	0.00	53364/53364	_store [14]
		2.03	0.00	1/1	_hcbinit [15]
		0.01	0.00	1/1	_ebufinit [28]
		0.00	0.00	1/1	_llinit [63]
-----	-----	-----	-----	-----	-----
		3.97	96.32	15850/15850	_main [2]
[3]	44.0	3.97	96.32	15850	_runcorr [3]
		96.32	0.00	45129/45129	_corr [4]
-----	-----	-----	-----	-----	-----
		96.32	0.00	45129/45129	_runcorr [3]
[4]	42.3	96.32	0.00	45129	_corr [4]
-----	-----	-----	-----	-----	-----

Figure 17.4. Example gprof output. The first four of sixty-five call graphs produced by gprof.

17.8 DEBUGGERS

A *debugger* is a program that helps you to remove some of the errors in your programs. Typical debuggers allow you to examine postmortem program dumps, execute your programs one step at a time, examine the values of variables in executing programs, and patch program images. Some debuggers take a machine-level view of the programming process. They let you step through a program one machine instruction at a time, and they have features geared toward the host machine's architecture. High-level debuggers operate nearer to the level of modern structured programming languages. They let you step through your program one source code instruction at a time, and they have features related to the original source code program.

The original UNIX debugger was db. It was a machine-level debugger that was replaced in Version 7 UNIX with adb, a much more powerful program. Both db and adb are machine-level debuggers. System V features a high-level debugger called sdb. It sports an ed style user interface—commands are single-letter mnemonics. On Berkeley UNIX there is a totally different debugger, dbx. The user interface of dbx is more verbose, and simple macros are available to allow simple customization of the user interface. Both debuggers allow you to run a program, set breakpoints, examine post-mortem dumps, view relevant source code, etc.

For finding subtle problems in a program, either sdb or dbx is usually preferable to adb. However, adb continues to be an oft-used tool, partly because it is almost universally available, partly because it is an excellent tool for patching binary files, and partly because many simple debugging tasks are managed adequately by adb.

When a program encounters a serious problem, such as a reference to a memory location that isn't part of the program's memory space, it usually "dumps core." A *core dump* is a file named 'core' that contains an image of the program's memory region at the time of the failure. The image also contains information about the state of the host computer at the time of the failure, such as the program counter and the values in the CPU registers. Many UNIX users are baffled the first time they run a program that produces a mysterious message such as "bus error, core dumped." The message simply indicates the general nature of the problem (e.g., bus error) and what the operating system has chosen to do about it (dump debugging information to a file named 'core').

Although some causes of core dumps are self-explanatory (divide by zero error), many are related to obscure features of the host computer that ordinary users seldom understand. (For example, a bus error typically refers to a data alignment problem, or an illegal use of a pointer variable.) If you have no intention of debugging the offending program, simply remove the core file, and try to avoid whatever activity led to the problem.

It is easy to get a little information about the cause of a core dump from adb. You must supply the name of the program to adb, unless the program that dumped core happens to be named 'a.out', adb's default file name. If the core file has a name other than 'core' (e.g., '../src/jim/core'), then that name must be supplied as adb's second argument.

The $C command to adb asks for a stack trace. It will show you what routines have been called, and with what values as arguments. Another useful command is $q, the quit command. Here is an example program containing a serious programming error.

```
$ cat clra.c
int a[100], b;

main()
{
    f(b);
}

f(a)
int *a;
{
    strcpy(a,"hello");
}
$ _
```

When the program is compiled and run, it dumps core. Here is the adb dialogue that shows how the trouble is discovered.

```
$ cc clra.c
$ a.out
Bus error - core dumped
$ adb
$c
_strcpy(0,830) from 99
_f(0) from 74
_main(1,7fffeea4,7fffeeac) from 5d
$q
$ _
```

The adb stacktrace shows that the function f is called with an argument of zero. From the source code it is obvious that f is expecting to be passed the address of an array, and since C arrays are never located at zero, something is wrong at this point. However, the actual termination of the program doesn't occur until f passes along its bad argument to the strcpy function.

CHAPTER 18

Make and the
Source Code Control System

Coordination is a major problem in large programming projects. When several (or dozens or hundreds of) programmers work together, communication among them consumes significant amounts of time and effort. Decreased efficiency in large programming projects has become an accepted fact in the software industry. However, the most costly result of poor coordination among programmers is a poor product. Some of the most entrenched bugs in large programming projects are due to subtle failures in coordination between the teams of programmers.

The UNIX system is not an error-free software system, but it is an inspiring and useful example of reliable programming. Part of the reliability of UNIX is due to its modular design. Most UNIX utilities are small and simple and thus much easier to maintain than the large and involved utilities that are common in other systems. Another lesson that can be learned from UNIX is that reliable software is easier to develop using an operating system with powerful *tools*. Many of the programs in the UNIX software tool kit are standard utilities for manipulating text files because text files are the original form of all software. Other programs in the UNIX tool kit analyze the binary files that are produced by the compilers (see Chapter 17). However, the UNIX system's most original software tools are for formalizing much of the knowledge about a software system—knowledge that would otherwise be locked in the subconscious of the major software developers. These tools are the subject of this chapter.

The first section of this chapter explains some of the problems that are common to large programming projects; the last two sections concentrate on the make utility program and the series of utility programs that comprise the Source Code Control System (SCCS).

18.1   LARGE PROGRAMS

Some programming languages allow a program to be divided into separate units (loosely referred to here as modules) that are worked on separately. For example, in C, the text of a program can be placed into separate files. Programming languages are often good at precisely defining and maintaining the integrity within a module; the problem usually lies in the relationship of one module to another. Separate modules are usually entwined by a network of interdependencies, and a change in one module can render another module obsolete.

Several types of problems can occur when program modules are placed in separate files. Consider a very low level module that returns mutually agreed upon values to some higher-level module. In a large programming project the two modules would probably be in separate files, so that they could be compiled separately. If the low-level module is changed so that it returns a different set of values, then the higher-level module must also be changed.

One technique for coordinating various modules is to put definitions needed by several modules into a common file called an *include* file or *header* file. In the case mentioned above, the include file would define the values that the low-level module could pass to the high-level module. Since the modules reference the same include file, you might think that the modules would automatically be synchronized.

Although include files solve many of the major problems of program modularization, they occasionally lead to an even more subtle problem—timing. Once you have a common include file and separate program modules, you run the risk of changing something in an include file without recompiling all of the affected program modules. If a program module includes a certain file, then we say that the program's object file depends both on that include file and on the program source file. If either the include file or the program source has been modified since the object was created, then the object file is out of date.

In a large programming project, the order and extent of compilation depend on the internal references of the modules. Very modern languages (e.g., Modula-2) are designed so that large groups of files are automatically coordinated based on the internal references of the modules. The program make can be used to enforce relationships between modules when languages other than Modula-2 are used. make accepts a specification that defines the relationships between modules and specifies the actions that must be performed to update the modules. Based on the specification and the modification times of the relevant files, make will automatically maintain the modules.

The advantage of make is that it saves time. Because make understands the dependencies in a software system, it can selectively compile only those files whose object modules are out of date. The alternative is to recompile everything, which is very time consuming for large programs.

Programs usually go through a shakedown phase where most of the errors are caught and fixed. The errors that remain after the initial shakedown are usually entrenched and much more costly to remove than errors that are caught early. After a certain point in the life of a major piece of software, fixing errors becomes very difficult because each fix is likely to cause several unexpected problems.

In the early stages of a software project, errors can be fixed with little regard for the integrity of the whole because the whole is not yet sound. However, in a mature product, each change must be considered carefully because the product as a whole is (we hope) basically sound. The Source Code Control System (SCCS) is a series of UNIX programs that make it easier to maintain and document a program as it evolves throughout its lifetime. Another problem in large programming projects is the need for different versions of a program. Naturally, SCCS is useful for maintaining different versions of a program.

make and SCCS are UNIX's two most powerful tools for maintaining large software projects. They are important tools both for programs built to run under UNIX and for programs developed for use on other systems.

18.2   MAKE

make is a program that accepts a specification of the interdependencies of the various modules of a program. Information about the relationships of one module to another allows make to infer what compiled modules are out of date based on the modification dates of the files. The specification also contains commands to update a module that is found to be out of date.

As a very simple case, consider a main program module stored in a file called 'network.c' which uses a few subroutines whose source code is contained in the file 'subrs.c'. Let's assume that both 'network.c' and 'subrs.c' include a file of common definitions called 'netdefs.h'. These relationships are shown graphically in Figure 18.1. (Include files are discussed in Section 15.7.)

The specification of dependencies for make is placed into a file called a *makefile*. In a makefile, a dependency is specified by placing dependent modules to the left of a colon and independent modules to the right of a colon. Let's try to determine the dependency for the 'subrs.c' module.

Since the 'subrs.c' module contains a compiler directive that includes the 'netdefs.h' file, the actual text that will be compiled is the text from 'netdefs.h' and from 'subrs.c'. Since 'subrs.c' isn't a complete program (it doesn't contain a main() function), we can't perform a complete compilation; instead, we perform a partial compilation. The result of the partial compilation will be placed in a file called 'subrs.o'. The ".o" suffix

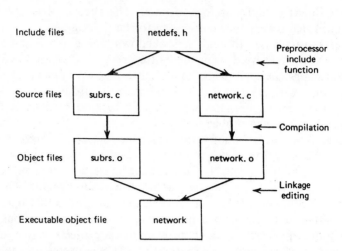

Figure 18.1.   The relationships in a small software system. The software for the network program is contained in six files: 'netdefs.h', which contains common definitions for the software system; 'subrs.c' and 'network.c', which contain C source code; 'subrs.o' and 'network.o', which contain the object code compiled from the source code, and 'network', which contains the executable program.

indicates that the file 'subrs.o' is an object file. (An object file is the result of a compilation. See Chapter 17.)

Since 'subrs.o' is created by compiling the text in 'subrs.c' plus the contents of 'netdefs.h', we say that 'subrs.o' depends on those two files. This can be expressed in a makefile as

```
subrs.o : subrs.c netdefs.h
```

In addition to the dependency specification in a makefile, you need to insert the UNIX commands that will update an outdated module. The UNIX command (or commands) is placed on a following line that starts with a tab. Thus, the entire specification for the dependencies and the script for recreation of the object module 'subrs.o' is

```
subrs.o : subrs.c netdefs.h
     cc -c subrs.c
```

The -c option to the C compiler (cc) directs the compiler to perform a partial compilation of the file 'subrs.c' and to place the object code in the file 'subrs.o'. Similarly, the specification for the 'network.o' object module is

```
network.o : network.c netdefs.h
     cc -c network.c
```

The 'network' program file depends on the two object module files 'network.o' and 'subrs.o', and it can be created as specified in this makefile entry:

```
network : network.o subrs.o
     cc -o network network.o subrs.o
```

The –o option to the C compiler instructs the compiler to put the executable output in the file 'network' rather than into the default file 'a.out'. All of this taken together leads to the following makefile for maintaining the 'network' program:

```
network : network.o subrs.o
     cc -o network network.o subrs.o
network.o : network.c netdefs.h
     cc -c network.c
subrs.o : subrs.c netdefs.h
     cc -c subrs.c
```

This makefile is used by the make program to create a table of dependencies and a similar table of remedies for rebuilding obsolete files. We can use this makefile to recompile the appropriate modules every time we change (using the text editor) a source or include module. For the following example, we assume that the makefile specification given above is stored in a file named 'Makefile'. (The name 'Makefile' is one of the default file names that the make program uses for makefiles.)

As a first example, let's see what make does when we modify the include file 'netdefs.h'. Once 'netdefs.h' is changed, all three object files in this software system are out of date, as illustrated in the timeline of Figure 18.2.

```
$ vi netdefs.h
-- netdefs.h is changed --
$ make
cc -c network.c
cc -c subrs.c
cc -o network network.o subrs.o
$ _
```

In this example, make deduces from the makefile specification and the file modification dates that all three object files are obsolete. Consequently, make executes the commands shown above to update the three object modules. Changing a single module provides a better example of the usefulness

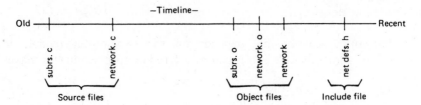

Figure 18.2.   A timeline for the network software system. According to the make specification in the text, this timeline indicates that the three object files ('subrs.o', 'network.o', and 'network') are obsolete because they are older than the include file, 'netdefs.h'.

of `make`. Let's suppose that the source code in the file 'subrs.c' is changed, producing the situation illustrated in the timeline in Figure 18.3.

```
$ vi subrs.c
-- subrs.c is modified --
$ make
cc -c subrs.c
cc -o network network.o subrs.o
$ _
```

Notice that `make` performs the minimum amount of recompilation to produce an up-to-date version of 'network'.

In this simple system, consisting of two source code files and one include file, using `make` doesn't lead to much of an advantage. However, maintenance of a system consisting of dozens of source code files and a rambling hierarchy of include files is much easier using `make`.

You might have noticed that the makefile specification given above is rather verbose. Since the object file 'subrs.o' usually depends on a source file named 'subrs.c', `make` contains internal rules to create 'subrs.o' from

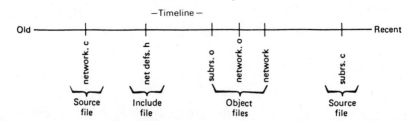

Figure 18.3.   Another timeline for the network software system. In this example, only two of the object files are obsolete. 'subrs.o' is obsolete because it is older than 'subrs.c', and 'network' is obsolete because it depends on the obsolete file 'subrs.o'. Notice that 'network.o' is not obsolete.

'subrs.c'. For example, make knows that the file 'subrs.o' is typically created by compiling the file 'subrs.c' using the -c compiler option. The makefile given above could be rewritten to take advantage of make's internal rules as follows:

```
network : network.o subrs.o
      cc -o network network.o subrs.o
subrs.o network.o : netdefs.h
```

make has a system of named variables that are very similar to the named variables that are available in the UNIX shell. If you include the line

```
CSOURCE=network.c subrs.c
```

in a makefile, then subsequently in the makefile you can use the word $(CSOURCE) to refer to all of the source files. Here is an example:

```
$ cat Makefile
CSOURCE = network.c subrs.c
network: network.o subrs.o
    cc -o network network.o subrs.o
subrs.o network.o : netdefs.h
listing:  $(CSOURCE)
    pr $(CSOURCE) | lpr
$ make listing
$ _
```

The make command issued above will produce a printed listing of the source code files. In all of the examples of make given previously, the UNIX command was executed only if certain items were out of date. In this example of creating a program printout, the UNIX command will always be executed, because there is no file called 'listing', so it is presumed to be out of date and the command is executed.

As a similar feature, consider the following excerpt from a makefile:

```
network.lint : $(CSOURCE) netdefs.h
      lint $(CSOURCE) > network.lint
```

The command

```
$ make network.lint
$ _
```

will process the C source programs using lint and place the output in the file 'network.lint'. Although a wide variety of tasks related to programming can be performed with the assistance of make, the most important use of make is documentation of the interdependencies of a complicated source code system.

18.3   THE SOURCE CODE CONTROL SYSTEM

SCCS is used to control and document text files by creating something analogous to an audit trail. The premise of SCCS is that most program source code files evolve and change over long periods of time as program bugs are fixed and enhancements are added. SCCS is in part a system to document these changes, in part a system for controlling who has the ability to make changes, and in part a system for recovering old versions of a file. The SCCS system can be used on any type of text file. However, since SCCS is usually used with program source files, most of the comments that follow will assume that the SCCS text is actually a program's source code.

SCCS works by keeping an encoded version of a text file in a special SCCS format file. The encoded format contains enough information to recreate old versions and to keep track of who is working on (or allowed to work on) specific revisions of the file. All SCCS format files are named using "s." as a prefix. Thus the SCCS file 's.network.c' is the encoded version of 'network.c'.

Let's generally describe the revision cycle using SCCS before we show some specific examples of using the SCCS programs. The complete cycle for a mature software product usually consists of a long idle period between revisions followed by a revision of the software, as shown in Figure 18.4.

During the idle period between revisions, only the SCCS format version of a file exists. When a revision becomes necessary, the get command is used to retrieve a version of a file from an encoded SCCS format file. The actual revisions are made to the retrieved version of the file. If the file is a program source file, then the programmer will probably go through a series of changes, compilations, and tests to verify the changes made to the file.

During the course of a revision, the SCCS format-encoded file and the recovered file both exist. When the revisions are complete, the new information contained in the recovered file is added into the SCCS format-encoded file using the delta command. A natural consequence of updating the SCCS format-encoded file using the delta command is the removal of the unencoded file. Leaving the open format version lying around between revisions is dangerous, because changes might be made to it in the false belief that the master copy was being updated. Therefore, only the SCCS format version of a file is available during the idle period.

It is best to apply the SCCS system at a mature point in the life cycle of a software project. If the SCCS system is imposed too early, many of the early versions of the software will involve repair of obvious flaws and inclusion of obviously necessary features. If, however, the SCCS system is

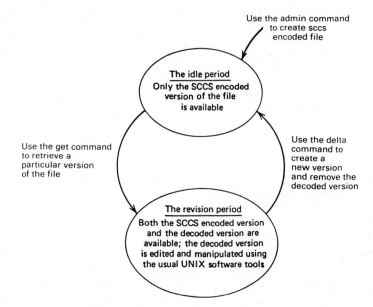

Figure 18.4.   The SCCS revision cycle.

applied too late in the lifetime of a software system, then much of the necessary information will be missing.

The SCCS system is initiated for a software system using the `admin` command. (Some of the major components of the SCCS system are shown in Fig. 18.5.) Besides the ability to create an SCCS format file, the `admin` command is able to control parameters of existing SCCS files.

```
$ ls s.SCCSsample SCCSsample
SCCSsample not found
s.SCCSsample not found
$ admin -n s.SCCSsample
$ ls s.SCCSsample SCCSsample
SCCSsample not found
s.SCCSsample
$ _
```

get	Retrieve a version of an SCCS file.
admin	Perform administrative functions on SCCS files.
delta	Place a new version into an SCCS file.
prs	Print an SCCS file

Figure 18.5.   The major programs in the SCCS system.

Other than the SCCS system information, the file is empty, and it is cataloged using the version number 1.1. (A variation on this command can create a file that is not created empty.) Before we can put some text in this empty file, we have to retrieve the file using the get command.

```
$ ls s.SCCSsample SCCSsample
SCCSsample not found
s.SCCSsample
$ get -e s.SCCSsample
1.1
new delta 1.2
0 lines
$ ls s.SCCSsample SCCSsample
SCCSsample
s.SCCSsample
$ _
```

The -e flag tells get to retrieve a file suitable for editing. The get command prints the version (1.1) of the retrieved file and the number of lines (0) in the retrieved file. All of this work has merely started the SCCS record-keeping system and fetched a blank file. We can use the ed editor to add text to the file.

```
$ ed SCCSsample
0
a
Doctor Foster went to Gloucester
In a shower of rain;
He stepped in a puddle,
Right up to his middle,
And never went there again.
.
wq
130
$ _
```

Now, assuming the revisions are complete we can save the new version of the file using the delta command.

```
$ ls s.SCCSsample SCCSsample
SCCSsample
s.SCCSsample
$ delta s.SCCSsample
comments?  Placed rhyme in file
No id keywords (cm7)
1.2
5 inserted
0 deleted
0 unchanged
$ ls s.SCCSsample SCCSsample
SCCSsample not found
s.SCCSsample
$ _
```

The changes will be saved under the version number 1.2, since the `delta`
command automatically increments the version number. The `delta` program will display the prompt "comments?" on the terminal and then read
a comment line from the terminal to add to the file. The comments are
used to specify the reason for the revision. In this example, the comment
"Placed rhyme in file" is entered. The `delta` program will remove the file
'SCCSsample' once its contents are safely added to the file 's.SCCSsample'.
`delta` prints out a statistical summary of the changes and an error message
that we can ignore concerning id keywords.

Now let's try retrieving version 1.2 of 's.SCCSsample' and then add
some text in order to create version 1.3. The `get` command will retrieve the
latest version, and the editor can be used to modify the file.

```
$ get -e s.SCCSsample
1.2
new delta 1.3
5 lines
$ ed SCCSsample
$a
   - Book of Nursery and Mother Goose Rhymes
by Marguerite deAngeli, Doubleday, 1953.
   .
wq
215
$ _
```

We can use the `delta` command to save the new version (1.3).

```
$ delta s.SCCSsample
comments? Added the citation.
No id keywords (cm7)
1.3
2 inserted
0 deleted
5 unchanged
$ _
```

Figure 18.6 shows the contents of the file 's.SCCSsample' after the preceding operations have been performed. Figure 18.6 is included here to give you an intuitive feel for the inner workings of the SCCS system; there is no reason for you to understand all of the lines. As you can see from Figure 18.6, the power of the SCCS system comes at some expense in storage use. Our seven-line text file contains 30 lines when stored in the SCCS-encoded format.

Any of the three versions of 's.SCCSsample' can be retrieved using the **get** command. The following dialogue shows how version 1.2 is retrieved.

```
$ get -s -p -r1.2 s.SCCSsample
Doctor Foster went to Gloucester
In a shower of rain;
He stepped in a puddle,
Right up to his middle,
And never went there again.
$ _
```

The **-s** flag suppresses the normal output of statistics, the **-p** flag indicates output to the terminal, and the **-r1.2** indicates that we want to see version 1.2 of the file 's.SCCSsample'. The latest version can be displayed on the terminal by entering the **get** command without specifying the version.

```
$ get -s -p s.SCCSsample
Doctor Foster went to Gloucester
In a shower of rain;
He stepped in a puddle,
Right up to his middle,
And never went there again.
   - Book of Nursery and Mother Goose Rhymes
by Marguerite deAngeli, Doubleday, 1953.
$ _
```

Although only a few of the features of SCCS have been shown in this example, the use of SCCS in managing source code throughout the mature lifetime of a software product should be apparent.

```
$ cat s.SCCS sample
<^a>h32774
<^a>s 00002/00000/00005
<^a>d D 1.3 82/04/17 11:57:30 kgc 3 2
<^a>c Added the citation
<^a>e
<^a>s 00005/00000/00000
<^a>d D 1.2 82/04/17 11:56:05 kgc 2 1
<^a>c Placed rhyme in file
<^a>e
<^a>s 00000/00000/00000
<^a>d D 1.1 82/04/17 11:47:26 kgc 1 0
<^a>e
<^a>u
<^a>U
<^a>t
<^a>T
<^a>I 2
Doctor Foster went to Gloucester
In a shower of rain;
He stepped in a puddle,
Right up to his middle,
And never went there again.
<^a>I 3
    - Book of Nursery and Mother Goose Rhymes
by Marguerite deAngeli, Doubleday, 1953.
<^a>E 3
<^a>E 2
<^a>I 1
<^a>E 1
$ _
```

Figure 18.6.   The file 's.SCCSsample'. The contents of the file 's.SCCSsample' following the operations mentioned in the text provide a clue to the inner workings of the SCCS system. All of the lines except the seven that are the actual contents of the file start with the Control-A nonprinting character, which has been shown in this figure with the notation <^a>.

CHAPTER 19

Yacc and Lex

This chapter discusses two of the UNIX system's most intriguing facilities—yacc (Yet Another Compiler Compiler) and lex. yacc and lex are widely referenced in the UNIX literature, and they are very important in the creation and maintenance of some of the key UNIX system utilities. Unfortunately, relatively few UNIX users understand what they do. This chapter describes yacc and lex at the "What is this stuff good for?" level. If you want to use yacc or lex, then you need to dive into the reference manuals and papers that describe the details.

Recognizing command languages is one of the most common problems in computer programming. Many computer applications involve a language that is used to control some process. Examples of command languages that are used in the UNIX system include the shell programming language, the C programming language, and the dependency specification used by the make program.

Some command languages, such as ed's, are very easy to recognize, but others require significant programming effort. Although it certainly is possible to write a C (or FORTRAN or PASCAL) program to recognize a complicated command language, much better techniques have been developed. This chapter introduces some of these techniques.

19.1 LEXICAL ANALYSIS AND PARSING

Recognition of a complicated command language is usually divided into two phases: *lexical analysis* and *parsing*. Low-level objects, such as numbers, operators, and keywords are recognized during the lexical analysis phase,

304

whereas higher-level entities, such as statements in a programming language, are recognized during the parsing phase. There is some leeway in deciding just which objects will be recognized during lexical analysis, and that will be recognized during parsing. Experience is often the best guide.

We use the term *lexical analyzer* to describe a program that performs lexical analysis, and we use the term *parser* to describe a program that performs parsing. Lexical analysis and parsing are explained in more detail in the remainder of this section. `lex` and `yacc`, the UNIX utility programs for producing lexical analyzers and parsers, are discussed in the last two sections of this chapter.

The input to the lexical analysis phase is a stream of characters. These characters might come from a terminal where someone is interactively entering commands to control some process, they might come from a file, or they might even come from the output of another program. In any case, the lexical analysis program scans the input according to a set of rules. When the lexical program recognizes an object, it outputs an indication of the type of object that it has just encountered. The indication is usually called a *token*. Given the input

```
25    * (16/2   )    +    15
```

a lexical analyzer might output something analogous to

```
NOLNONRON
```

Here the token "N" stands for a number, "O" stands for an operator, "L" stands for a left parenthesis, and "R" stands for a right parenthesis. The sequence "NOLNONRON" doesn't mean much to you or me—we prefer the original form—but it is just perfect for a parser that is attempting to deduce the form of an arithmetic expression.

The purpose of the lexical analysis phase is to smooth out many of the irregularities of the input, such as the spacing and the length of items, in order to produce an output that codes the sequence of items that have been encountered. Another input that would produce the "NOLNONRON" lexical sequence is

```
0x19*(0x10/0x2)+0xF
```

In this expression the numbers are in the hexadecimal radix instead of the decimal radix shown above, and the spacing of elements is different. Yet the basic expression is the same, so the lexical output is the same.

The parser phase of analysis is responsible for understanding the higher-level properties of the input. It verifies that a sequence of tokens, such as NOLNONRON, represents a valid expression, and it produces an appropriate sequence of actions.

The goal in specifying a parser is to list a set of rules that a command language must follow. If a command conforms to the rules, then some appropriate action is taken; if the command doesn't fit the rules, then it is in error. For example, if we were working with an arithmetic command language, we would want our rules to allow commands such as 7, 1+1, 5/8, and 6*7*14 and to exclude blunders such as 6 7, 5+*8, and 7k4.

Assuming that a good definition of number is already available, we might define an arithmetic expression as follows:

```
expression:
     number
     |
     expression "+" expression
     |
     expression "-" expression
     |
     expression "*" expression
     |
     expression "/" expression
     ;
```

In the list above, the vertical bar indicates an alternative rule, and number stands for any number. A colon is used to start the list of alternatives, and the semicolon ends the list. The standard arithmetic operators for addition, subtraction, multiplication, and division are shown in quotes, because they must appear literally in an expression. The definition shown above states that an expression is either a number or it is two expressions being added, subtracted, multiplied, or divided.

By defining an expression in terms of itself, we have created a definition that works for any size expression. Computer scientists have developed techniques for writing parsers that follow this type of rule. (In a more useful example, precedence rules would have to be added to our definition to resolve the ambiguity of an expression such as 5*8+1.)

The basic difference between a lexical analyzer and a parser is that a lexical analyzer follows rules to recognize certain sequences or groups of characters, whereas a parser follows rules that may be self-referential to recognize more complicated constructs.

19.2   LEX

The lex program is used to generate a lexical analysis routine. lex reads as input a specification of the lexical analyzer, and it produces either a C or a RATFOR subroutine as its output. The output must be compiled and combined with other programs to produce a complete lexical analyzer. As described in the previous section, the lexical analyzer takes a stream of characters as input and produces a stream of tokens as output. These three transformations are shown in Figure 19.1.

One of the important things to understand about both `lex` and `yacc` is that they produce subroutines, not full programs. The advantage of producing a subroutine is that it is possible to add application-specific code before, during, and after the lexical analysis or parsing. Programs similar to `lex` and `yacc` that produce full programs tend to be hard to adapt to a wide variety of uses.

The lexical rules that `lex` transforms into a program resemble the rules for forming regular expressions using the `ed` text editor. The rule

```
[0-9]
```

is a single-character regular expression that matches one digit. The rule

```
[0-9]+
```

matches a sequence of digits. The rules that are used in `lex` are a more powerful superset of the rules used in `ed` for specifying text pattern matches. For every rule in a `lex` specification, it is possible to code an action in the target language. The action code will be performed every time the rule leads to a pattern match. For example, the following line from a `lex` specification would generate code to print the message "found a number!" every time a number is encountered in the input:

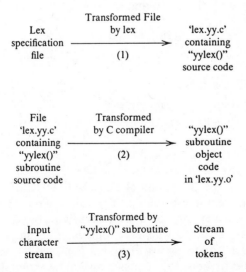

Figure 19.1.   **The elements of the `lex` system using C as the generated language.**

```
[0-9]+      { printf("found a number!\n"); }
```

This type of code is interesting but of limited practical value. A more general approach is to return a value each time an item is recognized. The value is called a token (as discussed above), and some routine is responsible for repeatedly calling the lex-generated subroutine yylex to acquire each token.

If the name "NUMBER" were defined appropriately, then the following line from a lex specification would generate code that would indicate that a number had been encountered in the input stream.

```
[0-9]+      { return(NUMBER); }
```

But what number? Obviously the code also has to indicate what number has been encountered. The usual method (variations are possible) is to put the value in an integer variable. In our case we will call this variable "yylval". In order to understand the following, you should know that lex makes the matched text (the digits in this case) available in a character string called yytext and that the standard C subroutine atoi converts a character string of digits into an integer value.

```
[0-9]+      {
        yylval = atoi(yytext);
        return(NUMBER);
        }
```

This code is quite representative of the contents of many lex specification files. Notice that both the value and the type of the object are made available in this specification.

A more complete example should make these ideas clearer. The example will be a lexical analyzer that can recognize the following items:

> Numbers (digit strings).
> The keywords set, bit, on, and off.
> Either a new line or a semicolon representing a command terminator.

The analyzer will ignore spaces and tabs.

The first thing we need to do is to define the tokens the analyzer will return. We will use the token names SET, BIT, ONCMD, OFFCMD, and NUMBER to represent these items. The token name ENDCMD will be returned whenever a new line or a semicolon is recognized, and the token UNKNOWN will be returned whenever something not identified by the rules is encountered. The following list of tokens is placed in the file 'y.tab.h' so that it is available to both the analyzer subroutine and the program that calls the analyzer subroutine:

```
# define SET 257
# define BIT 258
# define ONCMD 259
# define OFFCMD 260
# define NUMBER 261
# define ENDCMD 262
# define UNKNOWN 263
```

The particular values for these tokens are chosen so that they do not conflict with values assigned to the ASCII character set.

A lexical specification consists of at least two sections: the *declaration* section and the *rules* section. The two sections are separated by a pair of percent symbols. C language declarations in the declaration part of the lex specification must be enclosed within ''%{'' and ''%}'' delimiters. The following is the lex specification to recognize the items listed above:

```
%{
/*
 * a lex specification to recognize
 * numbers, 4 words, and delimiters
 */
#include "y.tab.h"
extern int yylval;
%}
%%
[0-9]+       {     /* rule 1 */
        yylval = atoi(yytext);
        return(NUMBER);
        }
;       return(ENDCMD);    /* rule 2 */
\n      return(ENDCMD);    /* rule 3 */
set     return(SET);       /* rule 4 */
bit     return(BIT);       /* rule 5 */
on      return(ONCMD);     /* rule 6 */
off     return(OFFCMD);    /* rule 7 */
[ \t]+     ;      /* rule 8 */
.        return(UNKNOWN);  /* rule 9 */
```

A few of the rules are worth discussing individually. Rule 8 causes spaces and tabs to be ignored. The notation [\t]+ indicates a sequence of spaces and tabs, and since the action part is null, any such sequence will be ignored. Rule 9 uses the metacharacter ''.'' to match anything that has not already been matched. lex works through the rules from the top down, so rule 9 will apply only when all of the other rules fail.

lex is quite happy to receive an ambiguous specification. When there are several rules that all seem to apply, the rule that specifies the longest match is applied unless several rules specify a match of the same length, in which case the topmost rule is applied. Rule 9, which specifies a one-character match, is the last rule in the specification and thus clearly has the lowest priority.

It would be fairly easy to write a C language subroutine to recognize the items shown above. However, even for a very simple set of items, the lex specification is shorter (and easier to change) than the equivalent C program. For someone who knows lex, this specification is easier to write than the C version. This specification only hints at the power of lex. For many applications, the equivalent C program would be quite difficult. More complicated applications provide even more incentive to use lex rather than a customized C program.

If this lex specification is placed in the file 'lex_demo.l', then the following shell command will produce the file 'lex.yy.c', which contains a C subroutine named yylex():

```
$ lex lexdemo.l
$ _
```

The name 'lex.yy.c' is the standard name of the lex output file, somewhat as 'a.out' is the standard name of the executable output of the C compiler. The file 'lex.yy.c' can be compiled to produce an object file using the command

```
$ cc -c lex.yy.c
$ _
```

Now that we have a lex subroutine, we need a method for testing it. In the next section you will see how this lexical analysis subroutine can combine with a parser created using yacc. However, for now we just want to see how it responds to various inputs. The following C language program was written to test the yylex() subroutine. The program repeatedly calls yylex() and then prints a message that depends on the returned token.

```
$ cat lextst.c
#include "y.tab.h"
int yylval;
extern char yytext[];
/*
 *          DEMONSTRATION
 * call yylex() to acquire tokens
 */
```

```
main()
{
int token;
while(token = yylex())
      switch(token)
      {
      case NUMBER:
            printf("Number: %d\n",yylval);
            break;
      case SET:
            printf("Set\n");
            break;
      case BIT:
            printf("Bit\n");
            break;
      case ONCMD:
            printf("On\n");
            break;
      case OFFCMD:
            printf("Off\n");
            break;
      case UNKNOWN:
            printf("Unknown: %s\n",yytext);
            break;
      case ENDCMD:
            printf("End marker\n");
            break;
      default:
            printf("Unknown token: %d\n",token);
            break;
      }
}
```

This main subroutine is just a multiway branch that prints a message based on the value of the token. The C main routine (in the file 'lextst.c') and the **yylex()** subroutine are compiled to produce an executable program.

```
$ cc lextst.c lex.yy.o -o lextst
$ echo "set bit 5     on;set20" | lextst
Set
Bit
Number: 5
On
End marker
Set
Number: 20
End marker
$ echo "set bit 3 On" | lextst
Set
Bit
Number: 3
Unknown: 0
Unknown: n
End marker
$ _
```

19.3   YACC

The yacc utility program is used to create a parser subroutine. yacc accepts a syntax specification and then produces either C or RATFOR source code for the parser subroutine. The parser subroutine must be compiled and then combined with a program that calls it to parse an input. The parser subroutine calls a subroutine named yylex() to acquire tokens. Notice that this works smoothly with lex, since lex produces a subroutine named yylex(). However, any subroutine named yylex() can be used, not just one produced by lex. The three transformations involved in using yacc are summarized in Figure 19.2.

The major difference between a lex specification, and a yacc specification is the format for the rules. In a lex specification, the rules are regular expressions similar to those used in many text editors. The rules in a yacc specification consist of chains of definitions that often are self-referential. For example, a command might be defined as

```
cmd:   SET BIT numb ONCMD ENDCMD
       |
       SET BIT numb OFFCMD ENDCMD
       ;
```

Definitions in yacc are introduced by a colon. The vertical bar separates alternatives in the definition, and the semicolon indicates the end of a definition. Tokens (returned by yylex()) are usually capitalized, and names that are defined within the yacc specification are usually lower-case.

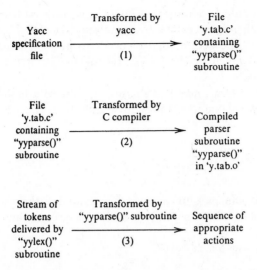

Figure 19.2. The elements of the yacc system using C as the generated language.

Since the two alternative definitions of cmd are almost identical, it would be wise to consolidate them as follows:

```
cmd:   SET BIT numb onoff ENDCMD
     ;
```

Now, of course, we must supply a definition for onoff that shows that onoff stands either for the token ONCMD or for the token OFFCMD, and we need a definition for numb.

```
onoff:     ONCMD
     |
       OFFCMD
     ;
numb:NUMBER
     ;
```

yacc specifications are the embodiment of top-down design. At the top of the specification is the most general definition, and subsequent definitions in the file expand and elaborate on the established definitions. Definitions that relate directly to the tokens returned by yylex() are usually found near the end of the file.

For each rule in a yacc specification, there may be an associated action. Like actions in lex, the yacc actions are executed whenever input corresponding to the given rule is encountered. Since rules in yacc may be written in terms of other rules, there is a mechanism in yacc for returning values from one rule to another. You can see why returning values from one rule to another is necessary by examining the definitions for cmd and onoff. Obviously the action for cmd needs to know whether onoff stands for the ONCMD token or the OFFCMD token, and it needs to know the value of numb.

A low-level rule (e.g., numb) can return a value to a high-level rule (e.g., cmd) by assigning a value to the pseudovariable $$.

```
numb: NUMBER
            { $$ = yylval; }
        ;
```

A high-level rule can pick up a value by examining the pseudovariable $1 for the first member of the definition, $2 for the second, and so on.

```
cmd:    SET BIT numb onoff ENDCMD
        {
        printf("Val %d returned by numb rule.\n",$3);
        }
        ;
```

Now that the basic elements of a yacc specification have been discussed, it is time to give an example. In many areas of programming, it is necessary to interactively assign values to elements of complicated data structures. For example, a program that controls a physiological stimulator may contain a data structure that controls the timing and amplitude of the stimulus. To use the program, the data structure must be loaded with the appropriate values. The process might be controlled interactively through a command language

```
set trial 3 amplitude 10;set bit 5 on trial 3 csr
```

The yacc specification that follows is the skeleton for this type of application. Instead of controlling an entire abstract data structure, what follows can set bits on or off in an integer variable or assign values to the variable. Each time a command is successfully recognized, the value of the variable is printed. The commands that are recognized by the following yacc specification include

```
set bit 3 on
set 10
set bit 4 off ; set bit 0 on
```

Just as in a lex specification, the first part of a yacc specification contains declarations, and the second part contains rules. The sections are separated by the %% delimiter. The third part of this yacc specification consists

of a very simple main subroutine in C that calls the generated yyparse()
subroutine to actually perform the parsing.

The declaration part consists of C language definitions enclosed in %{ and
%} delimiters and token declarations. In order for yacc and lex to agree on
token definitions, yacc can output a file of defined values for declared
tokens. In our case, this is the file 'y.tab.h', which was included into the
lex specification. lex and yacc work easily together.

The following yacc specification is longer and more difficult than most
examples in this book. However, if you understand the ideas presented
here and you are familiar with C, then you should not find it too complicated to understand.

```
%{
/*
 * Yacc Specification File
 *   - The First Part -
 *      Declarations
 */
int testvar = 0;
int yylval;
#define Off 0
#define On 1
%}
%TOKEN      SET,BIT,ONCMD,OFFCMD
%TOKEN      NUMBER,ENDCMD,UNKNOWN
%%
/*
 * - The Second Part -
 *        Rules
 */

session:           /* Rule 1 */
      |
      cmds
      ;
cmds: cmd          /* Rule 2 */
      |
      cmds cmd
      ;
```

```
cmd:    ENDCMD                  /* Rule 3 - Alternative 1 */
            { /* the null cmd */ }
        |
        error ENDCMD            /*  Rule 3 - Alternative 2 */
        |
        SET BIT numb onoff ENDCMD /* Alternative 3 */
                {
                if (($3 <= 15) && ($3 >= 0)) {
                    if ($4 == Off)
                            testvar = testvar & ~(1 << $3);
                    else
                            testvar = testvar | (1 << $3);
                }
                else
                        printf("Illegal bit number: %d\n",$3);
                printf("Testvar - %o\n",testvar);
                }
        |
        SET numb ENDCMD         /* Rule 3 - Alternative 4 */
                {
                testvar = $2;
                printf("Testvar - %o\n",testvar);
                }
        ;
numb:   NUMBER                  /* Rule 4 */
            { $$ = yylval; }
        ;
onoff:    ONCMD        /* Rule 5 - Alternative 1 */
            {$$ = On;}
        |
        OFFCMD                  /* Rule 5 - Alternative 2 */
            { $$ = Off; }
        ;
%%
/*
 *  - The Third Part -
 * Support Subroutines
 */
main()
{
     yyparse();
}
```

The following commands convert this simple **yacc** parser, stored in 'yaccdemo.y', into an executable program.

```
$ yacc -d yaccdemo.y
$ cc -o yaccdemo y.tab.c lex.yy.o
$ _
```

Note that yacc always places its output in 'y.tab.c'. Several of the rules are straightforward. Rules 1 and 2 simply explain that a session is either a null event or a sequence of commands, and a sequence of commands (cmds) is either a single command or several commands.

Most of the real work is in rule 3. Alternatives 3 and 4 of rule 3 implement the two types of command—the bit-setting commands and full-assignment commands. Alternative 1 allows null commands. Null commands occur rather easily, as in

```
set bit 3 on;
```

and they should not be illegal. (This input leads to a null command, because the command set bit 3 on is terminated with a semicolon, and then the newly initiated command is abruptly terminated with a new line.)

The second alternative of rule 3 illustrates a simple error recovery technique. The name error is built into yacc, and anytime an input error is encountered, it is as if the error token were recognized. Errors will occur in our simple language for inputs similar to

```
bit set 3 on
```

because the keywords are out of order. They also occur for inputs similar to

```
please set bit 3 off
```

because the word "please" is not recognized. In these situations the effect of an error is to complete alternative 2 of rule 3 by waiting until an ENDCMD token (either a semicolon or a new line) is encountered. The effect is to throw away the tail of a mangled command, a simple but adequate option for our simple command language. More sophisticated error-handling schemes can be implemented.

CHAPTER 20

===

Networking

A network is a group of similar individuals or systems that work collectively and share information. Examples are cells, spies, and computer systems. Communication is the essential aspect of a computer network.

20.1 UUCP

uucp, which is an acronym for *Unix to Unix CoPy*, is a suite of programs that was developed to help distribute software updates. The idea was to use uucp to transmit software over the phone lines rather than use the post office to transmit that information on computer tapes.

There are numerous advantages to the uucp approach. One is immediacy. A critical update can arrive within minutes of making a request. Another advantage is automation. When a system administrator receives a tape, it must be loaded onto the drive and read into a spare directory, and then the system manager must install the software. Many similar activities with uucp are more automated. Yet another advantage is convenience. uucp will send software to a site in response to a simple UNIX command. You don't have to arrange for mailing tapes.

Two UNIX systems can communicate via uucp if they are connected by a serial line or if they can call each other using the public phone system. The only hardware that a system needs for uucp is a serial port, and possibly a modem for accessing the phone system. uucp doesn't require kernel modifications; thus it will run on any UNIX system.

Today uucp's role in the UNIX community goes far beyond its original mandate. Virtually all major UNIX sites are connected by uucp connections to other UNIX sites, forming a worldwide network of UNIX systems. Electronic mail and other information travels on this network, enhancing the productivity of most UNIX users.

The original goal of uucp was to create a simple program that could manage unattended file transfers, using telephone connections to link one site with another. "Unattended" means that a person doesn't have to manually initiate the phone call, dial the number, log onto the remote computer, and perform the transfer. Rather, the user issues a request for a file transfer, and then uucp takes over, performing the necessary intermediate steps to carry out the request.

uucp has become the term to describe the entire system, but uucp is actually just the user-level program that accepts requests and for intersystem file copies. The other major user-level program in the system is uux, which accepts requests for command execution on remote systems. Both uucp and uux place the requests onto a queue of pending jobs. The internal heart of the uucp system is a program called uucico (copy in, copy out). It examines the work queues, makes the necessary connections with remote systems, and supervises the byte-by-byte transfer of information. uucico handles both ends of the conversations. When one system calls another, the uucico on the first system makes the call and logs onto the second. A uucico on the second system is started at the conclusion of the login, and from that point forward the two uucico programs interact, passing files and work orders between the systems until the work is completed.

Many people's primary interface to the uucp system is via mail. The UNIX mail program existed before uucp was developed, but when uucp suddenly provided intermachine links, the mail program was upgraded to take advantage of the new capability. Today uucp is still limited to single-hop transfers, but the mail software has been enhanced so that you can mail messages via a series of UNIX machines, enabling you to send mail to machines that aren't directly connected to your own.

uucp mail addresses are sequences of machine names separated by exclamation points (!) followed at the end by the user's name. Thus the network address 'rocky2!rna!kc' goes from the local machine to a machine called 'rocky2', from there to a machine called 'rna', and finally to the user called 'kc' on 'rna'. What actually happens is that each machine strips off the leftmost machine name (and the following exclamation point) from the network address and then ships the file to that machine. Thus the local machine will strip off 'rocky2!' from the network address before sending the message to rocky2, rocky2 will strip off 'rna!' before sending the message to rna, and rna will simply send the message to kc. On the uucp network each machine only knows how to send a message to a handful of neighboring sites. Thus messages often have to be routed through multiple machines before reaching their destination, and on most systems it is your responsibility to supply the routing information manually. Some machines have installed automated routing software, but automated routing software is far from universal.

A *gateway* is a machine that can forward messages from one network to another. The UNIX uucp dial-up network is "gatewayed" to various other networks. Access rights to these networks vary, and it is your responsibility to stay within the law. Most of these other networks have different conventions for network addresses. For example, on the ARPANET (a nationwide network administrated by the Defense Department's Advanced Research Projects Agency), an address is formed by the user's name followed by @ followed the user's machine name, followed by ".arpa". On the ARPANET it isn't necessary to use uucp style network paths, because each machine on the ARPANET knows how to get a message to any other machine on the net. Because of the way UNIX `mail` simply strips off the leftmost part of an address and then forwards the message, it is compatible with other styles of network addressing. For example, if 'cmclxy' is a gateway from uucp network to the ARPANET, the network address 'rocky2!rna!cmclxy!jacine@xphys.arpa' will send a message to a user named Jacine on the ARPANET machine named 'xphys'. The gateway, cmclxy, is accessed via rocky2 and rna. (This discussion of ARPA style addresses is not intended to imply that all UNIX users have access rights to use the ARPA net—they do not. My intent is to show the difference between UUCP style manual routing and ARPA style domain names, and also to show how a connection can be made from one net to the other, for those who are entitled to use such a gateway.)

One major uucp cost is administration. The system administrator must manage a set of configuration files for uucp. For example, there are files that tell uucp about the dialers that are connected to the ports, which ports are used to access which systems, and at what speed. The most critical configuration file is 'L.sys', which contains an entry for every site that your machine can reach directly. The entries specify when the site can be called, the login sequence for the site, and the login password.

The 'L.sys' approach, although important for a dial-up protocol such as uucp, is a major violation of the UNIX approach to password maintenance. The ordinary UNIX password file contains encrypted passwords, allowing it to be readable by ordinary users. Security of passwords is attained by the encryption algorithm, not by the relatively weak UNIX file access permissions system. The passwords in the 'L.sys' file are kept in clear text; the only protection is the UNIX file access system. The system can be compromised, for example, simply by stealing a backup tape containing 'L.sys' and reading it on another system. Perhaps the most troubling aspect of the 'L.sys' approach is that the integrity of a system can be compromised by sloppy system administration on any of the machines that dial in. Your system may be punished for a neighboring system's faults.

Although uucp is not perfect, it must be recognized as one of the milestones in the history of the UNIX system. Its universal use and distribution a decade after its original development are a remarkable achievement.

20.2   TCP/IP

TCP/IP is a protocol that was developed by the U.S. Defense Advanced Research Projects Agency (DARPA) to allow machines to communicate with other machines over many types of links, locally and over great distances. TCP, which stands for Transmission Control Protocol, is concerned with the details of information transmission. IP, which stands for Internet Protocol, specifies how messages should be routed between systems.

Although TCP/IP was developed by DARPA, it is currently available on many commercial and academic UNIX systems. It forms the basis for much of the Berkeley networking. Although TCP/IP was designed to work on almost any conceivable transmission medium, in the Berkeley environment the protocols are most often used for local area networking using *ethernet* hardware for the machine-to-machine connections.

Ethernet is a standard hardware communications interface that was jointly developed by Digital Equipment Corporation, Xerox, and Intel starting in 1980. Unlike telephone switching systems and other hardware designed for long-distance communication, ethernet is a local communications system, spanning a maximum distance of 2.8 km. Most ethernets are much smaller than the 2.8-km maximum. The raw transmission rate of ethernet is 10 million bits per second, but various hardware and software overheads provide significant overhead. Ethernet, a hardware connection, can simultaneously support multiple software protocols. On typical systems, TCP/IP is just one of several protocols running on the ethernet.

Berkeley's TCP/IP implementation resides principally in the UNIX kernel. This approach makes sense from a performance vantage point, but it makes it difficult to port the Berkeley networking software to other versions of UNIX. Thus the Berkeley networking is available only on Berkeley-derived versions of UNIX, whereas the user-level uucp protocols are universally available on UNIX machines. Unlike uucp, whose hardware requirements are minimal, Berkeley's networking requires an ethernet transport system, which typically costs $1000 or more per machine.

On Berkeley systems, the user interfaces to the networking facilities are `rlogin`, to log into a remote machine; `rsh`, to run a job on a remote machine; and `rcp`, to copy a file to/from (or between) remote machines. Besides these new facilities for networking, some traditional software, such as `mail` and `lpr`, has been modified to take advantage of the networking.

Berkeley's networking facilities provide a major improvement over the uucp protocols for local networking. (Of course, Berkeley's networking additions do not replace uucp for long-distance communication.) The connections are much higher in band width, and some facilities, such as remote login, are more transparent. Security is better, partly because one can make different assumptions in a local environment. However, Berkeley's networking is not perfect. It lets users run a program on a remote machine, but it doesn't provide finer-grained control, such as executing a procedure on a remote system. It also doesn't provide adequate flexibility in accessing files. Software can be written to access files on remote machines, but there isn't a transparent way to use existing software to access remote files.

20.3 NETWORK FILESYSTEMS

The ordinary UNIX filesystem is designed to support the needs of a single machine. Since disk drives are physically connected to CPUs, the original UNIX filesystem design closely tied filesystems to individual machines. In a networking environment, a more flexible arrangement is preferred. In a physical sense, a given disk exists on a given machine, and one might say that the files on that disk also reside on a particular machine. But the goal is to make file resources more generally available, so that machines can make their local files available to other machines and also access files physically stored on other machines.

The first widely available filesystem that was designed to meet the needs of a network environment is Sun Microsystem's Network File System (NFS). It provides file transparency by allowing users on one system to mount files on a remote system. Once a remote filesystem is mounted, its files can be accessed as easily as the files on the local machines. Ordinary processes don't need to know that they are using files stored on a remote machine.

NFS makes it possible to operate UNIX machines without an attached disk drive. Such a machine, usually called a *diskless workstation,* relies on the filesystem of another machine on the network. There are several advantages to diskless workstations, including simplified system administration. But the driving force behind diskless workstations is economics. It is cheaper to buy a single large disk to serve several diskless workstations than it is to buy several smaller disks. The CPU and memory, which are the principal ingredients of a diskless workstation, are all electronic and relatively inexpensive.

CHAPTER 21

UNIX on Personal Computers

Let's define a personal computer as "a computer designed to be used by an individual." That definition lets in a range of machines, from $200 home computers to $75,000 graphics workstations. These rough limits apply because few workers are so valuable that they warrant more than a $75,000 automated assistant, and few manufacturers can assemble a useful computer for less than $200.

The most successful personal computer family is the IBM PC. Based on Intel microprocessors, its hardware design was inspired by the older Apple II, and its operating software, MS-DOS (IBM's version is called PC-DOS), started out as a quick rewrite of CP/M, Digital Research's seminal 8-bit operating system. MS-DOS has the advantage of simplicity, but there are so many things it cannot manage that users must sometimes turn to the much pricier variants of the UNIX system. The second generation operating system for the IBM PC is called OS/2. It is blend of DOS compatibility, UNIX-like features, and new capabilities.

The original designers of the UNIX system didn't design it for minimal hardware, such as that found on the original IBM PC. However, later models of the PC family, such as the IBM PC/AT and the new generation of machines based on the speedy Intel 80386 CPU, are very adequate UNIX machines.

Besides the commercially successful IBM PC family, there are other personal computers that are often used for the UNIX system. For example IBM sells the RT/PC, a graphics workstation expressly designed to run UNIX. Sun Microsystems, Apollo, and Digital Equipment corporation all sell low-cost workstations that are in the personal-computer price and performance class.

This chapter will explore the uses of the UNIX system on personal computers and then discuss some of the tradeoffs of running the UNIX system on the IBM PC architecture vs. running UNIX on the low-end personal workstations.

21.1 UNIX ON THE IBM PC FAMILY

The introduction of the IBM PC/XT marked IBM's commitment to hard disk technology for the PC family. The original XT featured a modest 10 megabytes of disk storage, but subsequent machines from IBM and others contain several times as much disk storage. The introduction of hard disks into the personal computer marketplace is a big step forward from a UNIX perspective. The UNIX system needs a hard disk, because it achieves multi-tasking by temporarily swapping out to disk any executing programs that don't fit in main memory.

There are several difficulties running the UNIX system on an XT class computer. One problem is memory. Machines based on the Intel 8088/8086 processors are limited to a megabyte of memory, but other aspects of the XT design impose an even lower limit—640 kilobytes. Although the UNIX system can perform adequately with just over a half megabyte of memory, more memory would make it a much stronger product.

A second difficulty of the UNIX system on an XT class machine is processing power. Some vendors have XT class machines with a faster CPU, but the processing power of the Intel 8088/8086 CPU is marginal for the UNIX system. As a single-user workstation it is adequate, but nothing more.

A third difficulty is disk speed. The XT was designed as a better PC. The hard disk on the XT class machines has been described as a large floppy. That seemingly flip remark isn't far from the truth. Although the XT's hard disk performance is greater than a floppy's, it is a slow disk by most standards. The UNIX system relies on disk performance for swapping and program loading, and a slow disk is a major bottleneck. Of the three major limitations of using an XT class machine for UNIX, this is the easiest to overcome. Various vendors sell relatively fast hard disks for the PC family, and a faster hard disk will make UNIX run better.

Although the XT class of machines is a credible UNIX platform, my experience is that an XT class machine is usable as a multiuser UNIX system only if the demands of each user are very small. Demanding users, such as software developers, should have exclusive use of an XT running the UNIX system or perhaps shared use of an AT running the UNIX system.

An AT running the UNIX system is suitable for a broad range of applications. It can serve as a speedy single-user system or as a multiuser system for automating small businesses. AT class machines, based on the Intel 80286 processor, immediately dispense with the three objections raised above: the AT can be outfitted with several megabytes of memory, it has a much faster CPU than the XT, and its standard hard disk has good performance.

21.2   WHY UNIX ON A PERSONAL COMPUTER

There are two major reasons for running UNIX on a personal computer such as the PC. The first is features. People often need a feature found in UNIX, such as multitasking, that is missing from the PC's usual operating software. The UNIX system features multiuser database software, it comes with software for managing dial-in ports, it's a natural for electronic mail, it has traditionally been used for software development, it has powerful software for typesetting, etc.

Probably the most common use of the UNIX system on a personal computer is for small-business applications. A personal computer running the UNIX system equipped with a few terminals can easily automate a small business. The multiuser, multitasking features of the UNIX system make it easy to use a shared database. For example, there is a large auto salvage business in the Bronx that keeps its inventory on a UNIX system. Each salesperson is equipped with a terminal that is connected to an AT. Every major part in the inventory is logged into the database, enabling the salesperson to immediately deliver price and availability information to the customer.

Another example of UNIX business application was shown to me the last time I opened a bank account. The UNIX system provided each bank officer with access to the central accounts information, and it also provided convenient account information entry screens so that new account information could be entered easily. The bank officer who demonstrated the system explained that the current user interface, performed by the AT running the UNIX system, was much better than the previous user interface. An added advantage is cost; the UNIX system based on an AT and a few inexpensive terminals cost about the same as a single mainframe data terminal.

The second reason many personal computer users run UNIX is compatibility with minicomputer UNIX systems. Organizations or individuals with an existing investment in UNIX software, training, and expertise often prefer to run UNIX on their personal computers.

One example is a group here at Rockefeller University that used to perform its computing on the university's central UNIX computer facility. The main applications were word processing and simple database inquiries. As personal computer costs decreased, this group decided to move its operations off the central resource and onto local personal computers. Because UNIX on a personal computer is almost indistinguishable from the versions found on more powerful computers, it wasn't necessary to retrain any personnel, and none of their data needed to be converted. And whenever they need the extra performance of the central mainframe, they can switch back without difficulty.

However, there is another way for PC users to gain compatibility with minicomputer UNIX systems. Some traditional UNIX applications are now available running under MS-DOS. For example, MS-DOS users can purchase a vi work-alike text editor, the entire set of UNIX typesetting programs, work-alike versions of most of the UNIX programming utilities, and MS-DOS versions of the Bourne shell.

21.3 WHAT'S MISSING FROM PERSONAL UNIX SYSTEMS

Perhaps the question most often asked about PC/IX, XENIX, VENIX, Microport, and the other versions of the UNIX system on PCs is, "Is this really UNIX?" The answer is certainly yes, but there are a few caveats. Personal computers have fewer resources than minicomputers. Their disks are generally smaller and slower, and their processing power (especially their floating point performance) is lower. Within the bounds imposed by these hardware limitations, UNIX on personal computers can do the same jobs as the UNIX system on minis.

The first difference many users notice is that the UNIX system for personal computers is sold in pieces. There is some variation from one vendor to another, but typically the system is sold in three pieces: the basic system, the text-processing facilities, and the programmer's facilities. Minicomputer versions of the UNIX system invariably have the entire set of facilities, but on a personal computer you only need to purchase the parts you need.

Another difference is that on minicomputers the vendors routinely support a wide range of peripherals. That's because the minicomputer market has traditionally supported a mix-and-match approach to hardware configurations. Personal computer UNIX systems invariably support all of the standard peripherals, but they often don't support some of the more specialized peripherals.

Most vendors allow you to reconfigure (recompile) personal computer UNIX systems to add support for new devices. It's easy to add in a vendor-supplied device driver—for example, a tape backup unit software driver. However, the omission of source code from personal computer UNIX distributions makes it much harder to develop new device driver software.

21.4 MS-DOS AND UNIX

One of the most exciting trends in the personal computer marketplace is the increasing availability of MS-DOS and the UNIX system on the same computer. The first versions of the UNIX system for personal computers contained limited MS-DOS compatibility. They contained simple utilities to read and write MS-DOS format disks, and it was often possible to keep both systems available on the same hard disk so that either system could be booted. The major limitation of the early systems is that you couldn't run an MS-DOS application while UNIX was running. This limited capability was partly a result of the time allotted for getting a product developed and partly a result of the very limited ability of the Intel 8088/8086 CPU to switch from one environment to another.

The increasing sophistication of the Intel 286 and 386 processors makes it easier to have several separate sets of operating software available at one time. On the 286 it is possible, although somewhat difficult, to have MS-DOS running as a process under the UNIX system. Several vendors have 286-based systems that allow a single MS-DOS job to run on the machine as a task under the UNIX system. This allows a user to run an MS-DOS program while the UNIX system is running.

One of Intel's major design goals for its 32-bit CPU, the 386, was its support for virtual machines. Although the software is difficult to develop, the 386 can support a virtually unlimited mix of computing environments. A 386-based machine can run several MS-DOS and UNIX jobs simultaneously. This allows people to take advantage of the best that each system has to offer—the often superb user interfaces of the MS-DOS software, and the power and versatility of the UNIX software.

21.5 ADDITIONAL USER RESPONSIBILITIES

Running the UNIX system on a personal computer imposes an extra burden on the user. On a mini or mainframe, there is usually an operations staff that takes care of administrative matters, such as performing backups, installing software, configuring hardware and software, etc. On most personal UNIX systems, those chores usually fall directly on the user.

An extra degree of sophistication is needed to perform UNIX system administration. Users who have mastered the intricacies of `troff` may not be ready to install and maintain their own copy of the UNIX system. Vendors have responded by simplifying installation and providing improved system administration documents, but UNIX system administration remains a chore that is much more involved than MS-DOS system maintenance.

The first hurdle of using the UNIX system on a personal computer is installation. The instructions from the vendor are usually clear, but the size and scope of the UNIX system make it necessary to spend an hour or more following the vendor's installation script.

The most important system administration task, and one of the most ignored by personal computer UNIX users, is performing backups. Computers (especially hard disks) occasionally break, and information loss is inevitable unless you protect yourself by making routine backups.

There are several backup strategies, but probably the simplest is to put a copy of your work onto a floppy at the end of each session. This strategy works adequately on a single-user system if you modify just a few files each session, but it is not a good strategy for systems with multiple users or large databases.

The other system administration hurdle on personal computer UNIX systems is managing the routine chores. You must check the filesystems each time the system is turned on, add accounts for new users, keep the communication software properly configured, reconfigure the software as the hardware configuration changes, etc. Most of these chores are clearly detailed in the manuals that accompany the system.

21.6   UNIX ON PC'S VERSUS GRAPHIC WORKSTATIONS

Just as high-end minicomputers are beginning to compete with mainframes, high-end personal computers are proving to be stiff competition for low-end minicomputer workstations. Workstations started out as minicomputers. The first workstations had minicomputer price and performance. The only difference between a graphics workstation and a mini was the graphics. A mini with attached graphics and no provisions for adding a gaggle of users via serial ports was called a graphics workstation. Subtract the graphics and add the serial ports, and it was a mini.

As the graphics workstation market has matured, a wider range of machines has become available. Today there are low-end graphics workstations that sell for just a bit more than a well-configured AT class machine. Let's look at some of the differences.

The first difference is graphics, which has always been the primary concern of graphics workstation vendors. Although there are a few high-end graphics offerings for the AT family, the standard graphics fare on the AT is modest. The semistandard Enhanced Graphics Adapter (EGA) has a resolution of 640 by 350, much less than the 1000 by 1000 that is the minimum on a graphics workstation. Applications such as circuit design, VLSI design, mechanical design, and drafting work best at high resolution. For example, when designing a circuit, a graphics workstation can show about four times more of the circuit than an EGA-based PC.

Another difference is connectivity. Graphics workstations are designed with connectivity in mind. They are designed to share information with other workstations, and often to share processing burdens with a speedy mainframe. On graphics workstations from Sun, Apolio, and DEC, the networking is standard, and versions of the UNIX system for these machines routinely support networking protocols. Network adapters are available for PCs, but network software support of the standard personal computer versions of the UNIX system lags behind. It's possible to configure PCs to match the networking performance that is standard in traditional graphics workstations, but only with additional cost and effort.

CHAPTER 22

Benchmarking UNIX Systems

A benchmark is a measure of a system. But what do you need to measure? The apocryphal blind men with the elephant each chose a different metric. One might measure temperature, one might measure the smoothness of the skin, one might (attempt to) measure weight. These would all be valid measures, but little would be known about the elephant.

Similar problems confront those who attempt to measure computer performance. For a given system many different measures are possible, and each may be valid for a different purpose. For example, chip manufacturers debate the instruction timings of each generation of chips. Compiler vendors compare the efficiency of their generated code. Peripherals vendors talk about how fast their products get data into or out of main memory.

Your interpretation of benchmark information should be tempered by what you want to do with a machine. For example, if you are planning to run scientific programs that make heavy use of floating-point operations applied to massive data structures, you need excellent floating-point performance and excellent virtual memory facilities. Other performance aspects, such as disk band width, may be relatively unimportant. If you want a system for heavy multiuser loads, then fast context switching, large main memory, and fast disks are critical. If you want a personal UNIX system for software development, you want moderate overall performance coupled with low cost.

The goal of this chapter is to present a sample benchmark suite, the Ts'o benchmark suite, so that you can begin to see some of the issues in benchmarking. A secondary objective is to present results of the Ts'o suite for many current machines, so that you have a basis for comparison.

Performing the Ts'o benchmarks on new machines is discussed in Section 22.2, and the source of the benchmarks is discussed in Section 22.3.

22.1   THE TS'O BENCHMARKS

Researcher Dan Ts'o of the Rockefeller University has created a general-purpose benchmark suite for UNIX systems. The benchmark suite has been widely distributed, and individuals are encouraged to run the benchmarks on new systems so that the database of performance information can be expanded. His benchmarks have also been widely quoted by vendors, especially those vendors who have fared well.

The Ts'o benchmarks consist of standard chores, such as copying files, sorting files, and formatting documents, combined with a few more specialized programs that address specific issues, such as floating-point performance. The variety of chores in the Ts'o benchmarks is designed to reveal various aspects of system performance. Dan's benchmarks are not the last word on system performance; rather, they are easy to use, freely available, and based on typical chores, and a base of benchmark data exists for making comparisons. Dan claims only that his benchmarks provide a first approximation of UNIX system performance.

The Ts'o benchmarks contain 10 separate tasks. Each task is performed three times, and the results are averaged. The UNIX `time` command prints three time intervals—the total elapsed (real) time, the user time, and the system time. For the cpu-bound tasks, the user time is most important; the elapsed time is most important for the other tasks. The benchmarks should be performed on an otherwise idle system.

There are 10 separate tasks in the Ts'o benchmark suite.

Loop. The loop is an extremely simple C program that counts (silently) from zero to 1 million. It is compute-bound, and it provides the C compiler with significant opportunities for code optimization. This test measures the efficiency of the C compiler and the processing speed of the computer. Machines based on 32-bit (or better) processors (such as the 68020 and the microVAX) do better on this benchmark than machines based on 16-bit processors because the loop index must have more than 16-bit resolution to count to 1 million. (User time is most important.)

CC Loop. The C compiler, like many other UNIX programs, spends part of its time I/O-bound (mainly performing I/O, hence limited by the speed of the I/O system) and part compute-bound (mainly performing computations, hence limited by CPU speed). The I/O involves searching libraries and loading the compiler passes. The compute-bound part is the syntax analysis and code generation. The time it takes the C complier to compile a short program such as 'loop.c' is more indicative of I/O performance than of CPU performance. (Real time is most important.)

Sieve. The sieve of Eratosthenes is a method for finding prime numbers. The method relies on ruling out multiples of known primes. In the version here, which is identical to the version presented in BYTE magazine (9/81), only odd numbers are considered. Excluding even numbers makes this version efficient, but it is hard to understand the program. This task is most important to those who need good integer performance. Although the sieve is a widely used benchmark, it has several shortcomings. It penalizes 32-bit (or better) machines because it can be performed using 16-bit arithmetic. It also avoids all subroutine calls, which are a major ingredient of most programs. The sieve is probably most important as a compiler benchmark, because the nested loops and regular accesses to a small array provide many opportunities for compiler optimizations. As many people have noted, it is possible to rewrite the C language source of the sieve more efficiently. Unfortunately, many vendors have done just that and published the results. The only importance of the sieve is as a standard task, and results from hand-optimized versions can't be compared with past timings. (User time is most important.)

CC Sieve. This second C compiler benchmark is interpreted similarly to the first; the major difference is that the sieve is a slightly longer program than the loop. (Real time is most important.)

Float. This simple floating-point benchmark performs a series of multiplications and divisions 10,000 times. This task reveals a first approximation of a machine's floating point performance, but you should seek more information if you are planning to purchase a machine for intensive floating-point operations. For example, the float task doesn't exercise any of the standard math library functions, and it can't differentiate between machines where transcendental operations (such as *sin*) are performed in hardware and those where transcendentals are computed by software. The most widely known floating-point benchmark is the Whetstone, although it has been criticized for performing a more floating-point-intensive mix of instructions than most real floating-point programs. (User time is most important.)

Getpid. The getpid task repeatedly executes the simplest UNIX system call. It measures the efficiency of the system call mechanism, which is an important contributor to overall system efficiency. (Real time is most important.)

Grep. The grep task searches for a word in a large text file. This is a typical task on most UNIX systems. (Real time is most important.)

Machine	Loop	CC Loop	Sieve	CC Sieve	float	getpid	grep	copy	nroff	sort	Avg.
780	1.0	1.0	1.0	1.0	1.0	1.0	1.0	1.0	1.0	1.0	1.0
750	.49	.60	.61	.57	.76	.59	.5	1.0	.57	.55	.62
MVAXI	.21	.31	.28	.31	.10	.32	.32	.25	.34	.33	.28
MVAXII	.83	.89	.92	.91	1.0	.86	.97	1.25	.89	.83	.93
11/23	.10	.17	.26	.19	.034	.15	.24	.13	.14	.20	.16
11/73(1)	.24	.31	.67	.34	.16	.35	.59	.14	.29	.44	.35
11/73(2)	.25	.34	.67	.4	.16	.29	.59	.14	.34	.47	.37
11/34	.19	.25	.46	.27	.27	.30	.4	.13	.22	.34	.28
11/44	.27	.30	.71	.36	.31	.41	.44	.16	.33	.42	.37
11/45	.31	.29	.40	.2	.25	.28	.29	.05	.2	.23	.25
11/70	.35	.28	.86	.31	.62	.20	.24	.22	.46	.73	.43
MASS	.38	.38	.57	.4	.030	.76	.4	.25	.4	.5	.41
32016(1)	.23	.17	.36	.17	.33	.25	.2	.1		.22	.23
32016(2)	.81	.41	.58	.78	.34	.60	.46	.22		.74	.55
8088	.08	.073	.21	.075	.13	.22	.13	.047	.12	.16	.12
286(1)	.16	.17	.56	.19	.0029	.55	.39	.10	.27	.41	.28
286(2)	.22	.17	.58	.17	.0028	.71	.32	.19	.31	.56	.32
286(3)	.4	.28	1.1	.28	.14	1.2	.51	.23	.45	.92	.87
CALLAN	.4	.13	.59	.15	.031	.89	.51	.15	.29	.47	.36
G8750	4.20	1.10	8.0	1.5	3.3	3.1	4.1	2.0	1.4	3.4	3.2
PYR	2.10	.60	2.5	.67	.27	2.0	1.3	2.0	1.3	1.4	1.4
SUN(1)	1.56	.74	2.2	.92	1.0	1.74	2.0	1.33	1.78	2.25	1.55
SUN(2)	1.25	.38	1.88	.45	.52	1.3	1.46	1.18	1.69	1.46	1.15
RT	.53	.45	.96	.46	.17	.92	1.05	.67	1.0	1.01	.72
PE3220	.4	.38	.71	.44	.013	.36	.51	.2	.34	.51	.38
CRAY	12.5		13.3		40.6	14.4					

Figure 22.1A.   Benchmark results.

Copy. The copy task duplicates a 200,000-byte file. This is a good measure of I/O system efficiency. This test is especially revealing when performed on two configurations of the same machine, one with a fast disk and one with a mediocre disk. Disk I/O performance is especially important on machines that are expected to perform under heavy multiuser loads. In many (but not all) ways, UNIX performance is better on a modest CPU with a fast disk subsystem than on a fast CPU with a mediocre disk. (Real time is most important.)

MACHINE CONFIGURATIONS

780 Digital Equipment Corp. VAX 11/780, Fujitsu Eagle disk on Emulex SC780, FPA, 4.2BSD, 4k/1k filesystem.

750 Digital Equipment Corp. VAX 11/750, Fujitsu Eagle disk on Emulex SC750, FPA, 4.2BSD, 4k/1k filesystem.

MVAXI Digital Equipment Corp. MicroVAX I, RD51 disk on RQDX1, Ultrix 1.1.

MVAXII Digital Equipment Corp. MicroVAX II, Fujitsu Eagle Disk on Emulex QD32, Ultrix 1.2.

11/23 Digital Equipment Corp. LSI 11/23, USDC 40ms disk with read cache, FPU, no FPA, PWB/UNIX.

11/73(1) Digital Equipment Corp. LSI 11/73, USDC 40ms disk with read cache, FPU, no FPA, PWB/UNIX.

11/73(2) Digital Equipment Corp. LSI 11/73, Fujitsu Eagle disk, FPU, no FPA, PWB/UNIX.

11/34 Digital Equipment Corp. PDP 11/34, CDC 9762 disk, FPU, cache, PWB/UNIX (512byte/block).

11/44 Digital Equipment Corp. PDP 11/44, CDC 9762 disk, FPU, cache, PWB/UNIX (512byte/block).

11/45 Digital Equipment Corp. PDP 11/45, RK05 Disks, PWB/UNIX.

11/70 Digital Equipment Corp. PDP 11/70, FPA, CDC 9766 Disk, BRL UNIX (V6/V7/2.9BSD).

MASS Masscomp 500, Motorola 68010 CPU at 10Mhz., no FPA, 4kb cache, virtual memory System III.

32016(1) AIS 3210, National 32016 CPU at 8Mhz, PDP11/23 I/O Processor, 16081 FPU, GENIX (4.1BSD), no wait state mem.

32016(1) National 32016 ICM, 16081 FPU, UNIX System 5.2.

8088 IBM PC/XT, Intel 8088 @ 4.77 Mhz., 8087 FPU, Venix.

286(1) Intel 286/380, Intel 80286 at 6Mhz, Priam 3450 35Mb disk, no FPU, XENIX.

286(2) IBM PC/AT, Intel 80286 at 6Mhz, no FPU, XENIX System V 286, Release 2.1.

286(3) PC Designs ET/286i, Intel 80286 at 10Mhz, 80287, XENIX System V 286, Release 2.1.

CALLAN Callan Data Systems Unistar 300, Motorola 68010 CPU, Uniplus V7.

G8750 Gould Systems Concept 32/8750, 4.1c BSD.

PYR Pyramid, Fujitsu Eagle disk, no FPA, OSx (4.2BSD).

SUN(1) Sun 3/160, Motorola 68020 CPU at 16.7 Mhz., Fujitsu Eagle disk, FPA, Sun Release 3.0 (4.2BSD).

SUN(2) Sun 3/50 Diskless workstation, Motorola 68020 CPU at 15 Mhz., Motorola 68881 Floating point chip, Ethernet connection to Sun 3/180 NFS Fileserver with Eagle disk, Sun Release 3.0 (4.2BSD). (Floating point performance is .093 without 68881.)

RT IBM RT PC 6150 Model 25, Floating Point Accelerator, AIS (Berkeley) 4.2.

PE3220 Perkin Elmer 32220.

CRAY Cray X-MP/12, 1 processor, 9.5 nanosecond cycle time, UNICOS 2.1.

Figure 22.1B.   Benchmark results.

Nroff. The nroff task reads in the -ms macro package. Because -ms consists mainly of macro definitions, nroff must perform a large amount of processing as the file is read in, and the size of the -ms file makes nroff perform a large amount of I/O. Dan has noticed that this task is the best single predictor of a system's overall UNIX performance. Often the figure of merit for this benchmark is similar to the overall figure of merit for a system. On System V, the -ms macro package is often not available. A similar measure can be determined with the -mm macro package, which is always available on System V. If you do use -mm, you should be sure to use the noncompacted version, and you should compare your results to the other -mm times, not to -ms times. (Real time is most important.)

Sort. The sort task sorts a large file of words. Like the nroff task, this task exercises both I/O and computation. This task is probably the second best single indicator of overall system performance.

There are several aspects of UNIX system performance that the Ts'o benchmarks don't address. One area is multiuser performance. Although you can often estimate the suitability of a machine for heavy multiuser loads based on I/O performance, system call efficiency, and overall speed, there isn't a single test in the benchmark suite that specifically attempts to simulate a multiuser load.

Another omission is a test to determine the efficiency of the character I/O system. Some systems are able to service many terminals at a time, others slow down when more than one or two terminals are active.

For convenience, the Digital Equipment Corporation (DEC) VAX 11/780 is used for a reference system. The 780 is a widely admired and widely used machine. One of its most impressive features is its balanced integer performance, floating-point performance, and I/O performance. Although the 780 has been effectively replaced by newer machines from DEC, it's still useful as a reference point.

The data reported in Figure 22.1 show each system's performance for each task normalized to the time it took the 780 to perform the task. The most controversial part of the table is the column detailing the overall figure of merit for each system. The first caveat is that no single figure of merit warrants very serious attention. The individual task performance measures in the table are more reliable. The second caveat is that the figure of merit was computed simply by averaging the individual performance figures. The only advantage of this technique is simplicity. A weighted average would be better for most people, but the individual weights would depend on what features are important to you.

It has also been pointed out that an arithmetic average of normalized data overemphasizes the positive. For example, if a hypothetical machine performs task A twice as fast as the reference system, and task B half as fast as the reference system, common sense suggests that the machines be given the same figure of merit. But if one averages 2 and ½, the result is

1¼, indicating that the hypothetical machine is better than the reference. This difficulty notwithstanding, the overall figure of merit is presented as a simple average.

Compared to the balanced performance of the VAX 11/780, many other machines have an area of weakness. For example, many of the early machines based on the Motorola 68000 processor use software floating point, which makes those machines a poor choice for floating-point tasks (unless you add a hardware floating-point accelerator). Obviously, one area of interest is the deviation of a machine's performance from its average performance. A machine with low performance on one task and high on another must be evaluated carefully, because it is suitable for a narrower niche than a machine with more balanced performance.

About half of the tests reported in the table were performed by Dan Ts'o or myself; the other half were reported by various individuals who sent Dan a copy of the results. Although we have no reason to believe that there are any major errors in the table, you should independently confirm any impressions that you draw from these data.

22.2 RUNNING THE TS'O BENCHMARKS

The Ts'o benchmarks were designed to be easy to run. The hardest part is usually getting the benchmark software onto the machine to be benchmarked. If the machine has a UUCP mail connection, one way is often to mail the software in advance.

The shell script found in the following section will run the benchmark. All you need to do is to type the following to run the benchmarks.

```
$ sh bench.sh
```

The raw data will appear on your terminal. If you want to save the results in a file, you can enter the following command.

```
$ sh bench.sh >logfile 2>&1
```

There are three major difficulties that you may encounter: lack of disk space in '/tmp' for the copy task, lack of the -ms macros (absent on most pure System V machines) for the nroff task, and lack of the file '/usr/dict/words' for the grep and sort tasks. If '/tmp' doesn't have a quarter of a megabyte of free space but some other area does, you can set the $temp variable to indicate where cp should place its copies. If the -ms macros are missing, you can use -mm instead. The results in the table in Figure 22.1 are all for the -ms macros, but the reference time for the VAX 11/780 processing -mm is given below.

If the file '/usr/dict/words' is missing, a substitute can be constructed. One approach is to take a large text file, turn it into a word-per-line format using the deroff -w filter, and then catenate several copies of the file to form a file of about 200,000 bytes. Any ordering is fine for running the grep benchmark, but to run the sort benchmark, you should use a sorted file of words, so that sort -r will have a standard reversal task. If you do construct your own large text file, your results should not be directly compared to those given in Section 22.1.

You should be careful to compile the floating-point benchmark correctly. On many systems there are compiler options that control floating-point code generation. Some machines have floating-point hardware that will not be used unless specified by compiler options.

After you run the benchmarks, you must take the raw timing data that are output by the time command and normalize them to the VAX 11/780 times given below. Be careful to use the user times for the loop, sieve, and float tasks, but the real time for the other tasks. To normalize the raw times, you should take the VAX 11/780 time (given in the following table) and divide it by the raw time on your machine. To compute an average that will be comparable to those given in the last column of Figure 22.1, you should simply add the 10 normalized figures and divide by 10.

	VAX 11/780 (time in seconds)	Comparison Time
Loop	2.5	user
CC Loop	3.4	real
Sieve	2.4	user
CC Sieve	4.4	real
Float	1.3	user
Getpid	18.6	real
Grep	4.1	real
Copy	2.0	real
Nroff	4.1	real
Sort	37.8	real
Nroffmm	14.3	real

Note that the preceding table includes the time to execute the command nroff -mm /dev/null on the reference VAX 11/780. The -mm macros should be used only if your machine doesn't have the -ms macros. Although the -mm normalized performance figure provides useful information, don't compare it to the -ms normalized times in Figure 22.1.

22.3   THE TS'O BENCHMARK SOURCE

The shell script 'bench.sh' runs the Ts'o benchmark suite. You should redirect the script's output into a file if you need a permanent record.

```
$ cat bench.sh
: This benchmark shell script is for use with the Bourne shell
temp=/tmp
words=/usr/dict/words
who
echo No other users should be using the system.
echo Three CC LOOP
time cc -O loop.c -o loop
time cc -O loop.c -o loop
time cc -O loop.c -o loop
echo Three LOOP
time ./loop
time ./loop
time ./loop
echo Three CC SIEVE
time cc -O sieve.c -o sieve
time cc -O sieve.c -o sieve
time cc -O sieve.c -o sieve
echo Three SIEVE
time ./sieve
time ./sieve
time ./sieve
cc -O float.c -o float
echo Three FLOAT
time ./float
time ./float
time ./float
cc -O getpid.c -o getpid
echo Three GETPID
time ./getpid
time ./getpid
time ./getpid
echo Three NROFF
time nroff -ms /dev/null
time nroff -ms /dev/null
time nroff -ms /dev/null
ls -l /usr/lib/tmac.s /usr/lib/tmac/tmac.s
echo Ignore any tmac.s not found messages from ls.
echo The next series of benchmarks requires the use of the file
echo $words or a similar large text file. $words
echo should be 200,000 bytes long, plus or minus a few percent,
echo sorted in ascending order with one word per line.
ls -l $words
echo Three GREP
```

```
time grep zoom $words
time grep zoom $words
time grep zoom $words
echo The next few benchmarks requires sufficient
echo temporary disk space. There should be at least 300,000 bytes
echo or so e.g. 1000 512 byte blocks available in $temp.
df
sleep 5
echo Three COPY
time cp $words $temp/junk
rm -f $temp/junk
time cp $words $temp/junk
rm -f $temp/junk
time cp $words $temp/junk
rm -f $temp/junk
echo Three SORT
time sort -r $words > $temp/junk
rm -f $temp/junk
time sort -r $words > $temp/junk
rm -f $temp/junk
time sort -r $words > $temp/junk
rm -f $temp/junk
echo This concludes the benchmark^G.
$ _
```

The 'loop.c' and 'getpid.c' programs are simple indicators of CPU performance and system call efficiency.

```
$ cat loop.c
main()
{
    long i;
    for (i = 0; i < 1000000; i++);
    printf("Done.\n");
}
$ cat getpid.c
main()
{
    long i;
    for (i = 0; i < 100000; i++)
        getpid();
    printf("Done.\n");
}
$ _
```

The following version of the sieve of Eratosthenes is the same as the version in BYTE magazine.

```
$ cat sieve.c
#include <stdio.h>
#define NTIMES 10
#define SIZE  8190
#define FALSE 0
#define TRUE  1

char flag[SIZE + 1];

main()
{
    int i, j, k, count, prime;

    printf("%d iterations:", NTIMES);
    for (i = 1; i <= NTIMES; i++) {
        count = 0;
        for (j = 0; j <= SIZE; j++)
            flag[j] = TRUE;
        for (j = 0; j <= SIZE; j++) {
            if (flag[j] == TRUE) {
                prime = j + j + 3;
                for (k = j + prime; k <= SIZE; k += prime)
                    flag[k] = FALSE;
                count++;
            }
        }
    }
    printf("%d primes.\n", count);
    exit(0);
}
$ _
```

The 'float.c' program is a very simple floating-point performance indicator.

```
$ cat float.c
#define CONST1   3.1415926
#define CONST2   1.7839032
#define COUNT    10000

main()
{
    double a, b, c;
    int i;

    a = CONST1;
    b = CONST2;
    for (i = 0; i < COUNT; ++i) {
        c = a * b;
        c = c / a;
        c = a * b;
        c = c / a;
        c = a * b;
        c = c / a;
        c = a * b;
        c = c / a;
        c = a * b;
        c = c / a;
        c = a * b;
        c = c / a;
        c = a * b;
        c = c / a;
    }
    printf("Done\n");
}
$ _
```

CHAPTER 23

System Management

Managing a computer system involves more than just turning the power on before the users start logging in each morning. The system manager is responsible for maintaining the integrity of the system, installing new software, adapting software to local conditions, performing periodic backups of users' files, recovering lost data, informing the users of new services and features, and maintaining the security of the system. At some installations, these responsibilities are widely distributed; at other installations, there is a single person who accepts these responsibilities.

UNIX system administration is an increasingly important aspect of routine operations for many individuals because of the increasing use of the UNIX system on single-user workstations and personal computers. The chores described in this chapter are usually performed by professional computer system managers on large minicomputer systems, but they must be performed by relatively inexperienced users on many smaller systems.

Many of the operations performed by the system manager should be inaccessible to ordinary users. In the UNIX system this is accomplished by providing a special privilege level called *superuser*. The UNIX superuser is not restricted by the normal file access system and is allowed to perform all of the system maintenance functions.

A person can acquire the superuser privilege by logging in using the name *root* or by executing the su command. In either case, the user must enter the superuser password before the superuser privilege is granted. The superuser password should be known only by trusted and experienced users.

Maintaining the integrity of the system is probably the most challenging activity for a system manager; performing periodic backups is probably the most bothersome. This chapter does not explain how to fix every conceivable filesystem problem or how to set up a comprehensive backup policy. You must learn by a combination of trial and error, improvisation, and adaptation of the tried and true to your environment. If you have exemplary backups, then damage to the filesystem is not very important, and if you can patch even the most corrupt filesystem, then your need for comprehensive backups is diminished. The strongest defense against lost data is to keep good backups and to understand the procedure for repair of the filesystem, because eventually every UNIX installation has filesystem corruptions.

It is well beyond the scope of this book to provide a complete guide to UNIX system management. Rather, the goal of this chapter is to provide an introduction to some of the procedures and issues that must be understood by the system manager. Chapter 24 presents some of the utility programs that are often used by system administrators.

23.1 SYSTEM CONFIGURATION

Although some UNIX systems are stable over a period of years, it is much more common for configurations to change. Peripherals may be added, aging equipment is often replaced, and new machines are often purchased with a different mix of peripherals.

One of the major considerations when purchasing new equipment is its degree of support under UNIX. Some vendors are still unable to answer a simple question such as, "Do you have a UNIX device driver for your Mighty Fast disk controller?" Other vendors provide excellent UNIX support for their products.

Many vendors provide equipment that conforms to some established interface. For example, many third parties produce communications multiplexers that are functionally equivalent to the DMF communications multiplexer made by the Digital Equipment Corp. Some third-party gear mimics the original closely enough to work on a non-UNIX operating system but not closely enough to work with UNIX. When you are buying third-party hardware emulations, you should expect an informed answer to questions such as, "Is your emulation good enough to work with the standard Berkeley 4.3 device driver?"

One of the most common sources of software drivers is the UNIX community. If you're not up to writing your own, and the manufacturer hasn't heard of UNIX, don't despair. Support for even the most obscure hardware is usually available within the UNIX community. You can find out about such support from user groups, conference proceedings, and the USENET.

Acquiring your new peripheral and its software support is just the first step. The next is installation. You should be able to do the next two steps, hardware installation and software installation, in either order. Your computer system should still work even if unsupported hardware is installed, and you should be able to run a version of UNIX into which you have added new device support even if that device is not yet present. Of course some installations, such as installing a new root disk, or replacing one piece of equipment with another, are trickier.

Adding new device support to a working UNIX system is straightforward. Modern UNIX systems have a configuration file that specifies what support should exist in the kernel. All you need to do is to edit that file to reflect your new configuration, move the device driver files into their directories, and then recompile the kernel. Most of these steps are clearly detailed in the reference manuals, and today there aren't nearly as many ways to do it wrong as there once were.

23.2 THE STICKY BIT

Optimizing system performance is a constant objective of many system managers. There are many factors that influence overall performance, such as the performance of the hardware, the configuration of the kernel software, and the layout of the filesystems. These optimizations are common to most operating systems. However, there is one optimization that is unique to the UNIX system; frequently used programs can be stored on disk in a more efficient manner than that used for ordinary files. This optimization is controlled by an aptly named feature of the filesystem called the sticky bit.

Ordinary files are not stored contiguously on the disk. The information in a file is divided into blocks, and the blocks are stored throughout the disk. If you are having a file typed on your terminal, the system's overhead in retrieving the file from the various places on the disk is very low, because your requests to read the file are interleaved with other users' I/O requests. However, if the system is loading the file for execution, the overhead of noncontiguous disk storage is much higher. The sticky mode helps to reduce this undesirable overhead for frequently executed programs.

When a running program is temporarily suspended from execution (e.g., to let other processes run), the system may copy the process's memory image to temporary storage on a disk. This process is called swapping. The temporary storage on the disk is organized contiguously so that it can be accessed rapidly. In the UNIX system, a special mode can be assigned to a file so that an executable image of the program is permanently stored in the swap space when the program is not being executed. Since the program gets stuck in the swap space (i.e., never gets swapped out), the mode is called the sticky mode, and the bit in the i-node that controls the process is called the *sticky bit*.

Relatively few programs are assigned the sticky mode, because swap space is a precious commodity that will be rapidly exhausted if the sticky mode is overused. Frequently used programs (e.g., the editor, `ls`, `cat`) are often assigned the sticky mode. On large systems, where more swap space is available, more programs may have the sticky mode. On small systems, where disk space is limited, the sticky mode is seldom used.

On XENIX-286 System V, there are just three programs distributed with the sticky bit set.

```
$ ls -l /bin/sh /bin/ls /bin/vi
-rwx--x--t  6 bin    bin     17884 Nov 21 05:43 /bin/ls
-rwx--x--t  2 bin    bin     38001 Nov 18 15:13 /bin/sh
-rwx--x--t  5 bin    bin    126624 Nov 21 03:45 /bin/vi
$ _
```

The sticky mode is indicated by the character "t" in the last position of the file type/mode field of the ls command's long-format output. The sticky mode can be assigned to a file only by the system manager. Users cannot assign the sticky mode to their own files.

23.3 SET USER ID

Occasionally the sophisticated UNIX system file access protection scheme gets in the way of valid access requirements. The classic example is the requirement posed by games programs. Many games programs want to keep an auxiliary file that contains information for the game. For example, in an adventure program, the list of messages in an auxiliary file should be hidden from inquisitive adventurers. The UNIX system mechanism to protect this sort of information is to make the auxiliary file owned by the creator of the game and restrict access to the file. However, when a person plays the game, the information in the auxiliary file must be made available.

The problem is simple; when you are not playing the game, you should be prohibited from accessing the private game information. However, when you are playing the game, you should, within the structure imposed by the game, be allowed access to that information.

The set user id mode solves this problem. If an executable program file has the set user id mode, you acquire all of the privileges of the file owner when you execute the program.

Many of the programs that ordinary users use to find out about the system or to issue system requests, such as print requests, are set user or group id. For example, many people use the df program to print a list of the free space on various filesystems. The df program needs to access two key files in '/etc'—'fstab' and 'mtab'—and it needs to access the disk special file for each filesystem.

```
$ ls -l /etc/mtab /etc/fstab /dev/rhp0a /bin/df
-rwsr-xr-x  1 root     12288 Sep 27  1983 /bin/df
crw-------  1 root      4,   0 Aug 23  1984 /dev/rhp0a
-rw-r--r--  1 root       331 Jun  3  1986 /etc/fstab
-rw-r--r--  1 root       612 Feb 27 16:23 /etc/mtab
$ _
```

The listing above shows that the files in '/etc' could be read without df's set user id mode, but that it does need to have root privileges to access the raw disk interface special file '/dev/rhp0a'.

The owner of a file can set the set user id mode for his own files using the chmod command. The set user id mode is indicated by the character "s" in place of the file owner's execution ("x") character in the type/mode field of the long listing.

The set group id mode for a file allows the person executing that file to acquire the same privileges as members of the owner's group. The set group id mode is essentially a fine-tuning of the set user id system. The set group id mode is indicated by the character "s" in place of the file's group execution ("x") character in the type/mode field of the long-format ls listing. There is no set other id mode, because it would accomplish nothing.

23.4 FIFO FILES

Fifo files are used to allow one program to transfer information to another program. Typically one program will write into a fifo, and another program will read from the fifo. The fifo establishes a communication channel between the two programs. Information is stored in the fifo file only during the short period of time between one program's output to the fifo and the other program's input from the fifo. Fifos are only available on System V.

Fifo files obviously are similar to UNIX pipes. The advantage of using a fifo is that any two unrelated programs can use it to communicate. Pipes require the child programs at either end of the pipe to have the same parent. Usually this parent is the UNIX system shell. A fifo is used when it is not possible or convenient for the communicating processes to have the same parent.

Fifos can be created using the mknod (make node) command (discussed in Section 24.4). Fifos are owned by someone, and access to them is governed by the usual three-tiered protection system.

You have to create a fifo before you can use it. For instance, the following command reads data from the communication line '/dev/tty99' and then writes it out to a fifo file named 'fifo1.tel':

```
$ cat < /dev/tty99 > fifo1.tel
```

If the fifo file 'fifo1.tel' didn't exist when the command was entered, then the shell would have created an ordinary file named 'fifo1.tel' to receive the output of the `cat` command.

A command could pick up information from the fifo using input redirection:

```
$ sh < fifo1.tel
```

In these two examples, we have used the shell's I/O redirection to access the fifo.

23.5   SYMBOLIC LINKS

Both *symbolic links* and ordinary links provide pseudonyms for files. An ordinary link, which is available on all versions of UNIX, occurs whenever more than one directory entry references a given i-node (see Section 25.8). All references have equal weight; one can't say that one name for a file is its real name and that the other names are pseudonyms. The major limitations of ordinary links are that they cannot bridge across filesystems, and they cannot reference directory files.

A symbolic link, which is available only on Berkeley systems, is more powerful than an ordinary link because a symbolic link on one filesystem can reference a file on another filesystem, and because symbolic links can reference directories. The limitation on ordinary links occurs because directory entries can only reference i-nodes on the same filesystem. Symbolic links work by embedding a pathname into an almost ordinary file. "Almost ordinary" means that the file is marked as a symbolic link. Thus an attempt to access the file will actually access whatever file the link references.

One consequence of the Berkeley symbolic link design is that it is possible to point a finger at one file and claim that it is the original while claiming that symbolic link references to that file are pseudonyms. Although symbolic links can be used wherever ordinary links are used, they are slightly more expensive, because the kernel must fetch the symbolic link file, read its text, and then chase down the new pathname. Although this overhead is acceptable wherever the facilities of symbolic links are necessary, it is much more than the (nil) overhead of ordinary links.

Symbolic links are primarily used to provide systemwide aliases. For example, most UNIX programmers have grown accustomed to looking in the '/usr/include/sys' directory for C language include files for systems programming. On many systems the natural home for those include files is on the same filesystem that contains system source, which is often different from the '/usr' filesystem. The solution is to make '/usr/include/sys' a symbolic link to wherever the system include files are actually stored.

Programs can determine that a filename is a symbolic link, although few programs need that capability. One program that does is ls. It "follows" symbolic links while producing a short-format output, but it describes the link itself in the long-format output. An "l" (letter ell) in the first column of an ls listing indicates a symbolic link, and the target of the link is printed after the filename.

```
$ ls /usr/include/sys
acct.h      file.h      param.h      text.h      user.h
bk.h        fs.h        param.h.org  time.h      vadvise.h
^C
$ ls -l /usr/include/sys
lrwxrwxrwx  1 root    6 Jan 29  1984 /usr/include/sys -> /sys/h
$ ls /sys/h
acct.h      file.h      param.h      text.h      user.h
bk.h        fs.h        param.h.org  time.h      vadvise.h
buf.h       gprof.h     proc.h       timeb.h     vcmd.h
^C
$ _
```

(In this example, both ls listings are interrupted by Ctrl-C to reduce their length.) Notice that the length of the symbolic link is 6, which is just enough to store the text "/sys/h".

Symbolic links are created using the -s option of Berkeley's ln command.

23.6 SECURITY

The security of a system is its reliability in the face of adversity. If a system unexpectedly crashes, loses files, or allows unauthorized access to files, then it is insecure. A secure system works reliably and maintains and protects users' files. Security is a relative criterion; the world has yet to see the first completely secure computer system.

The reliability of the UNIX system (its crash resistance) is high. UNIX systems generated from standard software modules often run for months without a crash. This record compares very favorably with the reliability of the computer hardware. UNIX systems that are composed of standard software modules intertwined with locally modified software modules are sometimes less reliable.

The UNIX system is not inherently a fault-tolerant computer system (although versions have been developed that are fault-tolerant). It imposes heavy demands on computer hardware, and it is not forgiving (or informative) when hardware malfunctions. The later UNIX systems include error logging, and they tend to be good at spotting hardware malfunctions before they become serious.

There are three basic reasons computer systems lose files: the hardware malfunctions, the operating system software malfunctions, and the computer user makes mistakes. Hardware malfunctions are inevitable, operating system bugs are likely, and computer user mistakes are assured. The goal of computer manufacturers and operating system designers is to minimize the data loss caused by hardware and software; at the very least, these losses should be small compared to accidental file erasures by users.

One paradox of the UNIX system is that from a user's point of view, all I/O transactions are synchronous, whereas from the system's point of view, all I/O is buffered and asynchronous. The implication of the data buffering performed by the kernel is that data loss is likely whenever the computer stops unexpectedly. Another implication is that it is hard for the kernel to notify processes of write failures in all circumstances, because the process may have exited before the disk write occurs. These problems are undesirable but unavoidable if one wants to maintain the efficiency of the system.

Another aspect of system security concerns the malicious or mischievous user. Although beating the system is a natural human instinct, beating a multiuser computer system usually means interfering with other users and thus is strongly discouraged. Some simple precautions will prevent the great majority of problems.

In older UNIX systems, a user can usually cause a stoppage of service by gobbling up some resource (process table entries, filesystem storage space, etc.). It is always easy to examine the process table after the stoppage and discover the source of the problem, so most of the difficulties here are caused by buggy programs. These techniques are less effective in later versions of the UNIX system because of increasing use of quotas and increasing sensitivity to the problem.

There are several commonsense policies for protecting the security of a system. For example, you should remove the accounts of people who no longer need access to the system. You should also never allow an account to exist without a password. The common practice of allowing the user to install a password when he or she first logs in is bad—the password should be installed by the administrator when the account is created, and then the user can change it during the first login session.

Obviously, you should limit the number of people who know and use the superuser password. You should also limit access to the system console, and you should not leave the system console (or any other terminal) unattended and logged in with superuser privilege. Whenever the computer is running, it should be attended by someone who is trusted. For instance, someone using the computer alone at night can trivially break the security system by halting the computer and then rebooting the computer to single-user mode.

You should also prevent users from importing (by mounting tapes or disks) programs that run in privilege mode. One of the easiest ways to break the UNIX system's security is to import a privileged version of the su (see Section 24.1) command that doesn't require a password, or one that allows either the real password or a hard-wired code known to the perpetrator. Programs owned by root that use the set user id mode (su, mail, etc.) are dangerous. These programs should have write privilege denied so that they cannot be altered by an ordinary user.

The find program can be used to locate all of the programs in a system that use the set user id mode.

```
$ find / -perm -4000 -exec ls -l {} \;
---s--s--x  1 uucp      11264 Feb 14  1984 /usr/bin/uuname
---s--s--x  2 uucp      15360 Feb 14  1984 /usr/bin/uusend
---s--s--x  1 uucp      26624 Feb 14  1984 /usr/bin/uucp
---s--s--x  1 uucp      26624 Feb 14  1984 /usr/bin/uux
---s--s--x  1 uucp      12288 Feb 14  1984 /usr/bin/uulog
-rws--s--x  2 uucp      46080 Jun  1  1985 /usr/bin/tip
^C
$ _
```

The octal mask 4000 shown above finds set user id programs. You can alternatively use the mask 2000 to find set group id programs. Set user id is discussed in Section 23.3.

One of the most common ways to break system security is using a Trojan horse program. Any program executed by root can do anything, so it is very important to use the root privilege minimally. If root should execute a tampered program, security is gone from that point forward. Therefore, the search path for the superuser is critically important. It should never reference the current directory, and it should never reference directories that contain user-contributed software. The typical root $PATH is

```
# echo $PATH
/bin:/etc:/usr/bin
# _
```

Note that the $PATH shown above does not reference the current directory (the most common mistake), and it does not reference any insecure directories. The directories mentioned in the root search path should be as secure as possible, with write permission denied for the directory and for executable files in those directories.

Besides leaving Trojan horses lying around in the hope that a careless (or duped) root user will execute them, malicious users can also leave Trojan horses in source code. For example, a user might modify the on-line source code of a standard program to provide a security hole and then complain to the administrator about a trivial (but easy to fix) bug in that program. Then the administrator makes the fix and installs the updated program. A new security hole now exists. This technique has been applied successfully to ordinary programs and to the kernel. On-line source code directories and files should not be writable by ordinary users. Similarly, software distribution tapes should always be acquired from reliable sources.

Maintaining the correct access permissions for important files is a good first line of defense. Many standard attacks rely on lax permission monitoring. As mentioned above, you should keep very tight control over who can install software on the system. Executable's directories should be owned by root and writable only by root.

The permissions for the special files should also be carefully controlled. If raw disk interfaces are writable, all other permissions are moot, because a knowledgeable user can patch the filesystem to grant whatever access is desired. Disks and the memory special files should be owned by root and accessible only by root. The terminal special files should be writable by group and other, to allow programs such as `write` and `wall` to work, but they should have read privilege only for the owner.

Administrators should impress on the user community the importance of security awareness. Users should be aware of the following information:

- Correctly entered passwords that aren't accepted as valid are a common sign of password stealing programs.
- Passwords should be obscure. Names, dates, locations, words in the dictionary, etc. are to be avoided.
- Protect private files using `crypt`. Don't rely on file access permissions.

From the system administrator's view, the two most dangerous programs are probably `mail` and `uucp`. Both of these must be administered carefully to minimize the security risk. `uucp` should be installed conservatively in most environments. It is particularly dangerous because the `uucp` password for your system is stored on multiple foreign systems. A minor security breach on any of those systems can yield the `uucp` password for your system. You should limit the number of commands that foreign systems can execute, and you should try to use the call sequencing facility so that you can detect an attempt by an unknown system to masquerade as one of the permitted systems.

CHAPTER 24

The System Manager's Utilities

This chapter describes many of the programs used by system administrators. The intent isn't to provide a complete discussion of these programs, but to cover them at a more conceptual level that will be useful for those who want to find out where to look for more detailed information.

All of the programs discussed in this chapter should be owned by root, and the programs that can alter the state of the system (`volcopy`, `fsck`, etc.) should be executable only by the owner—that is, someone with the superuser privilege.

24.1 SU—BECOME SUPERUSER

The UNIX *superuser* is the most privileged user. The superuser is able to perform many operations denied ordinary users. Most of the operations discussed in the remainder of this chapter must be invoked by the superuser. In addition, several of the commands mentioned in other parts of this book function differently when invoked by the superuser. For example, ordinary users can use the `date` command to display the date and time, but the superuser can also use the `date` command to set the date and time.

Ordinary users are constrained by UNIX's file access mode protection system. However, the superuser is not constrained by the protection system. The superuser can change the mode of any file or access any file in any way. Inadvertent superuser commands can do great damage because the normal constraints don't apply. The superuser privilege should be limited to a few careful and trusted individuals.

There are two ways to acquire the superuser privilege. One way is to log in using the special name "root." The other method is to log in using your normal login name and then execute the su (superuser) command. In either case the system will ask you to enter the superuser password. If you enter the correct password, the system will display a different prompt (usually a #) while you are operating with superuser privilege. At the conclusion of the operations requiring the superuser privilege, you should strike Control-d. If you logged in as root, then you will be logged off; if you used the su command, you will be returned to your normal identity.

Don't do ordinary work while logged in as root. Simple mistakes can cause disasters. The su command makes it easy to log in as yourself, and then elevate your privilege temporarily to root, as often as necessary. Another good habit is to use a printing terminal whenever you need to perform many privileged operations. A paper record is often useful when something goes wrong.

24.2   MOUNT AND UMOUNT—MANAGE FILESYSTEMS

The mount and umount (pronounced "you mount") commands are used to control the logical connection of the disk storage volumes to the filesystem. Before we can talk about these two commands, we need to discuss a few terms. A *filesystem* is a collection of files and directories on a disk or tape in standard UNIX filesystem format, which is discussed in Section 25.8. Low-capacity disks (such as floppy disks) usually contain a single filesystem. Large disks are usually divided into several regions called *partitions,* each containing one filesystem.

There are several motivations for partitioning a disk into several filesystems. On very large disks, partitioning may be necessary because the kernel data structures for managing and accessing the physical blocks of data can't address the total number of blocks on a disk. Partitioning reduces the total number of blocks in a single region to a manageable number. Another reason for partitioning is modularity: partitions allow you to control the amount of disk storage that is allocated to each activity. Partitions also simplify chores such as backups because partitions can be backed up at appropriate intervals.

The process of loading the UNIX kernel into memory so that operations can start is called *booting.* The details of the booting procedure vary from one computer to another, but in all systems the result is that the UNIX kernel (usually stored in the file '/unix') is loaded into memory from the root filesystem. The root filesystem contains the most essential UNIX utilities and files.

The mount command is used to inform the UNIX kernel of the existence of additional filesystems that should be incorporated into the accessible filesystem structure. A filesystem that exists but is not incorporated into the accessible filesystem structure is said to be *unmounted*. One that is incorporated into the accessible structure is said to be *mounted*.

Unmounted filesystems can be attached to the active part of the filesystem by logically connecting them to an accessible directory. Usually the directory is empty and provided specially for mounting the filesystem. For example, on a small system the root filesystem might be stored on the '/dev/rk0' device. It might contain the file 'unix' and the directories 'usr', 'etc', 'dev', and 'bin'. The 'dev' directory contains all of the special files for the special I/O device files, the 'bin' directory contains the most frequently used commands, the 'etc' directory contains files for system initialization and system management, and 'usr' is an empty directory. The files stored on the '/dev/rk1' device can be attached to the empty 'usr' directory using the mount command.

```
# /etc/mount /dev/rk1 /usr
# _
```

(Note that the mount command is usually stored in the '/etc' directory. In many systems, the search string for the superuser includes the '/etc' directory, so you can use the name 'mount' instead of the name '/etc/mount'.)

The first argument to the mount command (/dev/rk1) is the name of a special device containing a filesystem. The second argument (/usr) is the name of the directory where the filesystem will be connected. Immediately after booting, the filesystems appear as in Figure 24.1. Figure 24.2 shows the filesystem after it has been logically extended by mounting the '/dev/rk1' device on the '/usr' directory.

It is possible to mount a filesystem so that it can be read but not written. This capability is used frequently when you are recovering data from a backup and you want to be absolutely sure that the backup is not disturbed. When a filesystem is mounted read/write, then the access dates of the files are modified whenever the files are accessed even if the files are not explicitly written. Mounting a filesystem read-only prevents this update, so a filesystem should be mounted read-only when you don't want to disturb the access dates of the files.

```
# /etc/mount /dev/rk2 /mnt -r
# _
```

Note that the flag option -r, which indicates a read-only mount, follows the other arguments. This is an exception to the usual UNIX convention of placing options toward the beginning of a command line.

The UNIX kernel is usually unaware of any write protect switches on the disk or tape drives. If you logically mount a filesystem as read/write and then use the switches on the disk drive to write protect the media, a flood of errors will occur each time a file is accessed because the write protect

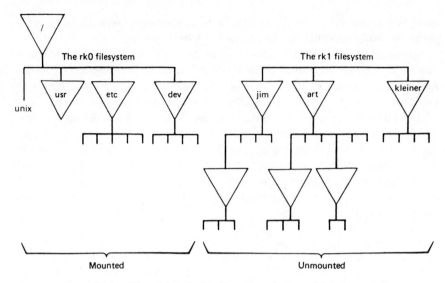

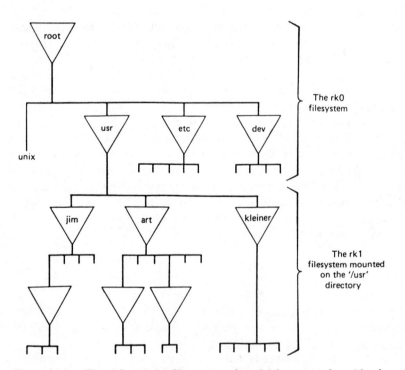

Figure 24.1. The rk0 and rk1 filesystems before rk1 is mounted.

Figure 24.2. The rk0 and rk1 filesystems after rk1 is mounted on '/usr'.

feature of the mechanism is preventing the operating system from updating the access dates of the files. The media won't be corrupted, but the voluminous console error messages may disrupt the operation of your system. If you use the write protect switches on a disk drive, you must also logically mount the filesystem read-only. The root filesystem can never be mounted read-only.

If the mount command is invoked without arguments, the names of all of the mounted filesystems are printed.

```
# /etc/mount
/dev/rk0 on / read/write on Thu Dec 3 19:08:21
/dev/rk1 on /usr read/write on Thu Dec 3 19:09:03
/dev/rk2 on /mnt read/only on Thu Dec 3 19:10:55
# _
```

The root filesystem, '/dev/rk0' in this example, can never be unmounted because it contains the programs and files that are necessary for basic system operation. It contains the binary executable file containing the kernel, plus the '/etc', '/dev', and '/bin' directories. All other filesystems can be unmounted, provided that they aren't being accessed by any active processes. The umount command unmounts mounted filesystems.

```
# /etc/umount /dev/rk1
# _
```

If anyone has an open file or a current directory on '/dev/rk1', then the umount command will complain that the '/dev/rk1' filesystem is busy. The only remedy is to find out who is accessing the filesystem (use the ps command) and then try again when the filesystem is idle. Occasionally a zombie process has an open file on a filesystem that you want to unmount. If you can't kill the process, you can't unmount the filesystem. The only remedy is to perform the other shutdown tasks, halt the system, and then reboot.

Occasionally you need to access data on a disk that does not contain a valid UNIX filesystem. Disks or tapes without a filesystem can be accessed by using the special device file, but they cannot be mounted. Mounting is an operation that logically extends the filesystem, so it is limited to disks or tapes that actually contain a UNIX filesystem. Although tapes can contain filesystems, they are usually treated as great big files without being mounted. Mounting a disk or tape that doesn't contain a properly formatted UNIX filesystem may cause a crash.

When you have mounted a filesystem, you must be extremely careful that the physical media (the disk) remain in the drive while the filesystem is mounted. When a filesystem is mounted, certain vital information about the locations of files on that filesystem is kept in memory with the kernel. Removing the physical media without performing the software unmount may cause the memory resident information about the filesystem to be lost. One purpose of the umount operation is to flush all of the memory resident information out to the physical media so that everything is consistent. Failure to logically unmount prior to physical removal is one of the major causes of corrupt (inconsistent) UNIX filesystems.

When you perform a mount operation, the information about the mount is recorded in two separate places. The UNIX kernel contains a memory resident table of mounted filesystems, and the attachment is recorded in that table. Unfortunately, the UNIX system contains no system calls that allow the contents of the internal mount table to be read by a user program, so it is difficult for a user program to really know what filesystems are mounted. Thus, whenever the mount command actually mounts a filesystem, it places a record of the mount in an ordinary disk file (usually '/etc/mnttab'). When this scheme works, it works well, but anytime you have information stored in two separate places it is possible for the information to get out of sync. When you enter the command /etc/mount, the information in the disk file is printed. Occasionally the internal system mount table (the gospel) contains different information. The problem is likely to persist until the system is rebooted.

24.3 SYNC—FLUSH SYSTEM BUFFERS

The sync command flushes the memory resident information about the filesystems out to the physical media. You should always execute the sync command before you halt the system. UNIX system lore dictates that you should sync twice just to be sure. The completion of the sync command is not a guarantee that the information has in fact been written out to disk, although it certainly has been scheduled. After executing the sync command, you should wait for the disk activity lights to cease (assuming you are at the console) before you actually halt the computer.

You should also use the sync command whenever you feel that a crash is inevitable. Perhaps you are about to run a program that uses some suspect feature of the UNIX system (beware of local modifications), or perhaps your intuition tells you that the system is about to crash. In any case, a prudent sync never hurts.

There is one exception to the rule that you should run the sync command before you halt the computer. When you repair the root filesystem (using the icheck program or the fsck program), the information on the disk is more timely than the information in memory. In this one instance, you should not sync before you halt.

24.4 MKNOD—CREATE SPECIAL FILES

UNIX *special files* are the link between the peripheral I/O devices and the operating system. There are two different interfaces to peripheral I/O devices: the block interface and the character interface. The block interface delivers data to a peripheral in blocks (512-byte chunks), and it is used primarily with disks and tapes. The character interface is primarily used to deliver data to peripherals one character at a time, and it is used mainly with terminals, printers, and other character-by-character devices. In addition to their block interface, disks and tapes usually have a character interface (also called the raw interface) that is used by many of the system maintenance programs.

Usually the special files are created when the system is generated or when the hardware configuration is changed. The special files are usually found in the '/dev' directory. If you enter the command

```
$ ls -l /dev
```

you will get a long-format list of all of the special files on your system. The mode field for all of the special files starts with either the "b" character, to indicate a block special file, or the "c" character, to indicate a character special file. Here is a partial list of the special files on one system:

```
crw--w--w-  1 bin    sys    0,  0 Jan 8 09:13 console
crw-rw----  1 bin    sys    3,  1 Jan 2 12:01 kmem
c-w--w----  1 bin    sys    5,  0 Jan 7 23:15 lp
crw-rw----  1 bin    sys    3,  0 Dec 7 11:11 mem
brw-rw----  1 bin    sys    1,  0 Jan 8 09:13 mt0
crw-rw-rw-  1 bin    sys    3,  2 Jan 8 09:00 null
brw-rw----  1 bin    sys    2,  0 Jan 8 10:15 rk0
brw-rw----  1 bin    sys    2,  1 Jan 8 10:15 rk1
crw-rw----  1 bin    sys    4,  0 Jan 8 09:44 rmt0
crw-rw----  1 bin    sys    6,  0 Jan 8 10:15 rrk0
crw-rw----  1 bin    sys    6,  1 Jan 8 10:15 rrk1
crw--w--w-  1 bin    sys    1,  0 Jan 2 03:20 tty
crw--w--w-  1 bin    sys    0,  1 Jan 5 15:49 tty1
crw--w--w-  1 bin    sys    0,  2 Jan 8 10:17 tty2
crw--w--w-  1 bin    sys    0,  3 Jan 8 10:20 tty3
```

In a long-format listing of an ordinary file, the size of the file in bytes is printed after the owner and group information. A special file doesn't have a length because it is not a storage region but a link to an I/O device. Instead of the length, the major and minor device numbers are printed.

The major device number indicates what type of hardware is associated with the file. The following table shows the major device numbers for the block and character special files listed above.

Character Special Devices

Major Device Number	Files
0	console, tty1, tty2, tty3
1	tty
3	mem, kmem, null
4	rmt0
5	lp
6	rrk0, rrk1

Block Special Devices

Major Device Number	Files
1	mt0
2	rk0, rk1

As you can see, there are often several interfaces to one major device type. The four communication lines (console, tty1, tty2, and tty3) all have major device number 0. This means that there are four identical hardware devices in the computer to handle the four communication lines. To distinguish the four lines, the four special files for the communication lines have the minor device numbers zero through 3. The minor device number indicates which device or which channel (port) when there are several identical devices.

What we have done in this section is look at the information in the '/dev' directory to deduce the major and minor device numbers used in this installation. To create the special files in the first place, you must look in the system generation files (often in a file called 'conf.c'). Once you know the major and minor device number, you can use the mknod command to create the special file. Let's suppose that you are creating the character special file for a communication line. Examining the system generation files reveals that the major device number is 7 and the minor device number is zero for the newly installed communication line. The following dialogue shows how you can use mknod to create the character special file '/dev/ttyk0' for the communication line.

```
# /etc/mknod /dev/ttyk0 c 7 0
# ls -l /dev/ttyk0
crw--w--w- 1 root     sys      7,  0 Jan 9 14:30 ttyk0
# _
```

On System V the mknod command is also used to create named pipes (fifos).

```
# /etc/mknod /dev/fifo1 p
# ls -l fifo1
prw-r--r--  1   root    sys     0  Jan 8 16:20  fifo1
# _
```

24.5   DF—DISK FREE SPACE

The df (disk free) command prints a summary of the free space on the on-line filesystems. The summary on System V includes the number of free blocks and the number of free i-nodes.

```
$ df
/        (/dev/root ):    14624 blocks    2161 i-nodes
$ _
```

In this example we see that '/dev/root' is the root filesystem and that there are 14624 free blocks and 2161 free i-nodes.

On Berkeley systems the format is slightly different.

```
$ df
Filesystem    kbytes    used    avail  capacity  Mounted on
/dev/hp0a      7415     4903    1770     73%     /
/dev/hp0d      7631      485    6382      7%     /tmp
/dev/hp0f     116655  103961   1028     99%     /usr
/dev/hp0g     116655   88895  16094     85%     /usr1
/dev/hp0h     116655  104478    511    100%     /src
$ _
```

df also allows you to specify which filesystems to examine, by specifying either a disk partition or the name of a directory where a filesystem is mounted. Without arguments, df prints information for all of the mounted filesystems.

The system manager should run df periodically to monitor the free space on all of the filesystems. Some systems need 20% or 30% free space, other systems only need 5% or 10%—experience is your best guide. Some systems impose limits on the disk space that is used by individuals. The du program can be used to check for compliance with these limits (see Section 6.9).

Individual users who are about to create very large files should use df to make sure that there is adequate room. You don't need superuser privilege to use df.

24.6   VOLCOPY, LABELIT, DUMP, RESTOR, CPIO—BACKUPS

There are numerous approaches to the problem of performing periodic backups. The goal is to be able to recover lost data. Infrequent backups mean that the backup is usually old and out of date; frequent backups can be disruptive of normal system operations. Each system manager has to find the middle ground based on the frequency of data loss, the value of the data, and the amount of effort that can be expended in the backup process. Each manager also has to find a procedure that works with the available hardware. With a minimal set of disks, then, the normal users have to be off the system for the entire backup procedure. With more hardware, the users have to be off the system for only part of the operation.

The UNIX system supports two major utilities designed expressly for backups: the `volcopy/labelit` system and the `dump/restor` system, plus general-purpose utilities such as `cpio`, `tar`, and `dd` that are often used for backups. The `volcopy` program copies whole filesystems from one place to another. `volcopy` scrupulously checks the labels (installed using `labelit`) on the filesystems to make sure that the correct media (disk pack or tape reel) are in place before performing the copy operation.

The `dump` program performs an incremental filesystem save operation. You can perform a full backup, which copies everything, or you can copy only the files that have been modified since the last backup. The `restor` program can examine the dumps created by the `dump` program to recover individual files or entire filesystems.

The `tar` and `cpio` programs package individual files into a great big file. Both programs have options for performing selective backups, based on modification date, filenames, etc. `cpio` works easily with the `find` program, which gives it more functionality than `tar`. With both `cpio` and `tar`, it's easy to restore one or two files from an archive.

One advantage of the `volcopy` system is that the entire filesystem is saved every time a backup is performed. This redundancy makes for very secure backups. Another advantage of the `volcopy` system is that it can be used to make copies to either disks or tapes. A disk-to-disk backup operation, which is extremely fast, is preferred for the most frequent backups. The final advantage of `volcopy` is that it is extremely useful for recovering lost data. Since an entire filesystem is saved, it is possible to mount the saved filesystem to recover a single file, or to copy the filesystem back from the backup medium, in order to recover an entire filesystem. `volcopy` backups from disk to tape are good for long-term archival storage of data, but they are inconvenient for day-to-day work because it is hard to remove a single file from a backup tape.

The advantage of the incremental `dump/restor` system is that fewer files are transferred to the backup medium during incremental backups. Thus the time spent performing backups may be minimized. (`volcopy` always copies entire filesystems, but it does so very efficiently. dump may copy less, but it has additional overhead.)

Recovering individual files using restor is tricky, since a missing file may be on any of several tapes depending on when the file was last modified. The restor program will browse through the set of dumped tapes and figure out which tape contains the missing file. Recovering entire filesystems is also difficult, because the backup is spread out over several tapes.

24.7 DD—CONVERT FILES

dd is a general-purpose data conversion and transfer program. It is often used to perform filesystem backups. Like volcopy, it is a very efficient way to copy entire filesystems from one place to another. Unlike volcopy, dd doesn't perform any label checking, but it offers many more options than volcopy for managing the transfer.

Another task that dd often performs is data conversion. It was designed with mainframe formats in mind, but it is useful for many data conversion duties. For example, punch-card (or other fixed-format) data are often transported from mainframes to UNIX systems. On the mainframe the punch-card data are probably transferred to tape in blocks of 80 characters, using the EBCDIC character coding system. To use such data in most UNIX systems, you would use dd to change the coding to ASCII and to terminate each 80-column card image with a new line.

24.8 FSCK—CHECK AND REPAIR FILE SYSTEMS

Sooner or later every filesystem becomes corrupt. The system manager is responsible for repairing corrupt filesystems. There are lots of reasons for corrupt filesystems, including intermittent hardware failures, power line surges or other irregularities, problems with the disk media, and turning off the computer without executing the sync command. Corrupt filesystems should be repaired immediately to limit the loss of data. Occasionally a filesystem is so corrupt that it must be discarded and recovered entirely from a backup, but usually only a file or two are lost, and sometimes nothing is lost.

A filesystem is somewhat like a general ledger, and like a ledger, a filesystem should be consistent. In a corrupt filesystem, something (perhaps a block of data) is not accounted for, or perhaps it is counted twice. Fixing a corrupt filesystem removes the inconsistencies. Filesystems should be checked every time a computer is booted, and they should always be fixed as soon as a problem is noticed. All filesystem checking and repairing should be done on unmounted (or quiescent) filesystems.

UNIX originally had a small fleet of programs for repairing filesystems, but on modern systems the `fsck` program is predominant. Fixing filesystems using the predecessors of `fsck` is difficult because you need to use several programs and good judgment to repair a corrupt filesystem. Using `fsck` is much easier because it recommends solutions when it discovers problems with a filesystem.

Repairing the filesystem will make more sense if you understand the format of the UNIX filesystem. The philosophy of `fsck` is to prune the dead or dying files. Pruning is simple and effective but usually results in loss of data and occasionally results in more data loss than is strictly necessary. An adequate file backup system makes data loss less painful.

Occasionally files and their names become separated. This is possible in the UNIX system because the names of files are stored in directories while the rest of the information for files is stored in a structure called an i-node. Files without names are called *orphaned* files, and `fsck` will attempt to place them in a directory called 'lost + found'. You should create the 'lost + found' directory in the root of each filesystem before you use `fsck`, and you should make sure that there are empty slots in the directory by copying some files into 'lost + found' and then removing them. If the 'lost + found' directory is not present, then orphaned files are discarded. In the 'lost + found' directory, `fsck` will use a number as the name of the file. You should attempt to determine the real name of the file based on its contents and either restore the file to its rightful owner or remove it.

You can check an individual filesystem by using its name as an argument to `fsck`:

```
# fsck /root
** Phase 1 - Check Blocks and Sizes
** Phase 2 - Check Pathnames
** Phase 3 - Check Connectivity
** Phase 4 - Check Reference Counts
** Phase 5 - Check Free List
1185 files 11782 blocks 14620 free
# _
```

Without arguments, the `fsck` command will automatically check all of the filesystems mentioned in the file '/etc/checklist'. Usually '/etc/checklist' contains a list of all of the active filesystems.

Every filesystem contains a list of free blocks. When a file is created, the blocks of data in the file are gathered from the list of free blocks. Occasionally the list of free blocks is damaged; sometimes blocks that are free aren't in the list, and occasionally blocks that are used in an existing file are also mentioned in the free list.

When you rebuild the free list of a mounted filesystem (usually the root file system), you must halt the computer immediately after the rebuild and then boot the system from scratch. Halting the computer immediately (without the usual sync operation) prevents the UNIX kernel from writing the old (bad) free list out to disk. Usually when fsck discovers errors in the course of checking a filesystem, it will ask your permission to rebuild the free list.

24.9 CRON—RUN PROGRAMS AT SPECIFIED TIMES

The cron program is used to execute programs at specified times. The cron program is usually started shortly after the system is booted, and there should be only one cron process running in a system. cron reads commands from the file '/usr/lib/crontab' (the crontab). Each line in the crontab specifies a command and the time or times when it should be executed.

cron periodically examines '/usr/lib/crontab' to keep up with new additions to the file. Thus the crontab file can be changed while cron is running.

Entries in the crontab file consist of five fields that specify when a command should be run followed by the command. From left to right the five fields represent minutes $(0-59)$, hours $(0-23)$, day of the month $(1-31)$, month of the year $(1-12)$, and day of the week (System V: $0-6$ with Sunday as zero; Berkeley: $1-7$ with Sunday as 7). The fields are separated by spaces or tabs.

The following line in crontab causes the date to be printed on the console every 10 minutes.

```
0,10,20,30,40,50 * * * * date > /dev/console
```

The numbers representing the time can either be a single number in the appropriate range, a list of numbers separated by commas (as in the example), two numbers separated by a hyphen to indicate a range of times, or an asterisk to indicate all legal values. The crontab specification to print the date on the console every hour weekday nights from 6 to 10 is

```
0 6-10 * * 1-5 date > /dev/console
```

The cron system is often used to run programs unattended during the wee hours, to perform periodic accounting operations, and so on. Some systems use cron to disable certain programs, such as games, during the peak periods to improve system response. (Berkeley 4.3 crontabs have an additional field following the date that specifies which user identificaton to use.)

CHAPTER 25

The UNIX System Kernel

The UNIX system kernel is a master organizer. The kernel schedules processes, allocates memory and disk storage, supervises the transfer of data between the main storage and the peripheral devices, and honors the processes' requests for service. This chapter examines the kernel in order to partially answer the question, "How does the UNIX system really work?" Note that some of the more specific information presented in this chapter may not apply to all UNIX systems.

Much of the information in this chapter has direct practical applications for UNIX managers and system programmers. The more theoretical aspects of the UNIX system, its avoidance of deadlock, its techniques for mutual exclusion, and so on, are discussed in the papers written by Ritchie, Thompson, and others. Most of the material in this chapter is relevant to any version of the UNIX system, although two version-specific topics, Berkeley sockets and System V streams, are discussed in the last two sections.

The kernel is the memory resident portion of the UNIX system. Compared to most mainframe operating systems, the UNIX kernel provides a relatively small repertoire of services. However, compared to microcomputer operating systems such as MS-DOS, the UNIX kernel provides a large repertoire of services.

The basic user services, such as copying files or displaying the time, are provided by utility programs, which provide the interface between users and the kernel. This has worked out extremely well because utility programs are easier to create, maintain, and customize than the kernel itself.

The UNIX Version 7 kernel contained about 10,000 lines of C code and about 1000 lines of assembly code. The more modern System V and Berkeley kernels are larger but still small compared to many other operating systems. Many UNIX systems are distributed with the source code for the kernel and the utilities. This allows programmers to study and tinker with their own system. In contrast, most other operating systems are too large to be understood and maintained by an individual, and most other operating systems are distributed "as is"—tinkering is not allowed.

25.1 OVERVIEW

The traditional UNIX system kernel consists of two major parts: the process management section and the device management section. Today's networking kernels have an additional section that manages network operations. The process management section allocates resources, schedules processes, and honors processes' requests for service; the device management section supervises the transfer of data between the main memory and the peripheral devices. One of the great triumphs of the UNIX system is the fact that widely different computers use almost identical process management sections and very similar device management sections.

The device management section for a given computer contains a module for every peripheral device attached to the computer. Every time a computer is configured with a new type of I/O peripheral, a program module has to be added to the device management section. Whenever the UNIX system is moved to a different type of computer, the device management section has to be partially rewritten because different computers usually have different peripheral devices with different control principles.

The process of configuring the UNIX system for a particular set of peripheral devices and default options is called *system generation*. The major work of system generation is creating a list that describes the exact hardware environment and prescribes a certain set of options for the system.

Typical applications programs have a beginning, a middle, and an end—somewhat like a good novel. The UNIX system is more like a woven tapestry than a novel. The UNIX system does not have a single plot that runs from beginning to end; instead, it has a number of interrelated threads that are woven in response to the needs of the moment. The fact that the kernel is not a simple sequential program makes it inherently more difficult to understand than most programs.

The UNIX system kernel maintains several important tables that coordinate the actions of the interrelated threads of execution. In fact, the UNIX system is an excellent example of a program where the data structures the program. Understanding the UNIX system begins with an understanding of the tables that the kernel maintains. Surprisingly, much of the work of the kernel is routine table searching and table modification. The following sections describe the major functions of the kernel and the relevant tables of information.

25.2   USER MODE AND KERNEL MODE

At any given instant, a computer is either executing a user program (a process) or executing system code. (I prefer to reserve the word *process* for entities that are in the kernel's process table.) We say that the computer is in *user mode* when it is executing instructions in a user process and it is in *kernel mode* when it is executing instructions in the kernel. While most modern processors have distinct hardware privileges for kernel mode, the distinction is the source of the instructions, not the privilege level of the hardware.

Several mechanisms can prompt a switch from user mode to kernel mode. Perhaps the most important from the point of view of system integrity is the system clock. The system clock periodically interrupts (usually 50 or 60 times per second) whatever is going on. (An *interrupt* is a hardware signal that can divert the computer to a special software routine.) During the service routine for the system clock, the process priorities are reevaluated, and a switch from one process to another is possible. In the absence of other interruptions, the system clock performs the basic time slicing that enables a computer to be shared among many users.

Whenever a user program needs an operating system service, it executes a system call. The implementation details of system calls vary from one computer architecture to another, but the immediate result is always a change from user mode to kernel mode. System calls that perform I/O operations often lead to a suspension of the calling process while the data are being transferred. A different user process will be executed in the interim if possible. Thus the natural I/O requirements of programs often drive the time-slicing mechanism.

The service requirement of the I/O peripherals is the third mechanism that causes a switch from user mode to kernel mode. I/O peripherals typically have a response time that is much longer than the normal instruction execution time of a computer. The details vary greatly from one computer architecture to another, but on most UNIX systems an interrupt occurs each time a transfer is complete. (At various times a transfer is either 512 bytes, a single byte, or a variable-length string of bytes.) The transfer completion interrupt typically updates various status elements in certain tables and then possibly initiates another transfer.

25.3   SCHEDULING AND SWAPPING

In a time-sharing computer system, processes compete for execution time slices. *Scheduling* is the series of actions that decides which of the competing user processes to execute. Obviously scheduling is one of the key elements of a time-sharing system. The fundamental act of time sharing is suspending a process and then restarting it at some later time. In most time-sharing systems (e.g., the UNIX system), the suspension/resumption activity occurs many times each second to create the impression that the computer is performing several functions simultaneously.

On a traditional single-CPU machine, at most one user process is active at any given time. All of the other user processes are suspended. We can divide the set of suspended processes into two groups—those that are *ready to run* and those that are *blocked*. A blocked process is said to be sleeping until an event occurs. Usually the event is the completion of an I/O request, although processes can also wait for (1) their children to die or (2) specified intervals of time or (3) signals from other processes. When the event occurs, the sleeping process is awakened. Awakening a process marks it as ready to run; it doesn't mean that a process will immediately start to execute.

Ideally, all of the user processes reside in memory, and the role of the scheduler is to select the active process from the group of memory resident processes. Unfortunately, the memory on modern computers is often not large enough to simultaneously store the typical number of processes that are active in a UNIX system. The solution is to store some of the suspended processes on disk, a procedure known as *swapping*. A process stored on disk must be reloaded into memory before it can execute. The scheduling system is responsible for two actions—scheduling the processes for execution and scheduling the processes for swapping.

The very simple explanation for a time-sharing system is that time is divided into a number of slices and the slices are parceled out to the processes. The UNIX system also takes into account that processes waiting for I/O may not be able to take advantage of their given slice. To avoid discrimination against processes that perform I/O, the UNIX system dynamically calculates process priorities to determine which inactive but ready process will execute when the currently active process is suspended.

Part of the priority calculation involves accumulated execution time starting when the process was last swapped in to memory. Processes that have accumulated a lot of execution time have less priority than processes that have been starved for execution time. Notice that processes that have just been swapped in and processes that have been waiting for I/O have not been executing, so they will have a relatively high priority. It is also possible for a user process to execute a system call that induces a bias in the calculation; ordinary user processes can only decrease their priority, but processes run by the superuser can increase or decrease their priority.

The net effect of this procedure is that I/O-intensive processes tend to execute until they can proceed no further. Computation-intensive processes tend to fill the gaps while the I/O processes are waiting for their I/O to complete. When everything is working, the system tends to balance itself to keep the processor busy and give all the processes some execution time.

In the UNIX system there is extremely little overhead for a suspended process. This crucial fact has had a profound impact on the nature of the system. The low overhead of suspended processes has enabled many "operating system" functions to be exported from the UNIX system kernel and placed in ordinary programs. One reason for the low overhead is that programs can be compiled so that their text is shared. Another reason for the low overhead is swapping—idle processes often reside in swap space, not in main memory. The only data structure that must be maintained in core for each process is its process table entry, which is an insignificant amount of memory on today's computers.

Consider the `getty` program. The `getty` program prints a login message on a communication line and then waits for a user to start logging in. There is a (usually suspended) `getty` process for every communication line in a UNIX system that can be used for logging in but is not currently in use. Many systems have 50 to 100 such `getty` processes. This design wouldn't be possible if suspended processes required significant overhead. Instead, a more complicated design would be necessary, probably involving one process to manage all of the lines, or possibly involving kernel code to manage this function.

25.4 PROCESSES

The UNIX system supports two powerful illusions: that the filesystem has "places" and that processes have "life." The strong visceral connection of directories with "places" makes it possible for people to master the filesystem. Similarly, the illusion that processes have "life" and thus can perform useful work makes it easy to think about and control processes. We say that the shell runs programs, that the editor creates text files, that the `ls` program lists the contents of directories. All of these processes are described as if they were active, vital organisms. The gift of life that we bestow on processes is a convenient illusion. A computer scientist might describe a process as an execution of an abstract data structure. The energy in a computer is in the hardware, but the intelligence is in the programs, so it is reasonable to transfer the life force to the software.

The process is the fundamental organizing concept in the UNIX system. Even though the instructions are executed by the CPU and stored in memory, even though the disks and tapes are spinning furiously, we say that the process is executing, and we ignore the obvious—the computer hardware is actually doing the work.

The UNIX kernel exists to support the needs of processes. From a process's point of view, the kernel's operations are a sort of overhead that must be endured; the view from within the kernel is that processes are just cataloged data structures that are manipulated according to a set of rules. The description of processes that follows might seem dull because the view from within is that processes are just data, more like an accountant's worksheet than a vital force.

A process is a program in a state of execution. For a given program there may be zero, one, or several active processes at a particular time. In this work we will confine the term process to entities that are cataloged in the UNIX system kernel's process table. Hence the activity of the UNIX system kernel is generally excluded as a process.

The vital information for processes is stored in two places: the *process table* and the *user table* (also called the per-process data segment). The process table is always in memory. It contains one entry for each process; each entry details the state of a process. The state information includes the location of the process (memory address or swapped address), the size of the process, and information about received signals. Each UNIX system is generated with a certain number of entries in the process table; each process consumes one entry in the table, and it is impossible to have more processes than there are entries in the process table.

Less timely information about each process is stored in the user table. One user table is allocated for each active process, and only the user table of the active process is directly accessible to the kernel routines. See Fig. 25.1.

The process table is referenced during all of the life crises of processes. Creating a process involves initializing an entry in the process table, initializing a user table, and loading the actual text and data for the process. When a process changes its state (running, waiting, swapped out, swapped

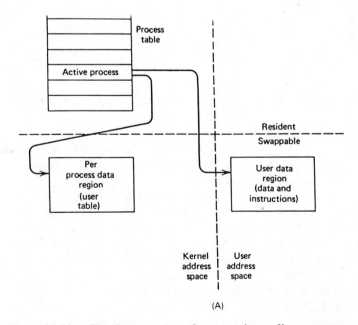

(A)

Figure 25.1A.   The data structures for managing ordinary processes.

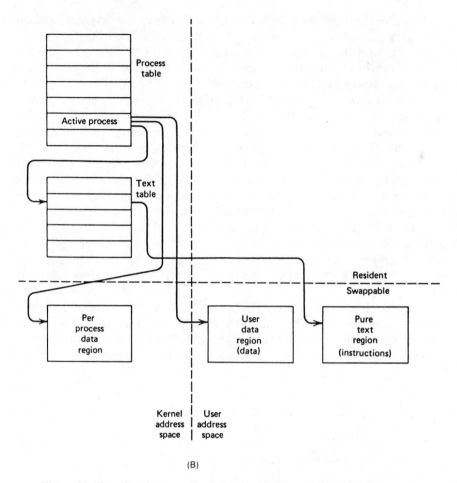

(B)

Figure 25.1B.   The data structures for managing proceses with pure text.

in, etc.) or receives a signal, the interaction focuses on the process table. When a process dies, its entry in the process table is (eventually) freed, so that it can be used by future processes.

The process table must always be in memory, so that the kernel can manage the life crises of a process even while the process is swapped out. Many of the events in the life of a process occur while the process is inactive. For instance, a process is sleeping while waiting for I/O. The I/O completion causes the process to be awakened and marked as ready to resume execution. The information necessary to manage the wake-up of a sleeping process is contained in the process table.

The kernel allocates one user table for each active process. The user table contains information that must be accessible while the process is executing. While a process is suspended, its user table is not accessed or modified. The user table is part of the process data region, and when the process is swapped out to disk, the user table is swapped with the rest of the process image.

Most of the user structure contains current information about the process. For example, the user table contains the user and group identification numbers for determining file access privileges, pointers into the system's file table (see Section 25.8) for all of the process's open files, a pointer to the i-node of the current directory (see Section 25.8) in the i-node table, and a list of responses for the various signals.

The information in the user table is often manipulated very simply. If the process executes the chdir system call, then the value of the pointer to the current directory i-node is changed. If a process elects to ignore a certain signal, then the appropriate entry in the table of signal responses is set to zero. Most of the manipulations of information in the user table are so simple that you might expect the program to perform the manipulation rather than the kernel. In part, these simple manipulations are performed by the kernel for the sake of uniformity, but the important reason is system integrity. On a computer with memory protection, the user table is inaccessible to a process (except via system calls), even though it is part of the process image.

Many programs, such as the shell and getty, are often being executed by several users simultaneously. Each process must have its own copy of the variable part of the process image, but the fixed part, the program text, can be shared. In order to be shared, a program must be compiled using a special option that arranges the process image so that the variable part and the text part are cleanly separated. Sharing program text allows the UNIX system to use the main memory of the computer more effectively. To keep track of the program text segments, the UNIX system maintains a text table. When a program uses shared text, the process table entry contains a pointer into the text table, and the text table actually points to the location of the process text. Keeping a single pointer to shared text, instead of one per process, makes the kernel simpler and more reliable.

25.5 FORK, EXEC, WAIT, AND BRK

There are two fundamental system calls that shape the UNIX environment. The first, the fork system call, is used by a process to create a copy of itself. fork is the only mechanism in the UNIX system for increasing the number of processes. After the fork there are two processes where once there was just one: the parent and the child. The major difference between the two subsequent processes is that the two processes have different process id numbers and different parent process id numbers. The two processes share open files, and each process is able to determine whether it is the parent or the child.

The second major system call for managing processes is exec. The exec system call is used to transform the calling process into a new process. The total number of processes in the system isn't changed; only the character of the calling process changes. After an exec system call, the process id number is unchanged, and open files remain open. The exec system call is similar to the chaining feature in other operating systems, which allows a process to choose its successor.

A fork followed by an exec is commonly used by a parent process to spawn a child process with a new identity. For example, this sequence is used by the shell each time the shell runs a program for you.

The wait system call is commonly used in conjunction with fork and exec. The wait system call allows a parent process to wait for the demise of a child process. This is used by the shell when you execute a program in the foreground. First the shell forks, then the shell's child execs the program, and then the parent shell waits for the demise of the child. When the child dies, the parent shell prompts you to enter another command. The shell runs processes in the background simply by omitting the wait for the demise for the child process.

The major routine for expanding a process's data segment is brk (break). When a process requests more memory, the kernel attempts to expand the process in place. Occasionally the kernel is successful, but more often the kernel swaps the process out and then eventually swaps the enlarged process back in. Thus, calling brk can be very time consuming because of the likely swap. Although the brk system call is fundamental, most programmers actually use the malloc subroutine, which provides an efficient and convenient interface to brk.

25.6 SIGNALS

From its earliest days, UNIX has contained a simple yet effective signaling system. A *signal* is a message from one process to another. Unlike messages that have content, the only information content in a UNIX signal is "It has arrived" or "It has not arrived."

There are predefined meanings to most signals. For example, the hangup signal is sent to your processes if your telephone connection drops carrier. Other examples are sigint, which politely asks a process to terminate; sigquit, which asks a process to terminate and produce a core dump; sigfpe, which informs a process of a floating point error; and sigkill, which forces a process to terminate.

Some signals may be caught or ignored by a process. For example, when you strike the interrupt key on your keyboard, which is usually <Ctrl-C> or <DEL>, the current process receives the sigint signal. By default, processes terminate when sigint arrives, but a process can alternatively arrange to ignore the signal or to activate a special signal handler routine. Other signals cannot be caught. For example, the `sigkill` is guaranteed to terminate a process, provided the process is not hung up waiting for a kernel service.

Two kernel data structures, the process table and the user table, are key to understanding the kernel implementation of signals. The user table contains a list with one slot per signal. If the value in the slot for a particular signal is zero, the default action will occur if the signal arrives. If the slot contains a 1, the signal will be ignored. Any other value is presumed to be the address of a signal handler routine in the user process. Processes can manage their responses to signals using the `signal` system call.

When a process sends a signal, by using the `kill` system call, it specifies the process id number of the target process and the number of the signal. On a single processor system, the target process is not running; rather, the originating process is running. Since the user table of a not-running process may be in core or swapped out, it may or may not be easily accessible. Therefore efficiency dictates that the signal arrival be recorded in a guaranteed resident structure; hence it is stored in the process table. Only the arrival of the signal is cataloged. Other possibly useful information, such as the sending process id, the time of arrival, the number of times the signal has arrived, etc., is not recorded.

When the target process gets its next chance to execute, the kernel checks its slot in the process table to see if any new signals have arrived. If there are fresh signals, the kernel decides how to handle them. For some signals, such as `sigkill`, the action is fixed. However, for catchable signals, the kernel checks the user table to see if the process has arranged to catch or ignore the signal. If a signal handler has been installed by the process, the kernel starts the execution of the process with a call to the signal handler. When the signal handler exits, the process resumes where it was last suspended.

The `fork` system call doesn't alter the list of signal actions in the user table. However, the `exec` call is forced to deal with the signal dispositions in the user table. When an `exec` occurs, caught signals are reset to their default state, but ignored signals remain ignored. If ignored signals were reset during an `exec`, programs such as `nohup` wouldn't be able to leave a signal ignoring legacy for their offspring.

25.7 BOOTING, PROCESS 0, PROCESS 1

Now that some of the basic ideas of the UNIX system kernel have been introduced, we can turn our attention to what happens when the kernel is first started. Several unique actions must be performed early in the course of execution in order to progress to the steady-state condition discussed above. By the time process 1 is initialized and started, the system is running normally and working according to the laws established by system calls.

The act of loading the kernel system image into memory and starting its execution is called *booting*. Booting occurs whenever the system is started for the first time following the initial power-up of the computer hardware. Booting is also performed following crashes and intentional stoppages of the Unix system.

Booting occurs in several phases. In the first phase, the computer hardware arranges to have the first block of the disk in the bootstrap disk drive loaded into memory and executed. As you will discover in the next section, the first block of every filesystem is reserved for special purposes, usually a short bootstrap loader program. Thus, in order to boot, you must have a bootable disk (i.e., one with a valid loader program in the first block) installed in the bootstrap disk drive.

The purpose of the short loader program is to find and load the file named 'unix' in the root directory ('/unix'). (The name 'vmunix' is used on Berkeley operating systems.) The file '/unix' contains the machine instructions for the operating system kernel. It is created by compiling and linking the operating system source code files. Phase 2 of the boot procedure starts once the file '/unix' has been loaded into memory and starts to execute.

The first thing the kernel does is initialize a few hardware interfaces. On machines with memory management hardware, the memory management needs to be initialized, and on all systems the clock that provides periodic interrupts needs to be initialized. The kernel also initializes a few data structures including the pool of block buffers, the pool of character lists, the pool of i-node buffers, and the variable that indicates the amount of main memory.

Following these rather mundane initializations, the kernel begins to initialize process zero. Processes are ordinarily created via the `fork` system call, which instructs the system to make a copy of the calling process. Obviously, this method is not feasible for creating the first process, process zero. The kernel creates process zero by allocating a per-user data structure and installing pointers to the data structure in the first slot of the process table. Process zero is unique for several reasons. First note that there is no code segment for process zero: its entire being is a per-user data structure. All other processes contain code that is executed to perform some function; they are images resulting from the compilation and subsequent execution of a program. Process zero is just a per-user data structure that is used by the kernel; it is not an image. Also note that process zero is created anomalously and persists for the life of the system. Finally note that process zero is truly a system process; it is active exclusively while the processor is in kernel mode. Process zero is called a process only because it is cataloged in the process table. You should keep in mind that process zero really a kernel data structure, not a process in the normal sense of the word.

After process zero is created and initialized, the system creates process 1 by making a copy of process zero. The copy of process zero is made by following essentially the same procedure that is followed when a user program executes the fork system call. Although process 1 is hand-crafted, at least the hand crafting is beginning to resemble the ordinary process creation scheme.

Initially, process 1 is an exact copy of process zero; it has no code region. The first event that occurs after process 1 is created is that it is expanded in size. The size of process 1 is increased by executing the same code that would be executed if the process had issued the break (increase memory allocation) system call. Once again, process 1 is acted on anomalously but in imitation of the procedure that is followed by an ordinary program executing a system call. Notice that up to this point both process zero and process 1 have yet to execute.

The third event in the creation of a viable process 1 is the copying of a very simple program into its newly created code region. The program that is copied into process 1's code region essentially contains the machine instructions to perform the exec system call to execute a program called '/etc/init'.

At this point the initialization of processes 0 and 1 is essentially complete. Process zero is a per-user data structure that is used by the kernel during the scheduling and process management operations. Process 1 is a viable image that might have resulted from the compilation of a program, although it actually was created uniquely by the kernel. Once the UNIX system has initialized a necessary data region (process 0) and a viable first process (process 1), it proceeds to execute the usual scheduling routines.

At this point, the initialization of the kernel is complete. However, the initialization of the system is just beginning, and we will conclude this section with a description of the first few events in the life of the system. The *scheduler* is responsible for deciding which process to run and which processes to swap in or swap out. This first time the scheduler is called, the decision making is very easy, there are no processes to swap, and there is only one process that is anxious to run—process 1. Executing process 1 immediately leads to the exec system call, which overlays the original code in process 1 with the code contained in the file '/etc/init'. Now that process 1 has attained its final form, we can call it by its usual name—the init process.

The init process is responsible for setting up the process structure of the UNIX system. init is usually able to create at least two distinct process structures, the single-user mode and multiuser mode. (On some systems init is able to create more than two distinct process environments.) Usually init starts by attaching a shell to the system console and giving this shell superuser privilege. This is commonly called *single-user* mode. In single-user mode the console is automatically logged in with root privileges, and none of the other communication lines will accept logins. Single-user mode is often used to check and repair filesystems and to perform basic system testing functions and other activities that require exclusive use of the computer. (On some systems you must enter the superuser password to enter single-user mode.)

At the conclusion of single-user mode the init process sets up the multi-user process structure. init does this by creating a getty process for every active communication line. (getty is discussed in the next paragraph.) init also creates a shell process to execute the commands in the file '/etc/rc'. The '/etc/rc' file contains a shell script that contains commands to mount filesystems, start demons, remove outdated temporary files, and start accounting programs. The commands in '/etc/rc' vary widely from one UNIX system installation to another.

During the life of the system, the init process sleeps, waiting for the death of any of its children. If one of init's children dies, then init awakens and creates another getty program for the relevant communication line. Thus init not only creates the multiuser process structure, it also maintains that structure during the life of the system (Fig. 25.2).

The final actor in the system initialization story is the getty program. Each getty program waits patiently for someone to log in on a particular communication line. When someone does start to log in, the getty program performs a few basic adjustments to the line protocol and then execs the login program to actually check the password. If the password is entered correctly, the login program execs the shell program to accept commands from the user. When a shell program exits, the init program (its only living relative) awakens and fork-execs a new getty program to monitor the line and wait for the next login (Fig. 25.3).

25.8   THE UNIX FILESYSTEM

The hierarchical filesystem is one of the UNIX system's most important features. The most basic function of any filesystem is to partition the storage on disks and tapes into named units that we call *files*. In many systems, there are several types of file with distinct access methods for each type. In the UNIX system, all files are a simple sequence of bytes. Sometimes files are referred to as text files or binary files, but the distinction is the content of the file (text files contain ASCII values only), not the structure of the file or the access method.

From the system user's point of view, a directory is a group of files. In some operating systems (other than the UNIX system), all of the files on a storage volume are contained in one directory. Still other filesystems, admitting that today's disks store very many files, partition the disk into a number of directories and parcel the files into one of the directories. Both of these methods create a flat filesystem. Everything is at one level. Flat filesystems are usable, but they are messy because they don't make it easy to organize your files.

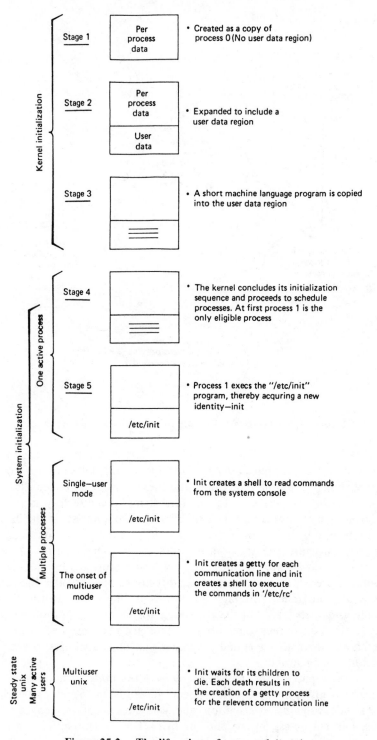

Figure 25.2.   The life crises of process 1 (init).

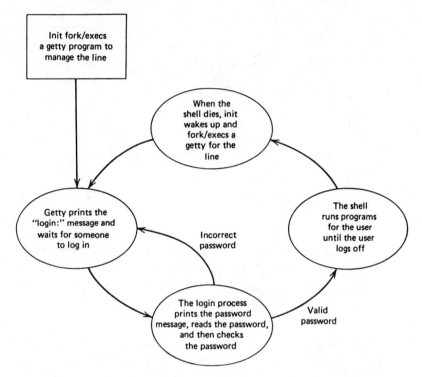

Figure 25.3.   The cycle of events for each communication line.

The UNIX system contains a *hierarchical* filesystem. Files are not stored at one level but at multiple levels, and the filesystem supports the illusion of "places" within the system. In flat filesystems, the directory is the chief organizing structure of the system; the directory contains all of the information about files including their name, length, location, access dates, modes, and types. Because directories in flat filesystems contain all of the important information about files, they are hidden and protected by the operating system. However, in the UNIX system, directories are just files that can be read by any program. Although directories are the visible structure of the UNIX filesystem, they are not the repository for all of the information about files. In the UNIX system, directories contain just two pieces of information for each file: the file's name and a number that the kernel uses to access the hidden filesystem structures.

The hidden part of the UNIX filesystem is the *i-node*. I-nodes are where the action really is in the UNIX filesystem. There is one i-node for each file. Each i-node contains information about a file's location, length, access modes, relevant dates, owner, and the like. The casual UNIX system user is well insulated from i-nodes, at least until the i-node structures become inconsistent and need repair.

Let's talk about the internal structure of the UNIX filesystem starting at the front of every filesystem (see Fig. 25.4). For now, we will concentrate on the filesystem structures that are actually stored on the storage disk. Later in this section we will concentrate on the structures that are stored in memory by the kernel.

The first block of any filesystem is the *boot block*. For filesystems that are involved in bootstrapping, the first block contains a short bootstrap program. Typically this bootstrap program reads in a longer bootstrap or perhaps the UNIX system kernel itself. The exact details of bootstrapping are very system-dependent. On filesystems that aren't involved in the bootstrap process, the first block is usually unused.

The second block of a filesystem is the *superblock*. The superblock (also called the filesystem header) contains a variety of information about the filesystem. In particular, the superblock contains the size of the filesystem, the number of i-nodes in the filesystem, and several parameters regarding the free list. When a filesystem is mounted (using the mount command), an entry is made in the UNIX system kernel's mount table, and the filesystem's superblock is read into one of the kernel's large internal buffers. The superblocks of all of the mounted filesystems are accessible to the kernel because the kernel needs the information in the superblock to access the files and the i-nodes in the file system.

The i-nodes are stored on a filesystem starting at block 2. Different sizes of filesystems contain different numbers of i-nodes; the exact i-node count is stored in the super block. Since i-nodes are fixed in size and numbered consecutively from zero, it is easy to locate any i-node, given its number.

Each file is defined by an i-node, which contains all of the information the system keeps about each file. The i-node contains the mode and the type of the file, the length of the file in bytes, the identification numbers of the owner and the group, the location of the file, and the times that the file was created, last modified, and last accessed. Notice that the i-node does not contain the name of a file; the name is stored in a directory.

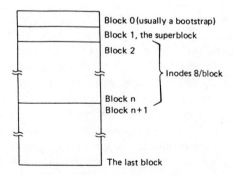

Figure 25.4. The filesystem layout.

The location information stored in an i-node needs to be examined in some detail. The UNIX system locates files by maintaining a list of the blocks in the file. Some operating systems locate files by maintaining the starting block number and the final block number, and the file is stored contiguously on the disk. Contiguous filesystems are unpleasant because files cannot grow without bound but are confined by the starting location of the next file. Contiguous filesystems tend to waste space because small holes between large files usually can't be used until they are collected during a garbage collection operation. By maintaining a list of the blocks in a file, the UNIX system avoids the problems of the contiguous filesystems. The blocks in the file may physically be scattered throughout the disk, but logically the blocks form a long chain which contains the information in the file.

The details of how information in the i-node leads the kernel to the blocks in a file vary from system to system. The numbers in the remainder of this paragraph apply exactly to Version 7 systems, but they should not be taken as gospel for modern systems. However, the general idea described here does pertain to all UNIX systems. The key to the location of the file is a list of 13 disk block numbers stored in the i-node. The first 10 block numbers in the i-node list specify the first 10 blocks in the file. If the file is only four blocks long, then the first four entries in the list contain block numbers, and the last nine entries in the list contain zeros. If a file is longer than 10 blocks, then the 11th block number is used to specify a disk block that contains a list of the next 128 blocks in the file. This block is known as an *indirect block*. For files longer than 138 (128 + 10) blocks, the 12th entry in the i-node list contains the address of a block that contains the addresses of 128 indirect blocks. This block is known as a *double indirect block*. Finally, for files longer than 16,522 ($10 + 128 + 128^2$) blocks, the 13th entry in the i-node list contains the address of a *triple indirect block*. The maximum number of blocks in a UNIX system file is $10 + 128 + 128^2 + 128^3$, or 2,113,674 blocks (see Fig. 25.5). (As noted above, the details of this scheme vary slightly from one version of the UNIX system to another.)

Fetching information from very large files is harder than fetching information from small files because the indirect blocks need to be fetched to determine the addresses of the actual blocks in the file. This overhead is a small price to pay for the ability to accommodate very large files. For example, to read a 10,000-block file entirely, the system has to fetch the 10,000 blocks in the file, one double indirect block, and 79 indirect blocks.

Let's now turn our attention to the directories. A directory is a disk resident file that contains a list of filenames and a corresponding list of i-node numbers. Programs are prohibited from writing into a directory; reading of directories is permitted. The kernel manipulates the directory contents when programs issue requests to create or delete files. Each directory file is defined by an i-node just as any ordinary file is defined by an i-node. On

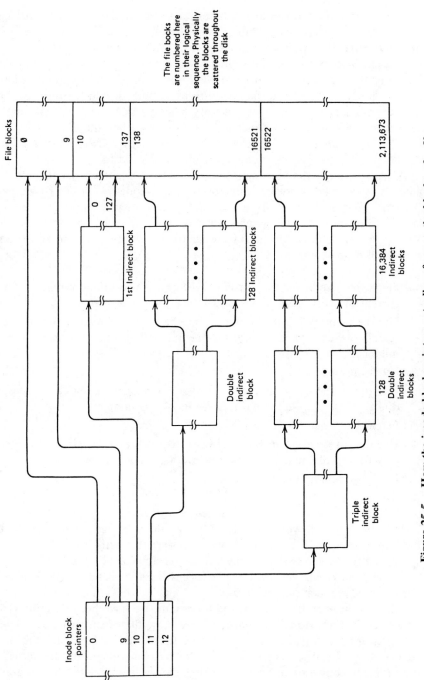

Figure 25.5. How the i-node block pointers actually reference the blocks of a file.

System V, directory entries are 16 bytes long: 14 bytes for the file name and two bytes for the i-node number. On Berkeley, directories have a more flexible format that allows filenames up to 255 characters long.

The first two entries in every directory are '.' and '..'. The '.' entry lists the i-node of the directory itself, and the '..' entry lists the i-node of the parent directory. (Note: in the root directory, both '.' and '..' reference the root directory because the root directory has no parent.) These two canonical entries are automatically placed in a directory when the directory is created by the system, and they cannot be removed by a user. A directory is considered "empty" when it contains only the '.' and the '..' files.

A path through the filesystem as viewed from the U<small>NIX</small> system kernel is actually a ricochet between directories and i-nodes. Consider the path '../a/b'. The path leads from the current directory to the parent of the current directory, to the parents subdirectory 'a', and finally to the file named 'b' in the directory 'a'. In order to follow this path the kernel performs the following steps:

1. Fetch the i-node for the current directory. (The i-node pointer for the current directory is in the user structure.)
2. Use the information in the i-node for the current directory to fetch and search the current directory for the name '..' and retrieve its i-node number.
3. Fetch the i-node for '..'.
4. Use the information in the '..' i-node to fetch and search the parent directory for the file 'a' and retrieve its i-node number.
5. Fetch the i-node for 'a'.
6. Use the information in the 'a' i-node to fetch and search the 'a' directory for the file named 'b' and retrieve its i-node number.
7. Fetch the i-node for 'b'.
8. Access the file 'b'.

This is a lot of work just to fetch a file (see Fig. 25.6). In a flat filesystem, the search for a file is much easier; this extra work by the U<small>NIX</small> system kernel is the price we pay for a hierarchical filesystem. Following pathnames is a relatively rare event; accessing the files that have already been located is much more common.

Thus far in our discussion of the filesystem, we have been describing the structures that are stored on a disk to create the filesystem structure. These elements are the superblock, the i-nodes, the directory files, and the ordinary and special files. These elements can be manipulated by the kernel in the ordinary course of operation, or they can be manipulated by programs such as fsck and fsdb while the filesystem is being repaired. Let's now conclude our discussion of the filesystem with a look at the structures that are maintained in memory by the kernel to access files (see Fig. 25.7).

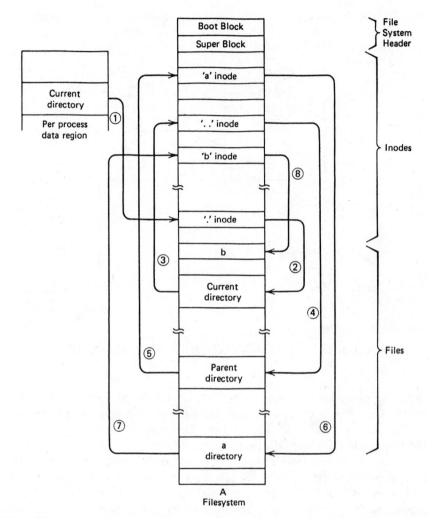

Figure 25.6.   Following a pathname. The eight steps (see text) in following the pathname '../a/b'.

We have already mentioned two of the structures the kernel keeps in memory: the superblock of each mounted filesystem, and a table of i-nodes. The superblock is kept in memory because it contains several key parameters for the filesystem including most notably the location of the list of free blocks. Each entry in the memory resident i-node table contains the key information for accessing a file including the mode of the file and the location of the blocks in the file.

There is one remaining table that the kernel keeps in memory for accessing files—the *file table*. Each entry in the file table contains a pointer to a

Peripheral Devices 253

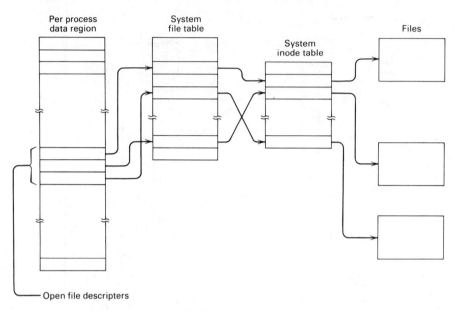

Figure 25.7.   The kernel's data structures for accessing files.

particular entry in the i-node table, and it contains the read/write pointer for the file. The per-user data area for each process contains pointers into the file table for each open file, and the file table points at the i-node table and the i-node table, actually points at the file.

This seems rather complicated; you might think that the per-process data area would contain pointers directly into the i-node table. Holding the read/write pointer for the file is the real reason for the file table. When a process with open files forks, the two subsequent processes share a single read/write pointer (stored in the file table) into the file. For example, this feature is often used in the shell. Whenever the shell runs a program, it fork-execs the new process, and then waits for the termination of the new process. Meanwhile, the new process reads from the standard input and writes to the standard output. The fact that the shell and the child process share the read/write pointers to the standard input and output causes the read/write pointer to be positioned correctly when the shell regains control.

25.9 PIPES

A *pipe* is an I/O connection between two related processes. At the user level a pipe is established when a process performs the following sequence of events. First, it executes the `pipe` system call, which returns two file descriptors: one for reading and one for writing. Second, it `forks` (often followed immediately by an `exec` in the child, the parent, or both). At this point, there are two processes sharing the file connections set up by the original `pipe` call. The final stage is for each of the two resultant processes to close one of the `pipe` file descriptors. If the pipe is to be from process *A* to process *B*, then *A* must close the read descriptor, and process *B* must close the write descriptor.

Notice that a pipe connection relies on the fact that open files remain open across `forks` and `execs`. Notice also that the use of a `fork` to create the two processes involved in a pipe forces pipes to work only between closely related processes. To remedy this shortcoming, System V has fifo files, which are locations in the filesystem that allow unrelated processes to have a pipelike connection, and Berkeley has sockets, which are communication end points.

In the kernel, pipe connections between processes are handled very similarly to ordinary I/O connections between a process and a file. Of course from a process's perspective, it is almost impossible to tell the difference between sending output to a pipe and sending it to a traditional output stream where seeking (moving the file's read/write pointer) is not allowed, such as a terminal.

First I am going to describe the traditional implementation of pipes in the kernel, and then I'll mention the new implementation provided by the Berkeley system. Traditionally the `pipe` system call causes the allocation of three kernel resources: an in-core i-node and two slots in the file table (see Fig. 25.8). One of the slots in the file table is reserved for input, and one is reserved for output. As with any file, the i-node records key information such as the size of the file and its type (pipe in this case). The file descriptors in the user table reference the allocated slots in the system file table, and those in turn reference the i-node, and the i-node will eventually reference the block buffers that will be allocated to hold the data as they flow through the pipe.

After the `fork` and the closing of the extraneous parts of the pipe connection, each process has the usual assortment of resources for I/O (see Fig. 25.9). When the writer places data in the pipe, the pipe's i-node records the amount of data and the block buffers that hold the data. The maximum size of the buffering allocated to the pipe is always made to be small enough to be directly addressable by the block pointers in the i-node. This is enforced in the kernel routine that writes data into a pipe. The kernel's read routine is careful not to take out more data from the pipe than the writer has deposited. When the writer has written as much into

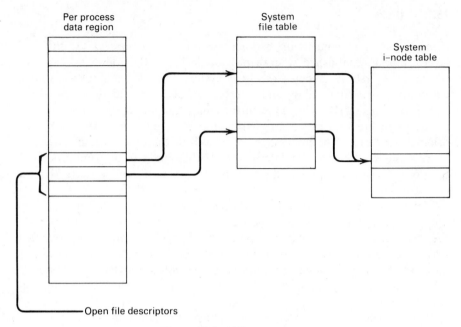

Figure 25.8.   Pipe creation.

the pipe as allowed by the maximum pipe size, it blocks and waits for the reader to catch up. When the reader catches up and notices that the pipe has reached its maximal size, the reader truncates the pipe to zero size and the process repeats.

In Berkeley UNIX, pipes are implemented using sockets. The two entries in the file table are allocated as usual, but then a socket is opened to act as the communication end point. This scheme works smoothly with the other Berkeley communication features, which are also organized around socket-to-socket connections. Sockets are discussed in Section 25.14.

25.10   DEVICE DRIVERS

A *peripheral device* is something that is attached to a computer, usually for performing input or output (or both). Disks, tapes, communication lines, and printers are typical peripherals. The UNIX system includes two strategies for managing I/O peripherals: the block I/O system and the character I/O system. The block model is usually used for devices that can be addressed as a sequence of blocks, which usually contain 512 bytes. Usually the block model is applied to disks and tapes.

The point of the block model is to allow the kernel to use buffering to reduce I/O traffic. The kernel maintains a set of block buffers. Whenever

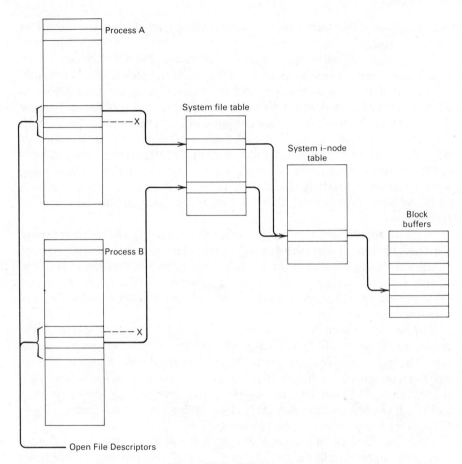

Figure 25.9.   Pipe usage.

a program requests a transfer, the internal buffers are searched to see if the block is already in memory. If the requested block is not in one of the internal buffers, then the system will free one of the internal buffers and transfer the requested block between the internal buffer and the I/O device. Frequently used blocks tend to stay in memory, thereby reducing I/O traffic.

The character model is used for all devices that don't fit the block model. Usually the character model is used for communication lines, printers, and so on. Most devices that have a block-structured interface also have a character interface in order to access the device without using the kernel's buffering facilities. Accesses to character devices that transfer a character at a time, such as a terminal, are usually buffered by the kernel in *character lists*, whereas accesses to character devices that transfer chunks (usually blocks) of data are usually not buffered at all by the kernel. Some of the major elements the kernel uses to access peripheral devices are shown in Figure 25.10.

There are two major difficulties in developing the I/O portion of an operating system. The first difficulty is that each peripheral requires slightly different management techniques. All of these different techniques need to be programmed into the operating system. The second problem is that the peripherals of most computers are constantly being rearranged. The operating system needs to be modified each time a peripheral device is added or deleted. These two problems are solved in the UNIX system by using individual software modules to control each different type of peripheral and using a set of tables to logically connect the kernel to different device drivers. A more detailed discussion of these techniques is given in the remainder of this section.

A set of subroutines that works within the operating system to supervise the transmission of data between the computer and a particular type of peripheral device is called a *driver*. The UNIX system is distributed with the drivers for a dozen or so of the more common peripherals. Dozens of other drivers for the more unusual peripherals are available within the UNIX community.

Getting the correct drivers incorporated into the operating system is the major operation during a system configuration. Operating systems utilize many different approaches to the problem of reconfiguration. The UNIX kernel is reconfigured by modifying several key program modules and then recompiling. The UNIX system uses two tables, bdevsw and cdevsw, to control the I/O configuration process. These tables are usually contained in a C language source program file named 'conf.c'.

In recent versions of the UNIX system, there is a program called config that will automatically create a 'conf.c' file for any given hardware configuration. In earlier versions of the UNIX system, the file 'conf.c' had to be modified manually. Besides the bdevsw and cdevsw tables, 'conf.c' usually contains several parameters that control various resources such as the number of the kernel's internal buffers, the size of the swap space, and the lengths of some of the kernel's internal tables.

The heart of the 'conf.c' file is a pair of structures, bdevsw and cdevsw. These two structures are the key to the ability of the UNIX system kernel to adapt easily to different hardware configurations by installing different driver modules.

Let's first examine cdevsw. The cdevsw table is the linkage between the driver modules for the character oriented I/O devices and the UNIX system kernel. Each type of device is assigned a number, called a *major device number*, for reference. There is one entry in the cdevsw table for each major device number. The zeroeth entry in the cdevsw table is for the character I/O device with major device number zero, the next entry is for the character I/O device with major device number 1, and so on.

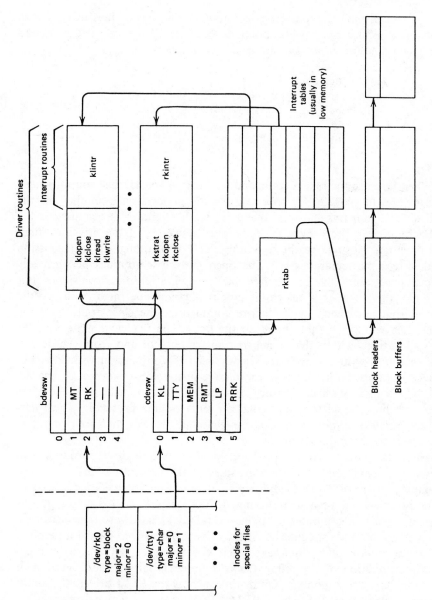

Figure 25.10. The kernel's data structures for accessing peripheral devices.

You can display the major device numbers for special files using the ls program. Because special files don't have a "size," the size field of the ls listing contains the major and minor device numbers.

```
$ ls -l /dev/tty0[0123]
crw--w--w-  1 root    1,   0 Feb 13 14:21 /dev/tty00
crw--w--w-  1 root    1,   1 Feb 13 14:21 /dev/tty01
crw-rw-rw-  1 root    1,   2 Feb  5 11:38 /dev/tty02
crw--w--w-  1 root    1,   3 Feb 14 11:44 /dev/tty03
$ _
```

When you use the mknod command to create a special file, you may need to examine the 'conf.c' file to determine the major device number for the device. The four ttys shown in the above list have major device number 1.

Each entry in the cdevsw table lists the addresses of the driver routines for opening, closing, reading, writing, and controlling the transmission mode for a particular device. The open and close routines perform any special processing that is required before and after data transfers. For example, the open on a telephone communication line might wait for the line to ring and then answer before completing; the close routine on the same line would probably hang up the line. The read and write routines are called from within the kernel to transfer data to and from the device. The read and write routines are usually used in conjunction with interrupt service routines, which manage the data transmission character by character. The transmission mode routine is used on communication line devices to adapt the channel to a particular terminal or line protocol. The transmission mode routine is not used for character devices that aren't sending characters to computer terminals.

The UNIX system drivers are designed so that one driver program can service the requirements of several copies of the associated hardware. For example, on the PDP-11 computer, an interface called a KL11 is used to transmit characters to a single terminal. Only one KL11 driver program is needed, even if a computer contains several KL11 hardware interfaces. To differentiate between the interfaces, the driver routines are passed a number, called the *minor device number*, which indicates the interface to be used. The interpretation of the minor device number is left to the discretion of the individual drive module. On drivers such as the KL11 driver, the minor device number indicates which KL11. Other UNIX system drivers use the minor device number for other purposes. An example is the magtape driver, which uses different minor device numbers to indicate the recording density or whether the tape should be rewound when it is closed.

The names of the driver routines usually start with a standard two-character prefix which is a clue to the associated hardware interface. For example, the driver routines for the Digital Equipment Corporation DL11 serial line interface use the prefix "kl" (because the interfaces formerly were called KL11). The line in the cdevsw table defining the kernel interface to the kl driver is

```
/*0*/ &klopen, &klclose, &klread, &klwrite, &klsgtty,
```

(The ampersand is the C programming language notation for the address of an object.)

Drivers frequently omit certain routines because the associated hardware device doesn't require (or allow) the operation. For example, there is no need for a special operation to open or close the UNIX system's memory device, and it is obviously impossible to control the transmission characteristics of the memory device, since it is not a communication line. When routines are absent from a driver, the special routines nulldev or nodev are referenced in the cdevsw table. The nulldev routine is used when a certain operation is not required, and the nodev routine is used when a certain operation is logically impossible and hence an error. The entry in the cdevsw table for the interface to physical memory is

```
/*8*/ &nulldev, &nulldev, &mmread, &mmwrite, &nodev,
```

This entry indicates that no operation is performed when the memory device is opened or closed, and it is an error to attempt to control the transmission mode of the memory device.

The bdevsw table in the 'conf.c' file is used to connect the I/O routines for block devices to the UNIX system kernel. Each entry in the table contains the address of open and close routines, the address of a strategy routine, and the address of a device table. The open and close routines perform any processing that is necessary when the device is first opened, and they are often unused (nulldev). The strategy routine is called to perform block reads and writes. The reason that a single routine is called is that the overall access time can often be optimized by rearranging the order in which blocks are fetched.

The device table, which contains pointers to the buffers for the device, is the central point in performing I/O to block devices. Performing an access to a block I/O device occurs in two stages. In the first stage, a buffer is allocated and the header of the block is initialized. The header contains the block number on the device as well as several flags and pointers to other headers and a pointer to the actual buffer. The second stage consists of the physical transfer of data between the buffer and the device. The order of the transfers between the buffers and the device may not be the order in which the requests were issued because of the strategy considerations mentioned above.

Many of the peripheral devices that are attached to UNIX systems use *interrupt* techniques for transferring data. A hardware interrupt is an electrical signal that causes the processor to stop whatever it is doing and go to an *interrupt service routine*. The interrupt service routine usually tends to the immediate needs of the peripheral device and then returns control to the interrupted program. Character-oriented devices often interrupt once per character, or occasionally once per line or once per block of data; block-oriented devices usually interrupt once per block of data.

An *interrupt handler* is the part of a device driver that actually supervises the transmission of data to and from interrupt-driven peripherals. These routines are activated when the I/O interface hardware generates an interrupt. In many computer systems, such as the PDP-11, the VAX, and the IBM PC, the addresses of the interrupt service programs must be stored in low memory at specified locations. The address locations are determined by options that are enabled on the actual interface circuit card.

25.11 CHARACTER HANDLING

The UNIX kernel's handling of character I/O to terminals is an excellent example of how good organization and the proper data structures can simplify a difficult task. Character I/O is deceptive. The overall mandate is clear; transfer character data between processes and terminals with maximum efficiency. However, there are a raft of details that follow immediately. Certain input characters, such as the ubiquitous erase, kill, and interrupt characters, are special. They cause things to happen other than simple data transfer from keyboard to process. Another difficulty is device management. Each I/O device has its own control sequence and timing requirements. Yet another difficulty is the large number of modes that are available. Just examine your stty manual page to see how many different character I/O processing options are available.

In the broadest sense, the UNIX kernel divides the problem into two parts: generic management of character I/O data, and specific management of I/O devices. Generic character I/O management is performed by the *tty* driver. The tty driver isn't a normal device driver—it doesn't manage any specific hardware device; rather, it handles erase/kill processing, most tty modes, etc. Character I/O device drivers handle the hardware-dependent aspects of character transmission. They catch the hardware interrupts, manage the device-dependent details, etc. There is one character I/O device driver for each type of communications hardware.

Character I/O drivers for terminals are written to automatically call the generic tty handler as necessary. For example when a device's open routine is called, it performs any necessary hardware management functions and then calls the generic open routine in the tty handler. The generic tty open routine performs some routine initialization plus one key initialization for init's offspring—it records the tty device in the user table and starts a new process group.

The major data element for managing a communications line is the *tty* structure. There is one tty structure for every communication line. It contains the key information about the state of the line, such as whether echoing is enabled, whether the line is in raw mode, the assignments for the special characters, etc. It also contains pointers to three clists: the raw queue, the canonical queue, and the output queue. A *clist* is a buffering mechanism for character data. Each clist contains a small buffer plus forward and backward pointers to other buffers in the chain. Thus, although the capacity of each clist is just a few dozen characters, a linked list of clists can store a considerable quantity of data.

The raw clist contains information that is received from the communication line. Each time a character is received, the device driver performs standard error checking and such and then calls the tty handler's input routine to deposit the character into the raw clist. The tty handler then performs all of the input processing and eventually deposits the character into the raw clist. In line-oriented operation, when the tty handler is passed a line termination character, it copies the raw clist to the canonical clist and makes it available for reading by the user process. In raw (or Berkeley's cbreak) mode, each character is made immediately available to the user process.

The output queue collects characters from process's write requests and also from the character input routines. Characters are processed as they are placed into the output queue. The processing includes mapping of tabs to spaces, mapping lowercase to uppercase, and adding delays to accommodate hardware limitations.

The various operational modes of the tty character-handling system are controlled using ioctl (sometimes pronounced *i-o-cuttle;* sometimes pronounced *i-o-c-t-l*) system calls. (In older systems, the ioctl functions were handled using stty and gtty, but both System V and Berkeley use ioctl.) When a device driver gets an ioctl, it first calls the tty handler's ioctl routine. The tty handler gets first chance to handle the request. If the request is not in the tty handler's domain, then the device driver tries to handle the request. Only if both fail is an error returned to the calling process.

A process that wants to read or write the controlling terminal, regardless of I/O redirection that has been supplied by the shell, can always open the '/dev/tty' special file. There is a trivial device driver associated with the '/dev/tty' special file that knows how to use the tty device information in the user table to call the appropriate routine in the actual device driver.

The character-handling system is directly involved in the UNIX process group mechanism. As mentioned above, when an offspring of init opens a tty device driver, the generic tty handler creates a new process group. The new process group id is set to the pid number of the process. All offspring of this process, which is usually getty, will inherit that group affiliation. Process groups are important because certain signals, such as the hangup signal, are distributed to all of the members of the process group. You can send a signal to all of the processes in your process group using the special pid number zero instead of an actual pid number. It is possible for background demons to establish their own process group.

25.12   SLEEP AND WAKEUP

sleep and wakeup are two of the kernel's most important routines. sleep is called whenever a kernel process wants to wait for an event. When the event occurs, wakeup will be called to resume the sleeping process.

sleep takes two parameters—an arbitrary token and a priority. The token is usually the address of a data structure in the kernel. For example, if a process issues a read request on a teletype, it will usually sleep until an entire line is received. In this case the token will, by convention, be the address of the input queue. When the line terminator is received, the teletype driver will call wakeup using the input queue address as the token. This will wake up the appropriate sleeping process. Note that if several processes are waiting for a line of teletype input, each will be waiting for a different queue to receive a line, and each will use a different token.

The sleep priority is the priority the process will have when it resumes execution. Priorities below a given threshold make it impossible for signals to awaken the sleeping process. Routines that call sleep may be inadvertently awakened. Because of spurious awakenings, sleep is usually called within a loop that executes as long as the reason for sleeping persists.

A *zombie* is a process that persists forever, because it is waiting for an event that will never happen. This can occur because of a hardware fault or a software fault in a device driver.

25.13   STREAMS

Streams are modular, full-duplex character-processing elements. They were designed in the early 1980s by Dennis Ritchie, one of the two original UNIX architects, to replace the traditional character-handling system in the kernel. Ritchie first described streams in *A Stream Input-Output System* in the October 1984 issue of the AT&T Bell Laboratories Technical Journal. They are also described in a booklet from AT&T titled *UNIX System V Streams Primer* and in AT&T's *UNIX System V Streams Programmer's Guide*. Streams are available starting in System V.3.

There were several problems with UNIX's traditional character-handling system that Ritchie sought to eliminate with streams. The most important improvement is modularity. The traditional character-handling system is complicated and interconnected, but streams achieve the same facilities within a simpler and more modular framework. The second improvement is efficiency—characters are traditionally passed from one kernel routine to another individually, whereas in streams entire blocks of characters are passed.

A *stream processing module* is a kernel routine that performs some processing on a stream. Typical stream processing modules perform chores such as the traditional tty character management (character echo, erase, etc.), networking protocols, etc. Stream processing modules are bidirectional. Each handles data traveling in two directions. Data traveling from the user process to the hardware device (or to the pseudodevice) are said to be flowing downstream; data traveling the other way are said to be flowing upstream.

A user process can reconfigure the modules that process data flowing between it an a device (or pseudodevice). The standard ioctl mechanism is used to request specific stream modules. For example, while a networking protocol is being developed, it can reside in a user process, and a minimal stream module can connect the process to the hardware device driver. When the protocol is working, it can be transported to a stream module, thereby allowing a user process to access the protocol service simply by asking the kernel to insert the protocol module in the process to a device data path. Stream processing modules have a standard interface to other kernel routines. Thus a network protocol module can work with any appropriate hardware drivers. If you are familiar with the ISO seven-layer protocol model, you may have noticed that streams make it easy to write kernel software that corresponds to the standard layers.

25.14 SOCKETS

Sockets are a general-purpose communication facility that is present in Berkeley UNIX systems. A socket is a communication end point. When a socket is opened, the process specifies a particular communication domain. The two original communication domains are the UNIX domain, for sockets used as interprocess communication end points on a single machine, and the Internet domain, for sockets used to communicate with processes on remote machines.

Sockets are opened and initialized by performing a sequence of system calls. Each system call further specifies exactly how the socket is going to be used. Once a socket has been created and initialized, data can be sent to and from the socket using the standard read and write system calls, although the more flexible socket I/O system calls sendto and recvfrom are often necessary.

The Berkeley kernel contains a socket data structure for each active socket. It details the state of the socket and contains pointers to data storage and pointers to processing routines. Essentially, the socket data structure is the kernel's way of keeping track of where the data are going and how they are going to get there. This additional layer isolates a user process from the data source/destination, thereby allowing much greater flexibility in routing data. Remember that in the traditional kernel a process's I/O connections are rigidly tied to buffers, which are in turn rigidly committed to specific I/O devices (or to other processes in the case of pipes).

APPENDIX I

Vi Command Reference

The ex/vi family of editors has two major user interfaces: ex, which is a line-oriented interface, and vi, which is a full-screen interface. This appendix primarily discusses the vi aspects of the editor; ex is not discussed on its own in this book, although nearly all of the commands discussed in Appendix III, the ed editor, will work when you use ex. Appendix II, the vi Options Reference, has a list of the options that can be set to alter vi's behavior.

COMMAND LINE OPTIONS

-t *tag*   The editor commences at the tagged location in the appropriate file. This option usually replaces a command line filename. *tag* must be a tagname that is found in a tags file. The default tags files are the file named 'tags' in the current directory and the file '/usr/lib/tags'. Alternate tag files can be specified in the '.exrc' editor startup script. (The '.exrc' file is discussed in the Environment Variables section of this appendix.)

-r   When vi is terminated by a hangup or by a system crash, it saves the current edit buffer and then sends mail to the user notifying him that an edit buffer has been saved. A list of saved edit buffers is printed by vi when you specify the -r option without mentioning a filename. The -r option combined with a filename tells vi to recover that file from the recovery area.

-x   vi will prompt for a key, which will then be used to decrypt all files that are read in, and encrypt all files that are written out.

-R   The input file will be considered read-only. All write commands will fail unless you use the w! form of the write command to override the write protection. You can unset the read-only mode by setting the noreadonly option. If you invoke vi using the name view, then the read-only option will be set automatically.

+*excmd*   The editing session will commence by executing the given ex editor command. The most common uses of this option are specifying a search target (e.g., +/Jones to find the first occurrence of *Jones* in the file) or line number (e.g., +50 to start editing on line 50). The editor will be positioned on the last line of the buffer prior to executing the command.

-l   Sets the showmatch and lisp options so that it is easier to edit lisp programs.

-w*n*   Sets the window size to *n*.

-           Sets the noautoprint mode. This makes ex quieter, which is useful when processing edit scripts.

OVERVIEW

vi attempts to portray, on the screen of your terminal, a window showing the current appearance of the file being edited. There are two major vi modes: visual command mode and text entry mode. (There are also several ex-specific modes, but they are not discussed here.) During visual command mode everything that you type is interpreted as a command. Visual commands are not echoed on the screen; just their effect is visible. In text entry mode, everything you type (with a few exceptions) is added to the text. Entering a Text Entry Command (Section 5) changes from visual-command mode to text entry mode; entering <ESC> terminates text entry mode and resumes visual-command mode.

While you are editing a file with vi, you are actually working with a copy of that file, which is stored in the edit buffer. Changes made to the edit buffer don't alter the original file until you issue a write command. You should periodically write out the edit buffer to the disk file so that your work will be safe—from computer crashes or your own mistakes. If you make a disastrous alteration to the edit buffer, do *not* write out the buffer to the original file (you might want to write it out to another file, just in case). At the end of your editing session, you should write out the buffer to the original file. vi will warn you if you try to exit without saving a modified edit buffer.

Before using vi, you must properly set the environment variable $TERM to indicate what type of terminal you are using. If $TERM is unset—or even worse, if it is set incorrectly—vi will not be able to function properly. The $TERM variable is often set in your '.profile' (or '.login' for csh users) login script. The second chore that must be done before using vi is terminal initialization. The importance of terminal initialization depends on what terminal you are using; some will not operate properly until initialized, and on others the initialization is superfluous. On System V, there is the tput program. The most recent versions of tput have the command line option init which will perform the initialization. On older versions of System V, the sequence of commands tput is1;tput is2;tput is3 will usually be sufficient. Berkeley systems have the tset program. It will gladly perform the initialization, but the syntax is awkward.

Commands in visual-command mode are typically one or a few keystrokes long. You do not have to enter a final <CR> for most commands; rather they are executed as you type the keys. Because visual-mode commands are not echoed on the screen, and because they are executed immediately, it is very easy to enter commands incorrectly, thereby producing surprising results. It is especially important to strike the correct keys, because there is no way to take back a keystroke (or to even see what you have typed). You can always cancel a partially entered command by striking <ESC>.

Since vi has several modes, it is possible for the novice to move unwillingly from one to the other. All of the commands in this reference assume that you are in vi visual-command mode. That's where you want to be, unless you care to learn the powerful ex line-editing commands. If you accidentally get into ex command line mode (you know you are in ex command line mode if a : is printed each time you hit <CR> or if <ESC> is echoed as ^[), enter the command vi<CR> to reenter visual mode. (If that doesn't work, try <CR>.<CR>vi<CR>.) If you accidentally get into open line-editing mode (you know you are in open line-editing mode when cursor movement commands constantly redraw the bottom line of the screen), enter the command Q (or <ESC>Q) to move to ex command line mode, and then enter the command vi<CR> to return to visual mode.

Commands that start with a : or a ! are displayed on the bottom line of the screen as they are entered. For these commands, you can use the backspace to make corrections as you enter the command, you can abort the command by striking the interrupt character (usually ^C or <DEL>), and you must hit <CR> (carriage return) when the command has been completely entered.

Many vi commands accept an optional *numeric prefix*. For most commands, if you enter a numeric prefix, the command will be executed that many times; otherwise the command will be executed once. The exact meaning of the numeric prefix is detailed below only when it does something other than repeat the command. Commands that accept a numeric prefix are indicated in the following table with a bullet in front of the citation. As you enter a numeric prefix, vi sits there silently, refusing to acknowledge the value visually on the screen. Type carefully.

The commands c, y, d, <, >, and ! (change, yank, delete, shift left, shift right, and filter the buffer) are called *operators,* because they operate on regions of text. An operator must be followed by a suffix, symbolized by § in the following table, that indicates the text region. The suffix may be any of the Cursor Movement Commands, any of the Text Search Commands, or either of the *goto* Marked Text Commands. (The suffix need not be a single keystroke.) The <, >, and ! operators always affect whole lines; thus they allow only suffixes that specify line positions. When an operator is doubled, its text region is the entire line. Thus cc will change the current line, and 5yy will yank five lines starting with the current line.

Many people who use vi extensively over long periods of time don't take advantage of vi's operators. That's unfortunate, because the operators are relatively easy to use, very powerful, and very flexible. The most important part of using an operator is knowing the cursor movement commands well enough to know exactly how to specify a given region of text. Once you've mastered cursor movement, you've nearly mastered operators. For example, d$ will delete from the current cursor position to the end of the line, d^ will delete from the current cursor position to the end of the line, dfq will delete from the current cursor position to the next letter *q* on the line, dG will delete from the current line to the end of the file, and d100G will delete from the current line to line 100. Take some time to learn to use vi operators; they are easier than you think and often useful.

Several conventions are used in this appendix. The notation ^X means Ctrl-*X,* where *X* may be any character. The notation <CR> signifies a carriage return, <DEL> is the delete key, <ESC> is the escape key, and <SP> is the space key. The notation *text* in the Text Entry Commands means any printable characters, any escaped (using Q or ^V) control characters, or tabs, spaces, or carriage returns. While you are entering *text,* only the controls described under Commands Used During An Insertion are available. You must terminate the insertion before using the full visual command set.

1.   CURSOR MOVEMENT COMMANDS

h j k l	• Cursor left, down, up, right
← ↓ ↑ →	• Cursor left, down, up, right
^H ^N ^P <SP>	• Cursor left, down, up, right
^J	• Cursor down
+ <CR>	• Cursor to first nonblank on following line
-	• Cursor to first nonblank on previous line
G	• Goto line (go to end without preceding count)
w b e	• Move forward word, backward word, or to end of word (a *word* is a sequence of letters and digits, or group of punctuation symbols)
W B E	• Move forward word, backward word, or to end of word (a *word* is any text delimited by white space)
0	Cursor to beginning of line
^	Cursor to first nonblank on line
|	• Cursor to column 1, or column specified by count
$	• Cursor to end of line, or if count is supplied then cursor to end of count-th following line
( )	• Cursor moves backward or forward to beginning of sentence
{ }	• Cursor moves backward or forward to beginning of paragraph
[[ ]]	• Cursor moves backward or forward to beginning of section
H M L	• Move cursor to home (top line of screen), middle line or lowest line. For H a count means move to that many lines from top of screen; for L a count means move to that many lines from bottom

2.   MARKED TEXT

m*a*	Mark location with mark named *a*, where *a* may be any lower case letter
' '	Goto line from previous context
'*a*	Goto line marked *a*
``	Goto character position from previous context
`*a*	Goto character position marked *a*

3. TEXT SEARCHES

f*c* F*c*	• Move cursor forward or backward to find character *c* on current line
t*c* T*c*	• Move cursor forward or backward to position left of character *c* on current line
;	• Repeat last intraline search
,	• Repeat last intraline search backwards
/*pat*\<CR>	Forward search for pattern *pat*
?*pat*\<CR>	Reverse search for pattern *pat*
n N	Repeat last search in same or opposite direction
%	Search for balancing parenthesis () or brace {} when cursor is positioned on parenthesis or brace

4. SCREEN MANAGEMENT

^F ^B	• Forward or backward screenful
^U ^D	• Up or down half screenful (preceding count, which is remembered, specifies how many lines to scroll)
^Y ^E	• Up or down one line
z\<CR> z. z-	• Move current line to top, middle, or bottom of screen. A numeric prefix to z specifies which line; a numeric suffix to z specifies a new window size
^R	Redraw screen. Closes up empty screen lines created during editing on dumb terminals
^L	Completely rewrite screen. Needed after a transmission error, or after some other program writes to the screen

5. TEXT ENTRY COMMANDS

r*c*	• Replace character under cursor with *c*
a*text*\<ESC>	• Append *text* following current cursor position
A*text*\<ESC>	• Append *text* at the end of the line
i*text*\<ESC>	• Insert *text* before the current cursor position
I*text*\<ESC>	• Insert *text* at the beginning of the current line
o*text*\<ESC>	Open up a new line following the current line, and add *text* there
O*text*\<ESC>	Open up a new line in front of the current line and add *text* there

s*text*<ESC>	• Substitute *text* for character under cursor
c§*text*<ESC>	• Change the given object to *text*. § is any character position specifier. For example, the command cwBob<ESC> will change the next word to *Bob*
C*text*<ESC>	• A synonym for c$. Replaces from cursor position to end of line with *text*
S*text*<ESC>	• A synonym for cc. Replaces lines with *text*
R*text*<ESC>	• Replace the original material with *text*
>§	• Shift lines right. § is a line specifier
<§	• Shift lines left. § is a line specifier
=	• Reindent line according to lisp standard
J	• Join lines together
!§*unixcmd*<CR>	• Filter lines of text through a UNIX pipeline. The pipeline's output replaces the original text. § is a line specifier
~	Change the case of the character under the cursor, and move right one position
.	• Repeat the last change
&	Repeat last **ex** substitute command. A synonym for :&<CR>

6. COMMANDS USED DURING AN INSERTION

^Q ^V	Quote the next character. For example, in text insert mode ^V^L will put a linefeed (^L) in the text
\	Quote a following ^H, erase, or kill
^W	Erase last entered word
^H	Erase last entered character
<CR>	Start a new line
^T	In autoindent mode, indent shiftwidth at beginning of line
^I	Tab
^D	In autoindent mode, move back one tab from beginning of line
0^D	In autoindent mode, move to left margin and reset autoindent amount to zero
^^D	In autoindent mode, move to left margin, but don't change autoindent amount (caret Ctrl-D)
<ESC>	Terminate insertion

<DEL>	• Abnormally terminate insertion

7. TEXT DELETION COMMANDS

d§	• Delete the given object. § is any position specifier
x	• A synonym for d<SP>. Delete character under cursor. (Preceding count repeats, but only on current line)
X	• A synonym for d<BS>. Delete character to left of the cursor. (Count repeats, but only on current line)
D	A synonym for d$. Deletes from the cursor to the end of the line
u	Undo last change
U	Restore Line

8. BUFFERS

y§	• Yank text into buffer. § is any position specifier
Y	• A synonym for yy. Yanks lines of text into a buffer
p P	Put back text from buffer, and place it after (lowercase p) or before (uppercase P) current line or character position
"*a*	A prefix to yank (y), delete (d), put (p), or change (c) to indicate that the buffer named *a* should be used. (*a* is any lowercase letter)
"*A*	A prefix to yank (y), delete (d), or change (c) to indicate that the selected text should be appended to the buffer named *A*. (*A* is any uppercase letter)

9. SHELL ESCAPES

:!*cmd*<CR>	Escape to perform one UNIX command
:sh<CR>	Start a subshell. You may enter commands, then exit from the subshell to return to vi

10. STATUS

^G	Display filename, modified message, line number, and percentage location in file
^Z	On UNIX systems that support job suspension, this will suspend vi
Q	Change from vi mode to ex mode
\<DEL\>	Striking the interrupt character returns to vi command mode from a search or from inserting text. Many people prefer to use \<Ctrl-C\> as their interrupt character
\<ESC\>	Sound bell or terminate insertion
:set\<CR\>	List options set differently from default
:set all\<CR\>	List settings of all options
:set *opt = val*\<CR\>	Set option named *opt* to *val*. (*Options* are discussed in Appendix II)

11. MACROS

@*b*	Execute the commands stored in the buffer named *b*
:map *key repl*\<CR\>	Create a command macro that will be invoked when you hit *key*. *key* is a single keystroke, the escape code generated by a function key, or *#n*, which means function key *n*. When you hit the key, the commands stored in *repl* will be executed. Use ^V to escape special characters (e.g., \<ESC\>, \<CR\>) in *repl*
:map\<CR\>	List the current command macros
:unmap *key*\<CR\>	Delete a command macro
:map! *key repl*\<CR\>	Create an insertion macro that will be invoked when you hit *key* in insert mode. *key* is coded as detailed above for map. *key* becomes a single keystroke abbreviation for *repl*
:map!\<CR\>	List the current insertion macros
:unmap! *key*\<CR\>	Delete a insertion macro.
:ab *word repl*\<CR\>	Create an abbreviation for *word*. During a text insertion, whenever you type *word* surrounded by white space or new lines, it will be replaced with *repl*. *word* can be more than one character. Use ^V in *repl* to escape special characters

:ab<CR>	List the current abbreviations
:unab *word*<CR>	Delete an abbreviation
#n	Manually simulate a function key on a terminal that lacks function keys

12.   FILE MANIPULATION

:w<CR>	Write edit buffer to original file
:w *filename*<CR>	Write edit buffer to named file
:w! *filename*<CR>	Write edit buffer to named file. Overwrite existing file
:wq<CR>	Write edit buffer to original file, and then quit
:e *filename*<CR>	Start editing a new file. A warning will be printed if edit buffer has been modified but not yet saved
:e! *filename*<CR>	Start editing a new file regardless of whether buffer has been saved since it was last modified
:e #<CR>	Edit alternate file. The alternate file is the previous file that you were editing, or the last file mentioned in an unsuccessful :e command
:n<CR>	Edit the next file mentioned on the command line
:n *filelist*<CR>	Specify a list of files to edit, as if they had been mentioned on the command line
:r *filename*<CR>	Read a file into the edit buffer
:r !*unixcmd*<CR>	Read the output of a command into the edit buffer
:q<CR>	Quit. (A warning is printed, and you will remain in the editor if the edit buffer has been modified but not yet saved)
:q!<CR>	Quit. (No warning)
ZZ	Save edit buffer and quit. Equivalent to :x<CR> or :wq<CR>
:cd *dir*<CR>	Change directory to *dir*. A warning will be printed, and the move will not occur if the file has been modified but not yet saved

ENVIRONMENT VARIABLES

Before using vi, the environment variable $TERM must be correctly set for your terminal. If $TERM isn't set, then vi will complain when it starts to run, and you will be put in ex commandline mode. If $TERM is set incorrectly, then when vi starts, it is likely that your screen display will be garbled. If either of these two problems arises, you should probably enter the command :q<CR> and get help. Since there are several families of similar terminals that share similar control code sequences, it is possible for $TERM to be wrong but for everything to appear correct for a while. Get help from an expert if your screen doesn't seem to behave as expected.

On Berkeley systems, the screen management routines are based on the *termcap* terminal capabilities database. The most commonly used terminals at your site should be listed near the beginning of the '/etc/termcap' database to help vi start faster. If the environment variable $TERMCAP exists and its first character isn't a slash, it is checked to see if it contains the termcap entry for the $TERM terminal. Placing a termcap entry into the $TERMCAP variable lets vi start faster, because it doesn't need to sequentially search through the '/etc/termcap' terminal capabilities database. If the $TERMCAP variable does start with a slash, then vi assumes it names a terminal capabilities database file and uses that database instead of the default database.

On System V, the *terminfo* terminal capabilities database is used. Unlike a termcap database, which stores all of its information in a single large file, the terminfo database stores each terminal's description in a single file. The directory '/usr/lib/terminfo' is the root terminfo directory, the '/usr/lib/terminfo/a' directory stores termcaps whose name starts with *a,* etc. If $TERMINFO is set, vi will look in that directory for the root directory of the terminfo description files. If a description isn't found in the $TERMINFO subtree, the '/usr/lib/terminfo' subtree will be searched as usual.

The environment variable $EXINIT may contain the name of a file containing ex commands. If $EXINIT doesn't exist, vi will read commands from the file .exrc in your home directory. Then in either case the editor will read any commands in the file .exrc in the current directory. '.exrc' startup files typically contain set commands to set desired vi options.

Index of vi Command Characters in ASCII Order

Char	Sect.	Char	Sect.	Char	Sect.	Char	Sect.
^@		<SP>	1.	@	11.	`	2.
^A		!	5.	A	5.	a	5.
^B	4.	"	8.	B	1.	b	1.
^C		#	11.	C	5.	c	5.
^D	4. 6.	$	1.	D	7.	d	7.
^E	4.	%	3.	E	1.	e	1.
^F	4.	&	5.	F	3.	f	3.
^G	10.	`	2.	G	1.	g	
^H	1. 6.	(	1.	H	1.	h	1.
^I	6.	)	1.	I	5.	i	5.
^J	1.	*		J	5.	j	1.
^K		+	1.	K		k	1.
^L	4.	,	3.	L	1.	l	1.
<CR>	1.	-	1.	M	1.	m	2.
^N	1.	.	5.	N	3.	n	3.
^O		/	3.	O	5.	o	5.
^P	1.	0	1.	P	8.	p	8.
^Q	6.	1		Q	10.	q	
^R	4.	2		R	5.	r	5.
^S		3		S	5.	s	5.
^T	6.	4		T	3.	t	3.
^U	4.	5		U	7.	u	7.
^V	6.	6		V		v	
^W	6.	7		W	1.	w	1.
^X	4.	8		X	7.	x	7.
^Y	4.	9		Y	8.	y	8.
^Z	10.	:	9 – 12.	Z	12.	z	4.
<ESC>	5. 6. 10.	;	3.	[	1.	{	1.
		<	5.	\		|	1.
		=	5.	]	1.	}	1.
		>	5.	^	1.	~	5.
		?	3.	_		<DEL>	10.

APPENDIX II

Vi Options Reference

The ex/vi text editor has various options that can be set to customize its operation. The set command in ex/vi is used to display or change option settings. set can be used interactively, or set commands can be placed in the '.exrc' script so that they will be set automatically each time vi or ex starts to execute.

Many options are either on or off. For example, vi will ring the terminal's bell when it encounters an error if errorbells is set; otherwise it will refrain from making noises. On/off options are set using the vi command

    :set *opt*

to set the option or the command

    :set *noopt*

to turn the option off.

Many options have values, such as the term option whose value is the name of the terminal that you are using. Options with values are set using the command

    :set *opt* = *val*

You can see a list of all of the option settings if you enter the command

```
:set all
```

Alternatively, you can see a list of the options that are set differently from the default by entering the **vi** command

```
:set
```

Options settings are traditionally controlled using **vi**'s **set** command, but the following command line options also have an influence on the option settings.

-R
  Sets the **readonly** option.
-l
  Sets the **showmatch** and **lisp** options for lisp editing.
-w
  Sets the default window size.

Option	Abb.	Meaning
autoindent	ai	autoindent makes vi automatically indent each new line to the same level as the previous, or to the same level as the one the cursor was on when a new line was opened. ^T will increase the indentation one shiftwidth. ^D at the beginning of a line will cause the indent to retreat left one stop. ^^D will retreat to the left margin. The default is noai.
autoprint	ap	When autoprint is set, lines are printed after being modified by one of the following ex commands: d, c, J, m, t, u, <, or >. This option applies only in line-editing mode, and the effect is as if a trailing p were added to each of the above ex commands. The default is ap.
autowrite	aw	When autowrite is set, vi will automatically write out the current file before executing commands that might switch to another file, or before executing a shell escape command. The default is noaw.
beautify	bf	beautify tells vi to discard all control characters (other than tab, newline, and form-feed) from the input. The default is nobf.
directory	dir	directory tells vi where to place its temporary files. The default is /tmp.

edcompatible		This makes the ex substitute command more closely resemble ed's. The default is noedcompatible.
errorbells	eb	errorbells tells vi to ring the terminal's bell for a larger set of errors. The default is noeb.
flash		Flash the screen instead of ringing the bell on those terminals that are capable of flashing the screen. (Available only on newer versions of vi.) The default is flash.
hardtabs	ht	hardtabs defines the hardware tab stops for your terminal. The default is 8 spaces.
ignorecase	ic	ignorecase tells vi to ignore case distinctions in searches and substitutions. The default is noic.
lisp		lisp alters the indent strategy in indent mode for lisp programs. The default is nolisp.
list	li	list mode displays tabs and linefeeds explicitly. Tabs are displayed as ^I, and linefeeds are displayed as $. The default is noli.
magic		In magic mode, all regular expression characters are active. In nomagic mode, only ^, $, and \ are metacharacters. In nomagic mode, a metacharacter (e.g., ?) can be restored its power by preceding it with a backslash (e.g., \?). The default is magic.
mesg		mesg allows messages to be written on your screen during vi sessions. The default is nomesg.
number	nu	number numbers lines on the display. The default is nonu.
open		open mode allows you to issue the open or visual commands from ex line editing mode. noopen prevents these commands so that novices will be less confused by modes. (Called novice on System V.) The default is open.
optimize	opt	optimize uses cursor positioning escape sequences at the end of each line to move to the beginning of the next line. This is more efficient on many terminals. The default is opt.
paragraphs	para	paragraphs tells vi the names of the nroff/troff paragraph macros. When you move to the beginning or end of a paragraph (using the { or } commands), vi searches for the closest paragraph marker in the paragraphs list or for a blank line. In the list, pairs of characters are macro names (e.g., IP). The default is IPLPPPQPP LIbp, which

covers standard -ms or -mm paragraphs, -mm list items, and manual page breaks.

prompt

prompt tells vi to print the : prompt when it is waiting for line-editing commands. The default is prompt.

readonly   ro

When readonly is set, the editor will refuse to write to a file (unless you use the w! command). readonly can be set like any other option, or it can be set by invoking vi with the -R command line option. The default is noreadonly.

redraw

redraw tells vi to constantly keep the screen display up to date, even on dumb terminals. This option generates much output on a dumb terminal. The default is noredraw.

remap

remap makes vi repeatedly scan the text of macros to see if any further macros are invoked. noremap scans each only once, thus making it impossible for one macro to invoke another. The default is remap.

report

When a command modifies more than report lines, vi prints a message. The default is 5.

scroll

scroll is the number of lines the display scrolls in ex mode when you type the EOF character. The default is ½ window.

sections

sections is a list of nroff/troff macro names that vi searches for when you enter the [[and]] commands to move to beginning and end of the section. In the sections list, pairs of characters denote macro names (e.g., SH). The default is SHNHH HU, which covers the heading start commands of -ms and -mm.

shell   sh

shell contains the name of the default shell. When vi starts to execute, shell is copied from the $SHELL environment variable.

shiftwidth   sw

shiftwidth is the size of the software tab stop. The default is 8.

showmode

showmode displays the current edit mode on the status line. When terse is set, the mode is represented by a single character. (Only available on newer versions of vi.) The default is noshowmode.

showmatch   sm

When showmatch is set, vi will automatically move the cursor to the matching (or { for one second each time you type a) or }. This is useful for

		programmers, especially for lisp programmers. The default is nosm.
slowopen	slow	The slowopen mode is an alternate output strategy for open or visual mode. It improves vi on dumb terminals by reducing the amount of screen updating during text inputs. Its value and default depend on your terminal type.
tabstop	ts	Tab characters in the input file produce movement to the next tabstop boundary. Reducing tabstop to 2 or 4 often makes it easier to view heavily indented material, such as C programs. The default is 8.
taglength	tl	taglength is the number of significant characters in a tag. Zero means the entire tag is significant. The default is 0.
tags		tags is a list of files containing tags. The default list is '/usr/lib/tags'.
term		term is the name of the output terminal. Its initial value comes from the $TERM environmental variable.
terse		terse makes vi produce shorter error messages. The default is noterse.
timeout		When timeout is set, the complete character sequence invoking a macro must be entered within one second. The default is timeout.
warn		When warn is set, vi will warn you if you enter a ! (shell) command without first saving your text. The default is warn.
window		window is the size of the text display in visual mode. The default varies according to the baud rate. It is 8 lines at speeds less than 1200 baud, 16 lines at 1200 baud, and the full screen at more than 1200 baud.
w300		w300 is a synonym for window, but it is effective only if the baud rate is less than 1200. The default is 8.
w1200		w1200 is a synonym for window, but it is effective only if the baud rate is 1200. The default is 16.
w9600		w9600 is a synonym for window, but it is effective only if the baud rate is higher than 1200. The default is full screen.
wrapmargin	wm	wrapmargin specifies the number of columns from the right margin of the screen before which vi will

automatically move your text down to the follow-ing line. The vi-inserted line break will be between words. Using wrapmargin makes it easier to type continuous text because you don't need to periodi-cally strike return to keep your lines about a screen-width long. One disadvantage of wm is that once vi automatically moves the text insertion point down to the following line, you cannot back up to correct mistakes on the preceding line (with-out leaving text entry mode). The default is 0, which disables the wm feature.

wrapscan   ws   wrapscan makes vi examine the entire file every time you perform a text search. Searches always start from the current line and proceed to the end (or beginning) of the file. When wrapscan is set and a vi search reaches the end (or beginning) of the file, the search continues from the beginning (or end) to the current line. The default is ws.

APPENDIX III

The Ed Text Editor

ed is the original UNIX editor. Although it was available almost from the start, ed has changed very little over the years. Creeping featurism has always been a UNIX problem, but somehow ed has remained the same. Today there are more convenient editing programs, but none quite so universal as ed. Just as I can't imagine a UNIX system without mv, cp, and ln, it wouldn't be UNIX without ed.

Even though ed has been superseded by newer editing programs, there are still many reasons to learn it thoroughly. Although ed is idle most of the time on most UNIX systems, there are editing tasks for which it is ideally suited. Because ed doesn't care what type of terminal you are using, you can use it on a hard-copy terminal, an obsolete "glass teletype," or even on a terminal with a hopelessly corrupted entry in the terminal characteristics file. Also, on some systems ed is able to handle larger files than other text editors. But even more important is ed's heritage in the UNIX world. Programs that have liberally adopted its regular expression-matching code include the grep utilities, the sed stream editor, awk, lex, and the ex/vi family of editors. The shell has pattern-matching primitives that differ somewhat from ed's, and the diff program produces an output that resembles an ed script.

You can't really claim to know the UNIX system until you know ed, not because ed was important way back when, but because ed-related programs are important today. vi-like programs are more convenient, but if you want to understand why the UNIX system is here, now, master ed.

LINE EDITING

A *text file* is divided into elements called *lines*. The lines in a text file correspond to your intuitive understanding of a line. To put it simply, a line of a text file is the amount of a text file that usually appears across one row of a computer terminal. Occasionally a text file contains a line that is too long to fit on your terminal. Some terminals fail to display the end of overly long lines, and other terminals wrap around and display the end of the line on the next row of the screen. Although there is no firm rule, lines are almost never longer than 255 characters.

ed is called a *line editor* because it operates on lines of text. If you were editing text using paper-and-pencil techniques, you would always be focusing your attention on some particular part of the text. The same idea is true for editing text with a computer. When you are editing a text file, there is always a *current line*. The current line is the area of the text that will usually be affected by the editing commands.

In a line editor it is possible to change a single character of the file, but only by specifying the line of the file that contains the character and then specifying the change. Although this seems to be a lot of effort for a small result, you will see that it is easy and natural to work with the constraints built into line editing.

STARTING ED

You start ed by typing its name followed by the name of the file that you want to edit.

```
$ ed firstsession
?firstsession

    - editing session -

q
$ _
```

This dialogue portrays an ed editing session. The shell command line is used to start ed, then the session occurs, and then the ed command q is used to quit ed and return to the shell. ed dialogues are mysterious-looking, partly because ed doesn't print a prompt. When you look at the dialogues in this appendix, you will need to differentiate between ed commands, input text, and output generated by ed. As usual, lines typed by the user are in a heavier typeface than lines printed by the machine.

In the dialogue shown above, ed exhibits its penchant for mysterious messages. The ?firstsession message is ed's way of telling you that it couldn't find a file called 'firstsession'. (If 'firstsession' had already existed, ed would have printed its length in characters in place of the message shown above.) Since 'firstsession' doesn't exist, ed will create it for you.

While you are using ed, you are working with a copy of the file, not the file itself. If you make a major mistake, the original file is still available. However, since you are working with a copy of the file, you have to remember to update the original file at the end of the editing session. If you forget to update the original file, the editor will remind you as you attempt to exit from the editor.

ed has two modes of operation, *command* mode and *text-entry* mode. In command mode, the editor is waiting for you to enter ed commands. ed commands can change lines, print lines, read or write disk files, or initiate text entry mode. In text entry mode the editor is waiting for you to enter lines of text. Anything that you type in text entry mode will be added to the file. You can leave text entry mode and reenter command mode by entering a line of text that consists of single period. The period tells ed that you have finished entering text, and you want ed to start executing your commands.

When you are in ed command mode, all of the lines that you type are interpreted as editor commands; when you are in text entry mode, all of the lines that you type are added to the file. You should always be careful to remember which mode you are in. The most common problem for beginners is entering commands in the text entry mode or entering text in the command mode. You can always switch back to command mode by entering a line containing a single period.

BASIC EDITING COMMANDS

The first 10 sections in this appendix introduce the basic editing commands. A mastery of these commands will enable you to use ed; serious ed users should also know the commands in the end of this appendix.

All ed commands are invoked by entering a single-character mnemonic. Most commands refer to either a specific line or a range of lines in the file. For example, the "p" command can print one or more lines in the file. If you enter the command

    20p

you will print the 20th line in the file. Lines 20 through 30 can be printed by using the command

    20,30p

The period is a special editor symbol denoting the *current line*. If you enter the command

```
.p
```

you will print the current line of text. The same effect will occur if you
enter the command

```
p
```

because the default line for the print command is the current line.

```
$ ls /bin | tail > cmdwords
$ cat cmdwords
tar
tee
test
time
tp
true
vi
wall
who
write
$ ed cmdwords
44
3p
test
1,4p
tar
tee
test
time
.p
time
p
time
q
$ _
```

ADDING TEXT TO THE WORKSPACE

The append command (a) is used to change the editor from command mode
to text entry mode. When you are in command mode, every line you type
is assumed to be an editor command. When you enter the append command, the assumption changes: every line is assumed to be text that is
added to the workspace. The command

```
a
```

will put the editor in text entry mode. All subsequent input lines will be added to the text file until a line containing a lone period is entered.

The append command is difficult because it causes the editor to change mode. Suddenly everything you type is interpreted differently. One of the most common errors is entering editor commands in input mode or entering text in command mode. If things seem funny, you should try entering a period alone on a line. If you are in input mode, the period will return you to command mode; if you are already in command mode, the period will simply print the current line.

```
$ ed whosonfirst
?whosonfirst
a
Friday
exactly
.
1,2p
Friday
exactly
1a
tomorrow
.
1,3p
Friday
tomorrow
exactly
```

The append command, like many ed commands, takes either zero or one line numbers (addresses). If no line number is specified, then the new text is added after the current line. If a line number is specified, then text is added after that line.

LISTING LINES OF THE FILE

The list (l) command is a variant of the print command. It is used to display special characters that may be hiding in the text. By special characters I mean characters (e.g., the tab or the backspace) that are not directly visible when the line is displayed on the screen. Consider a line of text that contains the following eight characters:

```
a,b,c,<backspace>,d,<tab>,e,f
```

If you use the print command to display the line, it will appear as follows:

```
.p
abd     ef
```

The *c* is not visible because the backspace character that follows it essentially erases it, and the tab character is expanded into the appropriate number of spaces. However, the backspace and the tab are visible if you display the line using the list command:

```
.l
abc\bd\tef
```

The \b and the \t conventions indicate a backspace and a tab character.

Like the print command, the list command accepts zero, one, or two line numbers. Without an address, the list command lists the current line; when one address is given, list lists that line; and when an address range is specified, then that range of lines is listed.

UPDATING THE ORIGINAL FILE

Whenever you have made any substantial changes or additions to the workspace, you should use the write command (**w**) to update the permanent copy of the file. Remember that while you are editing, you are working with a temporary copy of the file. It is necessary to update the permanent copy in order to save your changes.

The write command is used to write the workspace to a disk file. The general form of the write command is

```
n1,n2w filename
```

where **n1** and **n2** are line specifiers and 'filename' is the name of a disk file. If no line numbers are specified, all of the lines in the file are written; if no filename is specified, the default file is the original file being edited. Therefore the editor command

```
w
```

will write all of the lines of the workspace to the original file. The number of characters in the file will be reported after the write succeeds.

Occasionally you want to save only a group of lines, or to save lines in a file other than the original file. The editor command

```
10,20w safety
```

will write lines 10 through 20 to a file named 'safety'. This might be a good safety precaution before making a major change to those lines.

You usually use the w command before you leave ed with the q command. Here is the editing dialogue shown above, completed by adding the w command to save the file.

```
$ ed whosonfirst
?whosonfirst
a
Friday
exactly
.
1,2p
Friday
exactly
1a
tomorrow
.
1,3p
Friday
tomorrow
exactly
w
24
q
$ _
```

ENDING THE EDITING SESSION

I mentioned above that the quit (q) command terminates your editing session. There are no options or line numbers for the quit command. You must be careful to save any changes in the permanent file if you want to retain the changes. The editor does not automatically write the text buffer to the permanent file when you enter the quit command.

Most versions of ed will remind you (usually by printing a question mark) if you have made changes to the workspace without updating the original file.

```
$ ed xx
?xx
a
Hi.
.
q
?
```

The second ? means that you haven't updated the permanent file. To let you update the permanent file, the editor will have ignored the quit command. At this point, you can enter a write command to save the temporary file or you can repeat the quit command to actually quit the editor.

Usually the command

```
Q
```

can be used to quit the editor without its checking to see if changes have been made to the buffer since the last write. This is useful when you really want to quit, even though the original file hasn't been updated.

LINES AND LINE NUMBERS

Most editor commands operate on lines or groups of lines. For example, the print command can print a given line or a given group of lines, the append command appends text after a certain line, and the write command writes a group of lines to the output file.

Since lines are so important to ed, you might expect a lot of ways to identify lines of text. Naturally you can identify a line by mentioning its line number. The first line of text in a file is line 1, the second line is 2, and so on. As mentioned above, the command

```
2p
```

tells the editor to print line number 2 (not two lines).

In a small file it is easy to identify lines by line numbers because there are just a few lines. However, it is cumbersome to use line numbers in a file with several dozen lines, and it becomes even harder in a file with thousands of lines.

One way to identify lines in a large file is by using *relative* line numbers. Whenever a number is preceded by a plus + or a minus - sign, the editor interprets it as a relative line number. A relative line number specifies a line relative to the current line. For example, if the current line is line number 3, then -1 refers to line number 2, and +2 refers to line number 5.

The ed command

```
-5,+5p
```

will print the five lines before the current line, the current line, and then the five lines after the current line. At the conclusion of the command, the current line will be the last line printed.

Another way to identify lines is by *context*. Context identification is a very powerful technique. The first line following the current line that contains the text pattern "hello" is referenced by typing

```
/hello/
```

in place of a line number. You can use a context pattern anywhere that you can use a line number. If you want to type the first line following the current line that contains the text pattern "program" you would type the editor command

```
/program/p
```

If you wanted to type all the lines from the first one containing "program" to the first one after that containing "PASCAL", you would enter the editor command

```
/program/,/PASCAL/p
```

When you enter a context pattern in place of a line number, the editor searches for that pattern starting at the line after the current line. If the pattern is not found before the end of the file, the editor jumps to the top of the file and searches down from the top to the current line. The first line where the pattern is found is used as the line number. If the text pattern is not found, the editor prints a question mark or a short error message.

Besides the forward search that we have already mentioned, you can tell ed to perform a reverse context search by surrounding the text pattern with question marks. The ed command

```
?world?p
```

will search backward from the current line to print the first line encountered that contains the pattern "world". During a reverse context search, if the editor reaches the beginning of the file without a successful match, the editor jumps to the end of the file and searches from there up to the current line.

The term *wraparound* is used to describe the process of jumping from the beginning to end (or end to beginning) during a search. Conceptually you can imagine the file as a list of lines linked into a circle. The last line in the file is just the line before the first line in the circular analogy. Of course the file is not really stored in a circle, but the way that text searches work makes it useful to remember the circular analogy.

You can combine context addresses with relative addresses as in

```
?world?-3,.p
```

which will search backward to find the line containing the pattern "world", then move three lines in back of that, and then print from there to the current line.

The editor also allows you to add trailing plus and minus signs to a line specifier. The ed command

```
?world?---,.p
```

is the same as the previous command. You can also back up a few lines in the file by entering the command ---- or forward a few lines with +++. Using trailing pluses and minuses is useful for browsing through a file.

Occasionally you need to convert a context line number into an absolute line number. The ed command

```
.=
```

will display the absolute line number of the current line. You can also use a context pattern like

```
/PASCAL/=
```

to discover the line number of the line contains the word "PASCAL".

Another shortcut is the use the symbol $ to refer to the last line in the file. For example, the ed command

```
1,$p
```

will print all of the lines in the file.

You can use absolute, relative, and context line specifiers interchangeably in the editor. The choice depends on what you are doing. Absolute line numbers are the safest, because there is no ambiguity; relative line numbers are pretty safe if you really are where you think you are in the file; and context line specifiers are very convenient but rather hazardous.

DELETING LINES OF TEXT

The editor delete command (d) removes one or several lines from the text. If no line numbers are specified, then the delete command deletes the current line. If one line number (or context pattern) is specified, then the delete command deletes the specified line. If two lines are specified, then the delete command deletes that entire range of lines. As examples, consider the following editor commands:

```
10d
+10d
d
10,15d
20,/there/d
```

The first command deletes line number 10, the second command deletes the 10th line after the current line, the third command deletes the current line, the fourth deletes lines 10 through 15, and the fifth command deletes from line 20 to the line containing the pattern "there".

You should be very careful with the delete command, because it is easy to delete lines by mistake. In modern versions of ed, the undo command (u) will undo the last command that changed the buffer. However, many versions of ed don't contain the undo command, and it is possible that you won't be aware of the damage until it is too late to use the undo command.

To avoid disastrous deletions, it is good practice to print lines before you delete them. If you want to delete lines 10 through 20, you should enter the command

```
10,20p
```

to make sure that you are referencing the correct lines before entering the command

```
10,20d
```

to actually delete the lines. Remember that the print command usually changes the current line, so you could delete the 10th line after the current line by entering the command

```
+10p
```

to make sure that it's the correct line and then entering the command

```
d
```

to delete the line.

Another good practice in deleting lines is to use absolute line numbers until you become an expert at using ed. If you want to delete the group of lines from the pattern "here" to the pattern "there", you might attempt to use the brash command

```
/here/,/there/d
```

It would be more prudent to first enter the command

```
/here/p
```

to find and print the first line in the deletion. If the line that is printed is correct, then enter the command

```
.=
```

to print the number of the current line (the first line in the deletion). For this example, let's suppose that the number 20 is printed. Then enter the command

```
/there/
```

to find and print the last line of the deletion. Again use the command

```
.=
```

to print the number of the current line (the last line of the deletion). Suppose that the number 30 is printed. As a final precaution, use the command

```
20,30p
```

to make absolutely sure that lines 20 to 30 are the ones to be discarded. Finally, enter the command

```
20,30d
```

to actually delete the lines. The approach shown here is extremely cautious, but it is usually easier to be cautious than to reconstruct 10 (or 1000) missing lines.

Context line numbers are great for finding text, but because text patterns such as "there" occur many times in most text files, it is risky to use context line numbers when you are altering text.

INSERTING AND CHANGING LINES OF TEXT

ed's insert command (i) is used to insert text before the specified line. Inserting is similar to appending (a), except that text is added before the specified line rather than after the specified line. If no line is specified, then the insertion is made in front of the current line.

The insert command causes the editor to enter text entry mode. After entering the insert command, everything that you type will be interpreted as text, and it will be added to the file. You can stop inserting text by typing a line consisting of a single period.

ed's change command (c) first removes one or several lines from the text, and then text is appended in place of the deleted lines. Like the insert and append commands, the change command causes ed to enter text entry mode.

```
$ ed days
17
1,$p
Monday
Wed.
Fri.
2i
Tuesday
.
1,$p
Monday
Tuesday
Wed.
Fri.
3,/Fri/c
Wednesday
Thursday
Friday
.
1,$p
Monday
Tuesday
Wednesday
Thursday
Friday
w
41
q
$ _
```

MOVING AND TRANSFERRING LINES OF TEXT

ed's move command (m) is used to move text from one place in a file to another. If no source lines are specified, then the current line is moved after the destination line. If one source line is specified, then the specified line is moved after the destination. If two source lines are specified, then the group of specified lines is moved after the destination.

The following commands show all three forms of the move command:

```
m50
30m31
/hi/,50m0
```

The first command moves the current line after line 50, the second command moves line 30 after line 31, and the third command moves a group of lines after line 0. The third command is interesting because the addressed text is moved after line 0. In ed the first line of text is always line 1, but line 0 exists conceptually, so that text can be moved to the beginning of a file. Any text placed after line 0 will always be at the beginning of the file.

The transfer (t) command is almost the same as the move command; the only difference is that the addressed text is not disturbed during a transfer. The move command takes the addressed text and removes it from one place and puts it back somewhere else; the transfer command makes a copy of the addressed lines of text and places the copy at the destination. The move command has no effect on the size of the file; the transfer command always increases the size of the file.

```
$ ed hk
33
1,$p
Walking
Break rhythm
Writing
Now
3m0
1,$p
Writing
Walking
Break rhythm
Now
3t1
1,$p
Writing
Break rhythm
Walking
Break rhythm
Now
w
46
q
$ _
```

SUBSTITUTING TEXT

The substitute command (s) is used to change one pattern of text on a line to another pattern. The general format of the substitute command is

```
n1,n2s/pat1/pat2/
```

where *n1* and *n2* are line specifiers, and *pat1* and *pat2* are text patterns. The command causes pat1 to be replaced by pat2 in the group of specified lines. The simplest form of the substitute command is

```
s/pat1//
```

which removes the text represented by pat1 from the current line.
   If line 20 in the workfile is "The URIX Operating System", then the command

```
20s/URIX/UNIX/
```

will change the typo "URIX" into "UNIX". If you are in the habit of typing "URIX" instead of "UNIX", then the command

```
1,$s/URIX/UNIX/
```

will change the first occurrence of "URIX" on every line in the file to "UNIX."
   If the current line in the workspace is "Who'ss on first?" then the command

```
s/s//
```

will remove the extra "s" from the first word.
   If the current line of the workspace is "Don'tread on me." then the command

```
s/Don'tread/Don't tread/
```

will change the line to "Don't tread on me." You need to supply only enough context to enable the editor to recognize the part of the text that must be changed. Therefore, any of the following commands would have performed the same repair as the preceding command:

```
s/n'tr/n't tr/
s/'t/'t t/
s/'/'t /
s/t/t t/
```

Be careful when you supply minimal context because you can easily get into trouble. Consider the following line of text.

```
The rain in Spain falls mainly on the plain.
```

The text pattern "he" occurs twice, the pattern "ain" occurs three times, and the pattern "in" occurs four times, and the patterns "a" and "i" each occur five times.

Here is a fragment of an editing session that shows how hard it can be to specify the correct context for the substitute command.

```
p
The rain in Spain falls mainly on the plainly.
s/ly//
p
The rain in Spain falls main on the plainly.
u
p
The rain in Spain falls mainly on the plainly.
s/plainly/plain/
p
The rain in Spain falls mainly on the plain.
```

The first substitute command doesn't achieve the desired result, because the substitute commands changes the first "ly" but, the "ly" in "plainly" is the second one. The solution is to specify a longer text pattern that clearly specifies the errant "ly."

READING TEXT INTO THE WORKSPACE

I discussed earlier the easiest way to get text from a permanent disk file into the editor's workspace. (The workspace is often called the editor's text buffer.) If your shell command to start the editor mentions a disk file, then the contents of that file are automatically read into the workspace. If the permanent file doesn't exist, then it will be created when you enter your first write command. The shell command

```
$ ed mydoc
```

will start the editor and read the contents of the file 'mydoc' into the workspace.

The same result is attained if you enter the shell command

```
$ ed
```

to start the editor and then you enter the ed command

```
e mydoc
```

ed's edit command (e) instructs the editor to clear the workspace and then read the contents of the named file into the workspace. Any previous contents of the workspace are lost. The e command can be used at the beginning of an editing session as in this example, or it can be used in the middle of a session to start work on a new file. The e command is just as dangerous as the q (quit) command; use it cautiously. Most versions of ed will warn you if the old workspace had been modified so that you can write it out to a permanent file before you start with a new file.

ed does not require a filename to function. It is acceptable to start ed without specifying an input file and then add text to the empty workspace. The filename can be specified later either by using the filename command (f) or by using the write (w) command with an explicit filename.

Sometimes you need to combine the contents of a disk file with the current contents of the workspace. The ed command

```
0r headerfile
```

will place a copy of 'headerfile' after line zero in the workspace. The read (r) command reads in the named file and places its contents after the given line. If no line number is mentioned, the information is placed after the current line. The difference between ed's read command and its edit command is that the read command adds text to the current workspace without clearing the contents of the workspace; the edit command always clears the workspace.

ed does not allow you to read in part of a file; rather, you must read in the entire file. If you need to read in just a few lines of a file, you must make a copy of the file, then use ed to prune the unwanted portion, and then finally edit the target file and read in the pruned version of the original.

THE FILE COMMAND

ed remembers the name of the file that is being edited. The file command (f) is used to either display or change the remembered filename. The ed command

```
f
```

will cause the editor to print the remembered file name, whereas the command

```
f myaltdoc
```

will change the remembered name to 'myaltdoc'.

There are three commands that can change the remembered file name: f, e, and w. The r (read) command has no effect on the remembered filename.

THE GLOBAL COMMAND

Most ed commands pertain to either a single line in a file or a local group of lines. ed's global command (g) is used to modify commands so that they pertain to all lines that contain a certain text pattern. Suppose you want to print all of the lines that contain the word "help". The ed command

```
g/help/p
```

will print all of the lines containing the word "help" (or "helping", or "helpless", etc.). The phrase g/help/ modifies the print command (p) so that it pertains to all the lines containing the text pattern "help". The g character introduces the global modifier phrase, and the text pattern ("help" in this case) is enclosed in slashes.

The global command (and its variants discussed below) is extremely useful. The errors and problems in a text file are often very systematic. If you can identify a text pattern that is associated with a problem in a text file, you can often devise a solution involving the global command.

The global command works in two phases. In the first phase, the global command searches through the text and makes a list of all lines that contain the given text pattern. In the second phase, the given command is performed on all lines in the list.

It is also possible to specify a range of addresses with the global command. If you want to print all of the lines containing the word "alpha" in lines 50 through 100, you can use the command

```
50,100g/alpha/p
```

Context addresses can also be used to specify the addresses for the global command:

```
/beta/,/dopa/g/zeta/d
```

This command deletes all lines containing the text pattern "zeta" from the first line (after the current line) containing "beta" to the first line after that containing "dopa". Lines containing "zeta" outside of this range are not deleted.

The v command is the negated version of the global command. The v command goes through the text and makes a list of all lines that don't contain the text pattern, and then it goes through the text again and performs the command on all lines in the list. For example, the command

```
v/-/s/330/340/p
```

would substitute "340" for "330" on all of the lines that contain no hyphens.

Besides modifying just one command, the global family of commands (g and v) can be used to modify a command list. Suppose you need to change "hat" to "cap" and "sweater" to "coat" and "glove" to "mitten" on every line that contains the word "clothes". Of course, you could use three separate global commands. However, it would be easier to enter the following imposing-looking command:

```
g/clothing/s/hat/cap/\
s/sweater/coat/\
s/glove/mitten/
```

This command will execute the three substitute commands on every line containing the word "clothing." Notice that every command in the command list (except the last) contains a backslash at the end of the line. The backslash is the clue that tells ed that there are more editor commands in the command list.

THE JOIN COMMAND

The join command (j) is used to glue two lines together. The ed command

```
-,.j
```

combines the previous line with the current line. (The minus sign is a shorthand notation for the line in front of the current line.) A group of short lines can be joined as in

```
10,20j
```

Be careful not to create lines that are too long (usually there is a 255-character limit).

The join command exists because it is too dangerous to allow people to combine lines by deleting new-line characters. The editor cannot handle very long lines, so the editor checks to make sure that the created line is reasonable.

Although ed will not join lines without using the special join command, it is possible to split lines using the general substitute command. Splitting lines is less troublesome than joining lines, because the resulting line is never too long to edit. If you want to split a line into two parts, you can substitute a new-line character at the appropriate point. The ed substitute command

```
s/time /time\
/
```

will split the line

```
A stitch in time saves nine.
```

into the lines

```
A stitch in time
saves nine.
```

by placing a new-line character after the word "time". In the above command, after typing the second "time," you type a backslash and then a return (or a new-line character) and then a slash and then a return to complete the command. The backslash before the carriage return removes (escapes) the return's special meaning to the system: the "line" of input is therefore not complete until you have typed the second return. If you imagine the command on a single line, you should recognize the familiar command "s/pat1/pat2/". When you strike the escaped carriage return, you will advance to the next line on the screen although you are still entering the same command. (This example also demonstrates that either pattern in a substitute command can contain an embedded blank.)

REGULAR EXPRESSIONS

Throughout this discussion of the editor, I have been referring to text patterns. Text patterns are very important to ed. Lines can be identified and changed using text patterns. A text pattern that is involved in pattern matching is called a *regular expression*. A regular expression matches one or more character strings.

Regular expressions are used in two situations in ed: as context addresses, and as the first part of a substitute command. When a regular expression is used as a context address, it is surrounded by either a pair of slashes or a pair of question marks. When a regular expression is used in the first part of the substitute command, any character other than space or new line may be used to delimit the expression, although slashes are very common delimiters.

The second text pattern in a substitute command (s/pat1/pat2) is called the *replacement* string. It is not a regular expression because it is not involved in pattern matching. The difference between a regular expression and a character string is that regular expressions are involved in text-matching operations and they may contain special characters that indicate certain classes of matches. Characters that are special when included in regular expressions do not have special meanings in replacement strings.

Special Characters in Regular Expressions.

Up to this point I have been careful to use very simple regular expressions. To use ed expertly, you have to understand the rules of regular expressions. The following characters are special when used in a regular expression:

```
.   Period
*   Asterisk
[   Left brace
\   Backslash
^   Caret
$   Currency symbol
```

If you studiously avoid the characters listed above in forming regular expressions, then your regular expressions will always match themselves, no more and no less. If the following five text patterns are used as regular expressions, they will match themselves because none of them contain special characters:

```
hello
bye
This is a long regular expression!
abcdefghijklmnopqrstuvwxyz
01234
```

The backslash can turn off the special meaning associated with the special characters. For example, the following text pattern matches the word "end" only when it is followed by a period:

```
end\.
```

If the current line of text in the editor contained the sentence "This is the end of the end.", you could change the last word to "middle" with the following substitute command:

```
s/end\./middle./
```

In this example, the regular expression is "end\." and the replacement string is "middle." If the period weren't escaped in the substitute command, then the first "end" and its following space character would have been changed to "middle." Note that the period in the replacement string does not have to be escaped. Remember, the replacement string is not a regular expression.

Suppose you were looking for a line of text containing the comic book expletive "!!&&*$$". The editor print command

```
/!!&&\*\$\$/p
```

would find and print the line. If you wanted to change the expletive to "heck", you could use the substitute command:

```
s/!!&&\*\$\$/heck/
```

Just knowing about ed's special characters and knowing how to turn off their special meaning allows most people to use the editor without major surprises. However, mastery of ed requires mastery of its syntax for regular expressions. The remaining subsections of this section can be skipped if you plan to avoid (rather than master) regular expressions.

Single-Character Regular Expressions.

Long, complicated regular expressions are built from single-character regular expressions. First we must learn the rules of single-character regular expressions. Here is the list of all of the single-character regular expressions that ed accepts:

A single character other than the special characters. All of the characters other than the special characters form one-character regular expressions that stand for themselves. The character "a" stands for "a", the character "b" stands for "b", etc.

Escaped special characters. The special characters (period, asterisk, caret, currency symbol, left square brace, and backslash) lose their meaning when they are preceded by a backslash. Therefore, the following pairs of characters are actually one-character regular expressions that match the named character:

\.	Period
*	Asterisk
\^	Caret
\$	Currency symbol
\[	Left square brace
\\	Backslash

The special character period. A period is a one-character regular expression that matches any single character except a new line.

The special character left square brace. A left square brace introduces a *character set*, and the end of the character set is indicated by a right square brace. The characters between the square braces define the characters in the set. A character set is a one-character regular expression that matches any one of the characters in the set.

Let's talk about character sets. The character set [abcd] matches any of the first four lowercase letters of the alphabet. A dash may be used to indicate an inclusive range of characters. For example, the character set [a-d] will match any of the first four lowercase letters of the alphabet. A dash at the end of the set loses its special meaning as in the set [ab-] which matches either "a", "b", or "-".

If there is a caret at the beginning of a set, then the one-character regular expression denoted by the set matches any character not in the set. The set [^a-z] matches any single character other than a lowercase letter. The caret loses its special meaning if it does not occur first in the set as in the set [a-z^], which matches any lowercase letter or a caret.

The characters period, asterisk, left square brace, and backslash stand for themselves in a character set. The character set [*.] matches either a backslash or an asterisk or a period.

Combining One-Character Regular Expressions.

Single-character regular expressions can be combined according to the following rules to form more powerful regular expressions:

Catenation. A catenation of single-character regular expressions matches any of the catenations of strings that the individual components match. Therefore, the regular expression abc matches only "abc", whereas the regular expression a.c matches any three-character sequence beginning with "a" and ending with "c".

The asterisk operator. A single-character regular expression followed by an asterisk matches zero or more occurrences of the one-character regular expression. Therefore the regular expression 12*3 matches any of the following:

13

123

1223

12223

In the case shown above, the "2" is the single-character regular expression that is acted on by the asterisk, so it may occur zero or more times in a matching target string.

The currency symbol operator. When a currency symbol is placed at the end of a regular expression, that regular expression is constrained to match the final segment of a line of text. It is not quite correct to say that a currency symbol placed at the end of a regular expression matches a new line, because the new line will not be involved in any text substitutions that occur. A currency symbol used in the beginning or middle of a line will match a currency symbol. The regular expression 123$ matches the character string "123" if it occurs at the end of a line. The regular expression $123 matches the character string "$123" anywhere on a line.

The caret operator. The caret is a special character in two situations: when it is at the beginning of an entire regular expression, and when it is the first character of a character set. In all other situations, the caret matches itself. If a caret occurs at the beginning of an entire regular expression, that regular expression is constrained to match the initial segment of the line. It is not quite correct to say that a caret matches the beginning of a line, because the result of such a match is not involved in substitutions. We have already discussed the use of the caret at the beginning of a character set. The regular expression ^Hello matches the character string "Hello" when it occurs at the beginning of a line. The regular expression Hello^ matches the character string "Hello^" anywhere on a line.

Note that one of the most unfortunate features of the UNIX system is the difference between the rules for regular expression matching in ed and the rules for filename generation. An asterisk in ed represents zero or more instances of the preceding single-character regular expression, whereas the asterisk in the filename generation process matches any (possible null) sequence of characters. In ed, the period matches any single character, whereas in the filename generation process, the question mark matches any single character.

MORE ON THE SUBSTITUTE COMMAND

The substitute command is probably the hardest ed command. Changing one word to another on a short line is easy, but changing the third asterisk on a long line in a C-language program can require more skill than writing the program. One typical solution to the problem is deletion and then laborious manual reentry of the entire erroneous line. (Another difficult-to-correct typo is often the result.) This section is designed to demonstrate a few of the useful, but advanced, techniques for performing text substitutions.

The caret and the currency symbol are frequently used to simplify substitute expressions. Consider the following line from a table of binary numbers:

1101 1101 1101 1101

If you had to change the last number (field) to "1011", you could use any of the following substitute commands:

```
s/1101 1101 1101 1101/1101 1101 1101 1011/
s/1101$/1011/
s/....$/1011/
```

The first of these amounts to typing the line twice, so it is obviously bad. The currency symbol in the last two commands forces the regular expression match to occur at the end of the line, so less has to be typed. The second substitute command explicitly states that the last four characters should be "1101" and that they should be replaced by "1011". The third substitute command just replaces the last four characters on the line with "1011". Note that the second and third substitute commands will not work if the line contains trailing blanks or tabs.

The caret forces a match to occur at the beginning of a line. You can use the command

```
s/^/-/
```

to place a hyphen at the beginning of a line. In this example, the regular expression consists of a lone caret. The replacement string is a hyphen.

The editor's *longest leftmost* rule determines what text is matched when several matches are possible.

Leftmost. The leftmost match is always preferred. The command
s/1/2/ applied to the line of text "111111" will produce the text "211111" because the leftmost match is preferred.

Longest. The longest match is preferred. The command s/1*2/3/ applied to the line of text "1111124" will change the line to "34" because the whole string of 1's followed by a 2 is matched. (Remember that the asterisk repeats the previous single-character regular expression zero or more times.)

A harder problem is the application of the command s/1*2/3/ to the line of text "2 1112". The leftmost rule here is in conflict with the longest rule. Clearly the longest match on the line would involve the "1112". However, the leftmost match on the line is the leading 2. Since the leftmost match is always preferred, the text "3 112" is produced.

Occasionally you want to make more than one substitution on a line. For example, you might want to change all of the "jacks" to "janes" on some line. The letter g following a substitute command instructs the editor to make all possible substitutions. The ed command

    s/jacks/janes/g

changes the line

    jacks jacks and more jacks

to

    janes janes and more janes

You need to understand the difference between the g option to the substitute command and the g global command. The g option specifies that ed should perform every possible substitution on a line, whereas the global command specifies a list of lines on which a command should be performed. If you wanted to change all of the "teh" text strings to "the" throughout an entire file, you could use the ed command:

    g/teh/s/teh/the/g

The leading g indicates the global command, which makes a list of all of the lines containing a "teh". The substitute command is then performed on every line in the list, and the g option specifies that every occurrence of "teh" on the line should be changed to "the".

Naturally the g option modifies the "longest leftmost" rule. Leftmost no longer applies, since all possible matches on a line are made. The longest rule does apply; each match is made as long as possible, and the matches are performed starting on the left.

The other options that are commonly available when using the substitute command are p and l to print (or list) the changed line. For example, the ed command

```
s/jack/jill/p
```

changes the first "jack" to "jill" and then prints the result.

Someday one of your text files will become the home of a nonprinting character. Weird characters usually creep in because of typing errors, but strange characters are occasionally caused by noise in dial-up circuits or inexplicable hardware problems. In any event, the problem of strange visitors is twofold—identifying their presence and removing them.

One of the most common unprintable characters is the backspace. Unsuspecting novices (and occasionally experts) sometimes type in backspace characters when they intend to type in the UNIX erase character. Remember, the erase character is the character (often a pound sign or a delete or a Control-H) that the system interprets as your command to erase the previous character. Typing backspaces often looks the same as typing erases, so it is easy to confuse the two operations. In any case, if your text file becomes populated with backspaces, the lines you see on your terminal aren't the lines that are contained in the file.

If your lines of text are making noises when you print them or if your substitute commands aren't working or if unexplainable things are happening, use the l command to look for unprintable characters. As explained earlier, the list command is similar to the p print command; the difference is that the l graphically depicts all of the unprintables.

Once you have found undesirable unprintables in your file, you can use the substitute command to remove them. (Just delete and reenter a really botched line.) The problem with using the substitute command is that typing unprintable characters is usually difficult. The easiest way to match an unprintable character is to use the period in a regular expression. If your text line contains a "1" followed by an unwanted and unprintable character followed by a "2", the following command will remove the unprintable and then list the resulting line:

```
s/1.2/12/l
```

Remember that the period in a regular expression matches any single character, including unprintables.

Perhaps you have noticed that the replacement string often contains text that is very similar to the regular expression. When you are adding characters to existing text, the replacement string is often the original regular expression plus the added text. For example, if you are changing the word "awkward" to "awkwardly", you might use the following substitute command:

```
s/awkward/awkwardly/p
```

If you ever try to type the command, you will feel as awkward as the command looks. To reduce typing errors, ed allows you to use an ampersand in the replacement string as a shorthand for the entire text that was matched by the regular expression. Using the ampersand, the command shown above could be entered as follows:

```
s/awkward/&ly/p
```

The ampersand in this case stands for the text string "awkward".

The ampersand notation works even when you are using complicated regular expressions such as in the following command, which places a plus sign in front of the first number on a line and places ".00" after the number:

```
s/[0-9][0-9]*/+&.00/p
```

The above ed command above applied to the line

```
The year end balance is 550 dollars.
```

produces the line

```
The year end balance is +550.00 dollars.
```

This rather extended form is not very useful for making a change on a single line, but it is a great advantage when you are changing many lines throughout a file.

Always be careful with the asterisk regular expression operator. The command

```
s/[0-9]*/+&.00/p
```

applied to the original line above would produce the line

```
+.00The year end balance is 550 dollars.
```

because the regular expression "[0-9]*" would match the leftmost null string.

In all the examples of the substitute command given so far, the regular expression and the replacement string have been delimited by slashes. In a substitute command (but not in a context pattern), any character other than space is allowed as a delimiter. The slashes are often used because they clearly delimit the expressions.

If you want to change the word "boy" to "adolescent" on the current line, you can use any of the following substitute commands:

```
s/boy/adolescent/
s,boy,adolescent,
szboyzadolescentz
saboya\adolescenta
```

In the four commands shown above, the delimiters are slash, comma, "z", and "a". Whatever character is used as the delimiter becomes a special character in that command. In the last command shown above, the "a" in "adolescent" has to be preceded by a backslash to escape its special meaning as a delimiter. Without the backslash, the editor would interpret that "a" as the final delimiter in the expression, and the trailing characters "dolescent" would produce an error message. As a rule, it is easiest to choose expression delimiters that are visual (e.g., slash or comma) and not present in the expressions.

THE SHELL ESCAPE

Occasionally while you are editing, you will want to perform a standard UNIX command. Of course you can write your file and quit ed and then perform the command and then reenter ed, but that's a lot of work. ed's shell escape command allows you run standard UNIX commands without leaving the editor. If you enter the command

```
!who
```

then the who command will be executed. At the conclusion of the command, the editor prints an exclamation point to indicate that it is ready for more input.

The editing session is not affected by the shell escape. You do not have to write the text buffer to a permanent file before using a shell escape. If you want to enter several commands, you can semipermanently escape from the editor by entering the command

```
!sh
```

to create a new shell. This new shell will allow you to enter as many UNIX system commands as you like. You might try the UNIX ps command to get a list of all the processes you are running. Your original shell, ed, your new shell, and the ps command will all be in the list. You can terminate the new shell by striking Control-D or entering the exit command.

Index